Setting Down the
Sacred Past

Setting Down the Sacred Past

AFRICAN-AMERICAN RACE HISTORIES

Laurie F. Maffly-Kipp

THE BELKNAP PRESS OF HARVARD UNIVERSITY PRESS

Cambridge, Massachusetts, and London, England · 2010

Library of Congress Cataloging-in-Publication Data

Maffly-Kipp, Laurie F., 1960–

    Setting down the sacred past : African-American race histories /
  Laurie F. Maffly-Kipp.

      p. cm.

    Includes bibliographical references and index.

    ISBN 978-0-674-05079-2 (alk. paper)

    1. African Americans—Race identity—History—18th century.   2. African
Americans—Race identity—History—19th century.   3. African Americans—
Religion—History—18th century.   4. African Americans—Religion—History—
19th century.   5. African Americans—Intellectual life—18th century.   6. African
Americans—Intellectual life—19th century.   7. African Americans in literature—
History—18th century.   8. African Americans in literature—History—19th century.
9. Black theology—History.   I. Title.

  E185.625.M314   2010

  305.896′073—dc22

  2009053861

For Joseph, at last

Contents

Setting Down the
Sacred Past

That which has been is now;
and that which is to be has already been;
and God requires that which is past.

—Ecclesiastes 3:15

Introduction

Nothing captures more succinctly the knotty saga of race and religion in the United States today than the story of the Reverend Jeremiah Wright, the former spiritual mentor of Barack Obama. Wright is pastor emeritus at Trinity United Church of Christ (UCC) in Chicago, a congregation that advertises itself as "Unabashedly Black and Unapologetically Christian." In early 2008, just as Obama's battle for the Democratic nomination for president was beginning to heat up, excerpts of some of Wright's fiery sermons appeared on the Web. In those brief clips, the preacher lambasted the American invasion of Iraq, a national history of racism, and the failure of Christians to live up to their own ideals: "Racism is how this country was founded and how this country is still run! . . . We [in the United States] believe in white supremacy and black inferiority and believe it more than we believe in God."

These words served as a Rorschach test for many observers. Conservative white pundits expressed alarm at Wright's—and, by extension, Obama's—revolutionary and racist zeal, as well as his criticisms of the U.S. government and his blanket condemnations of whites, which they read as dangerous and deluded. Some high-profile African Americans cringed and quietly shied away from his words, knowing that they would be interpreted as anti-American and racially divisive. Liberal intellectuals and scholars put Wright's jeremiad into biblical and historical context, arguing for his social relevancy and the important work required for justice in inner-city Chicago. Many regular attendees at predominantly black churches wondered just what all the fuss was about, since they did not hear anything unusually rancorous or startling—at least, they heard nothing that had not been voiced by African-American preachers for centuries.

What was so shocking and new about Wright's words? They seemed almost tame in a country where television preachers daily spoke of sin and damnation, and where Puritan preachers once referred to their parishioners as "sinners in the hands of an angry God." Surely the potent combination of race and Christianity helps explain the public outcry. Wright himself has argued that his church is a historically black house of worship in a black community. To shape its form of Christian worship, it draws on the resources of an African heritage as well as a black church tradition forged in an era of racial oppression. Wright also pays homage to his congregation's ties to the United Church of Christ, a predominantly white denomination that incorporates the legacies of New England Puritans, Midwestern German immigrants, and Southern white Methodists into a progressive, multicultural, and undeniably American mix. He points to a longstanding Christian prophetic tradition, dating back to John Winthrop, Cotton Mather, and other Puritan divines, of calling a nation to account for its sins. Wright sees himself as advocating African pride and naming white oppression, as have generations of African-American preachers. There's nothing new here, his words insist. But outsiders continue to be surprised, as though the news of African-American Christianity is a startlingly novel and dangerous development.

Even some of Wright's supporters have diagnosed his version of "Black and Christian" as intellectual pathology. W. E. B. Du Bois referred to this duality as an aspect of what he called the "double-consciousness" of the African-American experience, in reference to what he saw as the inevitable bifurcation of identity caused by white racism. This description of divided identity assumes that blacks, as a result of unequal power relations in the United States, have a split consciousness that is ever at work trying to unite into a harmonious whole. African Americans are forced to see the world through the eyes of their oppressors rather than freely through their own self-understandings. While the trope of double-consciousness sometimes suggests that blacks have a heightened awareness of the world around them and particularly of racial issues, it more often implies a fragmentation of self exhibited in a struggle to find a coherent sense of community.

It is certainly true that racial violence in the United States has long extended beyond physical brutality to include the most fundamental assaults on personal and collective identity. For nearly five centuries, enslaved Africans were systematically ripped out of their homes, transported across the Atlantic, and resettled in unfamiliar and hostile environments. White masters and missionaries attempted to destroy all semblance of African culture and repeated emphatically that slaves were an "uncivilized" people without a past. Euro-Americans committed identity theft on a massive scale.

Yet Wright's understanding of African-American Christianity reflects something much deeper and more intellectually coherent than Du Bois or other scholars would allow. It reflects a long tradition, one now all but forgotten, of African-American collective narration. Remarkably, and despite unremitting cultural assaults, enslaved Africans arriving in the New World almost immediately began to reconstruct a history for themselves. They found, in the collected shards of memory and the newer intellectual tools arrayed around them, elements of stories that helped to restore meaning and purpose to their lives. This process of narrating a past gave African Americans control over their identities, allowed them to refute the pervasive dictum of "black inferiority," and affected their ability to shape the future.[1] "We tell ourselves stories in order to live," according to Joan Didion, and such was the case with African Americans, who told themselves stories that allowed them to survive and even thrive amid unspeakable assault. Over time, the stories they told became naturalized and seemed like an inevitable aspect of collective existence.

In the eighteenth and nineteenth centuries these historical accounts took shape in the form of a rich and varied Afro-Christian intellectual culture that gave rise to an enormous quantity of literature on a wide array of genres and formats, including poetry, essays, songs, sermons, novels, and letters. While the notion of a common race, anchored in African origins, served as one unifying element for these stories, there were many other points of connection and divergence, many kinds of identities embedded in accounts of heroism and glory. African-American identity was not built solely on African foundations; rather, it was anchored in a Protestant bedrock. Central to all of these histories was Protestantism as a source of belief, practice, and institutional structure. The Christian tradition gave birth to a worldview and a way of interpreting circumstances that imparted meaning and value to the incoherence of cultural removal and chattel slavery. American patriotism also informed these accounts, embedding growing understandings of racial nationalism in myriad ways.

Communal narratives appeared first in the urban North among free blacks around the time of the American Revolution, but their formative power spread south in the decades after the Civil War, as freed men and women formed their own institutions and set their own future courses. History once again supplied significance and a trajectory for growth and development. At the same time African Americans moved out into the world, to the Caribbean, to Europe, and to Africa, and they spread their stories abroad and linked their destinies to international communities. Through Christian faith, through a legacy of African glory, and through a commitment to American democratic principles, African Americans creatively moored themselves in time and space even as whites sought to disrupt those foundations.

Du Bois's understanding of double-consciousness, as prescient and evocative as it is, hardly conveys the complexity, richness, and contradictory nature of this Afro-Christian tradition. Some of this oversight was purposeful and involved a concerted effort to transform images of black life. In the early twentieth century Du Bois and other African-American scholars, eager to present African-American culture to academic and elite audiences (and to present blacks to themselves in a new and improved way), represented this older tradition, and especially its religious elements, as a romantic but vestigial remnant of a dying way of life. By focusing on "spirit" and "culture," Du Bois embraced particular elements of religious experience while downplaying others. The practices that he noticed—the frenzy of the Southern preacher, the croonings of the spirituals, and the ecstatic ravings of the congregation—reflected a black Protestantism drained of the intellectual force that had been integral in shaping behavior and belief. This cultural work of forgetting made it impossible for those who accepted his descriptions at face value to understand the intertwined themes of nation, religion, and race that continued to animate pulpits, pews, and Sunday School pageants in black churches throughout the twentieth century. Du Bois, Carter Woodson, and others, with the best intentions of setting a course for the "New Negro," robbed communities of the religious piece of their past that could make sense of the rest. Even today, many listeners encounter Jeremiah Wright's sermons and do not know how to hear them, other than as disconnected and angry taunts.

The time has come to explore that older territory, the world of Afro-Christian history-making prior to the 1920s and the rise of academic narratives that fragmented the political from the religious and privileged the former. This examination will render more explicable the writings of vernacular religious thinkers, people like Lorenzo Dow Blackson, who, just two years after the close of the Civil War, published what he termed a "feeble essay" titled *The Rise and Progress of the Kingdoms of Light and Darkness*. Blackson, a self-educated African-American Methodist preacher, may have been personally humble, but he was eschatologically ambitious. His work stretched to well over three hundred pages. It opened with a recapitulation of the biblical account of creation described in Genesis, and then depicted the battle between "the kingdom of light and the kingdom of darkness" through key moments from the Old and New Testaments. From there Blackson proceeded to assay much of modern history (up through the recent war) in light of this supernatural contest, ending with a "description of the last great battle between these two great powers . . . a war of extermination." In the course of his story, Blackson discussed the Reformation, the American Revolution, the rise of Protestant denominationalism, the major world religions, the independent black church movement, and the persistence of racism following the abolition of slavery in the United States. He hailed Martin Luther, Quakers, black church leaders, John Brown, and Abraham Lincoln as sacred heroes. Under the guidance of divine inspiration, he predicted a war "which is to determine on which side the final victory will rest forever and ever."[2]

Blackson's work, with its juxtapositions of biblically based narratives, political commentary, and historical explanation, poses some of the same questions as—and elicits reactions parallel to—those evoked by Wright's sermons. But it has rarely been taken seriously as an intellectual statement. Vernon Loggins, in his exhaustive study *The Negro Author: His Development in America* (1931), categorizes the work as fiction, criticizes its "disjointed," "childlike" reasoning, and dismisses it derisively as a "revelation of imaginative playfulness" that is "charmingly folkloristic." Moreover, he portrays Blackson as not only uneducated but singularly unattuned to the larger world of black literary culture, writing in an intellectual vacuum. As recently as 1989, the noted literary scholar Blyden Jackson also dismissed *Rise and Progress* for its lack of social and political relevance, its "hodgepodge" of allusion, and its piety and biblically derivative nature. Although they agree on his lack of aesthetic sensibility, Jackson and Loggins, ironically, come to opposing conclusions about how to situate Blackson culturally: to Jackson his work is tediously imitative of evangelical Anglo-American preoccupations; to Loggins, he embodies a "pure African temperament."[3]

What stands out in these assessments is the concordant desire to connect Blackson's work with familiar, racially derived styles: designated African or Anglo-American, it is more easily dismissed as the cultural product of a particular race. Further, both writers unambiguously associate a particular "racial style" with religious affiliation: for Blyden, Blackson's work is inferior because it imitates evangelical (Anglo-American) patterns (presumably Blackson's own evangelical style could not be the source, if one were even to admit that African Americans were capable of an evangelical style); Loggins, in turn, rejects Blackson's African temperament as "imaginative" (as opposed to mature and realistic) and folkloristic (in the sense of being unsupportable and probably specious)—all the reasons that Euro-Americans traditionally have set aside indigenous African beliefs. We hear in both valuations echoes of Du Bois's paradigm of a double-consciousness.

Both appraisals reveal little about Blackson's sense of self, or about the narrative that he produced. The fact is that a free black man with minimal formal education, in a moment of national crisis, took on a history of the world, for he understood history as a crucial mode of communication relevant in a time of war. In exploring history, he drew on the Bible, classical traditions, nascent theories of nationalism, Protestant denominational accounts, and diasporic African political developments to create a world he thought would be relevant and restorative for his readers. Blackson's world was defined by much more than the fact of his race or his lack of education: clearly he saw himself and his audience in relation to many communities— Christian, Methodist, American, African American, Northern—all of which played a part in his eschatological saga. His work is, literally, a map of the world as he imagined it.

Blackson's book is hardly alone on the library shelf. In 1867, the same year that *Rise and Progress* appeared, another self-taught African American, B. Clark, published *The Past, Present, and Future, in Prose and Poetry.*[4] Like Blackson, Clark wove sacred narrative with other literary styles, in a manner that was similarly perceived as discordant with Euro-American historical and religious patterns. Several dozen more narratives by African Americans in the late nineteenth century have also been ignored until recently. W. E. B. Du Bois himself produced a sprawling and spiritually infused novel in 1928 titled *Dark Princess,* a work that traced similar themes of racial identity and destiny. Although Du Bois referred to the novel as his favorite book, it is rarely mentioned by the many fans of Du Bois's work who take inspiration from the political valences of his sociology and philosophy. They generally dismiss *Dark Princess* as aberrant or simply propagandistic piety.[5]

We are faced, then, with a remarkable and almost entirely forgotten group of texts that share certain thematic similarities, not to mention aspirations to encapsulate the entire span of world history. They are chronicles in the original meaning of that term, a type of historical writing that flourished in Byzantium by the ninth century C.E. In that empire the writing of history took on a political cast as a means of shoring up the authority of the government in the eyes of the cultured public. The chronicle emerged as a more popular form of historical treatment, one cast in simple language that ran against the grain of official accounts and aroused the imagination. Often authors of these tales started with the creation of the world and traced a story up to the present, revising and adapting older sources freely as they went along. Chronicles thereby allowed for an alternative to the official voice, one inflected with local meanings and personalized to appeal to a broad audience. According to historians of the ancient world, their recovery is a treasure trove for understanding Eastern Christianity and the development of Byzantine civilization.[6]

Beginning as early as the 1780s, African Americans—mostly male, Northern, and Protestant—began to write and publish a new form of chronicle, communal narratives that wove together racial and religious concerns into sweeping chronological accounts. Although their immediate contexts and content are diverse, they all identify a particular group of people and situate them in a linear narrative of descent. Many even predict their destiny. Some, particularly those written before 1860, are fragmentary and only allude to a comprehensive view of the world in which the individual account is implicitly embedded. Increasingly, as the century proceeded, these narratives became mutually referential, drawing on tacit agreements about shared features, events, and figures, even while they diverged in other important respects. By the early twentieth century, African-American writers had fashioned a distinctive historical approach and a new textual genre.

This literary excavation is much more than an effort to rescue forgotten texts and historians from the dusty shelves of libraries. These chronicles open us to a new world of American popular expression with race and religion at its center. They shed new light on the significance of the work of better-known authors such as Booker T. Washington and W. E. B. Du Bois, African Americans frequently hailed as the heralds of black intellectual modernism. The "pathbreaking" work of Washington, who coauthored *A New Negro for a New Century* (1900) and later penned *The Story of the Negro* (1909), and the prescient political insights of Du Bois, who published *The Souls of Black Folk* (1903) and *The Negro* (1915), represent only the most well-known conduits of ideas that had circulated in black intellectual circles for much of the previous century. Indebted as both were to Euro-American scholarly currents and as determined as they were to reshape African-American representations, they also swam in a sea of black intellectual discourse. Washington and Du Bois stood squarely on the shoulders of dozens of artisans, ministers, Masons, journalists, and poets who had self-consciously struggled to create and sustain a racially defined intellectual culture. When Du Bois declared to white audiences that race was the preeminent problem of the twentieth century, his work relied on collective narration dating back nearly 150 years. He reasserted the call of many black intellectuals and writers for whom race had *always* been an abiding concern.

In contrast to the more familiar "slave narrative," we have no readily available language that captures the ongoing effort to *narrate* African Americans as parts of larger collective entities. These "communal narratives" refer to a community beyond the self, be it defined by African descent, Christian communion, or, most commonly, both; and a more or less explicit linear chronology that situates the community in a wider history. Part political commentary, part grand narrative, and part prognostication, Blackson's work, for instance, attempted a grand synthesis employing a figurative style of biblical interpretation in which previously disparate stories were woven together into a common narrative that referred to a single history. Through such an undertaking, Blackson created new interpretations of historical causation.[7]

Communal narratives are never simply texts; they are also the artifacts—and the sculptors—of particular collective experiences and desires. These authors and their narratives afford an invaluable and previously obscured glimpse into the formation and articulation of black communities in nineteenth-century America. Through the exploration of a series of paradigmatic themes, collective narratives provide a lens into the intersecting worlds of African-American religion and race between the American Revolution and World War I. If we listen to these voices from the past closely, we hear them chafing against the oppositions and binary definitions that observers have attempted to impose. Indeed, not only are these black translators of the American experience impudent in their refusal to be disciplined into received intellectual and religious categories; but also many of their claims, when examined closely, threaten to upset the standard conceptual apple cart altogether. Reimagining the relationships among national identity, religious affiliation, and racial lineage, African-American writers proposed a radical overturning of fundamental "American" assumptions about everything from the family, to Jesus, to the Fourth of July.[8]

A strong tradition of *collective* stories existed alongside the now better-known conversion accounts, autobiographies, fugitive slave narratives, and other sorts of individual testimonies.[9] They contained tales filled with histories of ancient peoples, fraternal orders, individual churches, national denominational bodies, Protestant nations, and eventually, racial histories in the modern sense, that is, stories of people united by a shared biology, history, and sacred purpose.[10] Despite their many differences of subject matter and approach, the works of authors such as Blackson, Clark, Du Bois, and dozens of others reflect a common concern and a shared method: these writers harnessed the intellectual and material resources of African-American Protestantism for the purposes of defining and empowering African Americans and exonerating them in the opinion of Euro-Americans. Individually, these stories answered specific needs at particular moments in time: they simultaneously spoke to distinctions based on gender, class, and region, and addressed the overriding and unifying realities of racial discrimination.

Current understandings of African-American life have been profoundly shaped by the search for an independent political voice, one that has, in its telling, perhaps necessarily screened out the buzz of complexity and countervailing voices. Yet there is a richness and density to nineteenth-century discussions of collective history among African Americans before 1920. Studies of black nationalism and black historiography, focusing as they have on key figures—mostly male—leave the impression that debates about race and history were significant only for elites. Those figures and their range of concerns—often traced from activists such as David Walker, Martin Delany, and Edward Blyden to George Washington Williams, Booker T. Washington, Du Bois, and Carter Woodson—have come to be seen as the sole intellectual lineage of African-American communal life. While it is certainly the case that those with education possessed the means to write, publish, and travel, their prominence depended on a thick network of organizations, technologies, and grassroots supporters within black (and white) communities, both at home and abroad. Ordinary men and women, in Christian churches, newspaper offices, literary clubs, and black colleges, provided bases of operations that eventuated in published historical accounts. The intellectual cultures of African-American life, then, were (and are) more variegated and complex than studies of black political history have allowed.

The creation of a black intellectual culture encompassed a range of concerns that extended well beyond what concepts such as "black nationalism" or even "history" might suggest. While countering the negative image of blacks as a "historyless" people—an image that was promoted by nearly all Euro-Americans at the time—African-American discussions ranged broadly into problems of human destiny, cultural difference, and fundamental unity. This rich discourse evinced curiosity about other world religions, speculated about the origins of evil, and debated women's rights. Rather than "skimming off" racial and political concerns as the "cream" of black intellectual life, those crucial issues need to be recontextualized in a world that nineteenth-century African Americans might recognize: it was a world devoid of our contemporary borders between the secular and the religious, the theological and the naturalistic, the political and the mystical, the ethnographic and the historical, and the academic and the folkloric. In what is perhaps the most controversial element of this conceptual "messiness," African Americans did not *always* conceive of race as the most salient feature of their self-understanding, although whites continuously foisted restrictive legal definitions upon blacks that forced the matter of race. Collective narratives liberated blacks to envision and enact worlds premised on the loyalties of family, gender, American nationality, and religious conviction. Their world was one in which collective identities were relatively fluid, contested, and shifting, and in which blacks spoke and wrote on a range of subjects.

The introduction and spread of Protestant Christian beliefs and practices were critical to the fashioning of an intellectual world. Cognitive work is too seldom understood as a form of religious practice; an overemphasis on other expressive forms, for example, dance, music, and preaching, runs the risk of ignoring the efforts of many African Americans to fashion what Pierre Hadot refers to as "cosmic consciousness." In his study of Christian spiritual exercises, Hadot argues that one of the legacies of early Christian practice was the understanding of *askesis,* that is, the living of the Christian life as an exercise in a particular kind of self-consciousness, a constant vigilance and attentiveness to God and his purposes. By the late eighteenth century, U.S. evangelicals had zealously adopted and adapted this cosmic awareness; both white and black converts were encouraged through spiritual exercises, prayer, and hymns to locate themselves at every minute in relation to God. It is no wonder, in this regard, that collective self-awareness became a significant part of this spiritual practice; communal narratives could continually reorient believers to the larger story of God's plan for the world.[11]

The use of the Exodus narrative by African Americans presents one limited example of the ways that stories could provide cognitive orientation through historical consciousness. The tale of Israel's rescue from the travails of Egypt has served as a powerful and multivalent image within black communities for more than two centuries; it has inspired both patience in the face of enslavement and discrimination, and activism to combat them.[12] But nineteenth-century African Americans used a broad range of stories and texts that extended far beyond the Exodus theme. Some of those narratives, in fact, such as the tale of Africans as the heirs to a glorious Egyptian past, stood in tension with the Exodus account (were the ancient Egyptians oppressors, guides to civilized existence, or both?). Just as the Exodus tale furnishes an important window into black sacred identity during this period, we must put it into historical play with the awareness of ancient Egypt and contemporary Haiti as sacred sites, of Ham and Solomon as communal leaders, of John Wesley and Richard Allen, and even George Washington, John Brown, and Abraham Lincoln as harbingers of African-American freedom. Only then will we begin to appreciate the full variety and productivity of African-American intellectual discourse.

Brought into the British colonies from different parts of Africa and the Caribbean, enslaved men and women arrived with varying loyalties and understandings of community, social identities that are difficult to recover today, but that were clearly quite different from the single legal status of "slave" proffered by their Euro-American owners. In this moment of cultural translation and transformation, they encountered at least three forms of collective self-awareness: race, religion, and nation. African Americans began to convert to Protestant faiths in large numbers in the late eighteenth and early nineteenth centuries, at precisely the same historical moment that gave rise to both biologically based theories of race and new conceptions of the "nation" as a potent form of political identity.[13]

The simultaneous emergence of these concepts was not mere coincidence, and in subsequent decades, the three remained intimately connected. Notions of religious, racial, and political loyalty and belonging interconnected in the worlds of antebellum African Americans (as they did for Euro-Americans) and remained entangled as blacks sought to retain an awareness of their distinct communal identity for subsequent generations. To do so, they used at least two forms of preservation: first, written narratives, including histories of denominations, churches, and both geographically specific and diasporic communities, many of which they produced with the economic and technological support of church enterprises; and second, commemorations, ritualized feasts, fasts, and celebrations that captured stories of the collective past, present, and future.[14] At the same time that African Americans were preserving their shared histories, they were also defining present religious and cultural realities, constituting specific and varied communities, and facilitating the further development of corporate identities. By the century's end, for at least some African-American Protestants, conceptions of race, religion, and national identity were indistinguishable: the notion of the "African race" had been sacralized and understandings of national identity and purpose integrated into a sacred saga of emancipation, redemption, and salvation. For many Protestants, the black church as a theological construct was perceived to be coterminous with the salvation of the race.

Relationships among the racial, national, and religious identities of African-American Protestants in the nineteenth century were dynamic and complex, and religious identity among African Americans was inseparable from the others. Some have argued, either implicitly or explicitly, that Christianity has frustrated the political goals of African diasporic unity and historically served as a divisive force within the African-American community. Christianity, the concept to be explained away in the pursuit of a legacy of racial unanimity, has been rendered as a puzzling sidelight to the otherwise comprehensible thought of early black nationalists; or worse yet, it has been seen as a thin, inconsequential veneer stretched over African practices and beliefs.[15] Conversely, those who have taken seriously the importance of Protestant beliefs and practices to the emergence of African-American collective identity often accept at face value the sacralization of racial categories advocated by late nineteenth-century leaders: they thereby depict the development of black churches as a monolithic and harmonious progression, ignoring the realities of denominational, political, and confessional differences that have divided African Americans for the last two centuries. In both instances, racial and religious identities have served to obscure individual and collective understandings.[16]

In many respects the trajectory of collective narratives, and the stories of religious, racial, and national loyalties of which they are composed, may sound like one more version of the movement from African ethnic particularism to African-American culture—a racialized version of ethnic assimilation into U.S. ways of "becoming American." And it would be, if the story were one of gradual but steady movement toward cultural unity. But African-American communal narratives tell a different tale. Beyond legal definitions, African Americans have always disagreed, in fundamental and sometimes vocal ways, about what it means to be African American, to be Christian, and to be American. Paradoxically, just as concepts of religion and race furnished tools for a certain kind of rhetorical and cultural unity among African Americans—especially among literate, professional males in the Northeastern states—they also served to separate, to distinguish, and to divide in other ways. Collective narratives provoke cultural tension by their very nature, inasmuch as they separate an "us" from a "them." Black authors, then, were not employing terms with unambiguous—or uncontested—meaning. Embedded within their understandings of peoplehood were other signifiers related to class and economic status, religious affiliation, gender, nationality, and even regional affiliation.

Lorenzo Blackson's narrative provides a helpful illustration. It is not a simple tale of black virtue and white evil; race is only one of the factors that complicate his explication of collective struggle. In this story of the ongoing battle between the kingdoms of light and those of darkness, the author sequentially privileges the perspectives of Americans (who, by their nature, seem to be more allied with the forces of good in the world), of Protestants (who run up against the "Beast" of Catholic popery), of Methodists (who appear to be more intimate with God than are most other denominations), and of men (no women appear as foot soldiers in the divine army). Many fine and sometimes conflicting distinctions inform the work, rendering the precise subject of the heroic "we" a moving target. Race is important here, but not definitive. In the end, the narrative seems to free the reader from any easy conclusions about which group comprises the heroic survivors.

Individual writers shape whole worlds and situate entire communities in times and places. In doing so, they script narratives of behavior and activity, stories that make sense of their lives in relation to those around them. Those scripts are, in turn, composed in idioms made accessible to us by virtue of our connections with "significant others."[17] For African Americans, those "significant others" included a Euro-American society that stood as both oppressor and enabler. Blacks increasingly asserted themselves as a coherent social unit in part as a response to the social fact of enslavement and the ideological relentlessness of negative images promoted by white Americans. In other words, Africans *became* African American as a necessary response to Euro-American persecution. Yet that same Euro-American society, and particularly evangelical Protestantism in both its intellectual and its institutional guises, also furnished the media necessary to construct counternarratives of unity and sacred purpose. Ultimately, as is the case with all collective memories, this process of narration resulted in the affirmation of a group identity that came to be seen as "natural" and inevitable rather than humanly constructed, denying its own genesis in a particular historical circumstance.

These narratives reinforce the historical linkages between Euro-American and African-American notions of collective identity, for both were forged in a moment when national, religious, and racial philosophies were emerging. But they complicate, and even contradict, assertions of racial unity. African Americans lived in—and still live in—many different worlds and communities; their bonds of loyalty and obligation have been shaped by multiple forces.[18] This extraordinary variety of racial and collective narratives, a new era of chronicles, illustrates how African Americans worked to negotiate within and across boundaries while maintaining a voice within a Euro-American society that insistently demanded, and now still anticipates, a monolithic response. These narratives also suggest that the rest of our society is impoverished by forgetfulness. The Wright phenomenon is a symptom of the fact that we have lost the critical tools to help us speak across contemporary racial divides. Recovering those voices heard so eloquently in these pages is a crucial step toward a collective rehabilitation of memory.

1

Wonders of the Ancient Past

The voice of history is the voice of God.

PAULINE HOPKINS, *Colored American Magazine* (1905)

People are trapped in history and history is trapped in them.

JAMES BALDWIN, *Notes of a Native Son* (1955)

Jacob Oson (1778?–1828) was not a well-known or terribly influential man in the early American republic. But he had seen a lot. As a teacher at a school for African Americans in New Haven, Connecticut, Oson labored on the frontlines of the halting and uneven movement from slavery to quasi-freedom in the urban North. Like other free blacks of his day, Oson witnessed both the hope unleashed by the official abolition of the United States slave trade in 1808 and the growing collective despair as racial lines began to harden again. By 1816 he had seen the flowering of independent African-American organizational life—churches, fraternal groups, and schools—and increasing white-sponsored institutional support for the full-scale deportation of black citizens to Africa. It is not hard to imagine, then, that in 1817 Oson harbored many pressing questions about his life and the lives of blacks in his community. Would they have jobs to support themselves? Would free blacks be accosted on the streets by white mobs? Would people of African descent ultimately be allowed to stay in the United States?

These many nagging questions about the long-term survival of African-American communities make Oson's only published speech, an address delivered in the spring of 1817 in New Haven, all the more remarkable. Oson began his talk not with a political statement or a call to arms. He began, instead, with a profound and fundamental set of questions. Who are we? Where has our community come from, and where is it going? Oson delivered a speech about "his people" and their own search for history: "My thoughts run on my people and nations; and I wish to inquire, who was our common Father, and from whom we sprang?"[1] The oration's premise of "people and nations" summoned images of plurality, variation, and dispersion that remained evocatively ambiguous: Who were his people? To what did nations refer? The United States? Countries that contained diasporic Africans? The African continent itself? A month later he delivered the same speech in New York City, and soon thereafter published it at the request of Christopher Rush, a local minister in the African Methodist Episcopal Church, Zion (AMEZ).

Most intriguing of all was the intellectual range Oson displayed in his work. Filled with erudite references to the Bible, classical allusions, and the poetry of the late Yale president Timothy Dwight, Oson's speech linked the history of African peoples in America to an ancient past. *A Search for Truth* assayed biblical history, republican notions of virtue, and classical political precedents, querying the origins and nature of the community of African-descended peoples. Oson concluded his speech with a quotation from Virgil's *Aeneid,* translated by the British scientist Erasmus Darwin in 1794:

Earth, on whose lap ten thousand nations tread,
And Ocean, brooding his prolific bed;
Night's changeful orb, blue pole and silvery zones,
Where other worlds encircle other suns,
One mind inhabits: one diffusive soul
Wields these huge limbs, and mingles with the whole.[2]

Stepping back from an inquiry about racial particularity, Oson's final lines framed a vision of unity, the "diffusive soul" in which all differences were melded. Africa and America had been united.

That same year a Haitian of African extraction, Baron Pompée Valentin de Vastey (1781–1820), published the essay *Reflexions on Blacks and Whites.* Although it appeared initially in French, it was picked up almost immediately by the Tory *Quarterly Journal,* a London-based periodical published by John Murray.[3] A decade later an edited and serialized version appeared in the first African-American newspaper, *Freedom's Journal.* In his work Vastey combined the new intellectual currents of biblical interpretation, ethnography, and the natural sciences to refute charges of African inferiority and to assert proudly the significance of early African civilizations. His geographical scope was wider than that of Oson, who hewed closely to the republican nationalism voiced by Euro-Americans in the United States. Vastey's Gallic sensibilities and influences rendered him more sympathetic to monarchy as an ideal political model.

Despite their geographic distance and political differences, there are evident parallels between Oson's and Vastey's narrative tactics. Theirs were among the earliest accounts by diasporic African Americans to survey the origins and destiny of a group that Oson referred to as "the African Nation." They would not be the last. Over the following century, dozens of men and women, most (but not all) of them Protestant Christians in the United States, produced lectures, sermons, poetry, plays, and histories that posed similar sets of questions. Like Oson, some had little or no formal education; many were self-taught. Eventually, their efforts were forcibly overshadowed —but not entirely silenced—by the twentieth-century hunger for professionalization, careful documentation, and "modern" views of historical inquiry. Their efforts left their mark, however, and served as background and subtext for the intellectual efforts of virtually all subsequent scholars of African-American cultures.

What were these collective stories all about, and why did they become so important to people of color living on the margins of New World societies? Certainly they were a reaction to white oppression and to the belief common among Euro-Americans that African diasporic peoples, slave or free, had no past worth remembering, no stories, and no culture. White activists have long been credited with the emergence of African-American communal narration. Vernon Loggins noted in the 1930s, for example, that white abolitionists in the 1820s and 1830s, particularly Benjamin Lundy and William Lloyd Garrison, "did much toward awakening a racial pride in the Negro." More recently African-American publishing of the 1820s has been credited with creating a sense of common origin and destiny among peoples of African descent. Others have highlighted the importance of biblical tropes and particularly Exodus as a significant and enduring model for African diasporic community. Still, African-American collective stories, in most instances, have been framed principally as reactions to white racist structures and ideas.[4]

Black communal narrators were no doubt cognizant of white oppression, and they challenged it as best they could in print and in public. Collective identities are by necessity formed in relation to others, and whites insistently reminded blacks that they were second-class "others" within a system of Euro-American dominance. Forced migration and enslavement also shaped narratives: we are left to imagine what forms communal narration might have taken if more diasporic Africans, like Vastey, had been freed earlier and accorded justice within New World societies. But what about Oson's questions? Were they mere instruments of politics, attempts to work up his audience?

If Oson, Vastey, and other authors were motivated principally by the desire to instill racial pride and incite protest, their narratives also reflected an odd and elliptical choice of approaches. Why embed collective stories in such intricate narratives? Something beyond political expediency seems to have been at work. The questions asked and the answers proposed moved far beyond the realm of the American political scene to envision something much larger, longer, and more enduring. We might better liken Oson's and Vastey's authorial efforts to Cotton Mather's Puritan chronicles or the historical projects of George Bancroft, intellectual efforts that could hardly be considered simply straightforward American political replies to Old World critics. Oson and Vastey, much like Mather and Bancroft, were creating and enacting culture: African-American communal narratives responded to immediate circumstances, but they simultaneously summoned a new world into being. Their accounts of racial origin and destiny invested deeper significance into the lives of peoples who desired meaning beyond what whites were willing to bestow. That Oson and Vastey did so in different national settings, one newly republican and the other monarchical, influenced by distinct intellectual currents, makes their commonalities even more intriguing. Through common stories and an appeal to a shared African history, Oson, Vastey, and their colleagues produced racial identities intended to transcend national and political divides.

For all their similarities, however, this historical process was also fractious and even self-contradictory. The mechanisms that gave rise to a cultural consciousness both unified and divided free blacks during this period. The creation of a common language of memory (for this is what historical narratives impart) also encouraged personal and collective authority in areas that were not overtly racial, and that at times worked against what some "African Americans" understood to be the political interests of their "people." The most remarkable aspect of these narratives is not the collective unity they assert but the degree to which they, as symbolic presentations of collective unity linked to a particular time and collection of peoples, allowed free blacks to obscure or conceal many real social divisions.[5]

Free blacks, in fact, began to tell stories of a common origin as soon as they gained the means to do so, as early as the 1780s. Comprehensive racial and religious histories did not spring into being all at once. Indeed, African Americans did not begin to publish what might be termed "grand narratives" until at least the late 1840s; these book-length works became a much more prominent part of black intellectual life only after the 1880s, when authors such as George Washington Williams published volumes that attempted comprehensively to survey the history of the "African race." Yet nearly a half-century before the abolitionists seized systematically upon the power of the ancient African legacy, diasporic African authors engaged in "narrative acts," shorthand allusions to sacred and classical history in a way that signaled their knowledge—and creative reinterpretation—of much broader stories.[6] The dissemination of this collective knowledge was encouraged by the growth of technological and intellectual resources within free black communities. Over the next seven decades, in pamphlets, sermons, and other orations, blacks formulated increasingly elaborate historical arguments in defiance of the challenges of European and Anglo-American critics who denied that African Americans had a history of any value.

The first traces of narration can be located in the rise of Protestant evangelicalism and Freemasonry among African Americans. Speeches delivered in the 1780s and 1790s by Prince Hall and John Marrant, two free Northern black community leaders, evince a discernible pattern of storytelling reliant on both inherited and new knowledge: biblical and classical texts, narratives borrowed from Masonic lore, European and Euro-American scholarship of the late eighteenth and early nineteenth centuries, hymns, oral accounts handed down through families, and possibly models of historical narrative derived from African customs. Their histories linked a sacralized view of ancient Africa, principally signified as Egypt or Ethiopia, to a racialized lineage in which Africans figured as the custodians of true wisdom to the present age. This mode of historical narration would continue within the ranks of

Prince Hall Masonry for at least the next century in the writings of free blacks such as David Walker, John Hilton, and Martin Delany, and would, in turn, influence other renderings of a communal past.

By the turn of the century another generation of free black orators built upon this nascent tradition, embedding racializc[1] narratives in new contexts: the extensive use of classical authors, the history of the slave trade, new scientific discussions of human variation, and nationalist sensibilities fueled by the American, French, and Haitian revolutions. Beginning in 1808 with the closing of the U.S. slave trade, free blacks along the Eastern seaboard commemorated the past and diagnosed the present in parades and celebrations: Absalom Jones, William Hamilton, Russell Parrott, Nathaniel Paul, Henry Sipkins, and Peter Williams, among others, published speeches that blended intellectual strands from a wide variety of sources. Their histories, like those written by Jacob Oson, Prince Saunders, and the Haitian Baron de Vastey in 1817, reflected diasporic contacts fostered through churches, lodges, and mercantile exchanges.

This impulse was not limited to the United States but extended among free black communities from Canada to the Caribbean. It was, from its beginnings, an international process. Protestant missionary activity spread such accounts wherever African Americans loyal to Great Britain settled after the American Revolution; John Marrant himself evangelized in a black settlement in Nova Scotia in the late 1780s, among a group that eventually migrated to Sierra Leone.[7] Commerce also facilitated communication of these narratives as Africans moved goods and bodies around the Atlantic trade system. With the opening of Liberia after 1820, Prince Hall lodges dotted the West African landscape as well as the urban centers of Pennsylvania, Boston, and New York. By the 1850s, émigrés in Canada West published and reported communal narratives and hosted travelers who offered still more reflections on the past.

The year 1817 marks a significant turning point in this process. Like Jacob Oson, other urban free blacks by the mid-1810s were feeling the stirrings of an increasingly organized and differentiated community life. In 1816, Richard Allen and his fellow African Methodists had formed the first independent black denomination, the African Methodist Episcopal Church, from the proliferating number of Methodist churches between Boston and

Charleston. That same year saw the founding of the white-sponsored American Colonization Society (ACS), a development that led African Americans to turn to missionary work with new energy. Some blacks were sympathetic or at least willing to cooperate with the ACS, while others actively opposed the implications of black "removal" from the United States. But in both cases, the colonization movement opened the door to heightened interest in pan-African communication and cooperation.

Beginning in the 1820s numerous technological and social developments in the Northern states encouraged a still more fully developed strand of collective histories: the establishment of the black press, which made such accounts accessible to increasing numbers of African Americans (and whites); the growth of free black associations, including literary societies, Sunday schools, and lycea, afforded African-American women the opportunity to relate history in public spaces; the rise of the abolitionist movement, which offered financial support for publishing ventures and speaking tours; and the burgeoning colonization and missionary enterprises which, for good and for ill, facilitated the transmission of ethnographic knowledge about Africa. By the 1830s, African-American authors such as Maria Stewart, Hosea Easton, J. W. C. Pennington, R. B. Lewis, Henry Highland Garnet, and Frederick Douglass had many more tools—both intellectual and technological—at their disposal for their renderings of history. They looked back to the late eighteenth century and commemorated early authors and political figures; they drew on black abolitionists, ministers, and politicians as harbingers of collective vitality; and they published their narratives in a far greater range of forms that would be read by a wide variety of people.

By the coming of the Civil War, diasporic Africans did not have a canonical account of their past, for the process of historical narration itself was filled with conflicts and disagreements: the apocalyptic work of Lorenzo Dow Blackson and the messianic prophesies of Robert Young existed uneasily alongside the measured and diplomatic musings of Oson and the systematic chartings of J. W. C. Pennington. In these increasingly diverse settings, African Americans spoke with multiple voices out of a variety of interests. Yet they shared marked resemblances and common questions, queries that provided free blacks with a distinctive means of disseminating collective history that set them apart from Euro-Americans, and that related the story of

African and American origins in original ways. Like many Euro-Americans in both the South and the North, they shared the sense that they were part of a community with a sacred purpose in the unfolding of the divine plan of redemption.[8]

Black leaders understood themselves to be uncovering preexistent accounts of an African community bound by the "natural" ties of shared history, values, and traditions, features that distinguished them from Europeans, white Americans, and other "peoples" of the world. Yet in the course of recovery these intellectuals, like other Americans of their time, combined resources from a wide variety of places to create new cultural forms. Free blacks were not simply recovering a lost set of stories about Africa; they were defining a new community by building stories that constituted a sense of belonging to something that preceded them and would continue after their time. Africa, the place constructed in their accounts, played a critical role in this process as the primary site of origin and point of reference; there could be no "African Americans," in other words, until there were people who understood themselves as such through hearing and recounting stories about themselves.

The communal narrative tradition resides in attempts by blacks to make connections between the communities created in their accounts and the land and people of Africa. It seems reasonable to ask, then, what role the Africa of recent memory, and particularly indigenous African practices of narrating the past and making history, had on the development of these early American accounts.

African Americans did not begin their narration of the past with a blank slate, of course, despite attempts by Europeans and Americans to assert that Africa had no history of any importance.[9] A rich scholarship has developed in recent years that suggests the continuity of cultural forms, from music to art to speaking, which linked slave cultures in the Americas back to African patterns. In West African societies the most evident analogue to a historian is the figure of the *griot* or *jali*, the storyteller who sang or spoke tales of the ancestors, of family and kingship lineages, and of collective life, keeping alive the memories of the ethnic group. These traditions were passed along orally within slave communities in the United States, as narrators transmitted stories focusing primarily on tricksters, animals, and other figures dwelling in an "eternal present."[10]

The hunt for African antecedents was more complicated among free Northern blacks, who were generally more assimilated into white society than were their enslaved counterparts and retained fewer direct ties to African cultural groups. Beyond suggestive contours and patterns, it is exceedingly difficult to disentangle distinctly "African" elements of collective narration in the Americas. The reasons for this are both cultural and historical. A principal problem is the tendency to oppose "oral" African and "literate" Euro-American societies. Scholars have thus sometimes located "African" elements of African-American cultures in the uses of orality, often presumed to be more characteristic of Africa than of early America. In this line of thinking, oral forms of historical transmission were counterposed to the fixed print cultures into which Africans were being assimilated, yielding a different kind of history.

Eighteenth-century Africans had a complicated and varied relationship to literacy, owing in great measure to cultural diversity and religious transmission beginning well before the start of the transatlantic slave trade. Even if we speak only of West Africa, the area from which most enslaved peoples in the New World came, the array of cultural traditions, including the practices of literate Muslims and Christians as well as indigenous ways of life, and the varying degrees of exposure to print technologies make it difficult to draw firm conclusions. Many West Africans clearly had access to writing and printed materials before enslavement—and indeed, began to incorporate printed materials into their oral accounts almost immediately—because of the influence of Islamic education and Roman Catholic missions in certain regions. West African oral traditions, including understandings and representations of past events, changed shape rapidly in response to European domination: a characteristic tactic was to amplify the antiquity of a genealogy or king list by artificially lengthening it, and by including gods and heroes as human rulers.[11]

In a real sense, eighteenth-century West Africa was considerably more cosmopolitan and more closely linked to international currents of commerce, politics, and religion than was colonial British America, where orality and literacy were also intricately entwined in everyday life. British North America placed great value on the literacy of its population, but on the eve of the Industrial Revolution, before the advent of mass publishing, oral transmission of knowledge necessarily played an important role in everyday life.[12]

Thus diasporic Africans were not poised on a precipice between oral and literate communities. While literacy among African Americans was certainly more widespread in the urban Northern states than in the South, written texts did not spell the demise of oral accounts. Northern blacks often represented their direct experience of the African past, for example, by way of family connections. Some recalled little other than familial gestures: Phillis Wheatley, the famed Boston-based poet, reported that "the only thing that clung to her about Africa was seeing her mother pour out water before the rising sun." But many others recounted tales of beloved parents and other kin, particularly women, who imprinted elaborate stories of the past in the minds of their offspring. Martin Delany, decades away from Africa himself, loved to tell the story of his Grandma Grace. He was proud of the Mandingo songs and stories she had told him when he was a child. From her, too, he learned about his mother's father, an African prince from the Niger Valley who had been called "Shango." Late in his life, Delany noted that Shango was also the name of an African god, "the same to which ancient Egypt paid divine homage under the name of Jupiter Ammon."[13] Delany's account, with its linking of oral stories of the immediate past to images of Africa (in this case, signified as ancient Egypt), the latter likely acquired through print, illustrates that strands of oral and written knowledge were, in practice, deeply entangled.

African-American communal narratives reflected both oral and literate traditions. On the one hand, they were textual and material products: printed and published for a variety of purposes, they bore the marks of certain educational strands that could only have come from exposure to European and British American intellectual traditions passed on primarily through the reading of texts. On the other hand, they were embedded in oral performance, commemoration, and pageantry, circulating in a variety of settings from the United States to the Caribbean and Africa, and back again. It is most useful, then, to think about these accounts as both oral and liter-

ary, African and American, and as product and process that brought into being new communities, peoples who recognized themselves in these stories.

If this process of creation was dialectical, knitting elements of African and
Anglo-American knowledge-making, the subject of these accounts is clearly
the recovery—we might even say the *rediscovery*—of Africa, among those
blacks who were demographically most removed from African communities: Northern free blacks. The earliest traces of collective narration are located in the burgeoning free black communities in what would soon be
the Northern United States. Between 1760 and 1810, the number of free
blacks in the Northern states grew briskly, from several thousand to almost
200,000. By 1850, approximately 330,000 free men and women lived in
Northern, mostly urban, settings. Cities such as Boston, Providence, New
Haven, Philadelphia, and New York contained sizeable free black communities, although African Americans were still treated very much as second-
class citizens.[14] In these settings, the creation of narratives was closely connected to two social and institutional developments that might appear, on
the face of it, to be contradictory: the "re-Africanization" of free black communities in the late eighteenth century, and the growth of independent
black fraternal and Protestant religious organizations.

Slavery as an institution did not just die out gradually in the North;
rather, it experienced a boom in the century before it ceased. Growing de-
mands for labor in the early eighteenth century had increased dramatically
the number of Africans being imported directly to colonies in the North; by
the 1750s, approximately 70 percent of slaves arrived in Northern ports
from the African continent. Increasing numbers of migrants from the Caribbean also supplemented the population and provided a steady infusion of
cultural knowledge from African regions. Therefore, even as the percentage
of native Africans in the population decreased steadily and American birth
rates climbed, American-born blacks continued to have access to firsthand
African experience as a tangible element of everyday life. As late as the
1810s, most African Americans in Northern cities would have had personal
experience with many people who were African-born.[15]

It is no coincidence, then, that in the 1770s and 1780s, free blacks began
adopting the modifier "African" in the names of their schools, benevolent
societies, and churches. This implementation of an abstract African identity
(as opposed to the adoption of any of the many particular identities among

African peoples) may have been a new way of identifying with Africa and of expressing a psychic link to a homeland, even though some blacks were coming to view Africa itself as backward and heathen. It is also possible that this use of nomenclature represented primarily a political tactic, that "African" became a political symbol, a name adopted as a way of signifying equality with white Americans who thought about legitimate public acknowledgment of cultural difference in terms of national affiliation.[16] Another possibility is that African Americans were indeed identifying with Africa and were highlighting a collective consciousness. That homeland, far from being simply a convenient political label, signified a far more profound shift; its reclamation in the hands of free black leaders provided a way for them simultaneously to become participants in American life while retaining a distinctive cultural identity, an African heritage based on a reconstructed constellation of images.

In their narratives, Africa was a constant presence as subject—but not in a form that would have been recognizable to most eighteenth-century West Africans. This reconstituted Africa was ancient and heroic, and it was tied to the present through lineages of prophets and patriarchs who safeguarded noble characteristics. Indeed, one of the most striking characteristics of the earliest free black communal narratives is their silence about the recent African past. As with contemporary primitivist and restorationist religious movements that marked Euro-Protestant culture, black urban authors focused on the connections between the ancient world and the present condition of African Americans, skipping over recent history in favor of a distant, glorious civilization ennobled by the passage of time. Most of the images that African-American authors employed in their narratives were derived from biblical and classical historians, not from memories supplied from firsthand (or even secondhand) experience in Africa. In this sense, one African lineage was chosen in place of another, perhaps more troubling, image. These were silences in collective narratives that bespoke an increasing psychic distance from the motherland.[17]

Protestant and Masonic narratives provided the content of that new focus on an older and less morally problematic Africa. The homeland could simultaneously be renounced and gradually recovered through the lenses of the Bible, the Western classical tradition, the writings of Puritan ministers, fraternal ritual, and evangelical hymnbooks. This was a creative and sometimes contradictory re-creation of Africa on American soil, principally among those who had not experienced Africa for themselves.

The richest repository of resources for African Americans' formulation of a new Africa came from the institutions to which free blacks increasingly were indebted: the Masonic Lodge and the Protestant Church. Beginning in the mid-eighteenth century, African Americans, like their Euro-American counterparts, yielded to the heady calls for repentance and conversion proffered by evangelical revivalists. Aside from the many social and political advantages offered by Protestant Church membership, conversion also offered abundant intellectual and emotional resources. Among the most important of these was a new purchase on history itself, one that could help diasporic Africans make sense of their earthly plight. Conversion drew believers into membership in a comprehensive and sweeping historical drama.[18] Christian history, premised on a linear narrative, sited in a particular geography, and populated by a discernible cast of characters, provided a rich set of models for African Americans. Albert Ukawsaw Gronniosaw composed one of the earliest personal narratives written by a New World African: *A Narrative of the Most Remarkable Particulars in the Life of James Albert Ukawsaw Gronniosaw, an African Prince, as Related by Himself.*[19] Gronniosaw, an eighteenth-century African, was sold into New World slavery and converted to Christianity. After his master died, he was given his freedom and moved to England, where he married and reared a family. His narrative, first published in 1770, opens with a series of what we might call "origin" questions, queries that unnerved his mother as well as the rest of his family:

> My dear mother says I, pray tell me who is the GREAT MAN of POWER that makes the thunder? She said, there was no power but the sun, moon and stars; that they made all our country.————I then enquired how all our people came? She answered me, from one another; and so carried me to many generations back.————Then says I, who made the *First Man?* and who made the first Cow, and the first Lyon, and where does the fly come from, as no one can make him? My mother seemed in great trouble; she was apprehensive that my senses were impaired, or that I was foolish.[20]

They were questions, apparently, with no ready answers in his community of birth. Yet Gronniosaw, recalling those early events many decades later, after having lived for years within a Christian culture, frames his quest as a search for answers that have already been laid out in a sacred plan authored by a divine God. The world of his family, a community in which a narration of the past could not logically contain the elements detailed in his questions—cows, lions, humans, a "great man of power"—becomes in his telling a world without access to the reality of the "true" story. Gronniosaw's memoir is prefaced by a reference to Isaiah that spells out the extent to which his Christian understanding had, for the transplanted African, become a discovery of something preexistent: "I will bring the blind by a Way that they know not, I will lead them in paths that they have not known: I will make darkness light before them and crooked things straight. These things will I do unto them and not forsake them" (Isaiah 42:16).

Gronniosaw's narrative exemplifies the complex relationships between enslaved Africans and their homelands that developed, beginning as early as the fifteenth century, as a result of Christian conversion. Natal beliefs and stories became blindness, prior practices were rendered as darkness, and the ways of knowing in African ethnic subcultures were transformed, in the Christianized telling, into dead-end paths.[21] Yet even as Gronniosaw recognized "Africa" and "Europe" as distinctly different places, marked by opposing approaches to fundamental questions, his narrative reflects the fusion of forms: oral accounts embedded within printed texts, and Africa seen through the lens of a universalized worldview that relativized it. Gronniosaw does not forget Africa; instead he distances himself from its contemporary modes of knowledge. This characteristic denial does not prevent diasporic Africans such as Gronniosaw from reconstituting a viable African past.[22]

African Americans living in New England, in particular, would have been exposed to views of the Christian past inflected by Puritanism, with its emphasis on a transcendent and inscrutable God of judgment and justice. Anglo-American writers in the colonial era linked themselves to this religious heritage through narratives of patriarchal lineage, grace, and obedience to the will of an omniscient Creator. Figures such as Benjamin Franklin wrote themselves into an emerging capitalist world by connecting themselves to the past in their memoirs. So, too, did early African-American evangelicals such as Lemuel Haynes and Jupiter Hammon narrate themselves into Puritan historical models to understand their current plight. Stories of Israelite enslavement offered a sacred historical framework within which their own suffering made sense.[23]

Free blacks, many of whom lived in the homes of, or in close proximity to, whites, would have had frequent exposure to the symbols and stories of the Bible. Albert Gronniosaw's master, the revivalist minister Theodore Frey-linghuysen of New York, sent the young man to school, and Freylinghuysen's wife gave him evangelical books to read. Gronniosaw also reported having read books by Puritan leaders such as Richard Baxter and John Bunyan. Other slaves read and memorized hymnbooks.[24] The evangelical preacher and missionary John Marrant mentions in his journal taking the Bible and "one of Dr. Watts's hymnbooks" with him to pray, and singing those hymns in times of trial. Many other colonial African Americans reported on the importance of the Bible as an instructional manual when they learned to read. Even African Americans who did not convert likely gained varying degrees of biblical literacy through hymns, stories, and the mere fact of living in a society saturated with the metaphors and characters of the Christian narrative.[25]

By the 1770s, free blacks in Northern cities were also coming into contact with the Masonic tradition, a fraternal organization with close ties to Christian churches. Black or "Prince Hall" Masonry arose in urban centers such as Boston, Philadelphia, and Providence in the 1780s in response to waves of black migration into Northern urban centers. On this racial frontier, black leaders sought ways to aid the relocation of migrants, and Masonry served many of those instrumental functions. Refused membership into white lodges, black men gained the support of sympathetic British Masons, who brought them into fraternal association with the founding of the Prince Hall Lodge (named after its charter member). With its emphasis on the building of character, conveyed through the metaphor of architecture and the practice of charity, Masonry promoted a distinctive form of black manhood and participation within the free black community. By 1850, there were roughly twenty-five to thirty black Masonic lodges in major Northern cities from Louisville to Boston.[26]

Churches and lodges served as important sites for the social and intellectual creation of African-American community. Both movements spread quickly among free Northern blacks of some means and education, those who aspired to economic prosperity and social position, and those who sought to ensure collective aid and support in an inhospitable environment. Lodges also served the important functions of providing burial costs for widows, aiding in the education of surviving children, and encouraging the virtuous behavior (temperance and thrift, for example) of members. Because of the fairly narrow range of occupations open to blacks at the time, class distinctions were not well articulated in religious or fraternal settings; membership rolls reveal a variety of occupations, including unskilled laborers, merchants, barbers, and the few teachers and ministers within the community.

Membership in lodges and church affiliation were also intimately linked. Many leaders of the first Masonic lodges were active church members or clergy: in addition to Prince Hall, who was himself reported to have been a Methodist preacher (although no evidence supports this assertion), black Masonry claimed antebellum Protestant luminaries such as Richard Allen, Absalom Jones, John Marrant, James Forten, Richard Gleaves, and Martin Delany.[27]

Freemasonry and Protestantism encouraged self-transformation as a mark of membership; both emphasized the trope of newness, of the rebirth of identity within a new community. Black Freemasonry, in particular, drew on strains of Calvinist theology dominant in New England at the time to blend biblical and fraternal history into a potent mix.[28] They each relied on notions of kinship—of brotherhood and sisterhood—to unite members in a common cause. And although neither church nor lodge practiced racial equality as perfectly as they preached it, their rhetoric was infused with calls for egalitarian harmony. In May 1787 the *Massachusetts Sentinel* published a poem that encapsulates this melding of fraternal and evangelical traditions:

> THRO'OUT the globe's extensive round,
>   The fire of love extends,
> Which glows in true masonick hearts—
>   That family of friends!
> Ev'n AFRIC's SONS—ill-fated race!
>   Now feel its genial heat;
> With charter'd rights, from England's Duke,
>   THE SABLE LODGES MEET.[29]

Employing these themes in word and practice, churches and lodges very quickly changed perceptions of the immediate past for African-American members. For these neophytes, Africa and one's personal experiences there (or those of one's family) became the unenlightened foil to a newly moral self; African origins represented the old, the non-Christian, the sinful creature before salvation who had now been offered a way into the light. Christian and Masonic historical awareness thereby provided a mode of transformation, an intellectual framework for moving from contemporary African families and tribes to Christian communities. In addition, these traditions furnished narrative models, including significant figures and traditions, for the birth of a new Africa on American soil. By fusing biblical accounts of the ancient world, identified with Africa, with noble patriarchs common to both biblical and Masonic lore, these first African-American historians wove collective accounts of honor, wisdom, and hope.

Black Masonic history, like its white counterpart, drew extensively on biblical narratives to undergird its claims to legitimacy. Freemasons used scriptural accounts freely and creatively. Masons have never agreed on a single definitive history, but many accounts of the origins of Freemasonry center around the transmission of the ancient wisdom of architecture—and, by extension, the moral virtues associated with it—from the Israelites, to the crusaders and knights of medieval Christianity, to the artisanal guilds of "operative masons," and finally to the "speculative" Freemasons of the modern era. A favorite point of narrative departure, and a dominant theme in the initiation ceremonies of new Masons, was the account of the construction of King Solomon's temple, which was said to have been designed and built under the oversight of Hiram, a master builder and one of the first Masons. Thus Masons extended biblical accounts into the recent past in ways that connected contemporary lodge members to a distinguished sacred origin and lineage.[30]

This blending of Christian and Masonic imagery proved a potent mix, and it lent itself almost immediately to creative interpretation on the part of African-American members. The first African-American narrators, however, supplied an additional twist: they identified the point of Edenic origin with ancient Africa and the noble lineage with dark-skinned Africans. The first black Masonic account that has been preserved is an oration delivered by John Marrant in 1789. Born in New York City in 1755, Marrant is perhaps known best for his conversion to Christianity at the hands of the British itinerant revivalist George Whitefield, and his subsequent missionary work among American Indians in the Southeast and black loyalists in Nova Scotia. During a brief stay in Boston in the late 1780s, Marrant joined African Lodge No. 459 (the first lodge founded by Prince Hall) and served as its chaplain. In June 1789 he delivered a sermon on the occasion of the feast day of St. John, the patron saint of Masonry. This characteristic Masonic occasion was a day of festivity: lodges often sponsored a parade that concluded at one of the local black churches, where a sermon was delivered for the occasion. We know little about Marrant's audience, but it most likely included other members of the black community: wives and families of Masons, members of the church, and spectators intrigued by the sight of some of the prominent men in the community dressed in their regalia.

In his speech Marrant sought to establish the legitimacy of African-American claims to membership. To do so, he turned to history, weaving a narrative that fused scriptural authority, Masonic lore, and political commentary. Beginning with the creation of the world by the Grand Architect of the Universe, Marrant recounted select elements of the biblical narrative from the perspective of Egypt and peoples associated with the Masonic tradition. On the basis of his readings of Eusebius, Jerome, and other church fathers, Marrant placed the Garden of Eden adjacent to the Nile River, concluding that "Paradise did as it were border upon Egypt." The precision of his geography stressed the centrality of Africa to God's plan for the world. But Marrant also asserted that God had thereby marked off the peoples of Egypt—and by extension, of Africa—as sacred. When Euro-Americans enslaved African peoples, they risked divine wrath: "what nation or people dare, without highly displeasing and provoking that God to pour down His judgments upon them . . . to despise or tyrannize over their lives or liberties, or encroach on their lands, or to enslave their bodies?"[31]

From there Marrant moved through a biblical lineage that initially appears quite idiosyncratic. He related the story of Cain, who was cursed by God for the murder of his brother, but who also learned from his father "to contemplate and study God's works," that is, the knowledge of architecture and the arts and sciences. In his later years Cain found peace in building a city east of Eden. Marrant made brief mention of Noah, who demonstrated his knowledge of the craft by building the ark, and later passed his expertise to his sons. The orator then dwelt at length on Nimrod, "the son of Cush, the son of Ham," who became the grand master of all Masons by building many cities. Eventually Nimrod brought his builders to Egypt, where they constructed the Sphinx and other great treasures.

In this meandering speech, Marrant created a counterpart to standard Protestant interpretations of biblical anthropology. Cain and Nimrod, bestowed with Masonic knowledge in Marrant's account, were also the two biblical figures whom white interpreters most often associated with the diversity of human cultures. When eighteenth-century biblical commentators sought explanation for the variety of peoples in the world, they commonly pointed to the curse of Cain, who was marked with dark skin for his murderous act, or to the curse of Ham and his descendants (including Nimrod), whom God had punished after Ham viewed his father, Noah, naked. Throughout the period of North American enslavement, theologians used these passages to justify or explain the divine origins of slavery: Ham or Cain had been the first dark-skinned person, destined because of his sinfulness to a life of servitude. But Marrant, in recounting Masonic history to highlight these accursed peoples, subverted these dominant interpretations; in his account, Cain and Nimrod became the repositories of sacred wisdom from God, a wisdom passed down through those who had been marked. The more obvious blemish of divine judgment simultaneously served as an indication of ultimate favor and salvation. Curiously, Egypt also gained a new valence: more often characterized by blacks as a place of enslavement, Egypt had also become a place of paradise and a site for those dark-skinned peoples who were chosen by God. Themes of accursedness and slavery, then, had been inverted and transformed into signs of divine election.

Marrant's creation of an African sacred lineage was quite likely indebted to his readings in Anglo-Saxon history. In his speech he cited the Benedictine monk Bede's *Ecclesiastical History of the English People,* a medieval text that documented the Christianization of the Anglo-Saxon kingdoms between the fifth and eighth centuries C.E. Although Marrant used the text to argue that slavery historically had not been limited to African peoples (even the "white bodies" and "fair faces" of Britain had endured its horrors), he undoubtedly gleaned from its scope a host of other lessons: a grounding in Patristics, which he made good use of; and a narrative template that, like the Old Testament itself, associates a moral lineage with an ethnic-national tale. In Bede's account, the religious unification of the English people is thoroughly enmeshed with the emergence of a political entity, a people united before God. One could, in his telling, be both part of a universal Christian faith and also a member of a particular tribe, without feeling any conflict.[32]

Prince Hall, the founder of the Boston lodge who had invited John Marrant to deliver his sermon, was equally steeped in biblical stories, Protestant theology, and classical history. We have little information on Hall's life, beyond the facts of his manumission in Boston and his service in the Revolutionary Army. As the grand master of Lodge No. 459 in Boston until his death in 1807, Hall presided over twenty-three years of feast-day sermons. Moreover, as one of the founding members of Lodge No. 459 and a political activist on behalf of the city's African-American population, he had long contemplated the connections between black protest and collective unity. In two sermons from 1792 and 1797, Prince Hall displayed a parallel ability to combine scriptural and Masonic history in novel and complex ways.[33]

Like Marrant, Hall evinced considerable knowledge of the Bible and of subsequent church history, and he found ways to weave an African sacred history into his oratory. In his 1792 survey of church tradition Hall cited Tertullian, Cyprian (the bishop of Carthage), Augustine, and Fulgentius on matters of Christian fidelity, piety, and love of virtue. He then enjoined his listeners to have patience, citing the biblical text most familiar to African Protestants and most suggestive of collective racial destiny, Psalm 68: "Aethiopia shall stretch forth her hands unto me." From Masonic tradition, Hall extracted a message of interracial cooperation, from the taking of Jerusalem, to the order of St. John, to the knights of Rhodes and Malta. He then juxtaposed these two genealogies to the recent Revolutionary War effort, in which "fellow Christians and brother masons . . . marched shoulder to shoulder, brother soldier and brother soldier, to the field of battle." Hall's narrative assumed the interconnection of Christianity, Masonry, and African lineage in a comprehensive historical awareness.[34]

Five years later Hall had somewhat different concerns but incorporated many of the same tropes. Writing in the middle of the Haitian Revolution, he acknowledged the continuing horrors of the slave trade and the glimmers of hope evidenced in the West Indies, "which puts me in mind of a nation (that I have somewhere read of) called Ethiopians, that cannot change their skin: But God can and will change their conditions, and their hearts too." He followed with a scriptural exegesis of Exodus 18:22–24, describing how Jethro, an Ethiopian, instructed his son-in-law, Moses. Prince Hall Masons would immediately have recognized the significance of this passage: it was through the biblical line of descent from the Ethiopian (and thus presumably dark-skinned) Jethro, to Moses, and eventually to Solomon, according to their tradition, that both the worship of Yahweh, the god of the chosen people, and the ancient science of Freemasonry were transmitted to the modern world. African Americans were still enslaved in "Egypt," like the Israelites, but they also held the keys to their own redemption: "Thus doth Ethiopia begin to stretch forth her hand," noted Hall once again, "from a sink of slavery to freedom and equality." The hand of God was delivering captives "by the mutual help of their fellow men." Hall's choice of Scripture reflected both a more general pattern of African-American biblical exegesis, which tended to focus on identification with the Israelites in exile, and a particular Masonic reading of racial and Christian imagery, emphasizing the significance of self-help and benevolent activity. "Live and act as masons," Hall concluded, offering fellowship "even though whites do not acknowledge you."[35]

Whereas Marrant emphasized Cain and Nimrod as the dark-skinned keepers of ancient wisdom, Hall stressed Moses and his Ethiopian ties as a way of linking Christianity and Masonry to a shared African heritage. Both claimed that Africans were better Christians and better Masons than their white counterparts. And both suggested that the African-American community held a sacred status in the eyes of the Creator.

Free blacks were, of course, not the only North Americans of the day who associated Africa with a glorious past. Contemporary European and Euro-American intellectuals shared some of these preoccupations with racialized renderings of history. In the closing decades of the eighteenth century, white scholars expressed assurance that the study of northern Africa could unlock the mystery of the origins of "true" civilization. The English philologist Sir William Jones argued in 1794 that the geographical center from which all civilizations arose was assuredly "oriental"; although he located it in Persia (Iran), he also noted the significance of ancient Abyssinia (Ethiopia), which had been known by the ancients for its wisdom in the arts and sciences. A year later the French rhetorician Charles Dupuis, in his book *Origin of All Cults* (1795), argued that all mythologies and religions could be traced back to ancient Egypt, the fount of European civilization.[36] Claims of ancient Egyptian and Ethiopian wisdom and the origin of intellectual traditions, then, were hardly farfetched, although Euro-Americans did not make the simultaneous move, as did Marrant and Hall, of construing these sites as characteristically "African."

British and American Masonic lore also emphasized the transmission of the secret wisdom of Masonry down through generations and civilizations. Whites stressed the roles played in this transmission by particular peoples who had been set apart. A notable example is found in a popular history of Masonry first published in 1775 by William Hutchinson, a lawyer and master of the Masonic Lodge of Concord at Barnard Castle. In his book *The Spirit of Masonry,* the British author began his explanation of the craft with the creation of humanity outlined in Genesis 1:26 and 31, and emphasized the relationship between the transmission of ancient wisdom and certain peoples. Adam, he asserted, first learned the "ancient scientific arts" and passed them along to his offspring, who immediately corrupted them. Hutchinson mentioned Cain and Ham, men who were marked by God and whose sins before Him were most often singled out in the late eighteenth century as explanations for racial variation, as two progeny who had defiled the ancient wisdom. Nonetheless, this ancient knowledge found its way to the priests of Egypt, who guarded it "from the vulgar by symbols and hieroglyphics, comprehensible alone to those of their own order." After Moses deciphered and refined the sacred principles, with the help of an immediate revelation from God, he passed them to the ancient Israelites. From Israel, the wisdom was then passed on to the Druids, who held it in safe keeping for, presumably, the master of the lodge of Concord at Barnard Castle.[37]

British and Anglo-American Masons, however, did not yoke this ancient wisdom to specific racial origins. Egypt was revered as a great civilization and was even identified by some whites as the source of civilization itself. But by the early nineteenth century, discussion of the region among Anglo-Americans had been largely disassociated from connections to dark-skinned or Hamitic peoples. Biblical interpreters argued that Egypt had been a heterogeneous culture, and that its decline as a civilization was the result of its light-skinned leaders' mingling with its inferior, dark-skinned residents, leading to cultural decay. Unlike Marrant and Hall, they downplayed textual references to Cushites, Midianites, Ethiopians, and peoples from other areas of Africa where skin color would have been unambiguously dark.[38]

Marrant and Hall's distinctive interpretive glosses suggest the beginnings of what might be termed a hidden transcript, a countervailing narrative of human origins that both glorified Africa and connected African Americans, through blood and secrecy, to a sacred community of origin. For both Hall and Marrant the focus on lineage, the communication of occluded wisdom, the revitalization of ancient Africa, and the inexorable linking of African development to providential (biblical) history ingeniously united the destinies of African peoples and offered not only a vague hope of a brighter future but also an insistent obligation to preserve and ensure their legacy. These were transcripts birthed in opposition to white claims of African barbarism and denials of the historical significance of Africa and African peoples; in this sense, they were always in dialogue with currents of British and Anglo-American racial discourse. But in the telling, such accounts also invoked something new: mutual obligation, interdependency, and collective pride.

Both the potential power and the immediate diffusion of these narratives throughout the Northeast are suggested by the public reactions of white detractors. In 1788 the *Columbian Magazine,* a white-sponsored publication out of Philadelphia, produced a lengthy satirical send-up of an African Masonic lodge. Poking fun at Freemasonry generally, but aiming particular barbs at the very recent effort by local blacks to start a lodge, the author claimed to present a transcript of a meeting, "which was spoken in the *Mandingo* language . . . and is now translated into English doggerel by a gentleman." The scene opens with a description of a long table, on which sits an ivory model of an Egyptian pyramid. In one corner we see "a representation of the antediluvian city built by Cain"; in another, "Noah's Ark in basso-relievo." An orator delivers a lengthy poem, a familiar-sounding history:

> My sable friends, and brethren dear,
> To my instruction lend your ear,
> While from the purest source I trace
> The ancient story of our race.

From there, the orator recounts a story that traces a biblical account very similar to John Marrant's sermon, from Cain, to Noah, to Ham (the grandfather of Nimrod).[39]

The piece is a biting attempt to humiliate African Americans who styled themselves as Masons—a rank that was, the satire implied, beyond their station. The African Americans in the account are drinking heavily, and the oration is interspersed with toasts to Cain and Ham, concluding with the statement that "every true masonic soul, / Dilutes his knowledge in the

bowl." Like the popular cartoons of the early nineteenth century that deni-
grated African-American claims to civil rights and citizenship, the story
lampoons black declarations of a proud heritage in the guise of entertainment. Yet its startling accuracy about the content of black Masonic narratives and, more intriguingly, its acute awareness of the politics of such assertions suggest that at least some whites grasped the intellectual stakes and
were attempting to defuse them with ridicule.[40]

Even more interesting, the satire appeared a year before Marrant's sermon, the first such piece published by an African American. Their similarities are too numerous to be pure coincidence, and there are no published
sources that provided the basis for both. It is highly likely, then, that Philadelphia whites heard some of these accounts in the sermons or lectures
of blacks; communications networks among Masonic and Protestant black
leaders were quite effective in the late eighteenth and early nineteenth centuries. Absalom Jones, the first grand master of the first black lodge in Philadelphia, became a Mason after corresponding with Prince Hall in the mid-
1780s. Hall also visited his Philadelphia brethren to check on their progress
around the same time. Although we cannot recover the precise pathways of
these stories, this satirical piece provides strong evidence that Marrant and
Hall narrated stories that were simultaneously being retold in other places,
and that quickly took on a common currency within African-American
communities.

Stories that emphasized the role of African peoples in biblical and Masonic history continued to circulate throughout the antebellum period. Only
a few tantalizing threads of these stories have survived, but the Masonic
lodge was clearly a major conduit of their dissemination and persistence.
More than a half-century later, many corresponding themes are evident in
an 1853 Masonic oration given by Martin Delany. Delany, a black nationalist
leader and one of the founding members of St. Cyprian Lodge No. 13 in
Pittsburgh, delivered a discourse to his brother Prince Hall Masons that constructed a similar account of African Protestant Masonry. Delany was a well-
educated editor, physician, author, and committed member of nearly every
black benevolent organization in antebellum Pittsburgh. Born a free black in
Virginia in 1812, he attended school until age fifteen. After his move to Pittsburgh as a teenager, Delany enrolled in the first black-sponsored school in
the city, a small academy run by the Reverend Lewis Woodson of Bethel African Methodist Episcopal (AME) Church. There Delany first read classical

literature and made the surprising discovery that Egypt, a nation of dark-skinned peoples, had been a great civilization long before the rise of Greece or Rome. That historical revelation continued to inform his life: in 1832, he and a friend founded the Theban Literary Society, devoted to the appreciation of classical literature. Two of his many children were named after African leaders: Rameses Placido and Ethiopia Halle Amelia. Most revealing of all, the first paper he published in the 1840s, *The Mystery*, used on its masthead the passage that also had captured the essence of Prince Hall's combination of African, Christian, and Masonic historical consciousness: "And Moses was learned of all the wisdom of the Egyptians."[41]

Delany's 1853 address outlined a comprehensive history of Freemasonry among African Americans. Like Marrant's and Hall's orations, it commemorated the most sacred Masonic ritual occasion, the feast day of St. John. And like his predecessors, Delany began with a biblically based anthropology that fused religious, fraternal, and racial themes. He briefly outlined the pre-Solomonic and prebiblical story, arguing that Egyptians and Ethiopians were the "authors of this mysterious and beautiful order" of Masonry, established well before the birth of Moses: "Being a people of a high order of intellect, and subject to erudite and profound thought, the Egyptians and Ethiopians were the first who came to the conclusion that man was created in the similitude of God." To sketch this story, of course, Delany had to rely on the biblical narrative itself, and to reason backward from the fact that, according to Exodus 18 (the same passage interpreted by Hall), Moses had acquired his wisdom and ability from Jethro, a Midianite priest (or Ethiopian). Moses also furnished a connection to the future enslavement of the African people, Delany asserted: "Was not the man who became the *Prime Minister* and *High Priest* of *Ceremonies* among the wise men of Africa, a *Mason?* . . . Are not we as Masons, and the world of mankind, to *him* the Egyptian *slave*—may I not add, the *fugitive* slave—indebted for a transmission to us of the Masonic Records—the Holy Bible, the Word of God?"[42] Delivering his speech just a few years after the devastating imposition of the 1850 Fugitive Slave Law, Delany deftly re-created a Masonic history for a new generation.

John Hilton, Martin Delany, and other Prince Hall Lodge members continued and expanded the tradition of Christian and Masonic narratives through the antebellum period. The dissemination of new forms of collective histories that built on these accounts, however, accelerated dramatically after the turn of the nineteenth century. The British and North American abolition of the Atlantic slave trade in 1808 marked the emergence of a second important occasion for structuring new narratives of the past. From 1808 until at least the 1830s, blacks and sympathetic whites in Boston, New York, and Philadelphia crowded into churches annually to hear speakers relate the long history of the slave trade, express gratitude to the abolitionist cause, and hail the continued march of emancipation as part of the progress of divine providence.

Like Masonic ritual occasions, these events allowed for both the articulation and the public performance of collective unity. The morning of Monday, January 2, 1809, illustrates typical proceedings for the event. At 9:00 A.M. a large gathering assembled at Liberty Hall in New York City. From there the crowd marched up Leonard Street and down Broadway before arriving at the Lyceum on Warren Street. The parade was led by a grand marshal, the arrangements committee, featured speaker Joseph Sidney, the Wilberforce Band, and the Maritime and Musical Associations. After the service, which typically consisted of prayers, the singing of hymns, the reading of the act of abolition, and an oration, the procession reversed its steps and recessed from Broadway to Pearl Street, Wall Street, and back to Liberty Hall. Most such occasions attracted throngs of onlookers, many simply curious at the sight of a large assembly of African Americans sporting banners and badges and occupying some of the city's main streets. Others were hostile and threatening; in the first decade of these celebrations, the African Church in New York City petitioned for police protection on at least four occasions.[43]

These commemorations were, from the outset, more racially integrated than were the black lodge events or Sunday services in black churches. They hewed to the standard form for public commemorations in the United States by the early nineteenth century: a parade followed by a service that included a benediction, prayers, the singing of hymns, and a public speech. Some of the orations were given by whites, but the majority of sermons were delivered by African-American clergy, several of whom were also prominent in black Masonry. Even as these commemorations reflected assimilation to broader American patterns, they exhibited simultaneously a distinctive ordering of time and space within free black communities. Since the colonial period African Americans in the Northeast had celebrated and commemorated their own holidays, including Negro Election Day, a West African–derived celebration that culminated in the election of black kings, governors, and judges, who then exercised symbolic or real authority over free black communities; and Pinkster, a spring festival derived from the Dutch word for "Pentecost."[44] These occasions allowed blacks a time of relative freedom fueled by dancing, eating, and drinking. In the early national era, public commemorations of the end of the slave trade brought celebrations into the center of urban public life, incorporating sympathetic whites and announcing the presence and unity of African Americans.

Freedom celebrations were especially freighted events. Focusing on the complicity of the United States government in the slave trade (in more or less confrontational ways) allowed participants to highlight the unfulfilled promise of emancipation and the hollow ring of the federal celebration on July Fourth. As Frederick Douglass would phrase it succinctly some decades later, "This Fourth of July is yours, not mine. You may rejoice, I must mourn." Freedom celebrations offered an alternative narrative of justice, rewrote the official national script, and claimed a countervailing understanding of collective progress. After 1820, when white supporters of African colonization mounted a campaign to use July Fourth celebrations as an opportunity to acclaim African removal, some blacks commemorated New Year's Day to protest July Fourth festivities overtly.[45]

William Hamilton, a carpenter by trade and lay member of the African Methodist Episcopal Zion Church, used his 1815 address to educate listeners about the African continent. Speaking from the pulpit of the Episcopal Asbury African Church in New York City, he embarked on an extended description "of the country of our parents," including a technical account of its longitude, latitude, and shape. His purpose, he explained, was to recenter the map, to emphasize that Africa lay at the "center of the Globe, surrounded by the other continents, to wit, Asia, Europe, and America." Further, he suggested that with its climate and location, Africa would have been a fortuitous place—an Edenic spot—for humanity to have originated. With sly wit, Hamilton only implied the derivation that he could not prove; he suggested that each of those present should "answer the question for himself" about the source of human civilization. Having established the prominence and historical importance of the continent, however, he continued with a lengthy account of ancient Africa: "She can boast of her antiquity, of her philosophers, her artists, her statesmen, her generals; of her curiosities, her magnificent cities, her stupendous buildings, and of her once widespread commerce." Egypt, he observed, had a particularly ancient pedigree, having been populated by "an honest, industrious, peaceable and well-disposed people."[46]

Hamilton spoke with particular vitriol about European atrocities during the slave trade. While most authors gave stylized and somewhat formulaic accounts of white cruelty, Hamilton's anger was vivid and uncontained. He excoriated the "traders in African blood and sinews" who thought themselves better than Africans and boasted of their "superior understanding, their superior genius, their superior souls." Hamilton referred to slave ships as "floating hells manned with fiends" and explicitly and repeatedly stressed the horrors of captivity. In a most striking image, the lay preacher likened whites to devils: "Some nations have painted their devil in the complexion of a white man. View the history of the slave trade, and then answer the question, could they have made choice of a better likeness to have drawn from? All that low, sly, artful, wicked, cunning attributed to him, was practised by them. All the insulting scorn, savage cruelty, and tormenting schemes, practised by him, were executed by them."[47]

Echoing Hall and Marrant, Hamilton and others emphasized the innate goodness of Africa and the inherent evils of Europe as the Manichean drama on which history pivoted. Adam Carman, speaking in New York City in 1811, rhapsodized about Africa as a paradise not unlike Eden: "She exhibits a vast treasure of every thing valuable almost spontaneously . . . redundant with every necessary enjoyment of life." In this setting, Carman insisted, ancient Africans had lived in peace and abundance:

> How noble, how delightful the situation of our ancestors, when delineated by the pencil of truth, so emblematic of the grandeur of our first parents when in the paradisical garden, the contemplation of which is sufficient to influence the soul of a grave hermit in his solitary and sequestered retreat in the gloomy forest, and tempt him to leave his cimmerian cell, to participate [in]the almost unutterable joys of Afric's sons.

With the arrival of Europeans, however, this paradise was disrupted and its inhabitants dragged into slavery. The European and American slave trade,

Carman contended, was unrivaled in its cruelty and scope: "All the deleteri-
ous effects of superstitious paganism, popery, and mahometanism; or all the
enthusiasms of the ecclesiastical imposters, who have spread desolation . . .
is not its parallel: in a word, it has not its competition in all history, from the
inspired Moses to the present day."[48]

Carman's analogies aptly captured the conviction that the battle over African liberty was profoundly religious. Numerous orators cited the enslavement of Africans as akin to that of the Israelites in Egypt. Absalom Jones
played most extensively with that comparison in his 1808 sermon when he
declared that "the deliverance of the children of Israel from their bondage is
not the only instance in which it has pleased God to appear in behalf of oppressed and distressed nations, as the deliverer of the innocent, and of those
who call upon his name."[49] Egypt, in Jones's rendering, represented not glory
or advanced civilization but oppression and enslavement; only the divine
hand could rescue the Israelites from their captivity. Unlike the increasing
number of authors who conflated Egypt, Ethiopia, and other parts of the
continent into a homogeneous region, Jones distinguished Egypt as a place
of particular human suffering.

For all the utility of the theme of Israel in Egypt, a Christian awareness
of the universality of sin tempered some African-American judgments of
whites. As the black Episcopal preacher Peter Williams related, the real problem was the human love of gain. Once Europeans witnessed the riches available in the New World, their reason was cast aside; they "violated the sacred
injunctions of the gospel" and "frustrated the designs of the pious and humane" in their decision to enslave others to extract wealth from them. Such
actions were not only a violation of human rights, Williams asserted, but
also a corruption of biblical mandate. The problem was not the Egyptians,
per se: the problem was human nature, which could be tamed only by the
laws of the Gospel. Even Absalom Jones, whose oration was most dependent
on a collective accounting for human behavior, also reaffirmed that God was
ultimately impartial and just in His ways; all peoples would be called to account for their deeds.

The speeches of Williams and Jones indicate the crucial role that a belief
in universal sin played in African-American Christian narratives. Moreover, the commemoration of abolition prompted gratitude to both black
and white activists. A staple feature of most histories was the expression

of indebtedness to a lineage of antislavery crusaders. Peter Williams lauded the British abolitionist Thomas Clarkson and the Quaker activists John Woolman and Anthony Benezet. Others added William Wilberforce, Abbé Grégoire, Benjamin Rush, and Benjamin Lay. The clear implication was that they, too, were part of the historical narrative of the advance of freedom. Their exaltation reinforced the hope that slavery might indeed be fought by individuals of all races. Even William Hamilton, after rebuking whites throughout his speech for their wickedness, admitted that among whites there were a few good souls: "Our children should be taught in their little songs, to lisp the name of Clarkson."[50]

While orators differed markedly in their attributions of human responsibility for slavery, their speeches reflected logical and remarkably consistent extensions of the tropes initiated in the earlier Masonic tradition: the iteration of biblical themes; the demarcation of ancient Africa as sacred ground; the elaboration of a lineage (now including abolitionist heroes) linking past to present; and the concomitant reminders of the responsibilities that heritage placed on contemporary hearers and readers. Some (but not all) of the freedom orators took great license in directly criticizing the actions of slave traders and owners, but in general they emphasized both the distinctive legacy of African accomplishment and the contributions of white abolitionists to the progress of freedom. Neither racially exclusive nor wholeheartedly assimilationist, freedom speakers carved a space for African achievement within a broader Christian framework.

William Miller's 1810 oration gave voice to a particularly complex understanding of these issues, and moved right to the heart of the multiple interpretive possibilities of African lineage. He opened his narrative with the glories and "national greatness" of early Egypt, from which all Africans descended. Instead of leading him to extol African innocence and denigrate European ruthlessness, however, Miller's reading of Isaiah gave him another insight. Referring to the "Ethiopians," he cited not a promise but a warning: "We read in a number of the Psalms and Prophecies, of their being a very haughty people. Isaiah, speaking of their downfall, says, 'And they shall be ashamed of Ethiopia their expectation, and of Egypt their glory.'"[51]

Miller employed biblical principles and emphasized collective agency, but the AME preacher read in Isaiah a general warning to all nations. History is a cyclical process, he reasoned, and "the history of every age proves, that vice and immorality will keep pace with wealth and prosperity." Even slavery began long before Europe became involved, originating with the Assyrians; Miller likened forced captivity to a poison that would diffuse its effects throughout a human body. He was one of the very few black authors, moreover, to depict Africans themselves as complicit in the slave trade when he referred to the involvement of the "Moors," or Muslim traders. *We are all Egypt,* Miller suggested, citing Isaiah once again in the prophet's condemnation of that nation: "I will set the Egyptians against the Egyptians . . . city against city, and kingdom against kingdom."[52] Africa was, in some measure, responsible for its miseries.

But just as the biblical prophecy condemned all nations, it offered a host of consolations. During their enslavement, Miller mused, Africans were not in Egypt but in Babylon, "led captive into a strange land for their iniquity," separated from their God by their own sins. As if to stress the comparison further, Miller alluded to a prophetic passage from Jeremiah, another eloquent prophet of the Babylonian exile, when he compared European civilization to the "ravenous tiger of the desert."[53] The divine plan, however, called for mercy and justice; God would smite, but he would also heal. Miller found recent evidence for redemption in the founding of the colony of Sierra Leone in 1789, an act that would certainly begin "civilizing and improving" Africa once again. The fulfillment of Zion, the renewed Africa, was manifest in the preacher's invocation of another part of Isaiah:

> Then shall the wilderness and the solitary places be glad for them; and the desert shall rejoice and blossom as the rose; it shall blossom abundantly and rejoice, even with joy and singing: instead of the thorn shall come up the fir-tree, and instead of the briar shall come up the myrtle-tree. The Lord shall make her wilderness like Edon, and her desert like the garden of the Lord.[54]

Miller's sustained use of Isaiah, and particularly his employment of verses from a section that scholars call the "prophecies against the nation," is striking. In part, it reflected a continuation of the Puritan jeremiad tradition, the castigating of the community for its sins commonly encountered in earlier Protestant American rhetoric.[55] But Miller did not limit his criticisms to the acts of a single nation: Isaiah's prophecies, taken together, condemned As-syria, Egypt, Tyre, and other powers, alongside Judah itself. This litany has the effect of putting all nations on an equal footing, of both attributing blame and explaining the misfortune of everyone: today it is us; tomorrow it might be you. We are all Egypt, and we are all Israel. We are all "the nation." Before a final invocation of numerous verses from First Isaiah, Miller fashioned an alternative collectivity: "The general acceptation of the phrase, my people, in scripture, is commonly understood as being applied to the jewish nation but now to the servants of God, or Christians in every nation, comprising the church militant." Citing Acts 10:34, Miller judged that "God is no respecter of persons."[56] Black narrators like Miller stressed the distinctiveness of African lineage and the Edenic promise of Africa. But they also believed that biblical accounts of Exodus, Ethiopia, and Babylon contained messages for all humanity.

Freedom celebrations continued many of the themes initiated in late eighteenth-century sermons, but this second generation of authors also incorporated newer intellectual currents into their work that were quickly becoming available to urban blacks through the growth of schools and the increasing focus on history as a community resource. By the 1810s, scientific theories of race, ethnographic evidence, and emerging political theorizing about the nation-state were used to bolster the evidence supplied by biblical exegesis and church history for African collective identity.

It is difficult to know exactly how free blacks might have accessed texts beyond the Bible. The American publishing industry of the early nineteenth century was decentralized, with small numbers of books published in a wide variety of locations; most substantial books were still imported from England before 1830, and they were more expensive than the typical free black would have been able to afford. Yet the majority of urban dwellers would have been "touched by print" to some degree. Even Prince Hall and John Marrant in the 1790s displayed a remarkable literary range in a society in which large collections of books were not commonly acquired. Some may have heard texts read aloud. Others, living in close quarters as domestics with Euro-Americans, quite likely made use of their employers' personal libraries. Both Absalom Jones and Richard Allen, African-American community leaders in Philadelphia, owned copies of Josephus.[57] But they were most likely the exceptions at a time when books were scarce commodities and educational possibilities were haphazard.

The expansion of Northern black organizational life and the growing availability of texts in the first decades of the nineteenth century made possible more systematic forms of education. Increasingly, free blacks had at least some exposure to the growing number of church charity schools and Sunday schools that emerged between 1780 and 1830. The Society of Friends, compelled by the mandate that each individual should have the opportunity to come to Christ's teachings through the Bible, initiated the instruction of blacks in Philadelphia as early as 1770. While the earliest schools emphasized religious salvation with a minimal degree of literacy, they nonetheless provided texts and discussions of classical and Christian precedents. Other congregations followed suit: in 1796 the city of New York had six church charity schools. By 1810, free schools for blacks were operating in Boston, Baltimore, Wilmington (DE), Burlington (NJ), and New York; Philadelphia alone boasted twelve. Some independent black churches also sponsored schools staffed by clergy who charged a modest tuition; this was quite likely the kind of school where Jacob Oson taught.[58]

In turn, education prompted increased access to books and stories beyond the lodge and the church. To be sure, history as an independent topic of study was not taught widely to either black or white scholars during this period. Not until after the Civil War would American history appear in school curricula, and other facets of history were subsumed in the study of philosophy, rhetoric, or politics.[59] Nonetheless, students learned about history through listening, through rote memorization, and through recitation from primers, spellers, and other available texts.

Historical knowledge also was abundantly available in fables, oratory, and geography. Children and adults alike would most likely have learned to read not only from the Bible but also from Webster's *American Spelling Book*, first published in 1783. Webster's speller was ubiquitous in American schools of the early nineteenth century, having been published in Pennsylvania, New York, Connecticut, Vermont, and Massachusetts within five years, and then reissued every year thereafter. With fifty agents at work by 1790, the publisher distributed samples from Boston to Charleston in an unprecedented media blitz. By 1829, ten million copies of the speller had been printed, for its day an enormous figure. Along with scriptural injunctions, morality tales, and Aesop's Fables, beginning readers were introduced to classical peoples and authors, including lists of the Midianites, Chaldeans, Tyrians, and Egyptians, names of ancient African peoples that would later recur in African-American narratives. From there a pupil might progress to a reader such as Caleb Bingham's *Columbian Orator.* That volume, first published in 1797, contained oratories by Cato, Milton, and George Washington, among others. Lessons blended a geographic sensibility with practical knowledge of the biblical and classical worlds. Very little space, if any, would have been devoted to the subject of slavery or the condition of African Americans.[60]

Because the organizing principles of early textbooks focused not on chronology but instead on "timeless" moral precepts and virtues, historical figures and events typically were assembled haphazardly. Passages often were plucked from the middle of a play, story, or essay and lacked a broader context or even an introduction.[61] These books communicated history as cultural bricolage, a pastiche of moments from the ancient past that provided edification in the present. Free blacks and whites who learned about classical history would have pieced it together from a variety of sources—and would have learned these patterns of textual assemblage as part of their expectations of what history could be. It should come as no surprise, then, that in their own recounting African Americans plucked out examples of African achievement past and present from a variety of sources and entwined them in novel ways.

The experiences of Martin Delany exemplify this process and illustrate how one enterprising man found his way to literature on ancient civilizations. Delany, who grew up in Pittsburgh in the first decades of the nineteenth century, recalled that as a child he purchased *The New York Primer and Spelling Book* from a passing peddler. He could easily count the other texts owned by his family: the *Farmer's Repository,* a weekly paper published in Charlestown, West Virginia, and a Bible. Delany claimed that the first lessons he learned were Aesop's Fables, Socrates's defense before his judges, and the writings of Ossian, a third-century Gaelic poet. Later, he became acquainted with and recited Shakespeare. As an adult, he also mentioned his fascination with the Old Testament: he and his friend the Reverend Mollison Madison Clark loved reading and researching the relations among dark-skinned peoples and ancient Jews and Egyptians; they eventually turned this passion into a study group called the Theban Literary Society.[62] With a limited number of texts available, Delany nonetheless managed to assemble a historical understanding that provided the basis for his lifelong interest in African-American cultures.

In addition to classical texts, African Americans increasingly utilized contemporary scholarly currents in their narratives. The writings of Oson and Vastey illustrate the extent to which black intellectuals before 1820 incorporated new discoveries in ethnology, politics, and the natural sciences in their collective accounts. In part the invocation of European and Anglo-American scholarly discourses represented a defensive measure, coming as it did precisely at the moment that whites were first articulating a systematic and "scientific" ideology of black inferiority that would displace a biblical account of human difference.[63] Although African Americans were not necessarily satisfied with the Hamitic legacy, at least insofar as it implied a curse on all Africans, the Masonic narratives found ways around the stigmatization of the Hamitic line without giving up the notion of biblical lineage entirely. The newer scholarly theories in the hands of white intellectuals—first of intractable cultural differences and later of biological distinctiveness, both premised on the notion that blacks were inherently inferior to whites—seemed even more problematic, lacking as they did any connection to Christian notions of redemption, forgiveness, or spiritual equality. An active God could lift a curse or possibly reveal a just motivation for His prior actions; but the Enlightenment-informed understandings of human variation left little room for a miraculous overturning of social hierarchies. African Americans therefore needed to find positive ways of assessing racial commonality as a response to white claims of black insufficiency.

But invoking race was only partly a response to white racism; it also followed directly from the opening of free black communities to broader intellectual vistas through increased commerce and cultural exchange. Black mercantilists such as Paul Cuffe and missionaries such as Daniel Coker represented only the most visible part of the transit of African Americans around the Atlantic world, a mobility that increased greatly in the first decades of the nineteenth century. The founding of the American Colonization Society in late 1816 was catalyzed primarily by the desire of Southern whites to remove free blacks from the United States, but it had the unintended effect of bringing African Americans into contact with diasporic Africans and their sympathizers in the Caribbean, Europe, and Africa. Although many free blacks remained leery of ACS intentions, they benefited from the books and goods that arrived in American and African ports. Similarly, the establishment of black denominations, beginning with the AME Church in 1816, initiated missionary exchanges throughout the diaspora and thereby circulated newer intellectual currents to audiences from Nova Scotia to Haiti and over to Liberia. Such transnational ties would have fuller implications for free blacks who combined emerging understandings of nation, race, history, and science.

Biblical narratives, classical allusions, ethnological speculation, and republican ideals furnished the arsenal that Jacob Oson used to edify and inspire his African-American audiences. Oson's background and his interests place him comfortably within the circles of communal narrators. The place of Oson's birth is not known. He probably came to the United States from the West Indies, along with the influx of Caribbean migrants making their way to the Northern states at the turn of the century. We do know that he had settled in New Haven, Connecticut, by 1805. There he spent most of his life, serving as a teacher at a school for African Americans and as a catechist and lay reader at Trinity Episcopal Church until his death. Impressing whites and blacks alike with his intellectual and pastoral abilities, Oson came under the care of Trinity's rector, Harry Croswell (1779–1858), who encouraged his parishioner to seek ordination as a minister. In 1821 Croswell, along with two dozen prominent citizens of New Haven and members of the Diocese of Connecticut, urged Oson's consideration as a candidate for the rectorship of the African Episcopal Church of St. Thomas, Philadelphia, the position that had been occupied by the Reverend Absalom Jones for more than two decades. Despite strong support from the congregation, the Episcopal clergy of Philadelphia rejected Oson's nomination, explaining that his "want of a Classical or sufficient education" made the appointment objectionable.[64]

By all accounts, Oson was a popular man who exerted considerable influence among other African-American Christians, both in New Haven and throughout the Northeast. As one of a small number of African-American leaders in the Episcopal Church, Oson most certainly communicated with a network of blacks within the denomination. Croswell, rector at Trinity from 1815 to 1858, relied on Oson's friendships with blacks in the local community to further the work of the parish. Oson also served as president of the Union Society of New Haven, an interdenominational organization that promoted the interests of its black members. Connecticut was known to be one of the Northern states with the highest degree of antiblack sentiment, and members of the small black community in New Haven responded by organizing across denominational lines to protect their rights. Oson's efforts caught the attention of the black Quaker abolitionist and merchant Paul Cuffe, with whom he corresponded on matters of education. Oson's associations also extended to leaders in newly organizing independent black churches. Christopher Rush (1777–1873), a member of Zion Church in New York City since 1803 who would later become the second bishop of the AMEZ, was so impressed with Oson's address that he requested its publication.[65]

Oson's 1817 address, his only extant speech, displays familiar themes and influences. Most evident is his biblicism. Like many free blacks, Oson most likely learned to read by using the Bible as his principal text. The shaping of his questions, the frequent citation of specific passages, even many of his more elegant turns of phrase, reflect a mind steeped in the language and imagery of the King James Bible. Within the first paragraph alone, he references Christ's commandment to love one's neighbor and alludes to African Americans as the latter-day Israelites, "being in a strange land, and in captivity." Much of his story, then, in which he traces the origins and history of the African people, is drawn from a biblically based chronology.

Like other Christians, however, Oson knew that the biblical version of creation and the monogenetic account of human origins in particular had come under increasing attack by natural scientists. Although it is doubtful that Oson had access to the work of Continental theorists who challenged the singular origin of all peoples, he knew well enough the implications of the debate: if blacks were created separately from whites, it would be easier to argue for their inherent physical and moral inferiority. He may well have known of the first American attempt to counter polygenetic theories. Samuel Stanhope Smith, Presbyterian minister, moral philosopher, and president of Princeton, had delivered an address to the American Philosophical Society in 1787 entitled *An Essay on the Causes of the Variety of Complexion and Figure in the Human Species*. Smith's summation of contemporary arguments for the unity of the human species prompted a spate of articles in magazines and newspapers of the day, and in 1810 he published a revised and expanded edition in which he affirmed monogenesis even more insistently.[66]

It is difficult to say whether Oson knew of Smith's work. Smith's brother John had tutored a young black Presbyterian preacher, John Chavis, at Princeton, and thus word of Smith's publication quite likely circulated on the highly effective networks among black church leaders of the day. Oson, like Smith, clearly saw the affirmation of monogenesis as the cornerstone of any argument for black capacities, and he begins his address by facing the issue squarely. Unlike Smith, who was criticized by many, including the trustees of Princeton, for failing to reference Scripture in his reading of nature, Oson argued first and foremost from the Bible. Tacking back and forth between the Old and the New Testaments, Oson asserted that all human beings had originated from Adam (Genesis 9:19), and that God had made "of one blood" all the peoples of the earth (Acts 17:26).[67]

Oson then moved on to the charge that Africans, even if they had been created alongside other peoples, were inherently and perpetually inferior. This belief, too, sprang from the biblical argument of the Hamitic curse, a sign placed on dark-skinned peoples by God, but it had been revived as a justification for enslavement by eighteenth-century theorists.[68] Oson, like other black Protestants of his day, did not deny a Hamitic lineage for Africans. He averred that Africans were indeed the "children of Ham," and proudly so; but they had been raped and plundered by the "Christian nations (as they are called)." Further, he employed images of the ancient glories of Africa, punctuated by allusions to a lineage of African church fathers and potent civilizations, to prove that Hamitic peoples were not "barbarous and ignorant" at all. He cited Abraham's learning at the feet of the Chaldeans and the Nubian glories detailed by Josephus. He recited the litany of African Christian bishops: "Divinus, Turtulian, Cyprian, Julius, Africanus, Armobius, Sactantins, and St. Au[gu]stine."

Oson also incorporated republican theories about the fate of nations and the characteristics of a virtuous republic, borrowing not simply from classical authors but also from a figure much closer to home: Timothy Dwight (1752–1817), a political theorist, critic, and president of the local Yale College. Dwight had published a number of epic poems known less for their literary significance than for their sheer length.[69] One of a group of conservative (and evangelical) social critics known as the "Hartford Wits," Dwight was hardly an obvious source of inspiration for a black Episcopal protester. Yet in his *Conquest of Canaan* (1785), Dwight drew from the same biblical images that so captivated Oson to frame a republican ideal. In a lengthy allegorical piece based on the story of Joshua's struggle to enter the Promised Land, Dwight cast General Washington as Joshua and detailed the victory of the colonial struggle in America as a sacred drama.

Oson cited Dwight in describing ancient Egypt as the first seat of learning, and he adopted some of his republican language in his references to the evils of luxury and unrestrained commerce. Equally important, Oson embraced the art of the metaphor utilized by Dwight to glorify the American nation, employing a range of natural images to describe Africa as a caged animal, an uncultivated garden, and a tarnished metal. Also noteworthy is his use of the concept of the people of the veil ("take off the veil that has been unjustly cast over our eyes"), an image that would prove so powerful in the writings of W. E. B. Du Bois more than a century later. While his speech followed a clear rhetorical structure, it often meandered; penning something closer to poetry than to finely honed analysis, Oson built his argument through the repetition of a series of familiar and indelible images. In arguing that "the Race of Ham were not so barbarous and ignorant as they have been represented," Oson seemed intent upon producing another set of images, icons of achievement, grace, and ability—the majestic lion, silver and gold, and the strong tiger—that would put to lie his detractors.

The resuscitated image of a valiant Africa stayed with Jacob Oson. In 1823, Harry Croswell reported that Oson read aloud for him a new piece he was writing on the subject: "I was astonished to find how much he had laboured to make out the proper origin of that nation, and with how much ingenuity and success he had managed the few materials of which he had possessed himself for the purpose."[70] Oson never published that piece. But thanks in large part to Croswell's support and encouragement, Oson finally was ordained as an African missionary in 1828. He died seven months later, before he could fulfill his commission.

Oson's speech also reflected the importance of nascent forms of nationalism to the development of communal narration. The new currents of nationalist theory emerging from the age of revolutions furnished paradigms for discussing and commemorating the endurance of the nation-state. Nationalism as a term, in fact, was invented in the wake of the French Revolution, and the cultural mechanisms that reinforced it, including parades, memorials, public ceremonies, and holidays, increased dramatically in subsequent decades in both France and the United States. The rise of the "commemorative spirit" became integral to postrevolutionary programs on both sides of the Atlantic, resulting in the establishment of museums, libraries, and souvenirs. Indeed, the goal of public education in the early United States arguably had less to do with inculcating morality or developing technological skills for their own sake, and more to do with the creation of virtuous citizens who could protect and defend national interests. Many free blacks embraced national sentiments but also used them to their own collective ends, sponsoring alternative commemorations and furnishing counternarratives of communal progress. It is not hard to imagine that the very existence of these narratives represented a threat to white Americans, inasmuch as they highlighted the constructed nature of their own renditions of national development that had been cast as "true history."[71]

Oson's rendering reflected his submersion in American republican rhetoric. Steeped in a very different kind of intellectual milieu informed by French revolutionary thought, the Haitian narrator Vastey also imbibed nationalist currents and modes of historical narration. Ennery, Haiti, in the 1810s could not have been further away socially and culturally from the town of New Haven, Connecticut. Vastey wrote during the reign of Henri Christophe of Haiti, the revolutionary warrior and self-designated king of a divided country still in the throes of the recent conflict. No one promoted and publicized the fledgling monarchy's achievements more indefatigably than Vastey. The eldest son of a white French father and a colored créole mother, Vastey was born in the northern Saint Domingue town of Ennery, near Marmalade, in 1781. A well-to-do member of the *affranchis,* or free colored class in French colonial society, Vastey experienced both the privilege and the discrimination that came with that position. Despite the *Code Noir* (1685), which afforded French citizenship to emancipated people of color, Saint Domingue law by the late eighteenth century increasingly barred *affranchis* from the highest social and political spheres. Thus Vastey (and others like him) were excluded from pursuing certain professions, were not allowed to sit with whites in public places, and could not take European Christian names. This class distinction had as much to do with wealth as with color, and for Vastey and others, late colonial Saint Domingue was a peculiar and precarious social world.[72]

Nonetheless, Vastey was accorded the education due the son of a French colonist. We know little about his childhood, but reportedly he received some early training in Paris and was known in later years for his erudition. William Woodis Harvey, a British observer who spent a good deal of time in Christophe's kingdom, remarked that Vastey "displayed considerable information on all subjects connected with modern history, legislation, and political economy; and occasionally shows that he had not entirely neglected literature and science."[73]

Keenly sensitive to the violence inflicted on the slaves of Saint Domingue, the young Vastey was swept up in the revolutionary fervor of the 1790s. Toussaint L'Ouverture, the Haitian commander, used Ennery as a base for his operations, and Vastey, although not technically of the same color or class as the ex-slave, joined his cause at age fifteen. From then on Vastey associated himself with the plight of enslaved Africa, expressing hatred for the white presence on the island. In the postrevolutionary period Vastey remained loyal to President Jean-Jacques Dessalines and finally achieved a prominent position of leadership during the reign of Henri Christophe. Quick-witted, often charming, mercurial, and unquestionably learned, Vastey was a loyal defender of the king. By the early 1810s he had come to serve as one of Christophe's principal advisors, as well as the tutor for his eldest son. Henri, in turn, named Vastey to the Royal and Military Order of St. Henry, a position of knighthood established by the king shortly after his coronation.[74]

As the "official ideologist and apologist" for the northern kingdom, Vastey published widely and helped circulate knowledge of Christophe's achievements to an international audience. His views reflected fully the contradictory mix of egalitarianism and hierarchy that characterized Christophe's reign. Fiercely critical of French colonial atrocities and adamantly opposed to the continuing efforts by France to reimpose itself on the island, Vastey vividly related the horrors of the slave system in Saint Domingue to his audiences and championed the cause of equality and liberty for the ex-slaves. In sharp contrast to Christophe's careful and deliberate overtures to British philanthropists (a sympathy that Vastey actually shared and, in his *Reflexions,* acknowledged), Vastey gained a reputation for his scathing attacks on whites. Harvey noted that "the hatred which he entertained towards whites of all nations rendered him sometimes an object of terror. . . . on one occasion he was heard calmly to declare that if he were allowed to follow his own wishes, he would massacre every white man on the island."[75]

At the same time, Vastey was fully committed to perpetuating a class-based system within the kingdom, a social milieu evidenced most fully by Christophe's creation of an elite class, complete with dukes, earls, counts, and the knighthood of St. Henry. Vastey saw himself as the spokesperson for the ex-slaves, but he also championed the leadership of a privileged group that maintained its legitimacy by continuously invoking the struggle for liberation. In his writings he criticized the republican form of government and ideals of social equality, and he defended monarchy as a more stable political model. He was particularly disparaging of the neighboring republic of Alexander Pétion and served as one of its chief political opponents. Vastey argued that Christophe's limited monarchy, derived from the consent of the Haitian people, both allowed for some measure of equality and still provided the social stability of leadership by an educated cohort. At once radical and conservative, Vastey's vision supported the rights of freed Africans within a circumscribed and highly ritualized system.[76]

Reflexions on the Blacks and Whites, Vastey's most widely circulated work, was written in response to the published remarks of the French ex-colonist F. Mazères. By the mid-1810s Mazères was the secretary to Admiral Bruix, the French minister of marine. In a letter to J. C. L. Simonde de Sismondi (1773–1842), the noted Swiss historian and economic theorist who had publicly criticized French policies regarding slaveholding in the West Indies, Mazères put forth a series of challenges to the abilities of African peoples.[77] Vastey provided enough context to give us a clear indication of Mazères's purpose. Like many other defenders of slavery, Mazères questioned the innate abilities of Africans ever to rise above the position of slaves. He premised this notion on the assertion that Africans were, in fact, a species distinct from and lower than whites, created separately from them. This polygenetic theory, while not novel by the 1810s and more prevalent in French intellectual circles than in the Anglophone world, must have been particularly galling to the proud defender of an emancipated Haiti—especially when it came from the pen of one who had inflicted so much pain upon his fellow subjects.[78]

Vastey's reply to Mazères represented an adroit blend of contemporary intellectual currents in biblical interpretation, ethnography, and the natural sciences. Indicative of his broad-ranging knowledge in European sources (Vastey could not, as he indicates, read English, and thus did not have access to works that were not translated), he countered his adversary on three distinct fronts: the biblical argument for monogenesis, the cultural battleground over African historical achievement and its relationship to "civilization," and the current state of African societies. He concluded by turning to a discussion of Haiti. Like Oson, Vastey first asserted "the unity of the Human Race" on the basis of his reading of Genesis 1:16, as well as arguments derived from the writings of the noted French naturalists Georges Louis Leclerc Buffon and James Henry Bernardin de Saint Pierre, and Baron de Montesquieu.[79] Vastey, who in other contexts expressed little patience for revealed religion and shared more in common intellectually with the Enlightenment tradition adhered to by his opponents, nonetheless hewed close to the biblical account of creation, bolstering his reading of Scripture with natural history and social theory.[80]

His exposition of the theme of the physical similarity (and hence, equality) of blacks and whites was also derived from a reading of contemporary ethnographic sources. By the first decades of the nineteenth century, naturalists, missionaries, and explorers had begun to introduce the wonders of the African continent to a curious European audience. Vastey drew extensively on the work of two Scottish explorers: Mungo Park (1771–1806), a surgeon sent by the African Association in 1795–1797 to explore the Niger River, and James Bruce (1730–1792), the British consul in Algiers who explored Abyssinia (Ethiopia) and discovered the source of the Blue Nile.[81] Both men expressed admiration for the beauty and virtues of the African peoples they encountered.

Again echoing the outline of Oson, Vastey took on the argument for African inferiority on the historical and cultural stages. Because his own erudition was perhaps his strongest argument that blacks were not inherently inferior to whites, Vastey used the occasion to prove the range of his knowledge in classical and modern literatures. Among the ancients he cited were

Herodotus, Hanno, Porphyry, Lucan, Lactantius, and Tacitus, supplemented with readings of French intellectuals such as Baron de Montesquieu, Alain René de Le Sage, Palisot de Beauvois, Volney, and Chateaubriand.[82] Vastey demonstrated, by his own reading, that Africans were capable of "civility" according to the prevailing European definition: a working knowledge of ancient and modern literature and politics.

But his primary purpose was not simply to recite a list of authors. Vastey made two important historical points. First, he asserted that African peoples established civilizations long before the Europeans—indeed, ancient civilizations in Ethiopia and Egypt (claimed by Vastey as African) provided the model for societies in Europe. Second, civilization, in Vastey's rendering, moved from Egypt and Ethiopia, to Phoenicia (with its commercial and maritime center in Tyre, which made mercantile inroads into the southern part of Africa by sea), to Greece and Rome, and then northward to Europe. As Europe "rose," Africa "declined" with the spread of Islam and the destruction of Carthage.

Vastey's line of reasoning would not have been unfamiliar to European or American readers. With the steady movement of explorers and missionaries into Africa by the late eighteenth century, many historians had taken to speculating about the cultural and moral disparities, as they saw them, between Europeans and indigenous peoples in other parts of the world. Vastey's historical logic is most directly indebted to the work of Baron de Montesquieu, who, in book 21 of *The Spirit of Laws* (1748), drawing on a wide array of ancient authorities, detailed the rise and fall of commerce—associated, by extension, with civilization—in various parts of the world. These historical theories were used frequently by whites to demonstrate the evident inferiority of African societies by measuring them against the yardstick of European culture, leading to the conclusion that blacks would never be the intellectual or moral equals of whites. But by the early nineteenth century, antislavery advocates countered their narratives with alternative explanations, arguing that the course of history, beginning as it did with the noble legacies of arts and literature in Egypt and Ethiopia, could once again return to the African continent. William Wilberforce, the noted British abolitionist, penned a historical treatise in which he argued that, while civilization had moved north and west from its origins in Mesopotamia, it could certainly be introduced to Africa now via Europe and the United States; the lack of "civilization" in Africa, in his estimate, owed more to the accident of historical diffusion than to the inherent moral capacities of blacks.[83]

Writing well before the rise of the arguments for biological racism that stressed the immutability of racial and cultural characteristics, Vastey adhered to an older model of historical change that posited the inevitability of the rise and decline of civilizations.[84] The most sustained treatment of this theme before Vastey was found in the work of another French intellectual, Constantin-François Chasseboeuf comte de Volney (1757–1820). Volney, a second-generation *philosophe,* developed an early interest in history and ancient languages. After travels in Syria and Egypt in the 1780s, he published the two-volume work *Voyage en Syrie et en Égypte* (1787), in which he observed the "negroid" character of the Sphinx and speculated about the racial character of ancient Egyptians.[85] In his even more influential treatise of 1791, *Les Ruines, ou méditations sur les révolutions des empires,* Volney made the controversial judgment that the early kingdom of Ethiopia had first established the arts and sciences and had adhered most closely to the divine plan for the universe: "Those piles, said he, which you see in that narrow valley, watered by the Nile, are the remains of opulent cities, the pride of the ancient kingdom of Ethiopia. . . . There a people, now forgotten, discovered, while others were yet barbarians, the elements of the arts and sciences; a race of men now rejected from society for their *sable skin and frissled hair,* founded on the study of the laws of nature, those civil and religious systems which still govern the universe." Severely critical of social inequality, monarchy, and revealed religion, and disparaging of the "civilized" empires of Greece and Rome that had first instituted slave systems as a matter of course, Volney implied that European cultures were actually far less moral and humane than those of ancient Ethiopia and Egypt.[86]

Vastey cited Volney briefly once in his text, but it is clear that he adopted the historical thrust of this argument, focusing particular attention on the hypocrisies of "civilized" European nations that still allowed for the widespread mistreatment of millions of enslaved Africans. European barbarities, in Vastey's rendering, were well documented, from the heathen practices of human sacrifice among the Germans and the Druids in ancient Gaul to the horrors of the slave trade—only the latest in a long line of barbaric ritualized activity.[87] Like Volney, Vastey predicted the eventual downfall of Europe (and potential rise of Africa), according to natural laws, since "the supreme arbiter of the Universe, has set bounds to the duration of empires, no less than men."

Another important influence on Vastey's work was Abbé Henri Grégoire's *De la littérature des Nègres: ou Recherches sur leurs facultés Intellectuales,* published in Paris in 1808. Grégoire, a white French intellectual sympathetic to the plight of blacks, set out to prove, through the accumulation of classical and ethnographic data, that Africans were inherently the equals of whites. Not incidentally, he used the example of Haiti as singular evidence of African achievement in the modern world. Vastey mentioned Grégoire in the early part of his work and was clearly indebted to his readings of a variety of texts that demonstrate African historical achievement.

Whether Vastey introduced the work to Christophe or vice versa, the Haitian monarch apparently greatly admired Grégoire's writing. In June 1814, Christophe's advisor, the Comte de Limonade, wrote enthusiastically to Grégoire: "We have received your great work *De la Littérature des nègres;* His Majesty, in great admiration for the philanthropic principles you are defending, has always been an avid reader of it. . . . Everything makes us love it and instills in our hearts feelings of admiration and thankfulness for its venerable author."[88] Christophe subsequently ordered fifty copies of the book in London, offering them to Haitian magistrates and generals, and printed excerpts in Haitian newspapers.

The dissemination of Vastey's narrative in Haitian newspapers marked the beginning of his fame in Haiti. Within a decade, excerpts from his piece would be published in serial form in the first African-American periodical, *Freedom's Journal.* This textual mobility signaled the beginning of a new era of commercial production and consumption that would catapult communal narratives into the households of thousands of free blacks in the decades leading up to the Civil War. By the 1820s and the 1830s, with the rise of the black publishing industry, African-American newspapers such as *Freedom's Journal* and the *Colored American,* spearheaded by editors who had received some of the first classical educations afforded to free blacks, elaborated biblical arguments for racial equality, brought classical authors such as Herodotus and Josephus into common parlance, explained the latest findings in science and ethnology, and provided histories of African peoples around the world. The black press quickly became a voice for free black communities that united their cause with that of enslaved blacks and Africans abroad; editors published letters from Africa and the Caribbean that linked the interests of African-American readers to an international diaspora and afforded them the means to debate and strategize. This accelerated circulation of ideas amounted to a new kind of public power for free blacks.[89]

The effects of this technological revolution were far-reaching. To read the first issues of *Freedom's Journal,* with their juxtaposition of writings from French, British, and American sources containing literature, race theory, politics, and ethnography, is to marvel at the new intellectual opportunities they supplied. Yet it is also clear that the newspaper was reassembling tools that African Americans had been employing assiduously for a half-century to create communal stories. By 1817, the writings of Jacob Oson and Pompée Valentin Vastey exhibited all the discursive elements that would animate the works of later and better-known black authors, writers whose works would become the foundation of black abolitionist rhetoric. When David Walker published his *Appeal* in 1829, a manifesto that circulated widely in parts of the South as well as in the North, he drew on the same combinations of classical authors, biblical narratives, and Masonic-inspired references to ancient Egypt that had become a staple of the communal narrative genre.[90] Hosea Easton, author of *A Treatise on the Intellectual Character, and the Civil and Political Condition of the Colored People of the United States* (1837) prefaced his work with a historical exposition that reiterated the Masonic framing of Moses in Egypt through the works of Joseph and Diodorus Siculus as well as the findings of Volney and Vastey. Invocation of these by-now-familiar themes would continue to echo evocatively and incite political responses because they had become so deeply embedded in the consciousness of thousands of African Americans. Commenting on Walker's *Appeal,* the abolitionist editor William Lloyd Garrison acknowledged that "the historical facts which he has collected were too familiar to have required extraordinary research."[91] Given the ubiquity of these "facts," one wonders why the genre of the slave narrative has endured in scholarly memory as the representative "black voice" of this era.

Along with the rise in black publishing came an explosion of black literary and debating societies, library associations, and lycea in the 1830s, developments that further encouraged reading among African-American women as well as men. Philadelphia boasted a reading room for blacks by 1828 and a female literary society by 1831. That society joined the New York Philomathean Society (1830) and the Pittsburgh Theban Society (1831), and many more such associations were founded in the following decade. Some were fleeting enterprises, and most had fewer than fifty members, but their public lectures and debates attracted audiences that numbered in the hundreds.[92]

The rise of black print publishing marked the end of the early era of communal narration. The sheer proliferation of accounts, widely disseminated to black (and white) readers in Northern states, in West Africa, in the Caribbean, and even in the American South, presented diasporic Africans in America with usable histories that anchored them as both African and American. Because early print culture was dominated by Afro-Protestants, their narratives also marked them as Christians. While not every American black would have wholeheartedly accepted these accounts, their sheer volume and ubiquity by the 1840s and 1850s gave rise to shared discourses about African precedents and current realities and reinvented communities as African American in the transmission and performance of common tales. Judging by the eagerness with which free Northern blacks joined literary societies, attended lectures and sermons, and wrote letters to the editor, these narratives were received with enthusiasm and frequently debated. Moreover, with the focus of the black press on international developments, print culture also opened black Americans to diasporic African events, signaling both their resemblances to other African descendants as well as their distinctive concerns as Americans and Christians.[93]

This proliferation of narratives, however, also worked at cross-purposes with the growth of a racially defined community. The denominational robustness that undergirded print culture offered additional historical engagements, and the exposure to diasporic Africans presented possibilities for political and religious expression that ranged well outside of the American Protestant synthesis. Black communal narratives simultaneously encouraged racial loyalties and provided alternative affiliations that offered potentially conflicting messages. African Americans disagreed, debated, and argued over the appropriate ways of living out these interrelated legacies in the coming decades. Despite their divergent conclusions, their arguments were fueled by a basic set of tools furnished in these early accounts, tools to which writers would return repeatedly: ancient African precedents, biblical and Masonic images, Protestant Church history, and American ideals of republican virtue that were closely related to nationalist identities gaining force in the United States and France. Those intellectual instruments of liberation, more than the specific answers at which authors arrived, defined African-American collective discourse into the twentieth century.

2

The Children of Gilead

Wouldst know the history of the Church,
Come, gaze about with me,
And see where Richard Allen rose,
And struck for liberty.

Within the old St. George's church,
While black men bowed in prayer,
Behold them dragged up from their knees
Scorned and insulted there.

And as brave Allen left St. George
With lifted hand he vowed,
That 'neath their own fig tree and vine,
His Race should worship God!

KATHERINE TILLMAN, "The Spirit of Allen," 1922

In May 1857 the Reverend William T. Catto, pastor of the First African Presbyterian Church in Philadelphia, delivered a sermon commemorating the semi-centenary of the church's founding. Catto understood well the historical significance of his church as the first black Presbyterian church in the country, and when he published his remarks shortly after the anniversary he included with his speech an assortment of documents: a history of the church, including a biographical sketch of its first minister and a lengthy explanation of the split that resulted in the founding of the second African Presbyterian church in the city, and an annotated list of all eighteen African Protestant churches in Philadelphia. Catto declared that he felt called to his task because the church was one "harmonious whole" throughout the world: "To gather up the history of each individual church, then, should be the aim of each disciple of the Lord Jesus, in order that its existence may be known." Citing Paul, he beseeched his readers to consider the Christian church a family in which even the weakest members must be taken into account. Since no one had yet "undertaken even a brief sketch of this member of the Christian family," concluded Catto, he would obey the command of his Savior to "'Gather up the fragments, let nothing be lost.'"[1] Catto cared deeply about "the church" as a unified international community, in theory if not in current social reality.

The communal narrative tradition that centered on the historic accomplishments of African peoples represented a particular form of "knowledge gathering," as free blacks garnered strands of information about societies and lands from Scripture, classical and scientific texts, and newer political theories to fashion a collective account of origins and purpose. We might, then, assume that William Catto was following the same mode of inquiry as he "gathered up" the histories of individual black churches to form a larger collective consciousness. After all, Catto himself, born into slavery, had been freed and licensed by the Presbytery of Charleston in 1847 and was one of the few African Americans who could make that claim. Cognizant of ties to an African homeland, he had hoped to become a missionary to Africa but instead had settled in Philadelphia. There, he helped to establish a strong black Protestant community, and he noted with pride the growing number of African-American churches in the city. His collected fragments, like those of the earliest communal narratives, contained a diverse assortment of facts and parables reflecting many different concerns, from ecclesiology to confessional unity to race consciousness.

Yet while African unity was important to Catto, divisions within the Christian fold, particularly among Presbyterians, worried him immensely. He celebrated the proliferation of black churches, but he deeply lamented the lack of confessional unity that it demonstrated. "It is regarded as a very unhappy state where divisions exist in families," he asserted. "Is the church, then, for which the Savior poured out his life blood, to be considered less important, less interesting, and less in the eyes of the Redeemer's blood-bought family, than the relations existing among us in our domestic and social ties, however sacred and tender they should be?"[2] Other kinds of loyalties, denominational Christian loyalties, were as pressing to Catto as were the bonds of African lineage.

For many Americans today, steeped in a world of mix-and-match faith and expansive evangelical movements, the very idea of a Protestant denomination, with its formal discipline, rules of order, and creeds and confessions, sounds decidedly antique. Few contemporary individuals or communities count denominationalism, that celebration of organizational diversity within Christian unity that emerged as a distinctive feature of white and black American religious life in the decades after the Revolution, as pertinent to their lives. As a result, the hundreds of denominational and local church histories that sit on library shelves and in family attics are less beloved heirlooms than odd curiosities. Why did nineteenth-century Protestants care so much about preserving the tiniest details of church life, from the names of every minister to the minutes of each meeting? And what investments could they possibly have had in the constructed kinships and genealogies of Methodism, Congregationalism, or Presbyterianism?

The fact is, church identity—be it local or denominational—has been a crucial element of American Christian life since the founding of the nation. The loosening of ties among Methodists, Presbyterians, or Baptists in favor of the less organizationally specific "evangelical" or "Christian" moniker is a very recent development. With the dismantling of state churches following the American Revolution, religious groups in the new republic elevated the importance of voluntarily associating in Protestant churches that were self-governing and bent on preserving moral order. To do this, religious leaders had to emphasize the importance of loyalty to particular communities and institutions. Defining this new religious landscape became, for some Protestant leaders, a primary means of claiming as well as advertising an American religious identity. In the 1840s church historian and Presbyterian layman Robert Baird was only the first of many leaders to try to categorize the growing and bewildering religious diversity in the United States. By no coincidence, he arrived at a classificatory scheme that placed his own evangelical Presbyterian churches at the center of the American religious scene. Greater institutional visibility meant greater social and political influence and, possibly, an increase in numbers of adherents.

Beginning in the 1810s, at a time of uncertain freedom in the North and almost certain enslavement in the South, free blacks began to write and publish church histories that detailed the growth of new institutions, leaders, and schools. In 1817, just a few years after the organization of the African Methodist Episcopal Church (and the same year that Jacob Oson and Baron de Vastey published their accounts of African unity), the new denomination circulated its first publication, *Doctrines and Discipline of the African Methodist Episcopal Church.* The book opened with a nine-page section described as "a brief history of our rise and progress," which, the authors added, "we hope will be satisfactory, and conducive to your edification and growth in the knowledge of our Lord Jesus Christ."[3] In the decades that followed, dozens of African-American Protestant leaders produced historical sketches, albums, pamphlets, and books that linked their churches to broader Christian communities. They corrected other writers, argued over the appropriate interpretation of events, and built on one another's work. In fact, no genre of African-American communal narrative is quite as sedimented or intertextual as are church histories: authors vigilantly read previous histories of their church and used them as touchstones or foils, even quoting (and creatively editing) them at length.

Churches were places of respite, meeting points and organizational hubs for a wide variety of charitable and political activities in free black communities. They also provided one of the few avenues available for individual self-improvement and moral uplift through education, temperance, and other reform efforts.[4] For nineteenth-century African Americans, denominational affiliation formed a central component of African-American identity. Church was not simply an obvious route to racial liberation; it fostered a self-understanding that related in varying and even contradictory ways to race consciousness. Church histories nurtured the collective loyalties that made racial unity possible. But they also complicated and challenged racial affiliation in myriad ways, for they, too, reflected the working out of contemporary social relationships—among blacks, and between blacks and whites—in narrative form. Black denominational histories thus reveal the simultaneous articulation of racially defined Protestant, as well as interracial Christian, identities.

As Catto's sermon indicates, denominational histories were family stories, narratives that united individuals in church entities that were understood to be organic and persistent over time. In the nineteenth century in particular, churches were assemblies catalyzed not simply by a desire for self-help or individual improvement but by the imperative to worship, to gather, and to glorify their God in community. For many, and certainly for the authors of denominational and local church histories, Christian community had a significance that extended beyond the needs of the individual or the racial collective to an awareness of a shared spiritual past and future. Racial identity, as important as it was, could be seen as a temporary state; but churches, pulled together by correct forms of discipline and devotion, transcended the confines of human time and ushered African Americans into sacred time.

Denominational histories also reveal the fractures, the fissures, and the ongoing tensions over church-based identities that have animated the lives of African Americans. The fuller story of African-American religious history lies precisely in the enduring negotiations—articulated in narrative form—among race consciousness, denominational loyalties, and Christian commitments. That shared lineage was not identical to racial heritage, nor was the church merely a temple to racial unity. As Bishop Benjamin Tucker Tanner of the AME Church explained in the late nineteenth century, the primary aim of the church was "to help convert the world to Christ—the world, and not simply Africans, real or imagined."[5] Church histories, in turn, provide a fascinating window into the multifaceted nature of African-American communal life in nineteenth-century America. Black Protestants, excluded from virtually all the denominational accounts penned by Euro-Americans during this era, strove mightily to reconcile their deeply held Christian beliefs with their equally compelling commitments to racial equality. Their published narratives are the artifacts of this intellectual activity as well as a testimony to the making of a particular strand of social knowledge.

All Christian narratives serve present purposes. Individual conversion accounts penned by African Americans in this period, among other things, explained why a person ought to become a Christian in the first place by elaborating what faith had done for the author. Institutional histories served different but related purposes. They justified the separation of black from white Christians, and explained, *within the terms of their religious frameworks,* how and why it was acceptable to worship in a racially segregated setting. They sought to convince other African Americans that their church was both doctrinally correct and the most appropriate Christian institution for black believers. This latter purpose became especially critical after the Civil War, as black denominations embarked on intensive missionary activities among the newly freed slaves. Denominational histories announced a vision of how African Americans were to relate to the larger Christian world, especially their white American brothers and sisters, and staked a claim for the importance of black churches within African-American communities. Tedious as they often were in their lengthy recounting of idealized clergy and struggling local organizations, church histories were also profoundly political texts that opened up vital intellectual worlds in distinctive ways.

We might reasonably ask where to find the intellectual potency in hagiographic remembrances, lists of buildings, and the creation of catechisms—all prominent features of denominational histories. The trick is to see the potential for freedom embedded within the organizational form. The Christian message of individual and social liberation exerted a powerful pull for African Americans and represented an adamant repudiation of identities based on white-defined enslavement. Yet spiritual freedom and political freedom were hardly identical, and it is not so obvious why black churchgoers would voluntarily submit to white-controlled or historically Euro-American religious institutions, groups that had actively participated in African enslavement. For black Christians the problem with white churches was not a problem inherent in Christianity as a faith, which they understood to be a transhistorical phenomenon. It was a failing of individual Christians. Frederick Douglass voiced this significant distinction when he criticized the white churches of the South for not being truly "Christian." So, too, other black Protestants separated their faith in a God above and beyond mundane history from the ways in which believers lived out their understanding of that faith. Protestant churches, according to African-American members, were not the sole property or lineage of white Christians; they were communities ordained by God. In this sense, black believers wrote church history to trace the stories of the saved and to distinguish their lives from those of other people, be they persecutors, pretenders, or simply the religiously indifferent. They sought to parse the movement of the sacred through its historical development.

African-American believers also understood liberation and submission not as polar opposites but as potentially complementary goals for the Christian life. Submission, be it to a pope, a church council, a minister, or a spiritual discipline, is frequently experienced as a liberating practice that facilitates other kinds of freedom.[6] Freedom and submission are constantly entwined in human experience as well as in religious systems. Such was the case for African-American Protestants, for whom particular forms of institutional submission to white religious authorities proved a prerequisite for the achievement of spiritual salvation. On at least some level, many black Protestants saw themselves in Christian communion with white believers, a fact that deepened and complicated racial relations.

When African Americans voluntarily yoked themselves to Western and Euro-American–derived notions of Christian history and community, the process of narrative creation helped liberate them to discover the freedom culled from ingenious reinterpretation. Religious loyalties thereby provided many African Americans with a new sense of freedom and belonging—a freedom in Christ, a new identity within a Christian fellowship—and a freedom to appropriate and mold that tradition as they chose.[7]

Church histories ushered readers (and listeners, since some were delivered as sermons) into a rich world of biblical and historical imagery that described and shaped the development of black religious life. With their eyes trained toward the anticipated disapproval and condemnation of white Protestants as well as the competitive reach of other African-American religious organizations, black church historians created distinctive, and highly variable, accounts of sacred foundings. The images and themes they employed revealed a foundational set of stories to which African Americans would return repeatedly to explain and interpret their collective existence. African Americans re-created church histories in their own image.

From the beginning of their conversion to Christianity in North America in the mid-eighteenth century, African-American Protestants founded independent churches. The precise meaning of religious "independence" in those early decades, however, varied widely by tradition and locality. All black Protestants were affiliated with institutions that offered Christian fellowship in exchange for assent to collective discipline. In these settings, religious "independence" was always mitigated and defined in relation to submission to religious authority. Even enslaved Africans occasionally achieved a modest amount of organizational autonomy, circumstances that then allowed them to enforce their own communal regulations. Numerous reports of "African" Baptist churches surfaced in the Southern states before the revolution; these were societies in which blacks initially exercised a remarkable degree of control over church discipline and the calling of pastors. After several slave insurrections in the early nineteenth century white authorities rapidly curtailed any motion toward religious independence. Yet despite constant tensions surrounding authority and oversight, large black churches remained a noticeable feature of Southern life throughout the antebellum period.

In the North, early "African" churches were forged in response to the same set of circumstances that shaped the development of Euro-Protestant churches in the postrevolutionary period. Blacks, like whites, championed the newly bestowed rights of religious liberty and attendant opportunities for voluntarism and denominational establishment. Just as the revolutionary legacy of religious disestablishment brought tumult and revitalization to the biracial and predominantly white churches, so too were black church leaders and laity encouraged to assert themselves spiritually and ecclesiastically through the message of newly legitimated religious dissent.[8] Local black church studies and denominational histories from the nineteenth century reveal an ecclesiastical world filled with division, differentiation, and competition, an environment in which racial identity played a complex and even ambiguous role.[9] By the 1820s black Methodists, Presbyterians, Baptists, and Episcopalians had organized separate congregations, although they, too, wrestled with white church leaders over control of buildings and leadership issues. By 1821 three different societies of black Methodists had established their ecclesiastical independence from the Methodist Episcopal Church: the African Union Church (1813), the African Methodist Episcopal Church (1816), and the African Methodist Episcopal Zion Church (1821).[10]

Even in the Northern states, however, where blacks were free to congregate, the African Protestant church world was far more variegated and molded by ecclesiastical mandate than is suggested by the dichotomy between "independence" and "dependence." Autonomous black Baptist churches in New York and Boston, unfettered by the strictures of denominational oversight, chose their own ministers and regulated their own internal codes of discipline. Black Methodists by the 1820s worshipped as they chose but still retained Methodist discipline and hymnody as the basis of their worship. And those "fully independent" black churches were joined by a growing number of Episcopal and Presbyterian black churches that exhibited varying degrees of self-rule, including oversight by (white) denominational authorities and committees that owned their property and regulated ordination. "Independence," in other words, was a relative term and never entailed complete license to do as one pleased. In some instances, religious agency compelled black church leaders to yoke themselves firmly to disciplines and doctrines previously defined by white majority denominations.

Despite organizational variation, virtually all black Protestant churches felt themselves connected, spiritually and historically, if not locally and materially, to wider Christian circles of influence. This fact is substantiated most clearly by the elaborate biblical and ecclesiological stratagems that church leaders used to justify separation from white Christians. Even in local communities, freedom of action was determined as much by ecclesiastical imperative as by political principle: black Episcopalians, for example, at the most hierarchical end of the Protestant spectrum, remained obligated to a system of sacerdotal power that governed their ability to call pastors, as evidenced in Jacob Oson's failed attempt to be called as a minister in Philadelphia, where the white hierarchy regulated authority even within the all-black local church. Although blacks may have protested the grounds by which white church leaders determined ordination, they did not dispute the ecclesiastical model by which those decisions were made. African-American Protestants, in other words, lived within political worlds where the lack of racial freedom was a real, but not entirely determining, social constraint. Equally salient in daily life were the collective principles and covenants that governed their churches, rules that did not necessarily motivate them toward racial separatism.

Precisely because Christian community (comprising both the visible and the invisible churches) was so important, separation or independence from other Christians became a problem to be explained rather than a freedom to be celebrated. The first task of church leaders, then, was to interpret and clarify this growing phenomenon of separate racial churches for both skeptical white and potential black members. Why should Christians condone racial separation? It was not enough to argue that whites treated black churchgoers badly, since the bonds of Christian fellowship extended beyond democratic egalitarian precepts. As a result, the first writers of black church histories felt the need to justify—through pragmatic arguments, biblical mandates, and ecclesiological precedents—separation from whites.

Initially, they couched the issue of separation less in terms of white discrimination than in terms of procedural and aesthetic concerns. The first histories of the AME Church, those contained in the *Doctrines and Disci-*

pline of 1817 and Richard Allen's 1833 autobiographical narrative, focus more on monetary considerations and worship style than on racial discrimination. Race is a significant subtext, but these works overwhelmingly stress denominational description and difference. AME leaders framed the history of their dramatic split in terms other than that of race distinction. To be sure, the care of Allen's language, in particular, reflected his consciousness of the precarious nature of Northern "freedom" for blacks. Whites were always watching, and blacks knew it. Allen did not shy away altogether from criticisms of whites: he devoted the bulk of his narrative of the founding of the AME to the legal and monetary disputes with white Methodists opposed to separation. We are the real Methodists, his narrative implies, and we have played by all the correct legal and ecclesiastical rules.

The Methodist Daniel Coker published what was arguably the first "history" of African churches in the United States, in the form of an appendix to his *Dialogue Between a Virginian and an African Minister* (1810). The pamphlet itself was an extended religious argument against slavery, in which Coker refuted biblical arguments that supported the enslavement of Africans. But his most telling proof came at the end of the pamphlet in the form of direct evidence of God's divine handiwork. He prefaced this final demonstration with a passage from 1 Peter 2:9: "But ye are a chosen generation, a royal priesthood, an holy nation, a peculiar people; that ye should shew forth the praises of him who hath called you out of darkness into his marvellous light." Coker then followed this quote with a series of lists: "A List of Names of the Descendants of the African Race, who have Given Proof of Talents," "A List of African Churches," "A List of the Names of African Ministers in Holy Orders," and "A List of the Names of African Local Preachers." There he counted thirteen African churches from Charleston to Boston, as if his "gathering," his enumeration of these growing numbers of clergy and churches, in itself proved the righteousness of his cause.[11]

Not surprisingly, biblical precedent served as one of the most potent means of establishing the religious legitimacy of African Protestant actions. The foundational event of AME history to this day is the story of the "gallery incident," an episode from the 1780s in which Absalom Jones, Richard Allen, and other black members of the predominantly white St. George's Church in Philadelphia were interrupted during prayer and asked to move to the back seats. In response they exited the church after services, never to return, in a movement that became linked by later AME historians to the Israelite Exodus from Egypt. So, too, William Catto, in his 1857 address to the First African Presbyterian Church of Philadelphia, urged listeners to "arise and go forward," just as their church forebears had done: "What was commanded the people by the mouth of Moses was commanded by a greater than Moses to our fathers; they did go forward; they have finished their work, crossed over Jordan, and are now in Canaan and at rest."[12] Exodus, as many Jewish and Christian groups over the centuries have discovered, contained elements critical to a sharpened collective consciousness: undeserved suffering, divine vindication, and ultimate freedom.

More commonly, however, church writers invoked the Babylonian exile, a tale explicated in the lush poetry and prophecies of the books of Isaiah and Jeremiah. The story of Israel in exile and the model of social expulsion outlined in Isaiah and Jeremiah fit the ecclesiastical plight of black Christians in the United States better than did the story of the Exodus. In January 1816 the AME minister Daniel Coker honored the newly created denomination with a sermon that drew on the parallels between the Jews in Babylon and African Methodists who had been "bound" by the white Methodist conference, although "governed by the same laws" and subject to the same disciplinary penalties. Just as Israel had finally been freed and allowed to return home, so were African Methodists now offered their congregational freedom, a gift that some apparently refused. Coker wondered at this turn of events: "While you have prayed that Ethiopia might stretch out her hands unto God, now when God seems to be answering your prayers, and opening the door for you to enjoy all that you could wish, many of you rise up and say, the time is not yet come." Drawing on Isaiah, he called on African Methodists to rise up and gather in the AME fold, so that "we as a band of brethren, shall sit down under our own vine to worship, and none to make us afraid."[13] John Gloucester also saw in the Babylonian experience a precedent, although he believed that the dedication of the African Presbyterian Church in Philadelphia in 1811 represented the return from exile to the land of Canaan, a site where the latter-day Israelites had been allowed to rebuild their temple.[14] Through exodus or exile, Israelite enslavement stood as a salient marker not simply of physical captivity but of ecclesiastical control.

Not all African Methodists, however, conceived of separation as permanent or altogether negative. Perhaps the most creative and organizationally intricate biblical history was offered by John Prout. In 1818, at the third anniversary of the establishment of the AME denomination, Prout preached a sermon at the annual conference in Baltimore that spelled out his understanding of the appropriate relationship between white and black Methodists. Prout chose as his text the story of Reuben and Gad from Joshua 22, a tale that addresses the division of the children of Israel into distinct communities. Because of a shortage of land, Joshua commands several of the tribes of Israel to separate from the Israelites in Canaan and move to Gilead on the opposite bank of the Jordan. There they erect an altar, an act that is misconstrued by the tribes in Canaan as a rebellion against the Lord. After considerable negotiations and threats of war, the dwellers in Gilead convince those in Canaan of what the Lord already knows: that their altar is, in fact, a sign of loyalty to God and a witness to the collective unity of the tribes.

Prout's exegesis of this passage struck at the heart of the Methodist dilemma. Race, like the river Jordan, divided their organizational unity. White Methodists resided in Canaan, and some black Methodists, with all the right intentions toward their brethren, had removed to their "African Gilead." As with the tribes of Reuben and Gad, the Lord granted African Methodists this distinct inheritance in a contract that guaranteed them the same privileges as the other children of Israel. They were obliged to "build up African altars . . . as nearly as we could upon the great Methodist model," not as a means of sowing discord but as "humble monuments of our union and love; intended to bring millions yet unborn from every corner of this vast continent, to bend at the great altar of Methodist liberty." White Methodists claimed that their separation was illegitimate. But as the tribes in Gilead had done before them, Prout enjoined African Methodists to stand firm on Methodist principles and to use the history of the denomination as a means to fortify their resolve: "Look back to the times of ancient virtue and renown; look back to the mighty purposes which your fathers had in view when they planted this church. Recal[l] to your minds their labors, their toils, their perseverance, and let their divine spirit animate you in your actions."[15] Although their church was physically distinct, Prout advised AME members to see it as intimately linked to the larger Methodist collectivity, united by a shared history and a common evangelical purpose.

New Testament and early Christian history also provided black authors with powerful arguments for African Protestant separation. Ecclesiastically, early church precedents justified the manner in which black churches had organized themselves and called their ministers. Heirs to a form of government in which apostolic succession was a primary means of conveying sacred authority, African Methodists worried greatly about establishing the appropriate line of episcopal legitimacy in the face of separation. It was not enough to "be Israel" in an exilic sense; one also had to belong to an authentic Christian community. Christopher Rush, an early historian of the African Methodist Episcopal Zion Church writing in 1843, argued that his purpose was to demonstrate that his denomination held the "proper or authentic organization of Church Government, relative to Episcopacy, that we did not spring up like mushrooms (as some unfriendly persons would like to have it published and believed, to suit their own purposes), but that we came in possession of that title by deliberate gradation."[16] Drawing on the apostolic era, the Reformation, and Methodism's split from the Church of England, church historians rehearsed elaborate justifications for holding separate services, hiring their own ministers, and even withdrawing completely from fellowship with whites.

Noah Cannon's 1842 *History of the African Methodist Episcopal Church*, the first attempt at a full-scale history of the organization, took great care to link the development of the young association to the Christian past. Cannon, a second-generation AME minister from Delaware, dedicated his narrative to the memory of Richard Allen, and he plainly wanted to fashion a fitting tribute to his forebears. Much of his recounting followed closely the chronology of Allen's earlier memoir, but Cannon highlighted two features of the past that related the AME to ecclesiastical precedents. First, he cast the founding generation as an apostolic band, turning Allen into a "brave soldier" who battled with a "little crew" against "cruel persecutors." Citing 2 Timothy 4:5–6 ("For I am now ready to be offered, and the time of my departure is at hand"), Cannon described how—like the first disciples—the small gathering of AME preachers spread the work of Christ from Philadelphia to "various parts of Pennsylvania, Delaware, Maryland, New York, Ohio, Canada, the barren shores of Africa, and the Island of Hayti." Echoing Daniel Coker in a citation of Psalms 68:31 that would become a ubiquitous reminder of African promise, he concluded that "'Ethiopia is seen stretching out her hands to God.'"[17] Cannon linked the early spread of Christianity in the ancient world to the growth of his denomination, thereby establishing a biblical precedent for the new organization—as well as a righteous explanation of the opposition they had encountered. White persecutors were portrayed not simply as fellow Christians troubled by Christian schism but instead as enemies of the apostles of truth, the Rome to black AME apostles.

Second, Cannon affirmed the AME connection to both Reformation history and early Methodism. Using Methodist founder John Wesley as his champion, Cannon redacted a Wesley sermon within his own text that addressed the issue of Christian schism. As Wesley had pointed out, Methodists were heirs to a long line of false accusations. Roman Catholics had charged Protestants with being schismatics during the Reformation, just as Anglicans had leveled identical charges against early Methodists. Wesley insisted that both indictments contradicted biblical teaching: "'They have been fighting with shadows of their own raising: violently combating a sin, which had no existence, but in their own imagination, which is not once forbidden, no, nor once mentioned either in the Old or New Testament.'"[18] By extension, Cannon's appropriation implied, white Methodists were once again wrongly accusing AME members of schism. But at least the AME was in good historical company.[19]

Racial oppression was a constant in the lives of black church members and authors, and much of the time white society really was Pharaoh or Rome. But such politicized readings can be misleading, for they ignore both the persistence of white participation in black church life and the intraracial conflict among African-American Protestants over deep-seated organizational differences. Christian communal consciousness fostered intimate relationships with some Euro-Americans, as well as a desire to narrate a common Christian lineage that made sense of race-based separation. Sought out by African Methodists, early white defenders of separate African churches in cities such as Philadelphia and New York raised money and provided organizational support. Both Richard Allen and Christopher Rush repeatedly cited the participation of whites in their communal accounts. Allen referenced the crucial roles played by white Christians throughout his life and the growth of the church, from Jonathan Bunn and his wife ("a father and mother of Israel") during his youth, to the Germans in Lancaster, Pennsylvania, who composed his first preaching field, to Philadelphia's Mother Bethel AME Church benefactors Benjamin Rush and Robert Ralston, who "subscribed largely towards the church, and were very friendly towards us, and advised us how to go on."[20] Christopher Rush also depicted white Methodists as almost uniformly helpful and supportive to their cause, providing ways for the two churches to remain "in union with each other" but organizationally separate. In the first years of the establishment of the New York church (AMEZ), Rush recounts that a white elder preached there twice a week. Racial separation, in his narrative, was necessitated not by discrimination but by the rapid increase of the numbers of whites in John Street Methodist Church and the desire to evangelize among other African Americans. In the early years after separation, sympathetic white Baptist clergy in the Northeast preached in African and Abyssinian Baptist churches in the absence of qualified blacks.[21] Both intimacy and oppression marked the interactions of early American Protestants across the color line.

African-American church histories insisted on *both* racial difference and Christian connection; they continued to knit together Christians in ways that emphasized human redemption alongside racial particularity. Such elements can be found even in sites where blacks did not need to perform for whites. One ubiquitous and opportune place to render church history was through hymnody. In 1801, less than a decade after the founding of Mother Bethel Church in Philadelphia, Richard Allen compiled a collection of hymns for the use of his church and distributed them widely. According to AME Bishop Benjamin Tucker Tanner, who described the writing of this hymnal near the end of the century in his own history of the denomination, Allen told his congregation that new hymns were crucial for a newly established church: "Having become a distinct and separate body of people, there is no collection of hymns we could with propriety adopt. However, we have for some time been collecting materials for the present work."[22]

In 1817 the nascent AME denomination adopted the Methodist doctrines and discipline *in toto* for their own use, so why not use the Methodist hymnbook as well? We don't know what compelled Allen to compile a new songbook, but we do know what he wanted his church to sing about: the sweet love of Jesus, the one who suffered on the cross. The vast majority of the hymns he collected, in fact, highlighted the saving power of Christ. Of the more than fifty hymns in each edition, only a handful dealt with subjects that might have had any resonance with exodus or exile. One described the "land of pure delight" that humans would enter after death: "So to the *Jews* old *Canaan* stood, / While *Jordan* roll'd between." Another explicitly mentioned Exodus:

> Then let us well remember,
> How Israel was freed,
> When from the hand of Pharaoh,
> By Moses they were led . . .

Most, however, referenced sacred history as a way to highlight Christian suffering and redemption rather than national or racial liberation:

> Thus Sinai roars, and round the earth
>   Thunder and fire, and vengeance flings;
> But Jesus thy dear gasping breath,
>   And Calvary say gentler things.[23]

Like many Methodists of the day, Allen's congregation ranged widely in its attempt to place itself within a Christian history and to explain redemptive suffering as well as the problem of ecclesiastical separation. While the trope of exodus lent itself well to illustrating and protesting racial separation, Allen clearly intended to shift his denomination's gaze to a focus on the power of Jesus as suffering savior for all humanity. The Christian life, his choices seem to suggest, promised divine judgment of the oppressors, but it also required disciplined sacrifice and even personal suffering as part of the package.

From the first years of ecclesiastical separation, African-American scribes situated their denominational origins within broader biblical and Christian frameworks. They provided a means for members and other readers, many of whom had not participated in founding events, to place themselves collectively in biblical and ecclesiastical stories—of exile and expulsion, of early Christian persecution, and of organizational separation. Their stories reflected and shaped the multilayered contexts of African-American Protestant life, perspectives that fostered both a growing racial consciousness and a Christian worldview shared by sympathetic white believers.

Church narratives delineated another important feature of African-American religious life: intraracial disagreements. Substantive doctrinal, ec-

clesiastical, and social differences divided black church communities beginning in the earliest years of denominational formation. Disagreements
between Episcopalians and Methodists divided members of the African
Church of Philadelphia as they sought organizational independence in the
1790s. Richard Allen, in his autobiography, related that the congregation
held an election to determine which denomination to join; he recalled that
the "large majority" favored the Church of England, and only he and one
other preacher, the Reverend Absalom Jones, desired a Methodist affiliation.
When the African Church later requested his offices as minister, he explained his institutional commitments: "I told them I could not accept their
offer, as I was a Methodist. . . . I informed them that I could not be anything
else but a Methodist, as I was born and awakened under them, and I could
go no further with them, for I was a Methodist."[24] Political and social differences also divided black churches during the antebellum period, becoming, in effect, doctrinal issues. Arguments over the appropriate response of
African-American Christians to slavery led to schisms in African Baptist
churches in Boston in the 1820s and 1830s, with congregants disagreeing
over new abolitionist currents of thought. In that same decade, class differences led to rancor in Mother Bethel in Philadelphia over the "highhanded-
ness" of Allen and other church leaders; in protest, a disaffected group broke
away in 1820 and formed "Wesley Church" just ninety feet down the block.[25]

Christopher Rush's history of the AMEZ Church demonstrates the tenacity of some of these religious disputes among black congregations: for Rush,
conflicts among African Methodists posed an even greater obstacle to Christian community than ecclesiastical separation from whites. By 1813, two
groups had already broken away from the Zion Church in New York and divided the congregation. Even more trouble erupted with the arrival of the
"Allenites" (AME leaders) in the city; according to Rush, they held "secret
meetings" with selected church members in an attempt to form a united association. AMEZ preachers felt that Allen "had acted very unkind towards
the church," and according to Rush "the old man" refused to help with the
establishment of their organization unless they agreed to join the AME denomination. These early disagreements, which continued throughout the
century despite occasional gestures toward reconciliation, divided African
Methodists along denominational lines. Through Rush's history that division, framed as a dissatisfaction with the "general manner of proceedings" of

the Allenites, became part of the founding lore of the AMEZ denomination.[26] Ecclesiastical divisions among African Americans played a major
role in the formation of separate churches. For Rush and his fellow AMEZ
members, the "Allenites" were the foremost suppressors of their religious
freedom.

These contentions reveal African Americans' profound attachments to denominational identity, allegiances that existed alongside racial and cultural
ties. Rush's and Allen's histories provide glimpses of this effort to distinguish
among newly independent churches. In the years following the Civil War,
as black denominations competed for members among the free black populations of the Southern states, these disputes simmered among African-
American Protestants. Articulated most vividly in their denominational self-
descriptions, intraracial contests emerged as another decisive feature of
black religious life.

Despite early efforts to justify and memorialize their foundational moment
of religious autonomy, the writing of formal denominational histories began to flourish only after the Civil War, as freed Southern blacks swelled
the ranks of black churches. As members of the founding generation died,
church leaders looked to historical interpretation as a means to instill faith
in younger believers. But aside from this inevitable generational desire for a
sustained historical memory, black Protestants assessed the organizational
needs of the mission to the ex-slaves in the South, a campaign that required
clear statements of church history and purpose. Potential members had to
understand the differences among their many new religious options, and
church leaders used narratives as a tool of evangelism. What kind of Christian do you want to be? Joining the African Methodists or the African Baptists in the years following the Civil War, therefore, required not only testify-
ing to one's faith in Jesus but also entering into the life of a community over
time, joining a sacred history already in progress. Benjamin Tucker Tanner
voiced a common sensibility when he noted that AME history is

> such as our Church needs, and has needed for years. It is such as the
> Church has *demanded*. . . . The Church, by an intuition born from
> above, knows she has a history. From the high standing ground of to-

day she looks back and around, and lo! Israel is seen to be abiding in
his tents according to his tribes. . . . And with this vision of the Almighty upon her, with her eyes open, she has demanded of the men
who led her—men like unto Moses and Aaron—that they teach these
things diligently unto the children, and that they write them upon the
posts of the house and upon the gates.[27]

Through denominational texts, church periodicals, and Sunday school
primers, the growing legions of Southern black Protestants learned who
they were and from whence they had come.

The postwar geographical spread of black Southern churches was somewhat haphazard, and depended in large measure on where the most char-
ismatic and energetic ministers established an early base of operations. By
1906, four black denominations boasted the vast majority of African-
American Protestant members, according to the *Census of Religious Bodies*
published that year. The AME Church, by far the largest black Methodist
group, grew from approximately 20,000 members on the eve of the war to
495,000, and was particularly strong in South Carolina, Georgia, and Alabama. The much smaller AMEZ attracted its largest numbers of congregants
in North Carolina but had only 185,000 members by 1906. The Colored
Methodist Episcopal (CME) denomination, founded in 1870 as the first
black Methodist denomination of Southern origin, spread most effectively
in Tennessee and claimed 173,000 communicants. Altogether, those three
black Methodist groups accounted for just under one-quarter of churchgoing African Americans at the beginning of the twentieth century.[28]

Black Baptist churches spread even more quickly among freed men and
women, although the superior organization of the Methodist groups, especially their publishing houses, magnified the public voices of black Methodist leaders relative to their size for most of the nineteenth century. Baptists
traditionally were protective of congregational independence and therefore
came late to the pooling of resources and authority necessary to claim
denominational status. While there were plenty of powerful black Baptist
preachers, influential churches, and missionary enterprises before the 1890s,
it was not until 1895 that the first black Baptist denomination, the National
Baptist Convention (NBC), was formally constituted. This was quickly followed by the founding of a publishing house. Led by dynamic and savvy

men such as Richard C. Boyd, the nascent National Baptist Publishing Board shortly thereafter began to produce periodicals, Sunday school literature, and pamphlets that could spread the NBC message more broadly. By 1906, 61 percent of black churchgoers were NBC members, a strength of approximately 2.2 million people, most of whom lived in the Southern states.[29]

It would be difficult to overestimate the level of competition for members among these groups, especially in the first few decades after the war. Driven by Northern black and white missionaries and local leaders, all of whom were determined to rescue the ex-slaves using their own understandings of true religion, the Reconstruction South became a battleground for the souls of the race. Of course, competition necessitated advertising. Church histories reflected an important element of this marketing strategy. Pamphlets, books, and even catechisms contained considerable amounts of historical material as a way of grounding new members in the life of the community. If the driving question of these narratives before the war had been explaining racial separation from white churches, the compelling question in the postbellum era focused on understanding the increasing religious divisions among African Americans.

No one took up the mantle of church history more energetically than did the AME Church. With its publishing concern and nascent educational programs, the denomination was well positioned to proclaim—as it did into the first decades of the twentieth century—that it spoke as the "voice of the race." Between the AME Book Concern (est. 1817), the AME *Christian Recorder* (est. 1852), and the *AME Church Review* (est. 1884), few voices could effectively contradict its claims. AME leaders tried to secure their monopoly by pointedly emphasizing the moral distinction between written history— which they produced in abundance—and oral communication. As editor and AME bishop Benjamin F. Lee explained, every association must be able to answer questions about its origin, tenets, and goals. Replies had to be *written,* he stressed, "not dependent on *oral* tradition, for it is *written history* alone that unifies and conserves the true characteristics of associations, races and nations."[30] By this definition, AME modes of religious narration, many more of which appeared in textual form, were self-evidently superior to other black denominational productions—as well as to the vernacular (and frequently spoken) histories of the ex-slaves—by sheer dint of their form and volume.

The development of AME Church history affords a window into the creation of a historical consciousness among African-American Christians and the elaboration of a black sacred canon. Between 1866 and 1916 AME authors penned at least a dozen works that outlined the history of the denomination. Those texts were then sold by the AME Book Concern, advertised in the AME *Christian Recorder*, used in the growing number of AME Sunday schools, and even marketed from the pulpits of local churches. Three canonical themes that linked a new generation to the "AME story" emerged in these accounts: the gallery incident as a trope of exodus from white Christianity, the singular heroism of Richard Allen as a model of Christian manhood, and the "natural" appeal of Methodism to African Americans.

Ironically, the gallery incident, which had been given scant attention in antebellum histories, received its greatest boost from a dramatic and lengthy depiction of the event in an 1862 history penned by William Douglass, the rector of St. Thomas's Episcopal Church in Philadelphia. Within AME circles, the significance of Richard Allen and the exodus from the Philadelphia gallery grew dramatically in subsequent narrations. Benjamin Tucker Tanner set an entirely new tone in 1867 when he wrote that "Richard Allen, Daniel Coker and others, unable to endure the mad prejudices of their white brethren, which pulled them off their knees, drove them from the body of the church, thrust them into galleries, resolved to leave them in peace, and worship under such circumstances as would be to edification, and not condemnation—as would dignify and not debase." Postbellum writers also extended the exodus trope to the founding stories of scores of AME churches. In 1874 Benjamin Arnett, reporting on the origins of the AME Church in Cincinnati, recounted its establishment as an exodus from a Methodist Episcopal camp meeting in the 1820s. According to an early member of the church, two local black preachers attended the service and were forced to leave the communion table; thereafter they established a branch of the AME Church. At the three-week general conference of the AME denomination in 1916 that commemorated its one-hundredth anniversary, attention was repeatedly focused on Allen and the gallery exodus, which was characterized as an example followed by other blacks in New York, New Jersey, Delaware, and Maryland.[31]

The gallery incident was increasingly rendered as a vivid symbol of the white expulsion of African Americans from their churches. The event resonated deeply with the biblical story of Moses and the promise of liberation that figured prominently in Southern religious life during enslavement, and surely AME Church leaders recognized the power of its appeal to potential members. It also accorded neatly with the desires of independent African church leaders for freed blacks after 1865 to march out of the interracial Southern churches and form separate black bodies, just as the early leaders of these churches had done. As time passed, and ex-slaves themselves became church leaders, the narrative of the gallery incident was increasingly fixed as a potent and sanctified symbol of black agency in the face of white oppression. At the same time, the lead "Moses" figure shifted from Absalom Jones to Richard Allen, thus securing the AME Church a primary place in the story of black collective assertion.

As Allen and the Philadelphia gallery moved to the epicenter of the AME quake, Allen's leadership within the denomination grew in significance. Church historians compared him to Toussaint L'Ouverture, Moses, Jesus, Paul the Apostle, Martin Luther, John Wesley, and the Pilgrim Fathers. In the 1890s the denominational writer Frances Ellen Watkins Harper celebrated Allen in poetry. The AME minister Alfred Lee Ridgel visited Mother Bethel in 1892 before leaving on his mission to Africa, and he was overcome with emotion by the memory of the founder: "As I sat on that historic spot, made sacred by the tears, prayers, and labors of Richard Allen and his coadjutors, my soul became so full of the Holy Spirit that I could not restrain my tears."[32] Ridgel's comments underscore the sheer emotional power of historical association and its ability to create sacred space.

The commemoration of Richard Allen's birth or "Allen's Day" had become an important public occasion for the denomination by the 1870s, as church leaders amplified their narrative histories with public rituals and other nontextual approaches to appeal to Southern blacks newly emerging from the slave system. By the early twentieth century, AME members regularly memorialized this early history through public ceremonies and pageants. In 1901, three of Allen's great-grandchildren attended Mother Bethel as a one thousand–voice choir entertained the overflow crowds; the pulpit and chair used by Allen replaced the everyday furniture, and his own clock timed the speakers as they lauded their founder. That same year marked the completion and dedication of Allen's newly refurbished vault and sarcophagous.[33]

The valorization of Richard Allen served the important purpose of encouraging black youths to remain on a religious path and to emulate their forefathers. Josephine Heard, the wife of an AME minister who had been born in North Carolina just after the outbreak of the Civil War, composed a lengthy ode to the memory of Richard Allen, one of a series of poems produced by "a heart that desires to encourage and inspire the youth of the Race to pure and noble motives." In it she likened Allen, the freed slave, to the suffering Christ, and explicitly compared Emancipation, prefigured in Allen's liberation from bondage, to Christ's resurrection. Just as God lifted the bonds of enslavement from the patient and faithful Allen, he broke the chains of slavery from all blacks, whom she imagined carrying forth Allen's work to all lands over the intervening century:

As they march on you hear their steady tread,
With Allen's banner waving overhead;
The cause of Christ to distant islands borne—
O, flourish till the resurrection morn![34]

By placing Allen at the center of the story of salvation (both racial and universal), the AME Church occupied a crucial place in sacred history, ordained by God to fulfill his purposes.

As the United States reached a high tide of American imperialism and a racial nadir of Jim Crow at the turn of the twentieth century, church leaders also used Allen's legacy to link the AME connection to American patriotism. On the 145th anniversary of Allen's birth on February 14, 1905, church members executed the "first grand pilgrimage" to Allen's tomb and participated in a devotion and conference dedicated to his memory. While some speakers stressed his legacy among the "sons of Allen" in the church, the Reverend D. S. Bentley hailed him as a democratic hero, "one who stood for the cause of human rights and religious liberty for every soul on the face of the earth." He likened Mother Bethel to Plymouth Rock. Because of Allen's leadership, the orator concluded, the AME Church shares "the hopes and fears of all who believe in the principles of a Government, 'Of the people, by the people, and for the people.'"[35] Bentley thereby consecrated the AME

Church as the most American of institutions, and Allen as the forefather of that noble enterprise.

These stories divulge many of the crucial concerns of African-American intellectual life at the time. In the face of increased violence against blacks and the resurgence of Jim Crow, the AME Church offered a story of patriotic black male prowess. William Scarborough referred to Allen as "a man, every inch a man, a man of ideas, of principles, a man of convictions, and the courage of the same." As J. T. Jenifer enthused a decade later, "The Allen movement was not the impulse of an obstinate individuality; it was the promptings of pity, patriotism and piety, exerted through manly independence." African-American church leaders undoubtedly sought to counter the same concerns about the "feminization" of the church that were being expressed by white contemporaries. In response, male writers transformed church-building into a manly art fitted only for the most courageous souls.[36] For blacks in particular, turning Richard Allen into a masculine hero also reasserted black male agency in what was potentially a tale of demasculinization. By emphasizing Allen's actions in leaving the oppressive St. George's Methodist Church, authors highlighted the proactive role played by black church members in their own past. Rather than casting African Americans as the victims of white racism, these stories inscribed blacks as the creators—the pilgrims—of their own independence, and thereby linked them to the founding myths of America.

Narrators also linked the AME Church to the rising tide of American cultural expansion in the world, a development welcomed by both black and white Protestant church leaders. Christian civilization would spread throughout the world, aiding the "uplift" of benighted souls in other countries. The AME, proud of its missionary legacy, placed itself squarely within this Christian triumphalist tradition. Katherine Tillman's 1922 play "The Spirit of Allen" made explicit the geographical range of AME political and religious aspiration. The Illinois-born Tillman had attended Wilberforce (an AME school), married an AME minister, and written for AME publications throughout much of her life. Her pageant of the history of the church interspersed scenes in church history with the singing of negro spirituals. In a series of brief vignettes, Tillman outlined the confrontation between the "Spirit of King Cotton" and the "Spirit of Abolition," the selling of slave families on an auction block, and the career of Phillis Wheatley as preludes to the birth of African Methodism. The dramatic hinge of the performance brought the audience to the gallery of St. George's Church, where Richard Allen assumed the role traditionally ascribed to Absalom Jones. The second half of the drama then outlined denominational organization: Allen is consecrated as bishop, and soon the church missionaries are scattered throughout the world gathering followers. Among those indebted to the attentions of the AME are a "West African bush girl, Liberian, Haitian Girl, South African mother and babe, San Domingo, Jamaican, South American, Canadian, Bermudan." The final scenario celebrates American patriotism:

> And when we give honor
>   To whom honor is due
> We'll own that the Negro
>   Is American clear through.[37]

By linking the history of the church to broader themes of national expansion, denominational celebrations proved that AME members were true American patriots. Tillman's pageant, however, presents a pan-African twist on that imperial dream: she envisions AME leaders as the spokespersons for African diasporic peoples around the world.

African-American Protestants felt compelled to bring their religious beliefs to other diasporic Africans as well as to Africans themselves. Their Protestantism provided a language by which to understand and articulate shared identities; in turn, those shared identities prompted them to evangelize others of African descent. But as Tillman's pageant and other early twentieth-century histories suggest, American nationalism and notions of black masculinity figured prominently in denominational accounts. Nationalism, in particular, provided a model of democratic expansion that worked alongside the Christian "civilizing mission" to redeem Africans around the world. That grand vision of pan-African unity was underwritten by narratives of Protestant unity and American imperial progress.

While AME Church leaders persistently directed their narratives at broader communities (at other Christians, African Americans, and the United States as a political and even imperial ideal), they also sought to distinguish themselves from other denominational competitors and offshoots. The extensive historical work of two of the most ardent denominational partisans of the postbellum era highlights the complexities within AME identity, and the intellectual stakes of the battles.

Daniel Alexander Payne was the preeminent historian of the AME Church in the nineteenth century. Born in 1811 in Charleston, South Carolina, to free black parents, Payne was also the first AME bishop to receive formal theological training (at Gettysburg Seminary in Pennsylvania). Throughout his long career as a church pastor, founding president of Wilberforce (1856–1869), official historian of the AME Church (1848), and finally bishop (1852), Payne stressed the importance of educational training for the ministry, church organization, and "respectability" as a hallmark of African Methodist worship and comportment. He had first been ordained an elder in the Lutheran Church in 1837, but Payne defected to the AME Church in 1842. Thereafter he distinguished himself as the most fervent of denominational supporters, and he put his educational training and organizational loyalty to work in the extensive chronicling of the first seventy-five years of the AME Church.

Payne situated the virtues of the Allenites within the wider context of the Protestant spectrum. Rather than arguing for the distinctiveness of the AME as the only true church, he viewed his denomination as one among many, all of which were working toward the same end: "The different denominations may be compared to so many regiments in the 'Grand Army,'" Payne claimed, and "the African Methodist Episcopal Church is one of the regiments of the grand division of the 'Grand Army.'"[38]

Although the AME Church did not fight the Christian battle alone, it could claim a privileged status as the true heir of Wesleyan spirituality. Payne portrayed the AME Church as the direct spiritual descendant of British Methodism, the "saving remnant" that carried Methodism through a time of division and tribulation. The formation of the AME Church also paralleled that of the Wesleyan organization. Payne hailed the Wesleys as apostles who courageously battled the evils of the oppressive and corrupt church establishment, eventually separating to form a faithful and morally elevated religious body. Similarly, when American Methodism veered off course, falling away from its scriptural mission to "love thy neighbor as thyself," the persecuted but spiritually pure African Americans fled to preserve true religion in the AME Church.[39]

Payne thus relied on distinctly American and Protestant precedents for his justification of ecclesiastical separation. Religious liberty, for Payne, meant not simply the ability to establish a racially defined church but also the opportunity to extend and express the fundamental biblical principle of spiritual equality before God. In his brief description of the founding of Bethel Church in Philadelphia, Payne vaguely mentioned the "unkind treatment" afforded blacks by their white brethren, but he focused more extensively on the legal and ecclesiastical battles that led up to the organizational separation of the Allenites—battles that had counterparts in many Euro-Protestant churches.[40]

Yet the church spokesman did not ignore the question of race. He deemed Richard Allen a racial as well as a religious leader, "chief of the noble band of heroes. . . . a lover of liberty, civil and religious—he . . . felt himself highly honored and sincerely happy in doing and suffering to secure the blessings of ecclesiastical liberty for his despised and insulted race." Payne emphasized how beneficial the AME Church had been to the race as a whole, inasmuch as it had forced blacks to utilize their own resources, giving each one "an independence of character which he could neither hope for nor attain unto, if he had remained as the ecclesiastical vassal of his white brethren." But salvation was not, ultimately, a matter of color or culture, and the future of Christianity did not rest in the separation of the races: *"The Eternal sets little value upon races, but much upon humanity. . . . Races perish. Humanity lives on forever."*[41] For Payne, the question of race was only one part of a larger issue of Christian life and leadership.

Bishop Benjamin Tucker Tanner, editor of the denominational *Christian Recorder,* founder of the *AME Church Review,* and the author of scores of historical works, also ruminated extensively on the importance of denominational identity. Like Payne, Tanner objected vigorously to the racist "crime" of white Methodists, who had "locked, bolted, and barred" the doors of schools and conferences to the church's African-American members. But he, too, located the AME Church within a spiritually pure religious line from the Mayflower migrants to Roger Williams that superseded racial constructs, a line squarely rooted in the American Protestant tradition of "justifiable" religious separatism. The primary aim of the AME Church, in Tanner's view, was "to help convert the world to Christ—the world, and not simply Africans, real or imagined." In this respect, he agreed with Payne that the denomination was only one among many engaged in a common enterprise, albeit the most "attractive," "interesting," and "worthy" of the Methodist alternatives. Despite the inclusion of "African" in the organization's name, Tanner insisted that the church was "simply a Methodist Episcopal Church, organized largely of 'Americans' by 'Africans' and for 'Africans.'" He declared that the AME Church was not a "race church" but rather a place where the "doctrine of the Negro's humanity" could be fully realized.[42]

For both Tanner and Payne, the idea of the AME Church as a unique vehicle for racial uplift existed in some tension with their denials of racial exclusivity. Both believed that religious humanism would ultimately prove of more lasting importance than the temporary claims of race, and both understood the AME Church to be serving the broader needs of humanity. Ironically, Tanner flatly denied that the AME was a "race church," whereas Payne contended that all American churches were "race churches."[43] Both claims tended toward the same idea that race was a contingent factor within a larger field of ecclesiastical and historical considerations. Both churchmen encountered opponents within their traditions, men such as Henry McNeal Turner, who criticized their assimilationist positions. But their defenses of the AME Church point out that denominationalism and its relationship to racial identity were contested issues among African Americans.

Moreover, as both Tanner and Payne intimated, African Americans who joined "black" churches found themselves worshipping in multiracial congregations, albeit settings with many more blacks than whites. "Already we have them from alabaster to ebony. . . . In no sense are we a race Church. . . . whose people in color of skin, general contour of face and texture of hair indicate oneness," asserted Tanner, estimating that one-half of 1 percent of the membership of the AME Church in 1891 was "of pure European extraction."[44] These denials of racial exclusivity, coming from two prominent denominational leaders, countered the assumption that churches with African-American majorities were necessarily "black churches." Racial affiliation was viewed as a means to a broader, universalizing end in which race itself would be irrelevant.

Despite the dominance of AME authors in the world of black Protestant narration, other denominations told their own stories. Like AME accounts, many incorporated the familiar themes of a canonized patriarchal leadership, the Reformation as a justification for denominational particularity, and the statistical profiling of church growth. But it is useful to contrast these to AME accounts briefly if only to cast the dominant tales into sharp relief, exposing the diverse choices made by African-American Protestant authors as they related their own origins and development.

The AMEZ Church, with its similar name and parallel historical development to the AME, bore the heaviest burden of comparison. Its historians made the most effort to distinguish their origins from those of the media-savvy "Allenites." Christopher Rush's 1843 account signaled an early self-consciousness about black Methodist competition when he defensively reminded readers that the church "did not spring up like mushrooms" but instead possessed its claims to be authentically Methodist through appropriate apostolic blessing. Postbellum AMEZ histories by Bishop John Jamison Moore, Bishop James Walker Hood, and Benjamin Franklin Wheeler all related historical accounts of the denomination that defended it from criticisms by white Methodists and by AME detractors.

Published in 1884, Moore's history closely followed the model Rush had established four decades earlier. He began with a spirited apology for his project. "We cannot maintain our true ecclesiastical standing without a reliable history of our church," he explained. "For the want of such a work we are frequently being misrepresented, in other church histories or religious encyclopedias, that get their account of our connection from unreliable sources." There is little doubt that Moore was referring to the massive publicity machine of the AME Church. In subsequent chapters he situated the AMEZ branch of Methodism in Reformation and Wesleyan history, separating it from the corruptions of other Christians as had Luther, Knox, and Wesley. Whereas AME members focused on the gallery incident as a founding moment of their church, Moore evoked memories of the pure and despised manger in Bethlehem recapitulated in the small collection of followers holding a modest worship service in the loft of a craftsman. Just as the first Methodists had met in a rigging loft, he mused, so the first members of Zion worshipped in the room of a cabinet-maker: "There are remarkable coincidences between the Mother Church and Zion Church in the beginning of their history."[45]

James Walker Hood, one of the first missionaries to Southern blacks and chief organizer of the AMEZ Church in North Carolina, was always its most prolific historian. He began his first retrospective with the invocation of that early Methodist image, the meeting in "a sail loft in 1765." The message Hood extracted from this moment of origin, though, dealt directly with race. Early Methodists, he determined, had no thought of race distinctions. Only later did "Negro haters" infiltrate the church and force black members to take matters into their own hands. Gradually, Hood related, groups of black believers formed their own independent churches. He emphasized this movement as a collective racial enterprise: "God moved at once upon the heart of the race. . . . this was not a Presbyterian or Baptist movement; it was not a Bethel . . . movement; but it was a grand united Negro movement." He noted that just as God used Egyptian oppression to move the Israelites into the wilderness so that they could form a cohesive and elect race, so he used white oppression, characterized as "blacker in wickedness and more terrible than the hosts of Pharaoh," to motivate blacks to form their own church organization—which he referred to in the singular as the "Negro Church." Hood outlined the unique capacities of the race, which included military prowess, skill in physics, and diplomatic talents; he emphasized that a primary purpose of the church was to develop those racial capacities.[46]

Hood, a passionate advocate, saw the AMEZ Church as superior, with first claims to being the founding black Methodist denomination. In his list of independent black congregations, he placed Mother Bethel (AME) last, claiming that it was established in 1809, more than a decade later than Allen's followers professed. He detailed the many rounds of negotiations with AME leaders over a potential merger, in which the fault always lay with the AME Church. Hood also compared the AME denomination unflatteringly to the Roman Catholics: "We believe there are other Churches which have the disposition to swallow every other Church in as large a degree as the Church of Rome," Hood observed. He painted Allen himself as a power-hungry, arrogant, and avaricious man who set his sights on the takeover of the lowly—but spiritually superior—Zion connection. "That Church has through all its history been making attacks upon us from one standpoint or another," Hood explained in his diatribe.[47]

Hood was deeply aware of the role that black churches—all of them—had played in sustaining the spirits and political aspirations of African Americans for decades before freedom. "No mortal can tell how much the Negro Church contributed to the emancipation of the slave," he noted in 1914.

Given the racial politics of the time, it is likely that he saw a direct correlation between Jim Crow North Carolina and slave times: black churches remained valuable sources of collective strength. His histories paid homage to that sense of unified purpose. At the same time, his abiding dislike for the AME Church, and its claims to chronological and spiritual priority among blacks, compelled him to reassert the superiority of his own denomination. In this regard, he and his colleagues steadfastly maintained that they were truer Methodists than were members of the AME because they had remained on good terms with white communicants.[48]

According to Hood, there were Christian and unchristian ways to separate from whites; most offensive were blacks who stayed within the predominantly white Southern Methodist Church, a group that Hood implied was perhaps not entirely black: "You can almost at a glance see the shadow of the white man resting upon them." But this harsh assessment of nonseparating blacks was not uniformly shared within the denomination. In fact, many others downplayed oppressive white influences. Benjamin Franklin Wheeler, a presiding elder originally from Charlotte, North Carolina, disputed Hood's criticism in his 1906 historical treatment of James Varick, church founder. Early church leaders, he insisted, even after being refused the right to preach by white authorities, and despite having to wait until whites were served before they could take communion, were not bitter. Indeed, they "loved them" because whites had led them to God. The Methodist Episcopal Church, Wheeler concluded, was merely a "victim of circumstances," swayed by the evils of slavery to implement a segregated church. Varick and his followers, Wheeler seemed to imply, stuck to their Christian principles of brotherhood and forgiveness even when whites did not. Still other writers insisted that even though the denomination was led by blacks, it was a Christian church that was linked to all other Christian organizations. C. R. Harris explained in his *Historical Catechism* of 1922 that the term "African" in the denomination's name indicated that it was "controlled by descendents of Africans, in the interest of humanity, regardless of race, color, sex or condition."[49]

The Colored Methodist Episcopal denomination (renamed the Christian Methodist Episcopal Church in 1956) was founded in the Southern states in 1870 as a white-authorized offshoot of the Methodist Episcopal Church,

South, the Southern Methodist branch that had separated from its Northern counterpart in 1844, amid the denominational schisms preceding the Civil War. The CME faced both the stigma of its continuing close associations with Southern white benefactors and a severe shortage of funds, since Northern missionary sponsors preferred to support the establishment of their own churches and schools rather than assist a denomination tainted by association with former Southern slave owners. In the late 1860s, free men and women in the South often felt overwhelmed by the deluge of Northern black Protestant missionaries from the independent black churches. Those newcomers vied for the religious allegiance of African Americans, and the vast majority of Southern blacks joined AME, AMEZ, and independent black Baptist churches. But a small group of Southern Methodists decided to form their own, homegrown denomination, one that retained a degree of affiliation with white Methodists. To many other African Americans, this new church, the CME, remained entirely too sheltered under the patronizing guardianship of Southern white sponsors; but for at least some black Methodists, the CME represented a church independent of an even more oppressive force: black Northern elites who were attempting to control their religious destinies and rob them of regional pride.

Like other branches of black Methodism, the CME established a publishing concern immediately after its founding. But unlike either the AME or the AMEZ enterprises, which had a generation of ministers trained in Northern states, the CMEs started from scratch: they had neither education nor funds to bind and print their own books. In 1887 Fayette Montgomery Hamilton, a church elder who served as editor of the denominational periodical the *Christian Index* as well as the church's book agent, published *A Plain Account of the Colored Methodist Episcopal Church in America*. Eleven years later, Bishop Charles Henry Phillips followed with *The History of the Colored Methodist Episcopal Church in America* (1898), the first comprehensive historical treatment of the church.

In contrast to AME and AMEZ authors, whose narratives explained separation from white Methodists by invoking their links to the longer span of Protestant and Methodist history, Hamilton and Phillips felt the need to justify their origins as a "slave church." "The man of African blood has written his name upon time's ample scroll, and has learned to tell with pen and ink the story of the cross and the historical facts of his day," wrote Bishop

Lucius Holsey in his introduction to Hamilton's volume. Holsey thereby highlighted the Christlike qualities of the freed slaves, who could perhaps better understand the lessons of Christian suffering than could other people. He also admitted that the community was quite young and would require further maturation: "It is true he is in a transition state—going 'out of Egypt' into the promised land—but he is nevertheless being developed in interest, moral suasion, and experience."[50]

Hamilton's narrative indicates that for some ex-slaves in this era of transition, Methodist, regional, and family ties came first. The CME is a legitimate Methodist body, he insisted, because "she descended from the very father of Methodism regularly down the line without one broken link, or turning this or that way on account of trouble." The "trouble" to which he referred most likely meant the kinds of disputes the AME and AMEZ churches faced over the ordination issue. Unlike those bodies, the CME prided itself on a history of close relations with Southern whites and a separation achieved with good will and divine sanction. The report of the Committee on Church Organization delivered at the first conference of the new denomination stated:

> While we thus claim for ourselves an antiquity running as far back as any branch of the Methodist family on this side of the Atlantic Ocean, and while we claim for ourselves all that we concede to others of ecclesiastical and civil rights, we shall ever hold in grateful remembrance what the Methodist Episcopal Church, South, has done for us; we shall ever cherish the kindliest feelings toward the bishops and General Conference for giving to us all that they enjoy of religious privileges, the ordination of our deacons and elders; and at this Conference our bishops will be ordained by them to the highest office known in our Church. No other church organization has thus been established in the land.[51]

Despite frequent articulations of affection between black and white Southern Methodists, evidence of division remained. Hamilton mentions in passing that both sides considered the split a "wise act" because it meant that "each party could have a better opportunity to labor with and for their people."[52]

But just who were "their people"? This question looms even larger in the face of evident hostility between Northern and Southern black Protestants.

Facing pressures from black competitors who argued that the CME Church required the moral guidance of trained, (mostly) Northern elites, CME histories situated the church in a lineage of persecution from outsiders. "Many of the ministers were ridiculed, reviled, and abandoned by many who at one time claimed to be their friends," wrote Hamilton. "The organization was looked upon with contempt, regarded as being low, insignificant, and dishonorable." Yet he saw a precedent for their situation that gave him great hope: "Our savior was born low. He was poor, despised; but 'he grew and waxed strong,' and finally overcame all his enemies." Hamilton depicted his community as filled with pious but poor souls committed to doing the work of the gospel, just as Jesus and his disciples had been.[53]

Phillips and other church leaders charted a history of persecution at the hands of AME and Zion ministers, folding New Testament history into their own denominational saga. R. T. White, a preacher from the Georgia Conference, extended the parallels between the life of Jesus and the life of the CME Church still further. In an address published in the *Christian Index* in 1895, he likened the post-Emancipation era of the nascent church to the newborn Jesus: "At the time of her eventful birth, many Herods of every cast and color stood in the way inquiring of the wise men concerning the time and place of this newborn Church. Herod and his household were not a little troubled. They started out with vile forces to hinder, by all possible criticism and misrepresentation, to destroy, the life of this newborn sister of the Methodist family." Fortunately, he related, those who knew the most about suffering themselves could also correctly predict the outcome of the story of the church: "Her enemies thought she was dead; but, like Christ, her Captain, it has been more than three days since she arose from the dead; and, behold, she is alive forever more, and has the keys to the mystery of the cross, as much so as any of her sisters." The CME Church, then, reflected the span of Christ's earthly life: the political chaos surrounding his birth became the saga of emancipation, and his persecution, death, and resurrection figured as the literal antecedents to the travails of the CME. Eventually, that first history taught, the church would also triumph over its tormenters.[54]

African-American Baptist histories differed greatly from the stories told by Methodists. As with the CME Church, the black Baptist legacy was homegrown in the South and was not tied historically to the Philadelphia gallery incident or to conflict with other black churches. Southern African Baptist congregations had existed since the mid-eighteenth century, predating by several decades the formal separation of Northern free blacks. As a result, Baptist stories of origin were shaded not with tales of the heroism of Northern free blacks but with vivid memories of the battle to sustain faith under the slave system.

In the late 1880s black Baptists threw themselves into the process of collection, commemoration, and narration with gusto. On June 6, 1888, the black Baptists of Georgia launched a centennial celebration of the founding of First African Baptist Church in Savannah. The proceedings opened "most solemnly" at 9:00 A.M., when members, led by the minister and officers of the congregation bearing the church banner, marched from the church to the Centennial Tabernacle. Observers noted that the processional stretched over a mile as the congregants poured into the tabernacle singing "All Hail the Power of Jesus' Name." After the celebration clerical leaders published a number of commemorative documents. In 1888 Emanuel King Love compiled a *History of the First African Baptist Church, From Its Organization, January 20th, 1788, to July 1st, 1888,* a volume containing, in addition to many addresses, no fewer than four articles detailing the history of black Baptists. The 1888 celebration paved the way for the even more focused denominational sensibility that emerged after the founding of the NBC in 1895. In writings by denominational leaders and local pastors alike, including Charles Octavius Boothe, E. C. Morris, and Eugene Carter, black Baptists differentiated themselves from other Christians through historical accounts.[55]

Narratives functioned in distinctive ways in the Baptist world. Authors frequently contrasted the poverty and illiteracy of the first generation of believers with the intelligence and material well being of the current generation, a comparison that, many members insisted, served as testimony to their abiding faith and God's favor. The achievement of gathering data itself was hailed as a signal accomplishment. As a result of antebellum laws forbidding the education of slaves and the fact that centralization of the tradition had not been considered a virtue, simple record collection proved a formidable task. Indeed, compiling history was tantamount to its creation, as the Reverend C. T. Walker, chairman of the Executive Board of the State

Baptist Sunday School Convention, explained in his preface to the commemorative volume: "The time has come when the negro must make his own history, shape his own destiny, solve his own problem, act well his part in church and state and occupy a prominent place on the stage of progress."[56]

The prevailing theme of the black Baptist collective story was bodily suffering. This is perhaps not surprising given the central role of enslavement in the living memory of church leaders, but the frequency and tactility of accounts are nonetheless striking. Emanuel Love traced independent church beginnings to Brampton's barn outside of Savannah in 1788, when a white minister, a black leader, and a group of slaves met clandestinely to worship. The church "has endured indescribable suffering and has been wonderfully blessed and preserved by a hand divine. The first pastor, Rev. Andrew Bryan, was whipped until his blood dripped freely upon the ground, for no other crime than that he preached Jesus and him crucified to the poor negroes," Love narrated.[57] Integrating the story of enslavement into the history of the church, James Simms's description was even more graphic:

> Frequent, then, became the whipping of individual members by the patrol on the plea of not having proper tickets-of-leave, which finally culminated in the arrest and punishment of a large part of the members, all of whom were severely whipped; but Rev. Andrew Bryan, their pastor, and his brother, Sampson Bryan, one of the first deacons, were inhumanly cut, and their backs were so lacerated that their blood ran down to the earth, as they, with uplifted hands, cried unto the Lord.[58]

Black Baptists drew on a long tradition of persecution narratives dating back to seventeenth-century attacks by Puritans on Baptist dissenters. Translated into a racial context, those stories presented a powerful religious challenge to white Christian oppressors. The emphasis on violent suffering evoked a very different flood of associations and images than did the gallery incident. Whereas black Methodists posited the church "exodus" as the reassertion of black masculine authority, Baptist narrators highlighted the sufferings of Jesus and the history of Christian martyrdom, likening early black Baptists—and the church as a whole—to other humble and oppressed figures who had endured persecution for the faith. Andrew Leile, the founding pastor of the Savannah African Baptist Church, became a willing victim of the slave patrols and the emulator of Jesus' passion, declaring to his persecutors, according to James Simms, "that he rejoiced not only to be whipped, but would freely suffer death for the cause of Jesus Christ." W. H. Tilman explicitly placed the black founders in a line of Christian martyrs, called by different names in different times, beginning with "heretics in the first two centuries. They mingled with the Messalians, Euchites, Montanists; in the third, fourth and fifth centuries with the Novatians, and Donatists; in the seventh with the Paulicians; in the tenth, the Paterines; in the eleventh century, the Waldenses, Albigensis, Henicians and Christians. They have ever been in principle and spirit really the same people."[59]

This collective accounting served a number of important social functions. Like all historical martyrologies, from Saint Bede to John Foxe, it rendered enslavement as well as current suffering meaningful by placing it in a broader context, furnishing it with a deeper "truth." It also sharply defined the Baptist community as survivors of undeserved persecution, all the stronger for their experiences. In Love's estimation, "the more this church was persecuted the more she grew and thrived." Most important, the narrative of martyrdom inverted racial hierarchies by valorizing torture as a triumph not only of Christian community but also of blacks over the Southern power that enslaved them. The ritual of voluntary submission to whipping or even death is treated in these accounts as a heroic victory, subverting traditional views of authority and masculine power.[60] The Reverend E. C. Morris made this linkage of gender, power, and religion explicit in a 1901 sermon in which he contrasted great men "of the world" to the men of God:

> The world without Christ cannot see any greater men than those who have led great armies and sat as rulers of great nations. It points with pride to such men as Napoleon, Cromwell, Hannibal, Washington and Grant; and the Christian cannot help admiring the courage, pluck and brilliancy of these great warriors and leaders. But these great men had great armies to follow them to encourage and cheer them as they went from conquest to victory. But when we come to a John, a Peter, a Paul, a Silas, who, ofttimes alone, sometimes with shackles on their limbs, with a cross before their eyes and a guillotine over the head, would profess willingness to die, if need be, for the cause of the Master; and, as we

look into the face of the trembling governor and hear the testimony of the trial-king, that he is almost persuaded to be a Christian by the irresistible argument of a Christian in chains, we conclude that no just comparison can be made between these great characters as the former were great with men; the latter, great with God and man.[61]

Morris effectively countered claims that the "Christian in chains" was a lesser man than those who had captured him by lifting up a different model of masculine endurance—the lonely sufferer who gladly dies for a noble cause.

The narratives of black Baptists, like those of the African Methodists, posed their community as intrinsically American. Authors claimed recent Baptist figures and events, enfolding them in a militarized march of Christian soldiers for freedom. Their patriotic claims echoed those made by white Baptists—that liberty of conscience and separation of church and state, foundational national principles, had been most thoroughly and purely embodied in their church tradition. Blacks took this one step further, pointing out that white Baptists had not lived up to their own ideals, either, when they persecuted slaves for worshipping freely. Thus black Baptists saw themselves as the most consistent soldiers in the Lord's Army, following in the line of Roger Williams as well as the patriots of the American Revolution. They, after all, had continued to fight for freedom long after the last shots against Britain had been fired. Black Baptists repeatedly paralleled the multiple battles that they had waged: against slavery, against colonial oppression, and against other attempts to curtail the independent workings of the spirit. All these layers of meaning, their stories suggest, were folded into their self-understanding as Baptists.

For many Baptist leaders, history was more than a recounting of suffering and persecution; it was also a tale of the onward march of God's army through the ages, led by Christ the liberator. C. T. Walker declared, "Our captain is now riding on his white horse giving orders to the armies to move forward." On the one hand, military images represented a classic and aggressive evangelistic tool, invoking Christians to spread the gospel to all lands— a cause that black Baptists certainly took up. On the other hand, in the late nineteenth century, military calls to arms also roused a community to stand up for itself, to have courage amid rising lynchings and Jim Crow laws.

Flanked by the traditions of Christian martyrs and American patriots, black Baptists were enjoined in these accounts to continue spiritually, physically, and mentally. Walker continued:

> So let the gospel star-spangled banner rise. Let it rise. Let it rise until its magnetic influence shall draw all men to Christ. Let it soar till the attention of the African shall be called from his devil-bush, the Arab from his tent and the Jew from his wandering. Let it rise until the shouts of our triumphs be borne aloft to the ear of the redeemed as they shout from their high citadel of triumph. We want angelic messengers who come as the representatives of heaven to this centennial celebration to report to the heavenly hosts we are moving forward.[62]

Suffering and sacrifice, according to Walker, would ultimately be answered with reunion and celebration under the "gospel star-spangled banner."

African-American denominational historians created expansive visions of Christian fellowship, linking members to an international community across time and space. Through the use of scriptural analogy, Reformation history, and Christian tropes of martyrdom, African Americans created race-based communities that simultaneously denied the eternal significance of race and decried segregationist policies, but also valorized certain features of black leadership and promoted the diffusion of Christian values within the African diaspora. Some groups, most vocally the AME Church, made claims to speak for "the race" despite the evident and longstanding animosities among leaders of various African-American denominations.

It was not an accident of history that the term "Negro Church," displaced a generation later by the phrase "Black Church," came into common parlance in the twentieth century as a shorthand means of describing mainline black Protestant denominations. Indeed, this phrase is so widely used now that we hardly stop to think about the intellectual and cultural assumptions that its use connotes—or the differences and variations that it simultaneously obscures.[63] Its use by Euro-Americans has often indicated a failure to see beyond racial difference to the complexity and religious variation within African-American communities. By contrast, from the perspective of

African Americans the term "Black Church" often has more intentionally denoted racial, cultural, and religious unity, often in ways that obscure denominational boundaries.

Although the idea of a "racial church" appeared sporadically in nineteenth-century accounts of black Protestantism, secular historians, not denominational advocates, were principally responsible for bringing to life the concept of a "Black Church." W. E. B. Du Bois first popularized the plight of a race living behind the "Veil of Color" in his classic work *The Souls of Black Folk* (1903). In that study, the "Negro church" emerged as a social and cultural meeting point that allowed for profound expressions of hope, sorrow, despair, and joy. Despite the many differences Du Bois noted between Southern black folk religion and its Northern, more "civilized," counterpart, the commonalities of the "more important inner ethical life" of blacks largely eclipsed distinctions based on region, doctrine, or confession. "The churches are differentiating," he acknowledged at the conclusion of his chapter on religion, "but back of this still broods silently the deep religious feeling of the real Negro heart, the stirring, unguided might of powerful human souls who have lost the guiding star of the past and seek in the great night a new religious ideal." Du Bois had little use for denominational identity as such, but he realized the power that religious life exercised among African Americans, particularly in the rural South.[64] He characterized "Negro religion" as a continuous and organic development, beginning in "pagan" Africa and culminating in the rational and orderly worship patterns of Northern black churches.

Widely recognized as one of the most eloquent statements of African-American spiritual striving, Du Bois's depiction of a unified entity called the "Negro church" caught on quickly. His most famous intellectual opponent, Booker T. Washington, also adopted this terminology (and capitalized the "C" in "Church") six years later when he agreed that "the Negro Church represents the masses of the Negro people. It was the first institution to develop out of the life of the Negro masses and it still retains the strongest hold upon them."[65] In contrast to Du Bois, Washington placed more emphasis on the populist nature of Southern black religion and on the significance of the Negro Church as an organization controlled exclusively by blacks. But he, too, underscored the essential unity of the race by downplaying confessional or doctrinal differences. In Washington's conception, the "Negro Church" was historically significant because it articulated a vision of cultural cohesion and independence.

If the era of Du Bois and Washington gave birth to the notion of a unified organism called the Negro church, it was Carter G. Woodson's monumental *History of the Negro Church* (1921) that marked its coming of age as a scholarly paradigm. Ironically, Woodson's sprawling narrative of African-American religious history devoted the largest share of space to a decidedly traditional discussion of the specifics of denominational life in the nineteenth century: the account moves quickly from early efforts to evangelize the slaves to a study of the rise of independent African Baptist and Methodist churches, schisms within religious organizations, prominent preachers, the growth of religious education, and the relationship of politics to church life. Yet in the final fifty pages, as the story drew nearer to the present day, Woodson's language shifted into a broader discussion of the "Negro church." Here his personal passion was most apparent as he outlined tensions between progressives and conservatives, the impulse for urban reform of the Social Gospel movement, and contemporary challenges facing the church. Despite nearly two centuries of institutional separation and differentiation, the concluding chapters depict a Negro church fundamentally united in its common theological and racial struggle to carry the true banner of Christianity through an oppressive historical situation. Racial and spiritual destiny had become intertwined and were mutually reinforcing elements of African-American culture. "The Negro Church," wrote Woodson elsewhere, "whether rural or urban, is the only institution which the race controls. The whites being Occidental in contradistinction to the Negroes who are Oriental, do not understand this Oriental faith called Christianity and consequently fail to appreciate the Negroes' conception of it."[66]

For Woodson as for Du Bois and Washington, therefore, the concept of the "Negro church" functioned as much more than a sociological shorthand for a collection of independent religious organizations. In different ways, the notion of a single church reflected their assumptions about—and aspirations for—the cultural and racial unity of a people. Although the works of Du Bois and Woodson, in particular, were well grounded in nineteenth-century documentary sources and demonstrated a remarkable degree of historical specificity about the formation of black churches, they also promulgated normative assumptions about the organic and monolithic nature of the African-American religious community. For Du Bois, the "Negro church" was one step toward a morally enlightened, educated African-American community, an entity born in the polygamous clan life of Africa and gradually raised through evangelical frenzy to a "civilized" form in the African Methodist churches of the Northern states.[67] Washington extolled the virtues of an organization that sprang from the initiative of the black masses and symbolized their ability to function as an independent cultural force. Woodson's "Negro church" reflected his theological commitment to African-American Christianity as the "saving remnant" in an otherwise racist and unjust society. Ironically, Du Bois, Washington, and Woodson carried on the same cultural work of creating community as had denominational historians—but the former had changed the social unit and terms of discussion.

Despite divergent racial aspirations, development of the notion of the "Negro Church" in the first decades of the twentieth century set the terms for subsequent discussions of African-American Protestantism and greatly influenced the types of questions that later generations would ask about black churches. A book by Benjamin E. Mays and Joseph W. Nicholson in the 1930s and another by St. Clair Drake and Horace R. Cayton in the 1950s extended some of the metaphors of Du Bois's sociological work by searching for the "soul" or "genius" of the Negro church; they did so by emphasizing its role as a means of racial advancement, and by elaborating on the importance of the church as one of the few social and cultural institutions controlled and owned by blacks. Neither work ignored denominational distinctions; on the contrary, they provide some of the most valuable statistical information that we possess about individual black churches in the interwar period. But their ultimate concern, betrayed most evidently by their choice of terminology, was to paint a portrait of overarching race-based commonality. Indeed, Mays and Nicholson's conclusions came close to the theological formulations of Woodson a decade earlier: "This fellowship and freedom inherent in the Negro church should be conducive to spiritual growth of a unique kind. . . . The Negro church has the potentialities to become possibly the greatest spiritual force in the United States."[68]

Before the 1960s, then, discussion about African-American religion turned away from discussion of denominational distinctions within African-American Protestantism to a form of consensus history, best symbolized by the increasingly common use of the concept of the "Negro church" as a reflection of the desire for racial unity. Institutional divisions among black Protestants were not ignored, but the concept of a racial church shaped the types of questions scholars posed about their source materials. Even those who most adamantly asserted that Protestantism had been a source of oppression for African Americans, such as E. Franklin Frazier, also employed the notion of the black church as an organic entity with inherent qualities that separated it from other religious forms. In *The Negro Church in America* (1964), an extended overview of the history of African-American Christianity, Frazier conceded that the Negro Church historically provided racial asylum, facilitated a "structured social life" in which blacks were able to articulate deeply held feelings, and served as a "refuge in a hostile white world." But it did so at a tremendous cultural cost, because its otherworldly outlook prevented blacks from confronting white oppression directly and aided in black accommodation to an inferior social status. Frazier characterized the rise of independent African churches as the institutional manifestations of black exclusion from participation in white denominations.[69]

Frazier's analysis, in conjunction with the larger debate about "Africanisms" of which it was a part, shifted the dialogue but did not alter its fundamental premises. The overriding concern, for Frazier, was whether the Negro church, a "nation within a nation," had ultimately detrimental or beneficial effects for American blacks, and whether any African characteristics survived within it. As important as these questions were, they moved discussion still further away from the issue of whether the black church as an entity even existed, and whether one could reasonably generalize about it. Conferring upon it sovereign status as a "nation," one could hardly question the loyalties of the individual states of which it was composed.

Du Bois, Washington, and other African-American intellectuals, moving well outside denominational circles, saw different stakes in the battle to frame church history. Black churches, especially when united as a symbol of persistence and virtue in the face of white supremacy, furnished an inspiring and distinctive political model. Their power lay in their "authenticity" as an expression of African-derived traits, not in their attempts to negate racial difference or to harness themselves to Christian narratives of suffering, redemption, or persecution. Indeed, many of those Christian traits were

deeply troubling indicators of racial disunity, and thus their histories needed
to be subsumed in triumphant narratives of material and political progress
rather than stories of spiritual salvation.

In retrospect, however, we see that Woodson and Du Bois also flattened
the cultural work of a century of historical "gatherers," those nineteenth-
century black church leaders who limned the differences among confessions,
creeds, and polities, and who fought ferociously for the right to create their
own collective accounts that were not singularly wedded to racial identity.
By the dawn of the twentieth century, black Baptists and Methodists had
constituted narratives that contained numerous points of connection to a
variety of communities, past, present, and future. It was as if the new generation of professional scholars, driven by an ever-hardening sense of the
pervasiveness of race-thinking and the transformative promises of bureau-
cracy, reshaped webs of meaning into straight, taut lines, severing the many
intricate and flexible strands that give cultures their pliancy and resilience.
Looking back from the vantage point of another century, those webs encode
meanings that are now barely decipherable. Instead of resilience we see thin
threads of stories, untethered from a solid mooring.

3

The Serpentine Trail

Here in this black nationality of the New World, erected under such glorious auspices, is the stand point that must be occupied, and the lever that must be exerted, to regenerate and disenthrall the oppression and ignorance of the race, throughout the world. . . . Civilization and Christianity is passing from the East to the West; and its pristine splendor will only be rekindled in the ancient nations of the Old World, after it has belted the globe in its westward course, and revisited the Orient again. The Serpentine trail of civilization and Christianity, like the ancient philosophic symbol of eternity, must coil backward to its fountain head.

JAMES THEODORE HOLLY, *A Vindication of the Capacity of the Negro Race* (1857)

Blood flowed through the streets. The young woman, writing to her horrified friends back in the United States, described the actions of negroes during the final days of the Haitian Revolution. She did not spare any gruesome details of the actions of self-emancipated slaves, "rendered furious by a desire of vengeance," who set fire to towns, tore young children from the arms of their parents, and slaughtered women with bayonets. "Every one trembles for his own safety, and silent horror reigns throughout the place," wrote the author. Her vivid exposé of negro atrocities, published in 1808 as *Secret History, or, The Horrors of St. Domingo*, struck at the heart of white American fears about the possibility of black revolution.[1]

It mattered little that this epistolary account was fictional. The slave revolt that began on the Caribbean island of St. Domingue in 1791 and culminated in the creation of an independent black nation in 1804, filtered through such sensationalized fears and anxieties, transformed the imaginative worlds of blacks and whites in the United States. The prospect of "copycat" rebellions at home terrified slaveholders, who increasingly tightened strictures on slave movement and assembly. Whites in both the Northern and the Southern states harbored fears of widespread black insurrection and retribution.

As the first European colony to be overthrown by formerly enslaved peoples, the new republic of Haiti set a menacing precedent.[2]

For African Americans, the insurrection proved even more significant as an emblem of the potential for political and moral triumph.[3] More than a symbol, the Haitian Revolution became a new point of reference for many blacks, allowing them to understand themselves as a people united to other communities of African descent. Over the seven decades that followed Haitian liberation, black interest in Haiti—and public discourse about its religious and racial significance—continued unabated among a similarly broad cross-section of people, including ministers in Northern free black communities, newly freed slaves on plantations in Southern states, and white abolitionists. Haiti's proximity also made the thought of migration a real possibility. Over the nineteenth century, more African Americans resettled in Haiti than in Africa. Although most migrants were from the North, a significant number of freed slaves, many helped by manumission societies or sympathetic whites, also made the trip.

Haiti demonstrated the potential for African-descended peoples, and specifically those moving out of enslavement, to rebuild their lives and govern themselves capably. But it also provoked a complex and even troubling set of problems. Haiti was a real place, a land with political inclinations and a religious legacy quite distinct from the evangelical Protestantism of growing numbers of blacks in the United States. And it resembled less a republic of yeomen farmers than a highly stratified community of poverty-stricken workers ruled by a small group of elites. Rhetorically, Haiti stood for the magnificence of African self-determination and liberation; on closer inspection, its lessons proved more elusive.

After 1820, thousands of black Americans, disillusioned by the prospects of equality in the United States, contemplated removal to the fledgling republic. But this migration raised profound questions: what, exactly, was Haiti to American blacks? And who were the Haitian people? Marked by a succession of monarchs, presidents, and emperors, Haiti's political leadership did not conform to U.S. democratic ideals. Its religious milieu, shaped by French Catholic values and indigenous creolized forms of religious practice, was foreign, at best, and frightening, at worst, for the Protestants who championed migration. Black writers, taking their cues from scriptural paradigms, sought rhetorical models. Was Haiti a haven for blacks? A refuge? A new start? The Exodus story, a tale that resonated with so much of the African-American experience, suggested that Haiti could be viewed as a promised land and as a place of welcome. But other compelling images derived from the New World experience also emerged: was Haiti, instead, a (potential) Eden to be remolded, reshaped, and transformed? Some observers, influenced by American nationalist ideals and Protestant narratives of chosenness and sacred destiny, saw Haiti as both Eden and Exodus: a haven in need of transformation and moral enlightenment. All African-American writers believed that narrating the story of Haiti reflected directly on their own collective identity. In talking about Haiti they were talking about themselves.

Some of the most celebrated black writers of the antebellum period tried to answer these questions. David Walker's *Appeal* (1829) provides a riveting example of the way Haiti represented, simultaneously, both promise and predicament for black leaders. Perhaps no African American in the 1820s was more historically self-conscious than David Walker. A free black born in North Carolina in the 1780s, Walker eventually settled in Boston in 1825, set up a clothing business, and became an active participant in black intellectual life in the city. A writer, speaker, and agent for the first black newspaper, *Freedom's Journal* (1827–1828), Walker advocated African-American unity and militancy in the face of the slave system. In *David Walker's Appeal, In Four Articles: Together With A Preamble To The Coloured Citizens Of The World, But In Particular, And Very Expressly, To Those Of The United States Of America* (1829), his best-known work, the antislavery advocate fiercely condemned slaveholders and presaged a bloody uprising on U.S. soil. He repeatedly couched his words in a historical framework, comparing the United States to Egypt, Gaul, New Spain, and the British Caribbean, in order to prove that the contemporary American system of enslavement was the most brutal ever created.[4]

After many pages of history, he turned to the present. "What need have I to refer to antiquity," he ventured, "when Hayti, the glory of the blacks and terror of the tyrants, is enough to convince the most avaricious and stupid of wretches. . . . [Haitians] are men who would be cut off to a man, before they would yield to the combined forces of the whole world." The Haitian Revolution of 1791–1804 represented, for Walker, the pinnacle of African achievement, the culminating, victorious moment in a history of oppression. Like many other black writers, Walker linked the ideals of African-American masculinity to the rebellion of Haitian slaves, noting that the ability to rebel against white oppressors displayed the natural assertiveness and character of black *men*. Walker's rhetoric grew more subdued when he noted that Haiti "is at this time, and I am sorry to say it, plagued with that scourge of nations, the Catholic religion; but I hope and pray God that she may yet rid herself of it, and adopt in its stead the Protestant faith; also, I hope that she may keep peace within her borders and be united, keeping a strict look out for tyrants, for if they get the least chance to injure her, they will avail themselves of it, as true as the Lord lives in heaven."[5]

In addition to religious liberation, the *Appeal* strongly suggests that true "civility" and improvement also required Protestantization. For Walker, Protestant religion, and particularly African Methodism, represented the pinnacle of civilized, democratic life. All other religions fell short. He criticized Europeans for centuries of departure from the true faith, and castigated the Spanish Catholic missionary Bartolomé de las Casas as "a notoriously avaricious Catholic priest or preacher." By way of contrast, he extolled Richard Allen, the first bishop of the African Methodist Episcopal Church, as one of the greatest religious leaders since the apostolic age: "I do hereby openly affirm it to the world, that he [Allen] has done more in a spiritual sense for his ignorant and wretched brethren than any other man of colour has, since the world began." Ending on a worshipful note, Walker concluded his *Appeal* with excerpts from the Book of Common Prayer and several Wesleyan hymns.[6]

The irreducibly religious dimension to Walker's work concerning Haiti—his understanding of morality, race, and political necessity—was shaped by his Methodism. In much the same way that his literary exaltation of Haitian glory was encapsulated in a Methodist liturgy, so too was his commitment to a diasporic African community framed by Protestant notions of what constituted true culture and appropriate conduct. African Methodist piety (including its civil commitments to American democratic values) furnished the categories through which Walker interpreted race.

Walker's ambivalence—Haiti was glorious but lamentably Catholic and therefore uncivilized—suggests that despite their initial exuberance, African Americans could not rely upon Haiti as an unambiguous symbol of black glory. More was involved than racial affiliation. Black Protestants, those most committed to the promise of Haitian emigration, articulated conflicting and overlapping allegiances to multiple communities: to a nascent conception of a diasporic African race, to Protestant denominations, to the international "progress" of Christian piety, and to the unrealized democratic ideals of the United States. Like Walker's *Appeal,* other African-American discussions brought to light the deep-seated interplay among national, religious, and racial identities, and laid bare the interstices between the promises of African descent and cherished assumptions about democracy and evangelical morality. Black narratives of Haiti exposed myriad worries about French Catholicism, monarchical despotism, political tyranny, and, perhaps most unspeakably, vodou, the serpent lurking at the heart of Haiti's ancient past.

As entangled as Haiti's fate was with the slave question in the United States, it should come as no surprise that diametrically opposed opinions emerged among Europeans and Euro-Americans about the "lessons" of Haiti.[7] From the 1790s, unsympathetic observers gauged the republic's religious difficulties and publicized its shortcomings to an international audience. On all sides, discussion centered less on the political expediency or practicality of the establishment of an independent nation than on the inherent capabilities of African peoples: could they govern themselves? Would they usher their new society into the youthful fraternity of "civilized" nation-states? For Americans in particular, arguments for revolution rested squarely on a nation's virtuous citizens. As eager to justify their own nascent political projects as to evaluate the future of the Haitians, observers in the United States and Europe weighed the moral capabilities of black Haitians and the cultural prospects of Haitian society.

The most sensational accounts, such as the "secret horrors" of Mary Hassal, painted Haiti as a site of repeated violence and massacre, in which negro control necessarily resulted in political instability and despicable behavior. Reinforcing the opinions of slave owners in the United States, Hassal's narrative asserted that African peoples were little better than animals, incapable of self-rule. Other commentators focused specifically on religion as an emblem of Haitian (and, by extension, African) inadequacy. James Franklin, a British merchant in the 1820s eager to defend slavery in the British Caribbean, contended that Haitians simply had no religious feelings whatsoever, and that they would have been better off remaining enslaved. Others exoticized indigenous African practices, such as vodou. The French lawyer Médéric-Louis-Élie Moreau de Saint-Méry, outlining the final days of white colonial rule in Haiti, could scarcely find the appropriate terms to describe the mix of "superstition and some bizarre practices" he witnessed. His description detailed the "dark cabal," the "school where those easily influenced give themselves up to a domination which a thousand circumstances can render tragic."[8] Saint-Méry's ominous description was reiterated in essays and lectures throughout the antebellum period.

Some whites disagreed with these images of African peoples as inherently brutish and inferior. A vocal minority of antislavery activists portrayed Haiti in more positive terms, acknowledging its problems yet highlighting its progress toward civility. But even in their defense of the Haitians they ceded ground to their opponents by focusing on the inherent moral worth of the Haitian people, a rhetorical act that required comparative assessment. A writer in the liberal *North American Review* in 1821 commended the "invincible love of freedom" that had "instantly transformed [Haitians] into men." Any current unrest in the country, he insisted, resulted from French plots to overthrow the black government. Even the idea of a black monarchy, clearly a subject of general scorn among whites, was defensible in Haiti's current state of progress; the author insisted that the late king Henri Christophe (d. 1820) bore a strong physical resemblance to King George III. Religiously, Haiti was also improving: Catholicism was not deeply ingrained in the general population, and Protestants increasingly were tolerated if not welcomed. Altogether, this observer spied "tokens of approaching civilization" that demonstrated innate African potential for equality with whites.[9]

Other white sympathizers diagnosed the current debased moral state of the nation as the result of an imposed French Catholicism, which was slowly giving way to the intrinsic simplicity of the African people. Stephen Grellet, a white Quaker missionary who visited the southern republic in 1816 on an evangelistic tour, was shocked by the state of the culture. He found "books of the most demoralizing, vicious and obscene kind; as well as many deistical works of the French philosophers." Placing the blame squarely at the foot of vestigial Catholicism, Grellet also commented on the "general demoralization" of the priests, who seemed indifferent to spiritual concerns.

Nonetheless, he preached to large and apparently enthusiastic audiences, including a military regiment that he estimated at six thousand in front of the presidential palace of the mulatto ruler Alexandre Pétion. Grellet concluded that he preferred to preach to those Africans untouched by the European influence he observed in Pétion and the priests: "I frequently marvel in beholding how among these descendents of Africa, who have had so few advantages compared to many of the Europeans, the Gospel stream *does flow;* and the word preached appears to have an entrance; they receive it in the simplicity of their hearts, and in the love of it."[10]

Most white observers agreed that Haitians needed the right kinds of influence. For some British and Euro-American observers, this entailed permanent enslavement. But from the standpoint of more liberal writers, the Haitian people needed education and "proper morality" to raise their country to the level of other nations. At present, Haiti remained perched between the extremes of African heathenism and priest-ridden French culture. In significant respects white observers, most of whom were Protestants, viewed French Catholic society as civilization run amok, culture taken to its most ceremonial (and thus artificial) extreme. Steering Haiti between the Scylla of barbarism and the Charybdis of Gallicism would require the introduction of Protestant values and virtues.

In the decades after the Haitian Revolution, free blacks, primarily literate Northern male leaders, many of them clergy, articulated their own views of the island's significance. They approached Haiti with a variety of personal and communal concerns, not the least of which was the extent to which blacks in the United States could vocally support a slave uprising anywhere. Well aware of the range and volatility of white opinion, and cognizant of their dependence on liberal white supporters, blacks could hardly speak "freely" in the strictest sense.

African-American narratives of Haiti's revolution reflected a range of desires and conflicting loyalties. Like their white abolitionist counterparts, black writers felt compelled to counter negative impressions of African potential. But they also needed Haiti as a model for contemporary African diasporic community, an alternative social space apart from the increasingly racist society in the United States. From the early nineteenth century until at least the 1890s, Haiti was a crucial site for black explorations of collective enterprise and achievement. In these mental mappings, Haiti was a bridge that could link their yearnings to ancient history, African glory, and future salvation, themes already articulated in sermons and discourses since the 1780s. They understood Haiti as one aspect of a broader and more encompassing communal story. Like whites, African Americans were selective: they chose particular aspects of Haitian culture and society to valorize and highlight.

Prince Saunders (1775?–1839), born in Lebanon, Connecticut, was the first African American to compile an extended narrative of Haiti. With the support of white benefactors such as John Wheelock of Dartmouth College and the Unitarian minister William Ellery Channing, Saunders had become a prominent educational leader in Boston by 1810. An accomplished speaker and writer, he served as the secretary of the African Masonic (Prince Hall) Lodge, and as an administrator and organizer of the Belles Lettres Society, a literary gathering of white men. In Boston he met Thomas Paul, founder of the first independent black Baptist church in the city. Paul encouraged Saunders's growing interest in Haiti and the country's potential as a site for African resettlement. By 1816, at the behest of British abolitionists Thomas Clarkson and William Wilberforce, Saunders had traveled to Haiti, where he became the official courier for King Henri Christophe, ruler of the northern part of the island.[11] In that capacity, and even after Christophe's death in 1820, Saunders published and lectured widely on Haiti on both sides of the Atlantic, promoting it as a natural haven for African Americans. During his travels he was sponsored by a network of free blacks, including Paul, James Forten, and Richard Allen, to publicize the cause of emigration.

In his *Haytian Papers*, the American edition of which appeared in 1818, Saunders included the first English translation of the *Code Henri*, a set of laws established by the monarch Henri Christophe. The compilation of documents celebrates and elaborates on the heroic exploits of the king and the pomp and ceremony of his accession to the throne, including a royal parade "to the sound of drums and music" and a Catholic mass. Saunders ruminated on the historic significance of Haiti, relating it to ancient social traditions. The concluding text of the *Papers* argued that the "light of knowledge" had always traveled around the globe, enduring periods of instability and attenuation. Yet the ultimate wisdom and worth of African peoples had never diminished, although Europeans had attempted to convince the world that "Greece, Germany, and Gaul" were the original seats of learning:

> Our traducers pretend to have forgotten what the Egyptians and Ethio-pians, our ancestors, were: the Tharaca of Scripture, that mighty mon-arch who was the dread of the Assyrians, came from the interior of Af-rica, as far as the columns of Hercules, the records that attest their works, still remain: the testimony of Herodotus, of Strabo, and of other historians of antiquity, confirm these facts. More recent proofs bear ev-idence in our favour, and yet our enemies, with signal incredulity, feign to doubt all this, in order to preserve to themselves the odious privilege of torturing, and persecuting, according to their own will, one portion of the human race.

Linking the status of Haiti to the collective destiny of African peoples, Saunders traced the nation to its origins in ancient Ethiopia and Egypt.[12]

Unlike David Walker, Saunders did not express sorrow about the injection of Catholic ritual into Christophe's accession. On the contrary, the ritual so-lemnity of the occasion, accentuated by the Catholic liturgy, only reinforced the link between Haitian (and African) monarchy and an ancient, sacred past. Saunders's history was at once intensely Gallic and shorn of any rela-tion to popular religious life. Like the *Code Henri* itself, the account valo-rized the monarchy as a sacred office, one that elevated Haiti *above* the stan-dard set by another nascent New World nation, the United States. Taking the example of European nations, Saunders noted that the establishment of a monarchy paradoxically signaled the European cultural aspirations of the new Haiti: "The establishment of the throne . . . has, therefore, appeared to us necessary, as a sacred and imperious duty, as well as a signal mark of the national gratitude."[13]

Saunders introduced Haiti as a sacred model of independent black politi-cal destiny with ties to the most ancient of traditions. With a deft touch he narrated the ceremonial elements of Haitian governmental authority for an African-American public, and in this sense, the pageantry of Catholicism lent an air of spiritual gravity to his tale. His choices, on the face of it, seem odd: Saunders wrote in a period when the lines between Roman Catholics and Protestants, and between monarchists and republicans, were fiercely drawn in the United States. Yet he combined his admiration for Christophe's kingship with a decidedly Protestant approach to social and moral reform. Shortly after the appearance of the British edition of *Haytian Papers* in 1816, Saunders set about helping Haiti "raise" its educational and religious standards. He proselytized for the Anglican Church, promoted school reform on the English Lancastrian model, and enjoined Christophe to invite educated American settlers to migrate to Haiti. In 1817, Saunders enjoyed an extended stay in Philadelphia, where he served as a lay reader at the church founded by Absalom Jones, St. Thomas Episcopal Church, and visited local Protestant preachers. Soon considered one of the foremost proponents of black colonization, Saunders urged audiences in the Northeastern states to help save "the paradise of the New World" through settlement and moral uplift.[14]

A place of sacred and ancient import, a New World paradise, a society in need of civilizing and educating—these potentially contradictory images of Haiti worked well on the lecture circuit, where Saunders's eloquent rhetoric and elegant presence swayed some of the most wary listeners. African Americans could embrace the symbols that resonated with their own experiences and desires, imagining either a literal place of escape from the United States or a symbolic triumph for black peoples on the Caribbean island.

By the 1810s Haitian historians and politicians, stung by the refusal of the United States and other nations to recognize the island's independence, were eager to spread word of the country's rise to civility and its rightful place in international politics. Doing so, however, meant appealing to Europe and the United States on their own terms, and highlighting elements of the revolution and its aftermath that reflected classical notions of industry, valor, and Christian virtue. Saunders's work, then, legitimized Haiti by appealing to ancient authority and simultaneously stressed its present emergence as a civilized nation.

The creation of a nation, however, entailed conscious acts of omission: the legacy of the first Haitian leader, Jean-Jacques Dessalines, was particularly problematic. Dessalines, a black revolutionary hero, had taken out his wrath on thousands of French at the close of the revolution by calling upon black Haitians to slaughter them en masse. Emulating the political strategies of his French mentors, Dessalines built up the army, instituted a system of forced agricultural labor, and declared himself emperor. He also disestablished the Catholic Church in the Constitution of 1805, allowing vodou, which had long served as a religious system parallel to Catholicism within the country, to thrive.[15] Eschewing this legacy, historians such as Saunders and Vastey stressed the connections between Haitian political authority and Christian (specifically, French) culture and ceremony and downplayed mention of the use of vodou. By the 1810s, renarrating Haiti meant appealing to foreign missionaries to encourage the inherent potential of the Haitian people by helping to stamp out popular religious practices, especially vodou, among the populace.[16]

Before 1820 Saunders was one of the few African Americans who could speak about Haiti from personal experience. As a result, he shaped domestic images of the island in the minds of black communities eager for arguments with which to counter white stereotypes of African barbarism and incivility. Although Saunders tried to engineer a large-scale emigration of U.S. blacks to Haiti in the late 1810s, political instability, including the suicide of King Christophe in October 1820, thwarted his efforts. Haiti remained a distant symbol, one in which the potential problems of barbarity, Catholicism, and monarchical control had few material consequences.

African-American images of Haiti changed dramatically in the 1820s as the racial and religious terrain of the United States shifted. Central to this transformation was the emergence of the colonization movement as a powerful voice in U.S. politics. For a vocal minority of supporters, Haiti seemed an ideal location for African-American migration. An answer to Saunders's dream, the reality of Haitian migration provoked closer scrutiny of the nation—less as a symbol of freedom this time than as a place and a people to be negotiated. As a result, accounts of Haiti briefly moved to the forefront for many African-American leaders and their white supporters.

Colonization was hardly a new notion. The idea of large-scale movements of African Americans to other parts of the world had long circulated among Northern free blacks. Searching for relief for themselves as well as for those still enslaved, free blacks in the Northern ports of Boston, Newport, and Providence promoted schemes for emigration as early as the 1780s. In doing so, they drew upon a two-pronged argument: first, that blacks would never achieve true equality in the United States; and second, that emigrants, in the

process of building a new society elsewhere, could in turn carry "civilization" and education to less advanced peoples in other parts of the world.[17]
Africa was the first and most frequently mentioned site of emigrationist interest. Over the course of the ensuing decades, however, advocates championed a variety of locales, including Mexico, South America, California, and
Canada. Emigration fervor reached several peaks of activity: in the 1820s
both Haiti and Africa generated intense interest; Haitian emigration re-
surged briefly in 1861–1862; and African emigration resumed with the demise of Reconstruction in the Southern states after 1877.

Religion played a central role in the rhetoric of colonization as well as in
institutional formation. Protestants black and white, assured of the superiority of Christian civilization, associated the notion of the permanent resettlement of blacks outside the United States with the spread of Christian
culture, education, and churches. Many of the most active emigrationists
were ministers—and most often Protestants. Bringing "civilization" in most
cases meant evangelical Protestantism (though occasionally it meant black
Episcopalianism, whose members wielded a distinctive sense of civility),
with its attendant understandings of piety, industry, and morality. Like their
white counterparts, black Protestants retained suspicion of the societal "extremes," as they saw them: either too little civilization, evidenced by the
"primitive" peoples of Africa, or the snobbery and artificiality of many
European Catholic nations. Yet black authors were also thoroughly committed to the inherent potential of Africans to rise to a higher kind of existence, given the proper training. That guidance could, in their thinking, be
provided by African-American migrants, who would serve as teachers and
Christian exemplars.

Support for migration and evangelization outside the United States before 1816 remained largely a hypothetical concern for free blacks, who simply did not have the financial resources to mount such an undertaking.
In that year, backing came from a troubling source: the newly established
American Colonization Society, a group consisting uneasily of both abolitionists (clergy and philanthropists) who sought to free slaves and return
them to Africa, and white slave owners, eager to rid the United States of politically and socially problematic free blacks. Receiving financial assistance
from private fundraising and the U.S. Congress, the ACS began to ship emigrants to Liberia in 1820. While some African Americans supported the

ACS, many free blacks reacted defensively to its efforts. In their eyes it bore the marks of a white Southern plot to deport all dark-skinned peoples involuntarily from the United States.

Discussions of Haitian emigration are best understood in the broader context of acrimonious and divisive debates during the 1820s over colonization and resettlement abroad. In contrast to African colonization, deemed by many a cowardly and devious way to de-Africanize the United States, advocates characterized the movement to Haiti as an autonomous, voluntary, and black-led effort. Many free blacks who were unwilling to entertain the advances of the ACS nonetheless championed movement to Haiti. Encouraged by the official endorsement of Haitian President Jean Pierre Boyer (1818–1843), who hoped to gain recognition for his government from the United States, and by the speeches of leaders like Prince Saunders, the emigration movement received the backing of prominent black church leaders in New York, Philadelphia, Boston, and other Eastern cities. Richard Allen of the AME Church and James Forten, an Episcopal layman, both of whom had recently decried the efforts of the ACS, hosted the visit of Prince Saunders to Philadelphia in 1817 and came out in full support of movement to Haiti.

Many black clergy served as leaders of the growing number of "Haytien Emigration Societies" established in urban areas. As early as 1821, a group of Maryland blacks formed an organization to agitate for Haitian emigration. By 1824, local auxiliaries reached as far west as Cincinnati. Richard Allen called a meeting in the summer of 1824 in Philadelphia, and immediately thereafter he formed a chapter which he then headed. The group sponsored talks and facilitated communication with migrants; Allen himself personally paid for the resettlement of at least fifty-eight African Americans.[18]

A significant number of African-American church leaders relocated to or visited Haiti themselves, and they touted evangelization as a prominent motivation for resettlement. Benjamin F. Hughes, pastor of Philadelphia's First African Presbyterian Church, migrated in 1824. In the mid-1820s the Reverends Peter Williams, a prominent black Episcopal priest in New York City, and Thomas Paul, the Baptist pastor from Boston who had befriended Prince Saunders, took extended tours of the island to survey its religious condition and prospects. The son of Richard Allen emigrated to Haiti and remained there for many years as a printer. He aided the Methodist cause in the new republic, writing to his father frequently about the state of religious life in his adopted country. Clergy brought with them other settlers, including large groups of slaves manumitted by owners once they promised to move to Haiti.[19]

With the migration of the 1820s, the "highs and lows" of Haiti's symbolic importance merged into a cacophony of stories invested with heightened consequence. The increase of antislavery promotion in the United States, the competing voices of the ACS calling for resettlement in Liberia, the reenergized promotion of immigration from Haiti's president, Boyer, and the human dedication of between six and eight thousand African Americans who willingly uprooted themselves to make the Caribbean republic their new home in the 1820s, all ensured that debates about Haiti's meaning for African Americans would increase dramatically as the decade progressed. Not surprisingly, discussions hinged on questions of religion, morality, and freedom.

American debates over colonization set the general foundations for the ideology of African-American geographic movement, but internal Haitian politics ultimately dictated its timing and tone. In 1823, after President Jean Pierre Boyer united the Spanish and French parts of Haiti, he embarked on a sustained campaign to invigorate a stalled economy, reestablish an agricultural base, and gain international recognition for the nation. The economic policies of his predecessors, in combination with deepening social fissures between the north and the south and blacks and mulattoes, had left the country in ruins. What Boyer needed, principally, were industrious farmers to increase national revenue.[20]

In early 1824, prompted by a letter from Loring Dewey, a white colonizationist who had grown disaffected by the proslavery members of the ACS, Boyer officially welcomed free black settlers to the island. That summer he sent his envoy, Jonathas Granville, on a speaking tour of the Northern states to publicize his plan. In visits to Boston, Philadelphia, and other urban areas, Granville continually stressed commonality in matters of religious persuasion, even as he attempted to assure blacks that their denominational affiliations would be respected and tolerated: "Your religious belief differs, in some points, from ours . . . but we all worship the same God," he noted.

Insisting that all African Americans, "being children of Africa, shall be Haytians as soon as they put their feet on the ground," Boyer also offered financial incentives to those willing to migrate and settle on the island. Granville, a former junior officer in Napoleon's army, poet, and elegant diplomat, was appalled by the treatment of free blacks in the United States and disdainful of the lower classes in particular—some of whom he referred to as a "class of lunatics." Their queries about the possibility of Protestant worship in Haiti annoyed him and seemed, to him, a small trifle in the face of their treatment by white Americans.[21]

But his invocations served their purpose in raising interest. Letters printed in newspapers from Baltimore to Boston in 1824–1825 carried reports about the Haitian invitation. Benjamin Inginac, then Boyer's secretary general and president of the Philanthropic Society of Haiti, wrote frequently to whites and blacks alike in the United States about the desire of Haiti to welcome its "brothers." He adopted the language of family, encouraging African Americans to return home: "Announce to them that in Hayti all are entitled to equal privileges and immunities. . . . Hayti will become to them a tender Mother." Early reports of emigrants being welcomed included a speech given by General Inginac "in very affectionate terms," in which he argued that the ties of kinship transcended any cultural differences: "if we differ in language, we were born with the same interests, because we are of the same blood. The blood of the *Great Africa*, which ought to render our union indissoluble, equally circulates in our veins." Urging migrants (and U.S. readers) to be proud of their ties to Africa, he reminded them: "Was not Africa the source of light and science, when Europe, at this day so vain, was still plunged in barbarism!"[22]

If Haitian promoters beckoned African Americans with familial metaphors and images of a welcoming mother, black ministers and white antislavery supporters in the United States narrated the relationship to Haiti in somewhat different—but equally positive—terms. Instead of cultural resemblance they stressed difference; in place of familial protection provided by Haitians, they stressed African-American moral superiority and organizational independence from the Catholic establishment.

These latter interests reflected the closely allied values of U.S. evangelical supporters. Although blacks and whites organized separately, founding both white "societies" and black "auxiliaries," they shared common religious and

political assumptions. White promoters wielded the power of the press, and
newspapers such as the *National Gazette* and the *United States Gazette* in
Philadelphia, and *The Genius of Universal Emancipation* in Baltimore, served
as crucial venues for the dissemination of images of Haiti throughout the
decade. Editors of these papers regularly published letters and articles by
Richard Allen, Thomas Paul, William Watkins, and other African-American
spokesmen, as well as official missives from Granville, Inginac, and President
Boyer himself. Especially energetic in championing migration to Haiti was
Benjamin Lundy, a white antislavery activist and editor of the Baltimore-
based *Genius of Universal Emancipation* in the mid-1820s. His paper served
as a rhetorical meeting point for Haitian leaders, advocates of migration,
and African-American settlers; its pages contained dozens of letters, editorials, texts of speeches, and announcements about movement to the island republic. Lacking their own race newspapers, black promoters of emigration
needed these public venues to spread the word about Haiti.

Moreover, black and white advocates generally shared the sentiment that,
even as Haiti could provide a place of refuge, migrants from the United
States could help the island republic by setting a moral and political example. Their own nation's social and religious systems, in other words, were superior in theory if not in practice; all they needed was a hospitable environment in which to nurture them. In March 1824, amid the lengthy long-
distance exploratory communications that preceded the migration, Loring
Dewey wrote to President Boyer to request information "on every point that
looks like affording benefit to my unhappy coloured countrymen." In addition to inquiring about financial support, toleration of religious differences,
and the Haitian educational system, Dewey pointedly wondered about the
feasibility of a separate political system for migrants:

> Would your government allow the Society to plant a colony in your Is-
> land, having its own laws, courts, and legislature, in *all* respects like one
> of the States of the United States, and *connected with* and *subject to* the
> government of Hayti, only as each state is with our general govern-
> ment; and would land be furnished for such a colony?

Dewey's query revealed his own assumptions about the moral and political
superiority of U.S. institutions, as well as his belief that emigrants would be

best served by use of Haitian lands without the attendant adoption of Haitian institutions such as a state church or an active militia. His proposal met sharp resistance from Boyer, who insisted that any migrants would be subject to the laws of the Haitian republic. "That cannot be," Boyer wrote in April 1824. "The laws of the Republic are general—and no particular laws can exist."[23]

For Prince Saunders, Haiti's importance resided in the character of its inhabitants and their links to ongoing Christian and African traditions rather than in its existence as a geographic entity. Haiti had served as an emblem of black initiative, liberation, and civilization. But the logic of migration in 1824 dictated another way of imagining Haiti: as a site for future refuge and redemption. In this conceptualization, the nation's meaning rested in its potential and in the promises it could offer to U.S. settlers, who were presumed to be superior morally and culturally to its current inhabitants. Haitian culture, so prized by Prince Saunders (and by Haitian leaders), became a potential obstacle to the furthering of those objectives. It also conflicted with the familial language preferred by President Boyer, unless one allowed that the adopted stepchildren would soon be taking over the family.

Much debate, then, revolved around the ability of migrants to adapt to the Haitian environment. A minority of U.S. observers worried that African Americans would not be able to assimilate and would be forced to adopt "foreign" (implicitly inferior) ways of life. The notion that Haitians and U.S. blacks were "of one blood" was by no means undisputed. "Our free people of colour are in constitution and habits essentially American," wrote an abolitionist "gentleman in Philadelphia" to his friend in New York. "It is nothing that their fathers and grandfathers were born in Africa." Fearing a difficult adaptation to the tropical climate and to new jobs, the adoption of a new language, and the threat of military conscription in a country that many perceived still to be in danger of imminent attack by France, the writer felt that African Americans were better off in the United States than on Haitian soil. Rather than returning to family, they would instead be placing themselves at the mercy of a foreign power.[24]

By far the most vociferous criticisms of Haiti came from members of the ACS who favored migration to Africa. Some of their concerns were directed at the situation of "unfortunate" Southern slaveholders whose proximity to ex-slaves in Haiti would constantly remind them of the potential for rebellion among their own slaves. But they also claimed a moral high ground, attacking the political and religious foundations of Haiti itself. The *National Intelligencer* of Washington, D.C., published one such assault, in which the editor contended that "there is not in the Christian world . . . a more despotic government than that of Hayti.—Political and Religious freedom exist there in name only . . . those free people of color . . . have suffered themselves to be seduced from a land of freedom, to place themselves under the sway of a political and religious tyranny, of which they had no conception, until the prison-bolts were drawn upon them." Another friend of colonization fretted publicly about the welfare of Haitian emigrants, stressing the differences between African "freedom" and Haitian "despotism": "Is not the impediment of a foreign language which the colonists must acquire before they can understand their new laws, of a religion to which they are strangers, of a government which savours at least of military despotism, sufficient to turn the scale in favour of Africa, to which the colonists would in time impart their own manners, religion, laws, and language?"[25]

Responding in part to this rhetoric, proponents of Haitian emigration countered with their own stories. Admittedly, they insisted, echoing U.S. biases about the superiority of their own republican system, Haiti was not yet a democracy, and to be sure, its French Catholic traditions were in need of reform. Yet therein lay the opportunity for symbiotic exchange. The majority of newspapers that circulated within Northern black communities in the 1820s stressed the fortuitous reciprocity of the emigration scheme: Haiti would help U.S. blacks, and African Americans in turn would bring the blessings of democracy and true Christianity (Protestantism) to the island republic. Just as Haiti could liberate the bodies of U.S. free blacks and slaves, so could emigrants liberate the hearts and minds of the Haitian people.

Typical of this 1820s understanding was the thinking of the black Baptist missionary Thomas Paul, who publicized Haiti as a land of religious potential. Paul (1773–1831), founder of the Abyssinian Baptist Church in New York City, had visited Haiti under the sponsorship of the Baptist Missionary Society of Massachusetts in 1823. His intentions for the trip were clear: he was to bring the blessings of Protestant Christianity to the island, and he was not to "interfere with the civil or political institutions of the country." Outfitted with one hundred Bibles in French and Spanish donated by the American Bible Society, Paul found the natives, as he later reported, "eager to receive Bibles" and enthusiastic about his preaching. It was especially gratifying to Paul (who spoke neither French nor creole) "to observe the eagerness with which the hearers listened, and the regret they manifested at not being able to understand the preacher." He recounted that he obtained an audience with President Boyer and bestowed on the leader "an elegant Bible." According to Paul, Boyer fully supported his wish to preach and expressed his hope that Haiti would soon resemble its northern neighbor. Cultural and moral influence, Paul's reminiscence strongly suggested, would move from the United States to Haiti, from the African-American migrants to the Haitian people.[26]

Although many African Americans accepted in theory the notion of Haiti as a site for migration, specific techniques were necessary to attract potential settlers. Promoters of Haiti in the mid-1820s painted portraits of the island republic for black Protestant readers. In newspaper articles, and later in letters to and from migrants, a more popular understanding of Haiti emerged. Writers drew images from a variety of U.S. revolutionary and biblical narratives to frame the public understanding of the island. Through the repetition of particular themes—exile, chosenness, destiny—writers encouraged African-American readers to see Haiti itself as intimately linked to their own future. Yet by invoking the image of Exodus, and migration to Haiti as an entry into Canaan, supporters subtly shifted the emphasis from Haiti as a pan-African *people* or Haiti as an *ideal of freedom,* to Haiti as a *site of future significance.* The story of the Exodus, after all, is not the story of the mixing of the Israelites and the Canaanites: it is the tale of a single community moving from one place to another, only incidentally encountering others along the way. By privileging this tale, African Americans obscured the importance of the Haitian people to the future of Haiti.

In most renditions, Haiti was unique and sacred—not simply a land to be cultivated and inhabited, but a spiritual destination, a hallowed ground. For some, the island became a new Eden or, in a phrase that numerous writers fondly repeated, the "paradise of the new world." For the majority, however, Haiti was Canaan, the promised land of deliverance from bondage. Writing in the *Boston Sentinel* in July 1824, Paul noted that Haiti "presents to the eye the most romantic and beautiful scenery, and while its verdant mountains recall to our minds what we have read of ancient Gilboa, Tabor, Lebanon, Carmel and Sion, its fertile valleys present us with the rich luxuriance of the valleys of the Israelitish Canaan."[27] Like Canaan, Haiti would provide refuge to the modern-day Israelites fleeing the Egypt of the United States.

The proclamations of Haitian leaders linking the birth of the nation to sacred mandate encouraged such sentiments. When President Boyer observed that the development of an independent black republic demonstrated that "divine justice has manifested its pleasure," he confirmed the notion of the revolution as a consecrated act. African Americans, in turn, saw the hand of God continuing to work through the migration of the new black Israelites as the "natural" inheritors of this land. John Kenrick, a lawyer from Brighton, Massachusetts, composed and published a poem dedicated to U.S. emigrants that extolled the island as a latter-day promised land. As with Israel, God had given ex-slaves this new republic to possess and occupy:

> REPUBLIC of *Hayti,* the Queen of the Isles,
> Tho' tyrants may frown, 'tis your Father who smiles;
> Your bonds he has broken, remember his hand
> Has rais'd you to glory, and given you the land.
> . . .
> Your beautiful Country, like Canaan of old,
> Abounds in productions and blessings untold.

Yet like the biblical account of the Exodus itself, Kenrick's reverie lacked any awareness that the land of Canaan was already occupied, or that migrants would be subject to a foreign power. The trope of Canaan did not admit the possibility of assimilation into a preexistent culture but instead heralded the birth of a newly created people: "Let American people of color awake,/For Providence calls them to go and partake."[28]

The observation that a New World Moses had enabled the entrance into Canaan further cemented the bonds between scriptural precedent and American fulfillment. Benjamin Lundy was particularly fond of the Mosaic image, using it, at various points, to refer to different actors in the drama. In early 1825, he hailed President Boyer as a "second Moses," leading the African Americans out of Egypt: "Well may they look to the enlightened Executive of that Government, as a second *Moses,* raised up by the Almighty, to lead them out of the state of degradation, into which they were sold (like Joseph was to the Egyptians) by their cruel and hard-hearted brethren." In an open call to U.S. citizens, Lundy announced that "the door is now wide open for our slave-holders to send their slaves out of bondage . . . I am prepared to take them off their hands, and demand of them, like Moses did of Pharoah, to—'LET THE PEOPLE GO.'"[29]

Repeated use of the Canaanite and Mosaic imagery and knowledge of its power by sympathetic whites suggest that by the 1820s its salience within African-American historical memory ran very deep.[30] Used in myriad ways, it evoked a string of associations among bondage, Exodus, strong political leadership, and future liberation. Its rich resonances could be molded to suit the particular context of the Haitian migration, thus uniting the United States and Haiti in a broader narrative of African memorialization and anticipation. In this setting, the narrative lent sacred authority to a political cause. As Kenrick's poem suggested, the biblical account provided an example of people who were not "godly" enough to accept the divine blessings they had been offered:

> Such gracious proposals how can they refuse.
> And merit the curse of the cowardly Jews;
> Who afraid to go over and Canaan possess,
> Were subjected to sorrows no tongue can express!

Conversely, Canaan imagery sanctified a particular reading of Haitian destiny—as a triumph of black Protestant morality: "Be honest, be punctual, industrious, and clever," Kenrick concluded, "if you wish to live happy, both now and forever."[31]

Use of rhetoric and imagery that evoked the American revolutionary struggle also placed Haiti in a recognizable and related story of providential destiny. But perhaps not surprisingly, given the fears of American whites about the potential contagion of revolutionary fervor from Haiti, promoters made little direct mention of the realities of martial conflict. Instead, select images, or narrative "shorthands," induced more elaborate—and useful—memories. The iconography of the "Liberty Tree," also employed as a symbol for the abolitionist cause, proved especially popular for Haitian publicists. In the pages of the *Genius of Universal Emancipation,* Lundy printed a poetic invocation:

> Americans, plead for the rights of mankind—
>   Of the bond-man, as well as the free:
> Unrivet the fetters of body and mind,
>   'Neath the shade of your "Liberty Tree."

The cause of the Liberty Tree, a crucial symbol of popular agency during the American Revolution, resonated in a variety of ways, connoting both a sacred place of refuge and an earthly ideal in need of protection.[32] In a celebratory speech about Haitian independence in 1825, H. A. Webb reminded listeners of the tree's sacred origins in the face of international condemnation: "Though surrounding nations look with scorn upon the Tree of Liberty, planted in our isle, yet Heaven protects it, and its branches are gloriously spreading, to overshadow the land." Just as important, however, Haiti was a place of asylum:

> A giant oak, she lifts her lofty form;
> Grows in the sun, and strengthens in the storm.
> Long in her shade may Afric's children roam,
> And welcome such poor wanderers to a home:
> Long may she live, and every blast defy,
> 'Till Time's last whirlwind sweeps the vaulted sky![33]

As with the multivalent use of Exodus and Canaan, the richness of the image of the Liberty Tree had distinct advantages for middle-class African Americans, who wanted to promote the idea of black independence but also needed to stay in the good graces of white promoters and patrons. They had no desire to stir up the disturbing memories of revolution articulated by Thomas Jefferson, who insisted that "the tree of liberty must be refreshed from time to time with the blood of patriots & tyrants. It is its natural manure." Accordingly, public commemoration of the struggle and of Haiti's independence was surprisingly muted in the United States—much less so than the joyous and ceremonial recognitions of the abolition of the slave trade common in Northern black communities by the 1820s.[34]

In keeping with the rhetoric of the Haitian government, promoters narrated a tale of welcoming home family. All African Americans, the published letters and editorials promised, would be treated like family members. But more frequently, U.S. advocates encouraged the impression that migrants would be more than kin; they might, indeed, be the favored sons and daughters. In this respect, writers appealed to the middle-class aspirations and patriotic sentiments of many African Americans. While class distinctions in Northern black communities of the day were somewhat fluid, there is overwhelming evidence to suggest that educated and prosperous African Americans sought various means to differentiate themselves from their less affluent neighbors. Although continually reassured by Haitian leaders that "in Hayti all are entitled to equal privileges and immunities," U.S. advocates encouraged them to expect even more. In narratives of Haiti, writers appealed to a particular sense of unacknowledged privilege: migrants, they suggested, would be treated with the deference that was their due—as enlightened Americans, as Protestants, and as educated people.[35]

The silences within the narratives are also significant. The most obvious omission, despite the considerable attention paid to questions of morality in the abstract, is discussion of religious practice or institutional life, and more specifically the religious elements that distinguished native Haitians from African Americans. In the push to encourage migrants, Haitian and American authors alike glossed over fundamental differences.

When Haitian leaders from Christophe to Boyer continually asserted that religious differences among African-American migrants would be tolerated and that the Haitian government allowed freedom of belief, they clearly had something quite specific in mind. What Haitian laws did *not* allow, by and large, was the freedom to worship publicly. Officials repeatedly warned visitors and settlers from the United States in the 1810s and 1820s that they could not erect separate houses of worship: they could meet in private homes, and Protestant ministers, such as Stephen Grellet, could, upon invitation, preach in the local Catholic church. As an 1826 observer writing in the *Genius of Universal Emancipation* noted, "Public places of worship are not very numerous here. The Roman Catholics have a large commodious house, built expressly for the purpose; the Methodists have two places of meeting; and the Baptists one. The three last mentioned are houses built for private use."[36] Discussions about "freedom of religion" between emigration-ists in the United States and Haiti therefore often missed the point: Haitians did not define such freedom in the "American" way, and African-American migrants had little chance to exert moral influence in a situation where their worship was legally circumscribed.

The distinction between religious belief and practice had its roots in an-other characteristic feature of Haitian religious life: since long before inde-pendence, Catholicism had shared cultural space uneasily with vodou. Taken from the Dahomean term *vodu* or *vodun*, meaning "deity" or "spirit," vodou comprised a set of practices that enslaved Africans from the Kongo, Daho-mey, and other parts of West Africa brought to Santo Domingo in the seven-teenth and eighteenth centuries. In Haiti, enslaved Africans fused those cus-toms with Roman Catholic practices. By the early nineteenth century, for the vast majority of Haitians, vodou and Catholicism were coexistent and not readily differentiated. It is no wonder, in this sense, that Saint-Méry in the 1790s spoke about vodou as a dance rather than as a religion, and that oth-ers hardly talked about it at all: lacking formal creeds and the trappings of institutionalization such as organizations or formal religious communities, vodou eluded Euro-American linguistic categories.[37]

Nonetheless, vodou played a vital role in Haitian life, evidenced most prominently and insistently by the effort of civilization-minded leaders and priests to suppress it. The original impetus for the slave revolt that set off the revolution in 1791 was alleged to be a negro named Boukman, a priest of vodou. Perhaps because of this association of vodou with revolution-ary tendencies, later rulers made every attempt to stamp it out and down-play its influences. From the establishment of the African-controlled gov-ernment, Haitian leaders believed that vodou incited sedition. In 1800 Toussaint L'Ouverture outlawed all dances and night meetings in an effort to curb dissent. Later, Dessalines and Christophe banned only the dancing of vodou, fearing that its powers would be used against them.[38] Subsequent state-legitimated narratives of the revolution emphasized L'Ouverture's deep Christian piety rather than Boukman's illicit practices.

Vodou was also dangerous because its pervasiveness created a moral cli-mate in some senses inimical to Catholic ethical teachings. In turn, this perceived immorality contributed to charges that Haiti could never become a civilized nation. The case of marriage is instructive. In the years after independence, the island was populated largely by newly freed slaves who had never been formally married, and who saw little use for a marriage ceremony. As priests fled the island and later were withheld by Rome, the incentive to undergo a formal marriage ritual decreased, since the few priests left in the region were said to charge exorbitant prices for their services. Formal marriage thereby became a luxury rather than a religious duty. Henri Christophe, alarmed by this trend and eager to demonstrate his nation's acceptance of Euro-American ethical norms, labored to remedy the situation: he changed the laws that had allowed illegitimate offspring to claim family inheritances, thus forcing those with sufficient means to legalize their living arrangements. This change meant little, of course, for the nine out of ten Haitians who had no family wealth, and so the situation steadily deteriorated thereafter. By the 1820s, visitors and settlers regularly noted that Haitians lived without benefit of marriage.[39]

The experiences of U.S. settlers in Haiti must also be viewed in the context of internal struggles to define and regulate appropriate religious behavior in the island republic. Just as African-American migrants, a mix of newly freed slaves and lower-class workers with higher aspirations, found in Haiti a caste-based society with scant room for a middle class, they also found a novel religious culture that defied expectations. Black Protestant ministers had bid them farewell, counseling them to "avoid ardent spirits and laziness" and to "keep the Sabbath," all good evangelical injunctions.[40] In their new home, migrants found little public reinforcement for those religious precepts.

Even more noteworthy is the extent to which settlers, a people shaped by biblical teachings and in search of Canaan, discovered in Haiti a religious culture they had learned to associate with religious enslavement. Both Catholicism and African "heathenism," in different ways, had long been portrayed by Protestant evangelicals as forms of spiritual servitude—one to an illegitimate earthly leader, the other to the whims of idols and human ignorance. In keeping with David Walker's comments, representations of Catholicism by other black Protestants closely resembled stock images borrowed from a long history of anti-Catholic rhetoric in Europe and the United States. In this view, Catholicism in Haiti was a sham or a "puppet of the state," a repressive system imposed for selfish reasons by the few and believed by none. Ordinary followers were thereby blameless victims, caught in the autocratic grip of power- and money-hungry priests and bishops. At the height of white Protestant America's own anti-Catholic fever in the 1830s, the editor of the New York–based *Colored American* voiced an observation passed along by the British and Foreign Bible Society, a Baptist organization. The Haitian people "learn nothing useful or valuable from the priests, who officiate among them," the missionary commented. "Mummery and external show being almost the exclusive character of their miscalled religion."[41]

Similarly, both black and white evangelical observers in the 1830s and 1840s represented vodou as the immoral worship of idols and a capitulation to the senses. The black Baptist William Munroe, stationed briefly in Port-au-Prince in the mid-1830s, reported back to his supervisor: "I preached the first Sabbath . . . within the sound of the Marshal Drum, and lectured at night within sound of the Congo dance: for the Sabbath is not regarded in this place, it being the Market-day and a day of Merchandise." He also commented on a general climate of immorality: "We have here a few professors but they have lived rather loose, and . . . another difficulty is they sell rum and drink it themselves." An Anglican missionary from Jamaica also remarked negatively on the differences between his own station and the religious condition of Haiti. Visiting the island in 1835, he noted the equally destructive consequences of Catholicism and vodou: "There is no light . . . there is no gospel . . . no Christianity there."[42] To black Protestants, the religious freedoms entailed by Catholic customs and vodou—to drink alcohol or work on Sundays, for example—connoted religious enslavement.

But too much was at stake—racially, religiously, and nationally—for supporters during the migration of the 1820s to level criticisms against Haitian culture. There were several key reasons for this silence. The ACS, for its part, argued against Haitian migration by playing on the unbridgeable cultural differences between African Americans and Haitians. As one ACS supporter put it, "the emigrant will find a new people, speaking a new language, with a Government . . . having an established State Religion, new to him in every aspect." Haitian supporters, in turn, felt the need to stress cultural commonality and downplay differences to make their case.[43] Equally significant was the idiom of emigration itself, which traded on Haiti as a sacred location, not on Haitian society as a communal ideal. Ironically, the biblical trope of exodus, encouraged by the logic of a growing sense of racial unity, masked profound religious disparities. Class and allegiance to the United States shaped the assumptions of black Protestant leaders about Haitian culture, provoking the determination that African Americans would bring their own moral and political influence to bear on the young republic. In underestimating the tenacity of Haitian culture, ironically, African Americans distanced themselves rhetorically from the very people they revered for revolutionary bravery.

Ordinary African Americans acted on these narratives of exodus and promise, privilege and recognition. Initially, migration was a hard sell. The fact that Jonathas Granville toured the United States for a full six months, from June to December 1824, suggests that considerable effort was necessary to convince people that Haiti was a desirable destination. Repeatedly, Granville answered the same questions—about religious toleration, about working conditions, and about freedom. "I have said, and I repeat," he wrote in September of that year, "that religious toleration is cherished among us. . . . All rays terminate in the center, yet they do not all issue from the same point of the circumference of the circle; but, if any religious sect should disturb public order, or social harmony, there is not the least doubt but its eccentricity would be suppressed."[44] Whether such a qualified answer quelled the fears of potential settlers is disputable, but the reiteration of the question itself indicated prevalent concerns. Granville and his sponsors labored continually to paint a portrait of Haiti that conformed to the desires of potential African-American migrants.

Settlers did come, at least for a brief time. Between 1824 and 1826, an estimated six to eight thousand African Americans left ports in the United States bound for Haiti. Most of them came from the Northeastern cities of Boston and New York and the mid-Atlantic port of Baltimore. But some traveled even farther: one young man reportedly walked all the way from Wayne County, Indiana, to Baltimore in late 1824 to board a ship headed for Haiti. Several white philanthropists underwrote the expenses of whole ships, making the exodus more affordable for many. With the cost of passage approximately fourteen dollars for an adult and half that for a child, the trip was far more manageable than travel to Africa or even the Western United States.[45]

Although whites in the Southern states suppressed press coverage of the migration, a surprising number of enslaved blacks in the upper South also reached the island, primarily via Baltimore. Some were freed by sympathetic owners—a fact that promoters were eager to publicize. A slave owner from Virginia, described only as a young Presbyterian who had recently come into possession of slaves through inheritance, freed eighty-eight African Americans: he bought them farming implements, clothing, provisions, and cooking utensils, and paid their passage to Haiti. David Patterson, a lawyer from Orange County, North Carolina, freed an entire family of eleven slaves, including an elderly woman, her six children, and four grandchildren, and secured their transport to the island. Benjamin Lundy, in subsequent editions of the *Genius,* reported on the progress of "Patterson's slaves," and printed letters from Margaret Patterson describing their good fortune: the family had settled on the plantation of President Boyer himself and was there accorded "special notice and protection." The North Carolina Society of Friends, which had become the nominal "owner" of approximately seven hundred slaves, also worked to secure their passage to the island.[46]

If promotion of Haiti piqued the interest of migrants enough to propel them to the republic, reports from settlers back to U.S. publicists, both positive and negative, confirm that migrants took with them the biblically infused notions of Haiti that writers had encouraged. Archibald Johnson, happy in his new home, wrote to a friend in Washington, D.C., in May 1826. He would never return, he stated emphatically. "I have adopted myself a Haytian; and I bid an eternal farewell to America." Evoking a vision of Israel in the promised land, enjoying the height of its political and spiritual satisfaction, he reported: "Here I repose under my vine and banana tree, contented with Hayti and all its errors. I feel determined to live and die under the safe-guard of her constitution, with the hope of aiding to open the door for the relief of my distressed brethren." As Johnson suggested, with all of "its errors," Haiti could still be fitted into a narrative of exodus and ultimate fulfillment. "While some have been dissatisfied and troublesome," reported settler John Cromwell to Richard Allen, "others have been supplied like the children of Israel." Charles W. Fisher, formerly of Baltimore, wrote to his father that the trip had been as fraught with expectation and disappointment as had been the Israelites' journey. But he had patience: "We have plenty of vegetable food, tho' meat is not procured in such abundance here as it is in America. Many of the emigrants are dissatisfied on that account.—They are impatient, and indulge in complaints, like the children of Israel, when in the wilderness, not knowing the good prospect that awaits them."[47]

Popular tales about migration that played on the Exodus theme circulated among Southern slaves. The Reverend Alexander Wayman, a bishop of the AME Church after the Civil War, recalled hearing stories and songs about those who had made the journey. In particular, he recounted one anecdote from the migration of 1824–1825. Moses, the slave of George Calahan, had run away to the North. Later, Calahan encountered an African-American woman newly returned from Philadelphia, who reported that a young boy by the name of Moses had just boarded a ship to Haiti. Wayman reminisced that "the colored people composed a song about that circumstance, and I have heard them sing it often":

Poor Moses, poor Moses,
Sailing on the ocean.
Bless the Lord,
I am on my way,
Farewell to Georgia.
Moses is gone to Hayti.[48]

But dark clouds loomed, brought on, in part, by such lofty hopes. Charles Fisher had commented that "many" of the emigrants had grown dissatisfied. Within months after the exodus began, negative reports filtered back to the United States about poor living conditions and general disappointment. Settlers had been expecting Canaan to provide an easier life and to be a place where they would no longer be considered inferior to others. As a result, disgruntled African Americans related stories of ill treatment, hard working conditions, and limitations on their freedom. They all pointed to the failure of Haiti to live up to its billing as a promised land. Not long after his return to the island, Jonathas Granville informed U.S. promoters that increasing numbers of emigrants were unhappy: "They are lazy," he insisted, "wishing to do that which they are not capable." He was especially scornful of "the high pretensions of some servants, who have not found here the remains of splendid tables, and who thought that with the old coats and boots of their masters, they would be here gentlemen and Lords, their disappointed vanity not being able to bend to a hoe or to an axe."[49]

Many such grievances illustrate the pervasiveness of the assumption that Haiti should have been the promised land awaiting the arrival of the chosen people—and the frustration and anger upon discovery that it was not. Predisposed to think that the Haitian government would treat them as dignitaries, migrants complained that they were not afforded due deference. One returnee reported in the *Boston Patriot* that General Inginac was very unsympathetic to the settlers and blocked direct access of African Americans to President Boyer; the immigrant, it seems, had "waited on the secretary as often as every other day, *by appointment,* to be presented to the President, yet he never was presented, although he bore the best letters of introduction to many respectable men in Hayti." Benjamin Lundy responded with incredulity that an ordinary settler would presume association with a government official, but he also made it apparent that such presumption was widespread: "It is true that so many hundred frivolous applications are continually made to the President of Hayti, it has become an intolerable burden to him."[50]

Haitian leaders, too, were appalled at the lack of gratitude evinced by many of the settlers. Their complaints, in large measure, led to Boyer's precipitous decision to discontinue the emigration program in April 1825. Moreover, despite the initial brass bands and military salutes, local populations, less swayed by the prestige of luring American settlers than was the Haitian government, did not greet African-American migrants as mentors or redeemers. Indeed, they more often responded with pity or suspicion, and depicted the migrants in subsequent decades as an ungrateful band of poverty-stricken refugees. "Nothing was sadder than to see their old chests, their old trunks, their woolen rags, necessary in the climate of their native land, but useless for Haiti's," reported Beaubrun Ardouin in 1860. "One can further imagine the impression produced on the spirit of these unfortunates, by the view of a new country so little resembling the one they had left, with a population whose language they did not understand, even though of the same color as they were, and on whose faces they perceived a mocking smile, produced by their sad baggage, in spite of all the good will that she had shown them!"[51]

Immigrants endured occasional persecution at the hands of indigenous populations. Several returnees, responding less to official government reports than to local conditions, reported that "anarchy and confusion prevail in every part of the island, and each moment may bring forth a massacre of all the mulattoes and whites upon the Island."[52] While promoters readily dismissed such tales of atrocity, the long history of class strain between dark-skinned blacks and mulattoes in the nation renders these reports quite plausible. Haiti in the 1820s enjoyed a relative degree of political stability, but civil wars raged in both the decade prior to Boyer's rule and again in the 1840s. Class-based tensions were never far from the surface, and although it is difficult to ascertain precisely the role that African Americans played in this larger civil drama, migrants surely had their enemies within the population. Moreover, because the avowed intention of the Boyer government was to raise "morality and decency" as part of Haiti's own narrative of national progress, and the arrival of black Americans was anticipated to play a critical role in this internal transformation, native detractors were likely stifled but not entirely silenced.

Moreover, rather than casting any local conflict as a rift between African Americans and native peoples, reporters probably saw fit to describe it in other terms. For example, in the early 1820s, when British Methodists began missionary outreach to Haiti (at the behest of Boyer), they were jailed and subject to persecution by both Catholic priests and local Haitians. Although Methodist missionary journals reported these incidents as religious persecution, they were just as likely based on skin color or proximity to European mores. "Protestant" or "Methodist," in other words, could also serve as a synonym for European, Euro-American, or even African American. By the time of the U.S. migration several years later, Methodist sources reported that Boyer "issued an equivocal proclamation against subjecting Protestants to stoning and other outrages," revealing that violence toward "Protestants" (be they native Haitians or African Americans) did occur.[53] Indigenous peoples, apparently, did not accept African Americans as the children of Israel.

In short, the migration, catalyzed in large measure by narratives of Haiti as a New World promised land, presented a recipe for disappointment, if not disaster. African Americans with middle-class aspirations did not fit readily into the class-based racial system that had emerged in Haiti by the 1820s. As much as the government hoped that their presence would provide the nation with a "respectable" community to mediate the growing divide between land-owning elites (mostly light-skinned mulattoes) and the desperately poor peasants who constituted nearly 90 percent of the population, their numbers alone were certainly not great enough to make a significant difference. African Americans had little preparation for a socioeconomic system in which they would be free but not, for all intents and purposes, in charge of their own destinies. The trope of Canaan made no allowance for the reestablishment of landless poverty. Similarly, the religious distinctiveness of migrants only exacerbated the fact of their irreducible difference from native Haitians.

This strand of African-American narratives, betraying loss, disillusionment, and abandonment by Haitian officials, finally spelled the death of the emigration campaign. As early as the spring of 1825, black and white promoters such as Lundy and Allen vehemently and publicly criticized the inflated hopes of the migrants. If they recognized their own complicity in creating such expectations, they did not acknowledge it. Placing the blame squarely on the unrealistic dreams of settlers, Haitian officials and American supporters alike revealed biases of class, gender, and region. Benjamin F. Hughes, a Northern black Presbyterian minister, observed during his 1825 trip that "the mass of people have come wholly unprepared to endure the least privation or affliction. . . . Not to be allowed to dispose of things as they think proper, nor to be indiscriminately admitted into the social circle of the principal men of the country, even the domicile of his Excellency, is in their estimation, hatefully cruel, and not a whit better than absolute slavery."[54]

Benjamin Lundy reserved even harsher invective for dissatisfied migrants, though unlike Hughes, who seemed to be criticizing the upper-class aspirations of non-elites, Lundy cast his net of blame more broadly. He censured slave owners for schooling their slaves to prize leisure over industry; he criticized ex-slaves for their "effeminate" and gullible "aping" of Southern white manners; and simultaneously, he reinforced the notion that civilized life necessitated the observance of distinctions of rank and privilege, albeit as part of a hierarchy based on merit rather than on race or birth:

> Hundreds of effeminate, lazy wretches, taught by their *worthless tutors* to despise honest labour, and having learned to ape their manners, by "playing high life below the stairs," have palmed themselves upon the

generosity of the Haytiens, under the belief that they would be permit-
ted to figure away in style, at their expense, without so much as dreaming of the necessity of working with their own hands to support themselves. . . . Some of them, indeed, with all the arrogance and pomposity
of upper servants, have assumed the air and consequence of gentlemen
of rank, and have culculated [calculated] on immediate induction into
offices of honour, trust, and profit, and, also, on being invested with the
dignity and emoluments of Clergymen, Statesmen, Generals, &c. &c.
before they may have proven themselves worthy of it. . . . Let the effeminate drones, who prefer the *flesh-pots of Egypt,* return to them.[55]

After mid-1825, emigration to Haiti dropped off precipitously as the hopes
of settlers dwindled. The Haitian government, dissatisfied with the results
of its initiative and insulted by the responses of many migrants by 1826,
suspended financial support for migrants, effectively stopping the exodus.
When the Haitian government ended its promotional campaign, U.S. promoters were left with little choice but to curtail discussion of Haiti in local
newspapers.

Remarkably little information has been preserved about the fate of the estimated four to five thousand African Americans who remained in Haiti.
Occasional reports about Haiti filtered northward in the 1830s and 1840s,
but they were more apt to be accounts from Protestant missionaries than
letters from ordinary settlers. They told a variety of stories. Some reported
decline: "Our brothers and sisters that bid fair when we left the United States
for old Canaan have hung their harps upon the willows and have lost the
song of Zion." Others insisted that the small band of Protestant settlers
greatly desired missionaries from the United States to shore up their minority faith in the face of persistent heathenism and immorality.[56]

The 1820s had afforded many African Americans a close glimpse of Haiti,
closer than some desired. In subsequent decades, as the political and economic fortunes of Haiti deteriorated, African-American narratives of the island reinvigorated the revolutionary moment of racial glory. From the 1840s
through the late nineteenth century, blacks who wrote about Haiti avoided
the turmoil of the present in favor of a restoration of the past. Haiti, in
African-American renderings, became a symbol of African initiative and

courage. But it no longer served as a blueprint for an African communal future. Its current woes, inasmuch as they were discussed at all, were subordinated to a former glory that served (and continues to serve) as a symbol of collective initiative for African Americans.

In 1826, the same year that the migration came to a disastrous end, the black abolitionist John Russworm (who later emigrated to Africa) delivered the commencement address at his alma mater, Bowdoin College. He highlighted the effects of liberty on the formerly enslaved population of Haiti. After thirty-two years of freedom, he affirmed, they were a people transformed. "Restored to the dignity of man and to society," he stated, "they have acquired a new existence; their powers have been developed; a career of glory and happiness unfolds itself before them." Russworm concluded by likening the future Haiti to ancient Tyre, a prosperous commercial city: "her vessels shall extend the fame of her riches and glory, to the remotest borders of the globe."[57]

By the 1840s, few African Americans would have agreed with Russworm's optimistic assessment. After more than a decade of a declining economy and increasing social unrest, revolution broke out in Haiti in January 1843 and drove President Boyer from office. Over the following seventy years, Haiti endured numerous civil wars. Only one of the succeeding twenty-two heads of state served out his term of office: the rest suffered deposition, poisoning, bombing, or forced resignation. Caste conflicts increased as well, as economic deterioration cemented the social disparities of rich and poor. In 1847, Faustin Soulouque acceded to power and promptly transformed the republic into an empire. Over the next eleven years, Emperor Faustin I created a peerage with princes, dukes, counts, barons, and knights. Moreover, he further increased the national debt by waging war continuously against the neighboring Dominican Republic. Altogether, it was difficult for African Americans, wedded to evangelical and republican views of culture and politics, to see promise in Haiti's future.[58]

After 1840, African Americans (and their white sympathizers) found new ways to narrate Haiti. By far the most prevalent was to focus biographically on Toussaint L'Ouverture, the revolutionary hero of the Haitian cause. Infrequently mentioned in the first decades after independence, L'Ouverture came to stand for the bravery and initiative that could then be attributed to all peoples of African descent. By the 1850s, in keeping with a more pervasive historiographical turn toward the exaltation of "great men" as representatives of national or racial excellence, descriptions of L'Ouverture's exploits became commonplace. Orators and writers such as James Redpath, Wendell Phillips, James McCune Smith, Lydia Maria Child, and C. W. Mossell all published biographical pieces, and many other observers spoke enthusiastically of his virtues.[59]

William Wells Brown delivered and later published an oration that captures well the thematic elements notable in many of those accounts. Brown, a free black author and speaker better known for his fiction than for his speeches, lectured about Haiti on two continents. In May 1854 he spoke in London at the Metropolitan Athenaeum, and in December of that year he appeared at St. Thomas's Church in Philadelphia (where Prince Saunders had served as a lay reader thirty-seven years earlier). Although his announced topic was "St. Domingo: Its Revolutions and Patriots," Brown devoted most of his attention to L'Ouverture. In a swashbuckling tale that drew from a recently published British biography, L'Ouverture emerged as a hero descended from King Arradas, an African chief, "one of the most wealthy, powerful, and influential monarchs on the west coast of Africa." A born leader, L'Ouverture reflected the "soul" of Africa: "That soul, when once the soul of a man, and no longer that of a slave, can overthrow the Pyramids and the Alps themselves, sooner than again be crushed down into slavery."[60]

Yet if L'Ouverture symbolized the best qualities of African lineage, Brown also yoked his legacy to more recent precedents. The orator emphasized the innate religiosity of the war hero, likening him to a notable Protestant revolutionary: L'Ouverture, in Brown's words, "had a deep and pervading sense of religion, and, in the camp, carried it even as far as Oliver Cromwell. It might be said that an inward and prophetic genius revealed to him the omnipotence of a firm and unwearied adherence to principle." In his concluding comments, Brown emphasized the leader's career "as a Christian, a statesman, and a general," which, in his estimate, also bore comparison to the career of the great American revolutionary George Washington.[61]

Cromwell, Arradas, Washington, L'Ouverture. The lineage was striking in the way that it asserted the apparently "natural" collective traits of Europeans, Americans, and Africans in its romantic invocations of the "soul" of Africa (in keeping with the strain of romantic nationalism newly in vogue in

Germany and the United States), and then *fused* them symbolically in the figure of L'Ouverture.[62] It also justified the Haitian Revolution by associating L'Ouverture's cause with that of champions of other battles (the Protestants in England, the patriots in America), which, presumably, his audiences would have taken to be self-evidently righteous. It related L'Ouverture, by all accounts a faithful Catholic, to the hero of the English Protestant cause, Oliver Cromwell, referencing an "inward and prophetic genius" that further downplayed the Haitian's nominal Catholic affiliation.

Subsequent U.S. abolitionists followed suit as they introduced and domesticated Haitian history for public consumption. Seven years later the white abolitionist activist Wendell Phillips compared L'Ouverture to Mohammed, Napoleon, Cromwell, and John Brown, and stressed his "pure African" descent. In 1865 Lydia Maria Child, writing a book intended to impart "fresh strength and courage" to newly freed slaves, focused on L'Ouverture's royal African lineage and his "intelligent, sober, industrious" piety. In all these accounts, L'Ouverture's African nobility was wedded to his (innate, even Protestant) religious virtue. And just as clearly, L'Ouverture stood as an emblem of African collective potential and moral possibility.

Haiti remained important to African Americans throughout the century as a singular sign of collective accomplishment. But as a society Haiti was still a troubling symbol, impervious to the dreams of steady virtue and progress that marked black Protestant communal desire. As romantic theories of racial and national character became ascendant, however, the individual worth of Toussaint L'Ouverture became increasingly salient as a gauge of potential achievement. Even if Haiti, in practice, had not lived up to African-American hopes, the ideals for which the original black revolutionary fought could inspire a sense of united purpose.

By far the most complicated rendering of Haiti came from the man who would lead a second migration to the country in 1861. James Theodore Holly (1821–1911) later claimed to have spent much of his early life dreaming of the glories of the island. The son of a shoemaker who was reared Roman Catholic, Holly recalled that he had been interested in the nation ever since his youth in Washington, D.C., when he met Catholic missionaries who had returned from the newly independent black republic. Beginning in the early 1850s, the recent convert to the Episcopal Church wrote and spoke more extensively than almost anyone else about the significance of Haiti, a place he did not visit until 1855. In 1861 he spearheaded a migration to the black republic, where he lived for the rest of his life. His speeches and writings from the years before his move, taken together, evince the struggle of one African American to unite his admiration for Haiti with his loyalties to religious faith, American nationalism, and a diasporic African community.

Holly's early life illustrates the continuing attentiveness toward Haiti demonstrated by African American leaders in the antebellum period. Although born on the heels of the first Haitian exodus in 1829, Holly came of age in an era when African Americans throughout the Northern states and Canada once again debated the desirability of migration. He was attracted to the writings of Henry Bibb, Mary Shadd Cary, Martin Delany (who named one of his children after the Haitian "emperor" Faustin Soulouque), and other black leaders who wrote and spoke about the need for a safe haven for African Americans. At age twenty-one Holly queried the ACS about the possibility of becoming a medical missionary to Liberia, but he was not commissioned. He later served as the associate editor for the *Voice of the Fugitive*, an emigrationist paper. Holly, although trained as a bootmaker, also became interested in the ministry. After a move to Burlington, Vermont, in 1850, he joined the Protestant Episcopal Church, and in 1852 he met the Reverend William C. Munroe, the dynamic pastor of St. Matthew's Episcopal Church, an all-black church in Detroit. Munroe had also served as a (then Baptist) missionary in Port-au-Prince in the mid-1830s, and he remained committed to the cause of Haitian evangelization. Shortly thereafter, Holly became the fourteenth African American to take ordination vows in the Episcopal Church.[63]

By 1853 Holly had become an active proponent of Haitian emigration—a cause from which most blacks had shied away since the failure of the 1820s. The 1850s, which had seen the rise of Emperor Faustin I on the island, hardly seemed a propitious time to raise the banner once again. But the young minister, unswayed by Faustin's political maneuverings and encouraged by his colleague Munroe, pushed for renewed African-American attention to Haiti. Their cause was unreservedly evangelistic and restorationist; as high church Episcopalians, they hoped to restore the island's Catholic worship to "its primitive purity." Holly believed that the Episcopal Church, because of its intimate connections to Catholic worship and liturgy, was the more "natural" religion for the Haitian people. After convincing his church to sponsor an exploratory trip to the island in 1855, Holly returned home even more assured that Haitians would flock to his church. He noted how widespread Freemasonry was there, and argued that the Anglican ceremony would fill a similar need for Haitian men, in particular (who rarely went to church at all, by many reports). Moreover, Holly stressed, Anglicanism was close enough to Roman Catholicism to be seen as "religious" by the Haitian people.[64]

Holly's understanding of Haitian culture departed abruptly from the evangelical views of blacks in the 1820s, mostly Baptists and Methodists, who considered the ceremonial trappings of Haitian life to be a vestigial (and unhealthy) remnant of Gallic Catholicism. Like his Episcopal and Masonic predecessor Prince Saunders forty years earlier, Holly relished the pageantry. During his leadership of a Masonic lodge in Detroit in the early 1850s, Holly dedicated its new building "to the greatness of Haiti and her monarch." He defended Emperor Faustin, even though the sovereign had officially disestablished Catholicism and allowed vodou to claim a much greater public presence. Holly called this a necessary step toward religious freedom, and it thereby confirmed, in his estimation, Faustin's greater sympathy toward Protestant missionaries. The emperor "was even supposed to be secretly in favour of the success of Protestant missionary efforts in his dominions," preferring them to the work of the local Catholic priests.[65]

Holly's advocacy of monarchy as distinctly African echoed contemporaneous renderings of Toussaint L'Ouverture as a descendant of African kings. In the 1820s African Americans welcomed the arrival of President Boyer's republic as a symbol of Haiti's political progress, and they rationalized the earlier monarchy as a vestigial legacy of French colonialism that would be swept away in the fervor of revolutionary housekeeping. Later African Americans such as Brown and Holly instead claimed monarchy as an honorable heritage of African origin: Holly termed it "an ancient traditionary predilection of the race derived from Africa. . . . The gorgeous splendor and august prestige of aristrocratic [sic] rank and title, always attendant on this form of government, hold an imperious sway over the minds of this race of men who have such a keen appreciation of the beautiful."[66] As attentive to the aesthetics of ceremonialism as Baron de Vastey and Prince Saunders before him, Holly celebrated the concept of monarchy as a salutary restoration of an African trait.

The U.S. Episcopal missionary board initially refused Holly's requests to establish a station in Haiti. Instead, he accepted a position at St. Luke's Church in New Haven, Connecticut, a town with a large and politically active free black population. From that pulpit he continued his efforts to promote the Haitian cause. A favorite speaker at convocations, suppers, Masonic meetings, and church gatherings of both blacks and whites between 1855 and 1859, Holly toured throughout the Northeast and Midwest delivering several series of speeches, which he later published and circulated widely in church and emigrationist circles. In "A Vindication of the Capacity of the Negro for Self-Government and Civilized Progress" (1857) and the seven-part "Thoughts on Hayti" (1859), the pastor elaborated some of his most significant theological understandings of Haiti as a religious and racial symbol.

As it did for L'Ouverture's biographers, the Haitian revolution figured prominently in Holly's speeches as part of a long lineage of righteous revolutions that connected contemporary African Americans to an ancient (African) history as well as to American national heritage. Haiti should be seen, Holly affirmed, as the height of revolutionary success, eclipsing all other such justifiable rebellions: "The ancient glory of Ethiopia, Egypt, and Greece, grows pale in comparison with the splendor of this Haytian achievement." The appropriate comparison, he reasoned, seemed to lie much closer to home, with the only other nation in the Western Hemisphere that had shaken off European control in the preceding century: the United States. It was no coincidence, in Holly's estimation, that Haitians had figured in that crusade as well (as soldiers in the Battle of Savannah): "If the United States can claim to have preceded her in this respect, Hayti can claim the honor of having contributed to the success of American Independence, by the effusion of the blood of her sable sons, who . . . fought side by side with the American heroes." The subsequent uprising in Haiti, moreover, was even more historically significant than what occurred in the United States, since Americans were already "comparatively free." The Caribbean slaves fought a more momentous battle, since they had many more obstacles to overcome in the process, and they did so entirely on their own—with absolutely no help from whites.[67]

Holly expressed considerably more satisfaction than did most black narrators with the "progress" that Haitian society had made in the subsequent half-century. He saw little evidence of degeneration, and he felt confident that the government had dealt readily with social and political problems that inevitably had arisen. Dessalines, Christophe, Boyer, and the newly ousted (by 1859) Soulouque had not survived politically in Haiti because the "liberty-loving" nature of the people eventually had triumphed. If Haitians were innate freedom seekers, for Holly, they were also instinctively inclined toward piety. Holly read evidence of African religious practices, though morally repugnant, as a sign of the "natural religiosity" of African-descended peoples. "The African character is decidedly religious," he asserted. "It is therefore impossible to make him an out and out atheist."[68] Left to the combined influences of French colonialism and Catholic oppression, Holly concluded, Haitians had remained mired in heathen practices: "On the Sabbath, after participating in the ceremonial observances at the Roman Catholic temples in the forepart of that holy day, they assemble together in the afternoon and evening of the same day, in portable tents, and celebrate by dancing and singing the heathen mysteries of Africa."[69] With this fundamental religious trait as a foundation, Haitians now simply required the guiding influences of Protestant morality.

Holly's understanding of Haiti's importance encompassed past and future, the Old World as well as the New. As participants in a history that had moved from Ethiopia and Egypt and later to Haiti, African Americans were now called upon to bring true Christianity to the Caribbean republic, so that someday it could be brought back to Africa. Haiti would be the location where racial greatness and Christianity at last would meet and combine: "If Haytien independence shall cease to exist, the sky of negro-destiny shall be hung in impenetrable blackness; the hope of Princes coming out of Egypt and Ethiopia soon stretching forth her hands unto God, will die out."[70] Haiti had become, in Holly's rendering, an intermediate measure of the biblical Ethiopian prophecy.

In his discourses, Holly eloquently fused Christian salvation and themes of racial unity, with Haiti serving as the linchpin in the narrative. Shortly before his own migration he embraced an additional understanding of Haitian settlement: he likened it to the founding of Puritan New England, thereby linking it with U.S. national history.

The second mass migration, in 1861–1862, could not rival the 1820s movement numerically. Estimates of numbers run into the low thousands, but it is difficult to say with any certainty precisely how many African Americans chose to remove to Haiti in the early months of the long-awaited Civil War at home. Neither did it receive the sustained press attention of the earlier effort, although the white emigration agent James Redpath did his best to drum up support. The movement appealed principally to blacks in the urban North, who had grown disillusioned with the prospects of racial equality on U.S. soil (and may therefore have held out less hope for the success of emancipation). The second migration appeared to be more overtly evangelistic in tone, a feature that probably speaks more to Holly's talents at publicizing his own version of events than to any heightened commitment to Christianization.

Organizers, including Holly, were nonetheless careful this time to avoid some of the problems of the past. Holly recognized that the first migration had not been well organized, and that the migrants had not been selected carefully. Hence, many of them quickly "longed for the flesh-pots, the leeks, the onions, and the garlic of domestic servility" in the United States. This time, he reasoned, African Americans must send the "industrial civilizers of Hayti" in small groups, ready to do battle against immorality. Self-consciously rejecting the metaphor of the Israelite Exodus, he compared this project instead to the model of early New England, in which groups would band together in "well-organized religious communities, headed by an educated ministry, and backed and sustained by learned laymen." The Puritan paradigm, Holly reasoned, would provide diasporic Africans with a "powerful Negro nationality," which presumably would serve as a light for all to follow.[71]

Holly carried the Puritan image even further. Before his departure in April 1861, the Episcopal minister formed a *Madeira* Compact with his fellow migrants, self-consciously appropriating the political agreement of the first settlers of New England. Hoping for far more hometown support than that received by the first Puritans, he publicized the departure from New Haven (the point of origin of approximately half of the 150 first settlers) to the population at large by declaring in the pages of the *Weekly Anglo-African*: "Citizens of New Haven! Descendants of the Pilgrims! You are invited to rally to the hearty support of this *Mayflower* expedition of sable pioneers in the cause of civil and religious liberty, which it falls to your lot to Hayti in the name of New England." Demonstrating that his evocation was not simply a public relations ploy, Holly boosted morale during the early months of settlement (when illness killed nearly half the migrants) by likening the band to pilgrims and reminding them of the trials undergone by those early Puritans. The Rev. John Lewis, among Holly's small group, wrote from the newly established Episcopal church, St. Mark's, that he equated his position there to that of the early settlers of the Plymouth colony: "I take, as a precedent, the position of the Pilgrim Fathers of New England."[72]

Holly eventually would become the first bishop of the Episcopal Church in Haiti, and he would spend the rest of his life trying to instill in Haitians a love for the high church ceremonialism combined with a Protestant sense of moral discipline that he himself so revered. Yet he also harnessed Haiti to the narrative of American civil religion through his invocation of the Puritan paradigm. The *Mayflower* model countered the Israelite Exodus theme so prevalent in the rhetoric of the 1820s. Therefore, it may be useful to contemplate briefly: if Holly's migrants were Puritans (and Holly himself John Winthrop, presumably), who were the Haitians, and what was Haiti by 1861?

If we take Holly's image seriously, the Caribbean nation signified New England, a light unto the nations. This characterization certainly fit his sense that a Christianized Haiti would embody and demonstrate for others the pinnacle of African achievement in world history. Just as the early Puritan settlers presented America as a "new Eden," Holly and J. Dennis Harris, both employed as regional recruiting agents for the Haytien Bureau of Emigration in 1860, presented Haiti as a new sacred center that would reconfigure global relations. Holly consistently referred to the country as a new Eden, and Harris enthused about the providential coincidence of its location. "Central America," wrote Harris, "by common assent, not only realizes in its geographical position the ancient idea of the centre of the world, but is in its physical aspect and configuration of surface an epitome of all the countries and of all climes."[73] Inverting prevailing Euro-American views of the backwardness of the region, Harris transformed Haiti into the geographical standard by which all other regions should be judged.

But who were the Haitian people? Symbols of glory, they nonetheless were consigned in Holly's image to relative invisibility—much as their predecessors had been in the 1820s. The paradigm of the Puritans, just like the rhetoric of Exodus after which it was fashioned, contained little room for independent initiative on the part of native peoples; they played a secondary role in the grand scheme of African-American collective destiny. Similarly, too, African Americans would bestow upon Haitians the blessings of a superior culture, just as the Puritans had understood themselves to be aiding Native Americans through their own missionary programs. It would be a mistake to carry the Puritan image too far, since Holly himself more frequently referred to the sense of a unified African destiny implied in the movement to Haiti. Nonetheless, his invocation of the Puritans suggests the coexistence of multiple understandings of black identity, and of overlapping narratives that attempted to incorporate racial, religious, and national themes.

Holly's synthesis of Christian and racial understandings further underscores the extent to which black leaders used such narratives to critique Euro-American history and racial theory as they were being constituted in this period. African-American responses to Haiti and its religious practices are perhaps best viewed, then, as historical and ethnographic accounts that enabled black Protestants to articulate and reconcile potential conflicts among racial, national, and religious loyalties. Through these stories, African Americans challenged the shortcomings of a Protestant tradition that had been complicit in their enslavement without forsaking the religious truths that helped to define their understandings of the world. By contrast, the same stories could link them to a glorious racial past and to other dark-skinned peoples in the present, and yet simultaneously explain the awkward sense of foreignness they felt while encountering other African-based cultures.

By the end of the nineteenth century, black American promoters of Haiti acknowledged their lack of progress in realizing their dream. The second emigration of 1861–1862 ended in miserable failure, with hundreds of disillusioned migrants returning to the United States and scores more dying of disease in their new homeland. In speeches and letters eerily similar to those written in 1825, some African Americans mounted anti-emigration campaigns and roundly denounced the movement as ill-conceived. Even Holly, who remained a staunch believer in a Christianized Haiti throughout his life, lost his mother, wife, and young child, along with many members of his pilgrim band of immigrants, within the first year of settlement. Financial

support for Haiti from the AME and Episcopal Churches, which had increased significantly in the 1870s and 1880s, declined in the ensuing years as
interest in missions to Africa increased. Many promoters expressed the same
poignant combination of images of glory and dampened hopes voiced by
Solomon Hood of the AME in 1890: "As for patriots the world has produced
no greater than Toussaint L'Ouverture and Dessalines, and as for rulers, we
are not ashamed of the stern and mighty Christophe, and the wise and diplomatic President Salomon, but Hayti needs more than this."[74]

In 1873 the AME minister Theophilus Gould Steward was commissioned
by the denomination to make an official inspection visit to the Haitian field.
For some years he had been eager to visit Haiti, so moved was he by the inspirational example set by a community of slaves who had dared to overthrow their masters. Yet the realities of the nation proved overwhelming.
Surveying the religious state of the people, he was alarmed by the perils of
Catholicism and vodou and fearful about the power of those "false" religions over the souls of the Haitian people. Class disparities bothered him
even more. He was appalled by the abject poverty in which the vast majority
of Haitians lived while a relatively small number enjoyed prosperity and
wealth. He was so disturbed, apparently, that he quietly gave up his hope of
establishing a mission there, and avoided discussing the reasons for his
change of heart.[75]

We can only guess at Steward's state of mind. But it is reasonable to conclude that his experience of the discrepancy between Haiti as symbol and
Haiti as a realistic social model devastated him. His psychic investment in
Haiti was very high, and he chose to remain silent rather than publicize what
he had seen. Steward never submitted his final report to the church. But he
did return with a poem, which later appeared in a denominational publication. In it, he reiterated Holly's "serpentine trail," albeit with a somewhat
darker view of contemporary Haitian culture, and underscored the symbolic
value of Haiti as an exemplar of African liberty. If Haiti could help to rescue
African Americans in the United States from psychological thralldom, he
mused, then surely AME missionaries could return the favor by delivering
the blessings of spiritual liberation to the small island nation:

Will ye not heed their call
And to them send the pure and holy word—

That word that can and will
Speak light and life.
Oh, send it forth with prayers wreathed
And benedictions shall its steps attend;
And Hayti, Roman Hayti, shall be made
The Hayti of a people free,
The land a freeman's God will e'er defend.[76]

Fleeting as it was, the heyday of African-American public interest in Haiti had significant and quantifiable results. It has been estimated that as many as 13,000 migrants left for the republic during the 1820s, and another 2,000 set off in 1861–1862. These numbers may seem small in contrast to the total figure of more than four million blacks in the United States by the time of the Civil War, but compared with the movement of perhaps 10,000 African Americans to all of Africa before 1861 (most of them sponsored by the ACS), the less well organized and chronically underfunded Haitian cause was remarkably popular.[77] The messages disseminated by promoters spoke directly to the needs and desires of free blacks in Northern cities, people with the education and means to act upon a dream of African diasporic religious unity.

But Haiti endured longest, and still endures, as a mirror for African-American aspirations, a way of knitting various threads of racial destiny and religious truth in a single, proximate site. The movement to Haiti, be it a movement of bodies, religious practices and beliefs, or both, promised to bring together in time and space a story of African-American life. It was a narrative that gave history, pride, and community to black Americans in exchange for religious transformation, with a reciprocity that pledged to make the serpentine trail of African destiny complete. If African Americans could impart the blessings of Protestantism to their brothers and sisters in Haiti, then the Caribbean nation could in turn link blacks in the United States to a glorious racial destiny.

4

Exodus and Ethiopia

Dear brethren, I want you to examine yourselves well in the glass, and consider all things well, and thus you will discover what is good for you in time and in eternity. Let us think of Africa for a few moments. Know you not that, in the beginning, the blessed Lord gave this great quarter of the earth to our nation, and bade us keep the Law and live?

DANIEL H. PETERSON, *The Looking-Glass* (1854)

When Daniel Peterson, an AME minister from Baltimore, embarked on a tour of Liberia, Sierra Leone, and Gambia in 1853, he cited several reasons for his trip: to bring the gospel "to my brethren," to speak to the heads of government about the prospects for future emigration, and to see for himself the condition and potential of the "heathen." But he also wanted to communicate with African Americans—not just about Africa but also about their own situation. Peterson published his "report and narrative" the following year, and its title, *The Looking-Glass*, conveyed his intent. He called upon blacks to "examine yourselves well in the glass, and consider all things well, and thus you will discover what is good for you in time and in eternity."[1]

On the face of it, Peterson's emphasis might seem odd: why did the clergyman need to cross the Atlantic to call for self-reflection? What kind of mirror could such travel provide? The obvious motivation for his trip was the escalation of racial tensions after the passage of the Fugitive Slave Act of 1850. Increasing numbers of black leaders since then had given up on the notion of peaceful coexistence with whites in an integrated country, and blacks and whites alike turned to the prospect of African colonization with new interest. The American Colonization Society sponsored Peterson's trip and published his report in an effort to encourage African Americans to see Africa as a viable possibility for migration. With the collective future of blacks in the United States looking increasingly bleak, Africa also proved a fertile place to imagine the possibilities for cultural development.

Peterson's report went well beyond the mechanics of movement to weave a broader tale of history, kinship, and salvation. Africa would assist African Americans in their spiritual discernment, the preacher argued, because the fate of black Americans was entangled with the destiny of that continent, and knowing the divine history of the African people was necessary for their salvation. God's sacred intent was that African Americans would one day re-occupy their homeland. But it would happen only after they ceased their backsliding ways. Slavery had occurred for a reason, he insisted: "In the beginning, the blessed Lord gave this great quarter of the earth to our nation, and bade us keep the Law and live. . . . But our progenitors were rebellious and disobedient, and refused to serve the true and living God." As it had been for the children of Israel, exile from their homeland was a punishment and enslavement a divine chastisement. The salvation of the race, Peterson asserted, depended on the will of the people to follow God's ways and thereby reclaim Africa for themselves and for Christ: "I believe that great treasures are embedded in those lands, and that only understanding and enterprise are wanting to bring them to light. It remains for us to go forth, sons and daughters of Ethiopia, embrace our privileges, obtain the lands, dwell thereon, and become a great nation."[2]

Peterson was only one of many nineteenth-century African-American leaders to write about the significance of Africa. Motivated by political expediency, missionary fervor, and race consciousness, Peterson and others made connections—temporal as well as spatial—between the fate of American blacks and the destiny of African peoples. Their accounts in turn stimulated more travel and reporting back home. Whereas Haiti was seen as a New World exemplar and redeemer for the race, Africa was the motherland, the connecting link with family and history, the place of origin. While Haiti symbolized the future, Africa represented the past. Whereas union with Haiti represented a political and religious choice, *re*union with Africa represented ties of blood that were far more fraught and spiritually significant. By the middle of the nineteenth century, few African Americans had direct family connections with native-born Africans. But that hardly diminished the importance of Africa as a subject of desire and concern.[3]

Like all missionary accounts, the stories of Peterson and his comrades have a formulaic quality; in their desire to convince readers to support the cause, authors stressed the obvious urgency of the moral situation. In Gambia, Peterson related, "I walked through the markets and saw the people lying about in the sand like pigs, half naked, both heathen and Mahometans, loaded down with charms and idols, going about shaving each other's heads."[4] He juxtaposed discussion of Muslims and "others" who wore idols with a lengthy passage on criminality. These accounts reflect a curiously hybrid collection of history, ethnography, climatology, and demography, and that very eclecticism leaves space for the voices of missionaries to emerge in distinctive ways.[5] Some express prurient interest in African sexuality or religious practices; others spur readers to action; and still others entertain with daring exploits. On lecture tours, as well as in articles in black periodicals and published books, African-American missionaries taught home audiences about Africa and about themselves. By constructing particular kinds of relationships to a place and a people, missionaries hoped to shape the future of both Africa and African Americans.

African-American missionary narrators—Daniel Peterson, Thomas L. Johnson, Alexander Priestley Camphor, Amanda Berry Smith, and William Sheppard, among them—were popular in African-American communities. Southerners themselves, they spent much of their lives in the states, yet they lectured widely at black colleges and churches about the significance of Africa for everyday black people. Many had strong connections to white-run church organizations, and few had any real desire to sever those connections; indeed, they saw the cause of Africa as a Christian cause, one that might best be met by black evangels, but that ultimately served the cause of Christ, not simply the African race. Most of them were also colonizers, men and women who believed that American economic and political institutions run by African-American emigrants could bring African nations up to their own standards of civilization. Thus in writing about the meaning of Africa, missionary authors sought to create communities defined simultaneously by race, religion, and colonial interests.[6] Their accounts instilled a historical memory of Africa and ushered ordinary African Americans into both a global evangelical project and a localized colonial endeavor.

African Americans, both slave and free, had obviously thought about Africa for a very long time. Familial links to the continent grew increasingly attenuated by the early nineteenth century as the trafficking in slaves declined, but this did not stop slaves from continuing to pass along stories about returning "across grandywater."[7] For Northern blacks, even more removed from the direct experience of that homeland, the meaning of Africa began to change. By the 1810s their stories designated Africa as a homogeneous and sacred location rather than as a constellation of separate ethnic groups. Ancient Egypt and Ethiopia stood in for the continent as a whole as a symbol of collective accomplishment. Free blacks learned about Africa through contemporary Euro-American scholarship, although as late as the 1850s a centralized body of scientific knowledge about the continent simply did not exist. Instead, current knowledge consisted of highly dispersed and simultaneous discourses from travel writers, biologists, men of letters, and antislavery Christians, all writing for specific audiences with particular objectives.[8] This last source, abolitionist rhetoric, proved most accessible and influential for African Americans, inasmuch as it provided information circulated by leaders whose opinions they trusted. But despite myriad resources, free blacks' impressions of Africa continued to be shaped largely by classical literature and biblical prophecy rather than by contemporary accounts.

This base of knowledge changed as African Americans gradually began to return to Africa themselves, forging new connections to the homeland. In the late eighteenth century, Great Britain established Sierra Leone on the west coast of Africa as a place of settlement for its own poor blacks, but it soon served as a refuge for migrants from the United States and the Caribbean as well. Its founding spurred Northern free blacks to consider seriously the prospect of emigration. From the beginning, free blacks were divided over the wisdom of such a move. The black Masons of Boston, led by Prince Hall, agitated for assistance in helping free blacks move back to Africa in 1787, with more than seventy-five signatories in support; the Free African Society of Philadelphia, on the contrary, rejected the concept entirely. The movement for African settlement was further complicated by the formation of the American Colonization Society in 1816.[9] Although African Americans remained involved with the ACS throughout its existence, many black leaders roundly criticized the organization and retreated from emigrationism as a result. Throughout the antebellum period, debates over colonization, freighted by the overtly racist motives of some proponents, inevitably focused on agency and intention. Would blacks be required to emigrate? The actual number of emigrants to Africa before 1860 remained very small, much smaller than the number going to Haiti. Probably only 10,000 African Americans settled in Africa before 1861, nearly all under ACS auspices. Between 1820 and 1833, only 169 African Americans from the North emigrated to Liberia.[10]

More significant than the human movement was the new supply of knowledge about contemporary Africa that the founding of Sierra Leone (and in 1820 Liberia, under ACS auspices) provided. Paul Cuffe, a wealthy and well-connected Boston sea captain and merchant, was among the first African Americans to report back on a trip to Sierra Leone. Cuffe, ever the entrepreneur and missionary, envisioned an international commercial enterprise that would unite the economic and spiritual interests of Africans and black Americans. In 1812 he published an account of a trip in which he described meeting native peoples from various tribes in Africa, including the king of the Bullone tribe. Cuffe gave Bibles to the Bullone as a gift and told them how useful the books could be. But he concluded that "so accustomed are they to wars and slavery that I apprehend it would be a difficult task to convince them of the impropriety of these pernicious practices." He also related a more auspicious encounter with the Muslim "Mendingo" tribe, a group that in Cuffe's estimation exhibited the virtues of education and abstention from alcohol. They did, however, traffic in slaves, a vice that the Quaker Cuffe attributed to Islamic influence. Cuffe tried to convince them that the practice was wrong, but "the prejudice of education had taken too firm hold of their minds to admit of much effect from reason on this subject." From the beginning, Cuffe envisioned the encounter as an exchange as much spiritual as it was economic, an ongoing relationship in which African Americans could offer "civilized" customs and beliefs in return for renewed ties to their homeland.[11]

Between 1816 and 1850 the ACS emerged as the most consistent public voice on African emigration. Its official organ, the *African Repository,* served as a significant source of information about Liberia for those back home, influencing conceptions of the morality and inevitability of Christian progress. The paper was, of course, primarily a "testimonial for colonization," and it relied heavily on letters of praise and African travel books to make its point.[12] Its opinions about African natives were heavily influenced both by the Christian impulse to evangelize the heathen and by the desire to promote patriotic support for Americo-Liberians in their ongoing civil war with indigenous peoples, both of which contributed to consistent reports stressing the immorality of natives and the Christian valor of the new settlers. Typical were the sentiments of Hilary Teage, editor of the *Repository* from 1835 to 1850 and a Liberian missionary. Teage, an extremely influential figure on both sides of the Atlantic who would eventually write Liberia's declaration of independence, composed a hymn that was published in the *Liberia Herald* and reprinted in the *African Repository* in 1837. A paean to God, the song included in its verses the history of the civil war in Liberia between patriots and native peoples, the latter of which are portrayed as dimwitted and brutish heathens facing the forces of righteousness.

Other early black missionaries to Africa voiced similar understandings of the place of their African work in the longer span of Christian progress. The former AME minister and organizer Daniel Coker, en route to Liberia as a missionary in 1820, spent his time on shipboard reading *The History of the Propagation of Christianity and Overthrow of Paganism,* a missionary tract penned by the eighteenth-century Scottish Presbyterian Robert Millar. Coker clearly absorbed Millar's narrative of the global march of Christianity that would eventually enlighten the most ignorant heathen.[13] Coker's subsequent descriptions of the "Cruemen" he observed upon landing stressed their pitiable religious state: "They adhere to their superstition, of charms and witchcraft—I stood on deck and looked at these children of nature, till streams of tears ran down my cheeks."[14] Like most American observers of the day, Coker used stock images of the continent borrowed from evangelical missionary rhetoric: "I expect to give my life to bleeding, groaning, dark benighted Africa," wrote Coker to Jeremiah Watts of Baltimore.[15] Coker, Teage, and others saw the salvation of Africa as a matter of Christian enlightenment, a story in which they would be the benevolent bearers of civility and progress.

Yet constant publicity could have unanticipated consequences, and at times ACS publications conveyed more ambiguous information than the authors realized. The *African Repository* in the 1830s and 1840s featured numerous articles containing intriguing facts about African cultures that did not necessarily correspond to their tales of progress from darkness to light. Some gave fairly relativistic renderings of local religious systems, such as the piece by an anonymous writer who acknowledged dispassionately that "the idea of virtue differs in different countries." Providing examples from Scandinavian and Greek mythology, the author concluded that "savages have *their* virtues; and although they may exclude other nations from the benefit of their operations, still, as it regards themselves, they connect happiness with the practice of these virtues." His report critiqued the Africans' alternative ethical systems but still conveyed some awareness that they contained internal coherence.[16]

Through the late 1840s, the focus of missionary supporters—driven almost solely by the ACS and its public relations campaign—rested exclusively on Liberia and Sierra Leone. Among the majority of African Americans opposed to ACS politics, discussion of emigration—to Africa or elsewhere—languished after the failure of the Haitian movement in the 1820s. Although a small, steady stream of settlers continued to move to Liberia, the unstable political situation there, as well as the country's associations with the ACS, made it a poor prospect for support. The Southern Baptist Convention appointed its first missionary to Nigeria in 1849, but the effort was initially small-scale and lacked support from African-American leaders.[17] In the early 1850s, the domestic political situation for blacks deteriorated further with the Compromise of 1850 and passage of the Fugitive Slave Act, a measure that compelled whites to return fugitive slaves to their owners or face criminal penalties. Northern whites and African Americans saw this development as one more effort to restrict the freedom of all blacks, since it denied a fugitive's right to a jury trial and encouraged a cottage industry in slavecatchers who could stop any black person to ascertain his legal status. Free blacks were rounded up and sent to Southern states. The Act led tens of thousands of African Americans in Northern states, fearful for their communities, to flee across the border into Canada, and many others turned to emigration as a last resort. African-American leaders once again reinvigorated debates about resettlement, opening up discussion of movement to a much wider range of possibilities: Canada, Mexico, or the West Indies, as well as Africa. Liberia retained the taint of association with the racist policies of the ACS. But other parts of Africa were about to emerge as likely prospects for the civilizing mission.

The opening of Central Africa to evangelization and potential settlement was facilitated less by missionary interest than by the earliest wave of a new Euro-American breed: the imperial missionary explorer. Typified by David

Livingstone, the explorer was a hardy adventurer, naturalist, and publicist who brought the wilds of Africa into the living rooms of British and American readers. In 1857 the publication of two travel accounts written by European adventurers electrified audiences on both sides of the Atlantic. Thomas Bowen's book *Central Africa: Adventures and Missionary Labours in the Interior of Africa*, and David Livingstone's work *Missionary Travels and Researches in South Africa*, dazzled European and American audiences with tales of the travelers' courageous exploits in the "dark heart" of the continent. These narratives focused on the daring achievements of heroic masculine figures struggling against brute nature and animal savagery. Although the advent of exploratory expeditions owed as much to the widespread use of quinine to prevent malaria as to any intrinsic interest in the continent, it would be difficult to underestimate their appeal and power to fuel domestic interest. The texts would serve as touchstones for all subsequent missionary labor (and imperial expansion more generally) in Africa, and they were particularly important in reinvigorating African-American interest in emigration. Could other areas of Africa provide possibilities for settlement untainted by the motivations of the ACS? And, simultaneously, might not African Americans emerge as the heroic bestowers of light to their heathen brethren?[18]

Martin Delany thought so. A member of the AME Church, a Freemason, and an outspoken critic of the ACS, Delany had been converted to the cause of emigration in the early 1850s. After reading Bowen's and Livingstone's texts, he agreed to head an exploration party in 1859 that would trace Bowen's journey through the Niger Valley. Interested in prospects for black settlement, Delany was more attentive to the economic than the spiritual potential of the area; he reported on the vegetation, soil, local diseases, and trade more meticulously than he observed the people. Yet he couched his report in an unmistakably historical framework: alluding to Africa's ancient glory, he observed that Africans had once had a vibrant culture and now awaited "regeneration." His initial encounters with natives were quite positive: "They are shrewd, intelligent, and industrious, with high conceptions of the Supreme Being, only using their images generally as mediators." Delany concluded that they could be readily Christianized. In some respects, moreover, they were still exemplary; reading their significance through the lens of ancient African civilizations, he compared their buildings favorably with those of Babylon, Ninevah, and Tyre.[19]

Like other antebellum black missionaries, Delany assumed that the future of Africa lay in its ability to accept Protestant Christianity and political leadership from African Americans. Previous efforts by foreign missionaries, he asserted, had led to "visible evidences of a purer and higher civilization." It was now time for American blacks, who were by virtue of their shared race better equipped to launch missionary efforts, to provide substantial material aid and human labor to lead Africans toward civility. When he met with the king and chiefs in Abbeokuta, he promised them that "no heterogeneous nor promiscuous 'masses' or companies, but select and intelligent people of high moral as well as religious character were to be induced to go out [emigrate]." They would teach the natives Christian habits—to eat with utensils, to sleep in beds, and to wear more clothes—but would not compel them to change their names, a practice he considered abhorrent: "A loss of name, and so far loss of identity."[20]

But if black Americans could give Yorubaland the benefits of Christianity and civilization, as Delany understood them, Africa also had much to give back. Delany's report made it clear that only by returning to Africa would African Americans become fully human. In his text he quoted the words of a black teacher who had written to him in 1858: "'I have read Bowen's work, and shall to-day purchase Livingstone's. I am more and more convinced that Africa is the country to which all colored men who wish to attain the full stature of manhood, and bring up their children to be men and not creeping things, should turn their steps.'" The gendered language here is noteworthy; as was the case with the Haitian emigration movement, African-American men associated the move to Africa with the attainment of manhood, something denied them by the oppressive racial restrictions of Euro-American society. But as in Haiti, the paradox was evident even if unstated: to become human, blacks were to leave behind Christian civilization as they knew it and live among the heathen—those who were not yet fully "human" themselves.[21] Redemption lay not simply in a settlement of the land but in a symbiotic—if hierarchical—relationship: Africans and black Americans, working together, one as the subject to be enlightened and the other as the heroic carrier of light, would restore their common humanity.

For African-American Christians, the Bible provided vital and enduring paradigms about how communities became fully human. Yet as Puritan settlers in the New World had discovered previously, its communal lessons remained elusively inchoate. The Exodus theme had long been enmeshed in black Protestant thinking about the African-American community in the United States. Led by Moses, the Israelites were brought out of the place of enslavement—Egypt—into the land God had promised to them. That much was certain. But little mention is made of the peoples already inhabiting the land of Canaan, and little attention paid to what happened between Israel and preexisting inhabitants once the Israelites laid down their tents and settled.[22] Political and social harmony in Canaan is assumed, and the rule of Yahweh is tacitly understood to be the correct way to live. But what if others disagreed or refused to comply? Equally important as a trope for thinking about African missions was the Ethiopian prophecy, which declared that "Ethiopia shall soon stretch out her hands unto God." Just who "Ethiopia" referred to, of course, remained ambiguous: did it refer to all those of African descent? Or only to native-born Africans? And if Ethiopians disagreed about how to gain their own redemption, whose vision would win out? African Americans pondered those uncertainties, and after the Civil War, the questions became harder and more entangled. What was the relationship between the Exodus story, which emphasized the agency and fulfillment of the newly freed Israelites, and the Ethiopian prophecy, which at least suggested that there were other Ethiopians to take into account? Daniel Coker's response, at once pitying and paternal, said it all: Africans may have been Ethiopians, but they, too, needed an exodus away from their superstitions and into "civilized" behavior.

Exodus and Ethiopia were never far from the minds of African-American missionaries. Two of the best-known supporters of emigration to Africa, Edward Blyden (1832–1912) and Alexander Crummell (1819–1898), waded deep into historical waters. Both began their careers as Christian missionaries in West Africa in the 1850s, Blyden as a Presbyterian and Crummell as an Episcopalian. Crummell stayed in Liberia for nearly two decades, and Blyden remained in West Africa until the end of his life in 1912. Each produced a large corpus of work dealing with questions of African-American history, collective identity, and Christian agency, and each would have gladly accepted the label of "Pan-Africanist" that subsequently became associated with his ideas. Yet their basic historical frameworks, modified greatly over many years of teaching and writing, posited very different understandings of divine agency, race, and collective history.

Edward Blyden, born in the Danish West Indies in 1832, left for Liberia in the early 1850s under the auspices of the ACS, an organization to which he, unlike most of his African-American colleagues, remained committed for more than four decades. Through both regular contributions to the *African Repository* and speaking tours on behalf of the organization, Blyden worked tirelessly for the cause of emigration. Ordained a Presbyterian minister in 1858 (after receiving his education under Old School Presbyterian auspices), Blyden also became a formidable scholar of classical learning and a teacher of classics. Despite his absence physically from the American scene, he was no intellectual exile. In addition to the *African Repository,* his work was published and reviewed in black denominational journals, including the AME *Christian Recorder.* As a reader, Blyden kept up with American missionary literature and intellectual culture from across the political spectrum, including the *Princeton Review,* the *Presbyterian Quarterly, Harper's Weekly,* and the *Methodist Quarterly Review.* Nothing illustrates more vividly his love of learning than a letter he sent to the Right Hon. W. E. Gladstone, British chancellor of the Exchequer in 1860, asking him to forward to Blyden a small library containing the works of Cicero, Herodotus, Shakespeare, Milton, and "the Oxford or Cambridge Examination Papers for 1859."[23]

A supporter of the ACS who believed that only "pure" Africans should emigrate; a longtime citizen of Liberia who despised the mulatto ruling class; a Christian who believed that Islam was perhaps better suited to Africans than was Christianity; and a scholar of the Western "classics" who fought fiercely to preserve indigenous African cultures, Blyden was a multidimensional thinker living in binary contexts: native African / ruling mulatto; black / white; and Christian / heathen. As a historical theorist, Blyden favored a view that might be characterized as racialized particularism, a belief that racial distinctions are (or should be) permanent, and that each race has a distinctive role to play in world history. Given that he was raised in the strict Calvinist Dutch Reformed Church, it is little wonder that Blyden's outlook was thoroughly providential: "In the music of the universe," he wrote in

1887, "each shall give a different sound, but necessary to the grand symphony."[24]

If the orchestra needed many instruments, Blyden felt most connected to the particular song of Africa. He believed in the importance of racial purity, so much so that he tried to convince ACS agents that only pure-blooded Africans should be allowed to emigrate to Liberia. His desire for purity also contributed to his intense hatred of the mulatto ruling elite and his conviction that missionary activity ought to be focused on native Africans rather than on new settlers. Blyden saw a direct link between a biologically based definition of race and moral behavior: "For thousands of years before Ethiopia had been meddled with by any exotic interference her people were described as long-lived, tall and handsome; and this physical perfection was the basis of moral excellence."[25] He believed that physical dilution had contributed to moral dilution, an opinion shared by later pan-Africanists such as Marcus Garvey, as well as by many white racists. Blyden therefore promulgated a distinctive definition of racial history, a one-drop philosophy in reverse, in which interracial children had fallen from their original pure state and were no longer considered full members of the community.

From this premise followed his understanding of religious difference in Africa. Because he took the creation of racial identity as his historical touchstone, religious adherence flowed from this as a secondary and less determinative component of collective identity. There had to be one religion that was appropriate for the African race. If Africans in their original purity were morally perfect, after all, they must have adhered to the most appropriate religion. As a Christian, however, Blyden still believed that the Christian message surpassed cultural particularities; over the course of his life he struggled to distill the essence of Christianity, to find the elements of his faith that transcended differences of time and space.

Although Blyden revered pure African ethnicity, he found indigenous religious practices abhorrent. In 1887 he published *Christianity, Islam, and the Negro Race*, a compilation of essays that explored the interrelations of sacred history, religious faith, and racial identity. Islam attracted him, in part, because it represented an appropriately religious alternative to a "hoary and pernicious" paganism and an African alternative to a Christianity that had been tainted by Euro-American mores. Muslims "are without doubt the most influential people on the continent, and they cannot be ignored," he noted. Their worship, moreover, fit well into his sense of what constituted appropriate religious reverence. During a visit to Muslim towns in the interior of Sierra Leone, Blyden remarked on the seriousness and piety of the population. The evenings were particularly quiet, "entirely undisturbed by those terpsichorean performances, which, in most pagan towns, as soon as the sun disappears, drive away sleep from the weary traveller. In Mohammedan communities here all foolish dancing is prohibited. The only music I heard was vocal and of a religious character." He also expressed appreciation for the Muslim love of history and tradition that meshed with his own Abrahamic theology: "They hold the language of the Koran in the greatest veneration. They affirm that it is the language which was spoken by Adam, Seth, Noah, Abraham, Ishmael, Isaac and Jacob; that it was introduced into Arabia by Abraham and Ishmael."[26] Islam served an important historical and religious function for Africans, raising them out of the degradation of paganism to a higher moral ground.

Yet Blyden, despite his renunciation of his own Presbyterian ordination in 1866, did not view Islam as an endpoint. It was merely a necessary historical steppingstone for Africans. Muhammed, Blyden averred, will "prove a servant of Christ." Christ, of course, first had to be reconceived in the likeness of Africa. Blyden was increasingly bothered by the conflation of European cultural mores (dress, names, customs) with the worship of Christ. The Christian Church is not true religion, he argued, because it has been so "travestied and diluted," weighted down with the cultural accretions of white values. He thereby distinguished between the spirit of Christ and the historical development of Christianity, the latter a tale of enslavement and the enforcement of cultural imitation that Blyden so wanted to disavow. Liberia, he came to believe, should be Christian "in the Bible sense, in the theological sense." But it must do this "without the instruments called Churches, which European genius and necessities have invented, but which, for us, are only ornaments and the means of confusion and disintegration. . . . Liberia, in a word, can have religion without dogmatism—Christ without the church."[27]

By 1908, when he published *African Life and Customs*, Blyden's growing cultural particularism had led him closer to a belief that all cultures have their own manifestations of one universal faith. He cited the noted philologist and scholar of comparative religions Max Müller to assert that a foundational Christian faith could serve as a sort of religious essence that might still vary widely from place to place. He married this notion to a commitment to African originary preeminence: true religion, he affirmed, began in Ethiopia and gradually traveled to Egypt and down the Nile. Cultural dilution explained the Euro-American failure to recognize the essential truth of African belief systems. In this way, Blyden was able to meld pure religion and pure race into a historical narrative that placed Africans at the point of origin. All other cultures were, in a sense, faint replicas of that original perfection.[28]

It is difficult to see any place in this scheme for an exodus by the children of Israel. Rather, Blyden envisioned in Africa a return to Eden—or at least a return to a society in which those closest to that pure religious and racial state of nature, "untouched either by European or Asiatic influence," would take the lead.[29] Yet Blyden's intellectual trajectory remained squarely within a Western classical tradition. The fact that he used Müller's comparative philology, an intellectual model premised on the assumption that Euro-American societies represented the cultural apex of human development, as a lens through which to understand the evolution of African religions reveals how wedded he was to Euro-American scholarly paradigms.[30]

In January 1909 Blyden addressed the senate chamber at Monrovia about the state of the republic, and he spoke of the role that emigrants would play in the life of the country. American migrants have been a boon for Liberia, he stressed, and they have rendered Liberians far better off than civilized Africans in the European colonies on the continent:

> We bring with us the spoils of the house of bondage—a prestige of civilization with many of its useful appliances. We have shown to the aborigines the example of national organization, weak as it has been. They know that we are returned exiles, their own kith and kin, from a distant land. They know that we laboured in that land under serious disadvantages. But they see us, on our own initiative, establishing settlements, building substantial houses, planting farms, and enacting laws under which life and property are secure. . . . We are the main, if not the only, channel through which they have held intercourse with the outside world.

Despite the admirable example of the emigrants, Blyden still worried that the natives were not acting on their own initiative, that they were "slaves to foreign ideas." He longed for a Liberia in which emigrants and native Africans could be united in one community: "We must merge ourselves in the indigenous forces of the land and become one with them in a vast body social, political, and religious. They are ours and we are theirs."

If native Africans were slaves to foreign ideas, then they, too, needed an exodus from intellectual dependence. Religious faith served as a shorthand of sorts for Blyden's ideal of cultural union, and his efforts to find a common religious language reflected his desire for collective unanimity. But achieving this Canaan was a difficult task, and clearly the old missionary model of Christian conversion had not worked. "Missions after Missions have been established and Missions after Missions have gone down, leaving not a rack behind," he argued. Yet he would not give up the concept of Christianity's providing the basis for cultural coherence. He called on Liberians to find a way to promote Christianity without the trappings of the church. To gain Christ for Africa, he concluded, the country must "nationalize" Christ as the Europeans had done: "We must make Christ an African."[31]

Blyden's Liberian colleague Alexander Crummell shared equally in his passion to discern the future of Africa within a broad historical framework. Crummell claimed that he had always been possessed by Africa: "From my early childhood my mind was filled with facts and thoughts about Africa and my imagination literally glowed with visions of its people, its scenery, and its native life."[32] Born in New York City to free African-American parents, Crummell attended the Oneida Institute and Yale Seminary, and then trained privately for the Episcopal priesthood, into which he was ordained in 1844. Crummell also became the first African American to graduate from Cambridge University, receiving his A.B. at Queen's College in 1853. Shortly thereafter he left for Liberia, where he remained for nearly twenty years, working as an educator, farmer, and missionary. In 1872 he returned to the United States and settled into a position as pastor of St. Luke's Episcopal Church in Washington, D.C. Crummell continued to write and lecture widely, promoting support for African missions and development. He also helped to establish the American Negro Academy in 1897, a group dedicated to the historical and sociological study of the race.[33]

Crummell's understanding of the perseverance of race in human history closely resembled Blyden's. The scholars agreed that races are human com-

munities that have particular roles to play in world history, and that the time
for the African was near. As Crummell put it, history seems to be "converg-
ing, in this our day, towards the continent of Africa." Although Crummell
believed that a race was a biological entity, he did not share Blyden's concern
for an original physiological purity. Crummell attributed races to God because they were "like families . . . the organisms and the ordinance of God;
and race feeling, like the family feeling, is of divine origin. . . . Indeed, a race
is a family." Influenced greatly by the historical trajectory of the Hebrew
Scriptures, Crummell believed that nations (a term he sometimes used in-
terchangeably with "races") were subject to the "disciplinary and retributive
economy" of divine will. God has his hand in all things, Crummell asserted,
and he leads some nations to ruin because of their sins, and chastises others
as a way of preparing them for destined greatness. "Negroes," because of
their cultural adaptability and capacity to assimilate into other racial settings, were clearly being groomed by God for future sacred work.[34]

Unlike Blyden, Crummell posited a distinction between race and culture.
Whereas for Blyden racial identity based on biology was intimately linked to
a particular cultural style (of which religion played one part), Crummell saw
race as an organism that could adapt in a variety of ways to new situations,
taking on new cultural characteristics. The term "civilization" did not have a
negative connotation for Crummell, as it did for Blyden; becoming "civilized" in the classical Western style only demonstrated the remarkable malleability of the African race—an evidence of its chosenness. In this sense, the
race represented a historical parallel, albeit "in a lower degree," to the case of
the Jews. Still, Crummell held out for natural religiosity as an immutable racial characteristic. In descriptions of Africa published in the Episcopal organ
Spirit of Missions in the 1870s, he emphasized the spiritual beauty of Africans, seeing in them "very clear evidences of the presence and recognition of
the main institutes of natural religion." The people were superstitious, he
admitted, "but their superstition is but a thin incrustation; for immediately
beneath a thin surface one finds the ideas of GOD, His providence." Unlike
Blyden's universal religious sensibility, Crummell's "natural religion" was decidedly Christian. Crummell had absolutely no use for Islam or indigenous
religions, and he believed that the task of evangelization meant bringing
out the Christian essence residing just beneath the surface of African heathenism.[35]

In keeping with his reliance on the Hebraic model of historical progression, Crummell urged New World Africans to heed the example of the Jews and flee Egypt. In "Emigration, an Aid to the Evangelization of Africa," a sermon preached to Barbadian emigrants in 1863, he urged listeners to forget the horrors of enslavement, the "partial pictures of many a sad tale from the lips of your fathers and mine," and to "turn . . . to another and fairer page." Colonization was a fact of human existence from the beginning, he pointed out, not an exception: as evidenced by Noah's sons having been scattered over the earth, God used such movements in a providential way. In this case, the New World Israelites could aid in the enlightenment of their African brethren:

> We have gone out as the immigrants of this republic to the shores of heathen Africa, and re-created these free institutions and a nation modelled after your own. . . . The black race in this country, as they increase in intelligence, will have to think of Africa, will have to contemplate the sad condition of that vast continent; will have to consider their relation to the people of Africa; must per force do something for Africa.[36]

Crummell's employment of the Exodus model highlights the curious and conflicted relationship the reformer had to historical memory. He urged African Americans *not* to look back on the flesh-pots of Egypt. "For 200 years the misfortune of the black race has been the confinement of its mind in the pent-up prison of human bondage," he explained to the graduating class at Storer College in Harper's Ferry, West Virginia, in 1885. Given that he was at the time situated on one of the most hallowed spots of African-American memory, the site of John Brown's ill-fated 1859 stand against slavery, Crummell's reference to the "morbid, absorbing, and abiding recollection" as a veritable continuation of enslavement had a curious ring. He himself was possessed by history: what was the Exodus model if not a chronicle of God's relationship with the Jews over time and space? What Crummell seemed to be calling for was selective remembrance, a remembering that would strengthen rather than diminish the community. Slavery was not a useful memory, for Crummell, and it did not contribute to the development of the nation.[37]

Other paradigms, however, proved more constructive in building up the new Canaan in Africa. In a lecture before the Common Council and citizens of Monrovia in 1855, delivered in honor of Liberian Independence Day, Crummell placed the future of this promised land within a biblical framework, edged by the classical Western tradition. Although all human beings came from two original progenitors, after Noah's curse the world was divided into "three distinct forms of race and family." African peoples are part of one of those original nations, but they are also, he insisted, religious and cultural "heirs" of the Jews, the Greeks, and the Romans, cultures whose spirits form "the elements of our faith, of our culture, and of our national rule and State polity." Again rejecting the notion that race and culture were necessarily linked, Crummell told his audience that indeed, their society resulted from "the ceaseless energy of mind and body of all past nations."[38]

The speaker was insistent, however, that Liberia must be a Christian community, and part of the work of evangelization would be to bring native Africans back to their true religious nature. Here selective memory became extremely important for communal development. Unlike Blyden and many other African-American historians, Crummell had no interest in the glories of ancient Egypt, Babylonia, or Phoenicia; they were all debased cultures, "saturated with the spirit of brutality, lust, and murder."[39] Human civilization, in an important sense, began with the birth of Christ, and it was this legacy, Crummell asserted, that Liberians must claim as their inheritance:

> Our religion is the *Christian religion,*—PROTESTANT, God be praised, in its main characteristics; and it is harmonious, in all its utterances, as the music of the spheres. Our civilization, in its elements, is that of the world's Christendom. . . . and it makes as *our* inheritance, although of other blood and race than theirs, the large common sense, the strong practicalness, the pure and lofty morals, the genuine philanthropy, the noble wisdom, and all the treasures of thought and genius, with which ENGLAND has blessed the world.

In 1855, a point at which Great Britain had freed all slaves in the empire but the United States was still gripped tightly in the death throes of the slave system, it is no wonder that Crummell looked to England as a political and moral model. It represented the best of what a Christian society could be, a civilization that embraced true Christian values and spread them liberally around the globe.[40] Only when Liberia—and, by extension, all those of African descent—embraced Christ's legacy would the continent gain its true spiritual inheritance.

Blyden, Crummell, and Delany all articulated hard-edged critiques of American political history and life. They looked to prior moments (ancient Africa, biblical history) or alternative models (England) to see how Africa might best fulfill its promise. But American nationalism had its proponents in nineteenth-century African-American communities despite the various critiques leveled by black expatriates. A significant number of African Americans expressed deep appreciation for the role that the United States was playing in the unfolding of Africa's destiny. Recall Daniel Peterson, the AME minister whose 1854 journey compelled him to urge his African-American readers to repent so that the Ethiopian promise of Psalm 68 might be fulfilled. Unlike Blyden, Peterson had no official ties to the ACS. Yet he, too, argued vehemently for the importance of emigration to Africa. At the same time, however, he defended the many white philanthropists in the United States who were helping the cause. Peterson, whose trip to Africa had been sponsored in part by white benefactors, remained grateful for their help, although he was not unmindful of the three million Africans still in bondage.[41]

Peterson, like Blyden and Crummell, was perched metaphorically between Exodus and Ethiopia. His view of American philanthropical support was informed by the Exodus story, although his reading of that event brought him to a conclusion very different from that of Blyden and Crummell. Israelite enslavement, he argued, had been considerably more brutal than what Africans endured in the United States:

> The sufferings of the Israelites in Egypt, were much greater than ours in this country. Their children were put to death by oppression, and they lost the covenant of their forefathers which they made with the Lord. But Moses was an instrument in the hands of the Lord, in leading the people out of bondage. Those people were among the heathens, but we are in the midst of Christians: their taskmasters made no provision for improving the condition of the sufferers, but there is good provision

made for us by the true friends of the colored race, comprising many comforts and conveniences. . . . There is another advantage which you have over the Hebrews. The rulers of Egypt did not aid them in their religious worship by providing churches or any other conveniences: but the Christian community of these United States has ever been, and still is, very kind and benevolent towards us in all cases. They have ever aided us very kindly in obtaining places of worship for the religious instruction of our unfortunate people.[42]

Black Americans were not quite like the Jews, the AME preacher insisted. They had the resources of Christianity at their disposal, and these they would bring with them back to Africa. Peterson was more concerned with the matter of unity, with how African Americans and Africans would become one people in Liberia. Like Crummell, he compared the natural surroundings and resources of Liberia to Eden. But in his recounting, Liberian society most closely resembled Israel after the return from Babylon, not from Egypt. On December 22, 1853, during his stay in Monrovia, he preached on Psalms 133, "Behold, how good and how pleasant it is for brethren to dwell together in unity." That particular choice of text spoke volumes about Peterson's concerns for the new republic. Thought to have been written in the post-exilic period in Israel, the psalm stresses the problems of collective disunity; the author calls for a revival of the togetherness of the pre-exilic period, when families and communities were more stable than after the return. For Peterson (as for the prophet Jeremiah), the wickedness of Israel itself prevented the communion he so desired: "The great evils which we have suffered came upon us, our forefathers, and our nation, on account of our disobedience, rebellion, and neglect of God. Dear brethren, the remedy for these evils is righteousness and truth." Then, and only then, he noted, "Ethiopia will stretch her hands unto God, and the islands shall be filled with his glory."[43]

Blyden, Crummell, and Peterson, three African-American Christians from disparate denominational traditions, came to varied understandings of Africa, its past and future, and its significance for African Americans. At a time of unsettling political shifts and increased intolerance of black freedom of movement in the United States, African Americans looked to their religious and racial loyalties for new perspectives on their present and future. Configured in slightly different ways, those loyalties produced markedly different evaluations of historical development, the essence of communal identity, the role of the U.S. government in African "progress," and even Christianity itself. Nonetheless, all three men wrestled with the same set of tropes: Eden, Exodus, and Ethiopia; salvation and rescue; progress and civilization. All three endeavored to link their understandings of sacred history to the endurance of an oppressed people. And all hoped that Africa could provide a future for that people as well as a past. Africa could be both Eden *and* Canaan. And its future would redeem and reunify the race.

Emancipation dramatically transformed the lives of African Americans and began to reshape their collective stories and aspirations. Most obviously, the war's end signaled the beginning of different legal and social relationships between blacks and whites in the United States, on terms that would be worked out for decades to come. But the new political status of four million free blacks also necessitated myriad adjustments internal to black collective life. It forced a rethinking of the relationship between Northern and Southern blacks, since the former were no longer the sole advocates for their enslaved kin. It compelled different ways of characterizing community, based on the experiences and opportunities of newly freed men and women. It also affected the relationship of African Americans to Africa. Since they were no longer living in Egypt, the paradigm of exile or migration to Canaan did not carry the same force it once had. Africa was still significant, but it was incumbent on diasporic Africans to figure out just what it now meant.

Emigrationist rhetoric and advocacy died down during the exhilarating early days after Emancipation. Inspired by the martyred President Lincoln, whom many envisioned as their own Moses, African Americans believed that it might finally be possible to build Canaan on American soil. They set about to do just that, forming families, founding churches, establishing schools, and running for elected office. During the late 1860s and 1870s few narratives about Africa appeared, perhaps because blacks were so busy building the lives about which they had previously only dreamed. But that heady optimism was short-lived. After the failure of Reconstruction in the 1870s, as hopes were dashed for the racially egalitarian regeneration of the

South, the American missionary movement focused on Africa with new intensity. Exodus once again became a live prospect.

Perhaps because of the brief glimpse of equality afforded by Reconstruction, the late nineteenth-century emigration movement looked decidedly different from its antebellum predecessor. By the 1880s the push for Africa was no longer dominated by the now-moribund ACS but by African-American ministers and politicians. Black churches themselves played a much greater role, although disputes, sometimes tendentious, continued within sanctuary walls over the wisdom of emigration. Most profoundly, the movement now had a decidedly Southern accent. Southern black schools and periodicals established in the late nineteenth century furnished an ideal way to publicize, raise money for, and attract emigrants and missionaries to the cause. As black organizations shifted their efforts, resources, and leadership southward after Emancipation, the leading voices discussing Africa increasingly were those who had witnessed the horrors of slavery for themselves.[44]

Between 1877 and 1900 at least 116 African Americans served as missionaries in Africa: sixty-eight in Liberia, twenty in the Congo, thirteen in Sierra Leone, six in South Africa, three in Nigeria, three in Mozambique, and one each in Cameroons, Angola, and Rhodesia. Although the majority of missionaries were black, the effort remained, for the most part, an interracial cause. Fifty of those who served were sponsored by predominantly white churches, and sixty-five by black denominations. Most missionaries were Southern, well-educated, and had learned about Africa in black colleges and seminaries in the postwar years. They had been encouraged by white teachers and sponsors, as well as by the work of prominent African-American spokesmen such as Blyden and Crummell. White and black missionary advocates mounted speaking tours at black colleges in the 1880s and 1890s, reiterating the promise that Ethiopia would redeem the world and, like Crummell and Blyden, arguing that missionary work was the "duty" of African-American Christians. Their excitement generated the formation of "Friends of Africa" clubs in Freedman's Aid schools by the 1890s, beginning at Methodist-sponsored New Orleans University in 1890. In 1894 a white Methodist minister established the Stewart Missionary Foundation in Atlanta, organized to train African-American missionaries for Africa. Co-directed by the white president of Gammon Theological Seminary in Atlanta and a black professor, John W. E. Bowen, the foundation subsidized essay and hymn-writing contests, collected an African library, provided fellowships, and sponsored a Congress on Africa in 1895. Study of Africa became part of the standard curriculum at schools such as Wilberforce (AME) in Ohio and Lincoln Seminary (Presbyterian) in Pennsylvania, where students were required to write essays about the continent as a way of fostering interest.[45]

The African missionary enterprise consisted primarily of men, especially in its early phases. With the exception of Amanda Berry Smith, who was forced to look abroad for material support of her evangelistic tours in the 1870s, few women ventured into the mission field before the late 1880s without a husband to serve as the missionary figurehead. Those who did received little backing for their efforts. Yet postbellum black church women raised far more money for missions than did their male counterparts, a situation that became the subject of debate and conflict in many churches. In 1874, for instance, a group of bishops' wives in the AME Church formed the Women's Mite Missionary Society, an organization that quickly became the chief denominational fundraising arm for mission activity. The society initially devoted its labors to supporting missionaries in Haiti, but in the late 1880s Bishop Daniel Payne, seeing an opportunity, enlisted its support for work in Sierra Leone. In 1893 the society held its first national convention.[46] By the 1910s and 1920s a new generation of female recruits, women trained mostly in Southern black schools, catalyzed the creation of a rhetoric of sisterhood among black women in the mission field. Their labors as teachers and healthcare workers thereafter became an indispensable component of missionary efforts. But in the late nineteenth century women's voices were almost entirely absent from the public narration of Africa.

The call to Africa after Emancipation also necessitated a shift of the biblical paradigms that had impelled the antebellum movement. If Egypt had been defeated, then what would become of the Israelites? The binary relationship of Africa and African Americans now became a triad. There were, in the minds of many black leaders, at least three different groups of "Ethiopians": Northern blacks, freed Southerners, and Africans. What would it mean for all of them to reach the promised land? Could they do it together and form one racial community? If an exodus out of the United States was still necessary, who would lead the way and how could one build Canaan? In the growth of new missionary organizations such as the Consolidated American Baptist Missionary Convention, formed in Richmond in 1866, we see a renewed effort to come to terms with the past as a way of moving forward. In the minutes of their annual meeting for 1877, the convention targeted Africa as their primary field of influence, because "God signals the intelligent men of our race, to begin to occupy the land, lest the African soon become a wandering Jew, without Judea, and without Jerusalem."[47]

Missions and emigration supporters continued to frame the cause in historical terms, but the past took on new meaning. The stalwart ACS-backer Beverly Page Yates, in a letter advocating emigration to Liberia in 1873, argued that *"a peculiar claim then rests upon us"*:

> The work must be done by *us*, and done by you, brethren in America, who are enjoying the glorious advantages of education. . . . Here is a great land, and there is a great race, to be elevated, enlightened, and saved. . . . You will not come as the prodigal son, wasted, weary, and wretched; but like the Jews, hastening from the land of Egypt, laden with precious and valuable spoils. You are one in origin with us, and with the benighted tribes in whose behalf we plead—one in interest and one in worldly destiny.[48]

Yates adroitly used the Exodus tale to a slightly different end, meshing it with the Ethiopian prophecy to call for missionary volunteers. In a great reversal of worldly fortune, the lowest caste in the United States, the ex-slaves, would become the redeemers of Africa. Black Americans figured as divine agents of redemption, not merely the victims of "Egyptian" aggression. Simultaneously, Yates cast African Americans as Israelites fleeing Egypt—this time carrying much more than manna. White supporters, convinced that Africa was indeed a grave for Euro-Americans, also adopted the Ethiopian prophecy as a way to recruit African Americans. The white missionary C. L. Woodworth, speaking before an audience at Atlanta University in 1888, asserted that slavery had been part of the divine plan, preparing an elect in America who would then spread the gospel to Africa. This historical interpretation, known as the theory of "Providential Design," became a common theme of missionary rhetoric by 1900.[49]

Yates's plea also invoked another powerful communal narrative that had figured as part of African-American national memory: the echoes of John Winthrop, the leader of the Protestant mission to New England. Just as the Puritans had been chosen by God and had a particular obligation to fulfill, African Americans were subject to a "peculiar claim"—by God, by virtue of racial affinity, or perhaps by both. They were the chosen people, the New Israelites, called upon now to serve as an example for the benighted souls of Africa. Appealing simultaneously to racial and national loyalties, the tale of the New Israelites would lead black Christians across the ocean.

By the 1890s, black students in Southern schools and members of black churches could count on regular visits from returned missionaries on fundraising tours who described their adventures and championed the cause of Africa. Just as the historical paradigm had changed, so had the types of people who responded to the call. This younger cohort of advocates, a group that included the first black female missionaries to Africa, expressed less of a commitment to a pan-African vision than did their older comrades. With a few notable exceptions, they were at once more practical in their approach, more committed to the workings of the denominational bureaucracies that had sent them forth, and more concerned with immediate and formulaic priorities. Generally these narrators had no trouble identifying the saved and civilized (American Christians) from the unsaved and uncivilized (African heathens). This shift reflected, at least in part, the harder-edged scientific racialized ideology and the imperialist cant of the 1890s that further bifurcated renderings of race and nation. Rather than abstract theories about history and race, these later writers provided vivid descriptions, compelling anecdotes, and sometimes lurid tales of the dark continent—a "meet the natives" style of entertainment and education rolled into one. Good publicists all, missionary writers narrated the history of Africa and America to vast numbers of African Americans at the opening of the new century.

While their aims were ultimately serious, their messages were often delivered with the aplomb of the showman. In an age when P. T. Barnum's circus garnered enormous profits parading exotic animals and humans from Central Africa around the country, audiences black and white clamored for a glimpse of anything from the "dark continent." This was the high imperial era of the museum and the historical pageant, two sites where American and European audiences could gaze upon carefully orchestrated representations of "primitive" peoples and civilizations. Those performances reflected back for domestic viewers what they already knew about themselves: they were civilized people who lived in the most advanced society the world had ever seen. For African Americans, of course, this mirrored message was complicated by racial affiliation, by the knowledge that those poor dark souls on the other side of the glass or across the stagelights were not simply "other" than themselves. But the images also entertained, amused, and delighted, and black missionaries were smart enough to capitalize on the pleasure— and the concomitant dollars—they could generate.

Two of the most notable of these impresarios were Thomas L. Johnson and William Sheppard. Thomas Johnson inspired immediate sympathy for Africa in audiences from Denver to London in the two decades before 1900. Born in 1836 in Rock Raymon, Virginia, the son of a slave mother and a free father, Johnson was freed after the fall of Richmond and later became a Baptist preacher in Denver and Chicago. Intent on delivering the message of Christ to Africa and encouraged in his interests by British sympathizers whom he had met in Chicago, Johnson traveled first to London in 1876. In his memoir he later claimed to have always held a special love for Great Britain. ("We had the idea on the plantation that the Queen was black. . . . We had never imagined that a great ruler, so kind to coloured people, could be otherwise than black.") There, in the hands of supportive white Baptists, he received missionary training and his first formal education.[50] In 1878 he and his wife headed off to establish a mission station in Bakundu, Cameroon, under the auspices of the British Baptist Missionary Society. Within six months Johnson's wife had died, and he, seriously ill, had to be carried out of the interior on a stretcher and sent back to London. Warned by physicians not to return to Africa, Johnson instead served for the next several decades as one of the most ardent African boosters, giving lectures and eventually publishing his memoirs. That volume, significantly revised and expanded over the years, ran through more than half a dozen editions in the United States and England by 1909.

A moving speaker in the simple, heartfelt manner of his mentor Charles Haddon Spurgeon (1834–1892), Johnson became known for his affecting speeches. "He preaches Christ with a simplicity, an unction, and an earnest-

ness that win all hearts," wrote the Rev. T. Hamilton of York Street Presbyterian Church in Hillsborough, Ireland. Throughout Great Britain Johnson attracted enormous crowds at missionary meetings, and supporters likened
the pathos of his renderings of slavery to the most touching scenes in *Uncle
Tom's Cabin*. Back in the United States, Johnson helped organize an African
missions movement among black Baptists in the Western states and U.S.
territories. He served as its financial agent, speaking before large and receptive gatherings of African Americans throughout the West and Midwest. A
writer for the *Chicago Herald* described him as a "born entertainer." He traveled the country wearing a bright red fez and flowing African robes, which,
in combination with his long pyramidal shaped hair, cut a remarkable figure. Advance publicity promised that he would "exhibit many African curiosities, including maps, idols, pictures of natives, &c.," and that the missions
advocate would "don the African dress, and sing in the African language."[51]

William Sheppard's performance took a different tack. Like Johnson,
Sheppard was from Virginia, and he, too, gained fame by offering a story of
affiliation—as well as material elements of African culture and plenty of
drama—to his audiences. But his presentation was decidedly more flam-
boyant and heroic than Johnson's evocation of the "authentic" simplicity of
the ex-slave. Born in the Shenandoah Valley town of Waynesboro, Virginia,
in 1865, Sheppard enjoyed the best opportunities that the son of an African-
American barber could expect: a Presbyterian Sunday school education followed by formal training at both Hampton Institute and Stillman College.
With much fanfare and celebration of their interracial efforts, Sheppard and
a white colleague, Samuel Lapsley, were sent to the Congo in 1890 by the
Southern Presbyterian Church. Lapsley died within the first two years, but
Sheppard remained for the better part of two decades and built a substantial
mission station in Central Africa. After his "discovery" of the long-sought
kingdom of Kuba in the early 1890s, Sheppard was inducted into the Royal
Geographical Society, and on subsequent speaking tours he regaled audiences with his exploits. The self-styled "Black Livingstone" toured the South
with his former Hampton Institute classmate Booker T. Washington in 1893,
with Sheppard receiving top billing in local black newspapers. After that
campaign some half-dozen young black students, stirred by his message, returned with him to Africa. His fame, enhanced in the early 1900s by his vo-

cal opposition to Belgian atrocities in the Congo, spread throughout the Southern black population.[52]

Part of Sheppard's strategy was to bring Africa back to America, completing the circle of cultural influence. Sheppard claimed that the missionaries sought to convert the African soul "without changing the African heart."[53] He would, in turn, bring that heart home to Southern blacks. And deliver it he did, with famous anecdotes about buying and eating dozens of eggs as a way of ingratiating himself with the natives, stories of big game hunts and near-death experiences with wild animals, and plenty of African artifacts. In his journey to the interior of Congo, Sheppard had discovered one of the last of the ancient courts of Central Africa, a civilization of ornate and lavish artwork, elaborate monarchical and judicial systems, and clean, orderly streets. He returned with, quite literally, piles of souvenirs of his extended visit—pottery, weavings, and metalwork that toured the United States with him. He donated a collection to Hampton, to which he added over the years until it became one of the largest assemblages of Kuba art in the world. Sheppard entertained audiences with a dramatic re-creation of the time his life had been threatened by a prince brandishing a ritual knife. At just the right moment, Sheppard pulled out a replica of the blade and whirled it around, imitating the gruesome execution that he had narrowly escaped. With his dramatic flair, it is no wonder that Sheppard attracted large crowds wherever he went.[54]

The contrasts between the two men were striking: Johnson, the ex-slave who celebrated his humble origins and spoke in sentimental terms of saving the barbaric Africans for Christ; and Sheppard, the hunter who dressed in a white pith helmet and celebrated his heroic exploits in engagements with the natives. In different ways, both men simultaneously embraced and exoticized Africa, and both employed familiar racial narratives to inspire their audiences to action. Thomas Johnson had not spent more than half a year in Africa but always referred to himself in two ways: as the "ex-slave" and as the "African missionary." He literally put on the garments of the place he denoted as the "land of my fathers" and used maps to acquaint his audiences with the continent. His narrative was a tale of a people sunk in ignorance, in need of rescue just as Southern blacks like Johnson had been saved. He juxtaposed the shackles of enslaved New World Africans with the fetishes and idols of the "enslaved" heathens in Africa. The implication could not have been clearer: African Americans had a particular obligation to rescue Africans from the bondage of life without Christ.[55]

Sheppard's double message drew on very different collective memories and yearnings. His white linen clothing and his daring deeds celebrated U.S. national notions of progress and the triumph of masculine prowess, in line with the European and Euro-American explorers he so admired. But in the continental interior Sheppard recovered the ancient and glorious civilizations that African Americans had always known existed, those African societies that would prove, once and for all, the temporarily obscured potential of the race. In retrieving that grandeur in physical form for African Americans, in artistry, textiles, and photographs, Sheppard delivered confirmation of their own illustrious history. The dramatic rendition of his initial encounter with the Kuba king who immediately embraced the missionary, believing him to be a reincarnated member of the Kuba elite, fulfilled the fantasies of many African Americans about what it would be like to return to the homeland. "You are 'muana mi,'" explained the king, "one of the family." Although he protested consistently, Sheppard later mused, "They knew me better than I knew myself."[56]

Sheppard and Johnson were exceptional performers, and we might be tempted to dismiss their theatrics as entertainment with little impact on the hearts and minds of most African Americans. But they represented only the tip of the African promotional iceberg. From Arkansas to Georgia and north to New York, black church members and college students alike heard stories about Africa in the 1880s and 1890s. They read articles on missions or Liberian politics in the *Christian Recorder* or in one of the local black newspapers. Students might have written an essay or read a book (most of which were written by missionary boosters) that imparted some sense of African geography and history. The local chapter of the Women's Mite Missionary Society, the AME women's organization that raised money to support workers abroad, would have provided information about missionaries and what they were accomplishing in Liberia or the Congo. These occasions would have created great anticipation and excitement over the arrival of the returned missionary, perhaps Alfred Ridgel, who came to town and gave a talk about Africa and its importance for the local community. Perhaps the most striking news would have been the vivid and specific information about the African people, African cultures, and the land itself. Many African Americans, by the century's end, had never even seen an African. What did they look like? Where did they live? How did they dress? How did they act? The domestic demand for vibrant detail that brought Africa to life surged, and the diverse images that narrators employed as they described people, landscapes, and cultures created associations in the minds of their audiences, bringing them into common stories of a racial and religious sojourn.

Venturing to Congo in 1901, C. C. Boone later wrote a "little story" to refute the "many erroneous ideas held by the people at home in regard to African missions." Boone, a missionary and physician who received support from both the Lott Carey Baptist Foreign Missionary Convention and the American Baptist Foreign Mission Society of Boston, explored like a scientist, noting the flora and the fauna, discoursing about endemic fevers and diseases, and enumerating the "desires and appetites" of the coastal inhabitants, which he concluded were "very much like our own. Some like one thing and some want another." Boone framed his discussion of Congo as a naturalized paradise. "Think of a land of perpetual spring!" he exclaimed about the climate and geography. "No African can look out over those wealth-laden bowers without saying, 'Breathes there a man with soul so dead who never to himself hath said, this is my own, my native land!'"[57] Just as Haiti was figured as the Eden of the New World, Africa represented the original paradise.

Boone also had a clear aesthetic appreciation for native Africans: "Their language is the most euphonic and beautiful of any language that I ever studied; Hebrew and Greek not excepted." For a Christian, of course, unredeemed nature presented its challenges, some of which Boone discovered after reaching Mpalabala, his inland station. The natives in the interior, for all Boone's curiosity about them, emerged in his account as part of the darker, wilder, and more unpredictable side of the natural order, far removed from the civilization of African Americans or even those Africans living in coastal areas. His job, as he saw it, was to bring civilization and Christianity, to tame nature. But the environment proved menacing at times. One day, Boone related, he journeyed back to the station at dusk and got lost, wandering in the jungle until well after dark. He tried not to panic, although he realized that

"I was then in an awful condition; wet, tired and lost amidst the leopards, wolves and heathen." Spying a light in the distance, he came upon a group of natives who instead of helping him pulled out their knives. As Boone fled and struggled to make his way home, he described hearing the insistent beating of drums in the distance, a reminder that just beyond his small Christian town lay a vast expanse of moral and physical chaos.

Daniel Peterson's comparison of natives to other organic matter was less ominous and more direct: "The minds of the natives and the land are just alike while uncultivated. The lands want ploughing up and sowing down with grain, and the different kinds of herd grass, and it is necessary to cross the breed of their flocks and herds." Similarly, he argued, natives need the civilization of emigrants to cultivate them until "all become one people in manners, habits, and religion." For both Peterson and Boone, Africans, like other elements of the natural order, needed training to develop in concert with African-American emigrants.[58]

Extending the scientific metaphor, other narrators categorized various tribes according to their observable characteristics, such as dress, behavior, and language. On the one hand, this strategy complicated generalizations about the homogeneity of the continent and reintroduced African Americans to the notion of ethnic divisions within Africa. On the other hand, it also led to some oversimplifications, injecting a romanticized tribal consciousness into their accounts. William Sheppard instructed his audiences with helpful information and the latest racial categorizations, noting that the continent was divided into 683 tribes, "as they differ in name so they differ in habits, customs and conditions." He went on to offer some generalities nonetheless. "I grew very fond of the Bakuba and it was reciprocated," he reported. "They were the finest looking race I had seen in Africa, dignified, graceful, courageous, honest, with an open, smiling countenance and really hospitable."[59]

Whereas Sheppard and Boone described Africa as an untamed natural world, other narrators focused more intensely on African bodies. Crummell and Blyden had both emphasized the inherent beauty of African peoples; Crummell mentioned that "one of the first things which attracted my attention . . . was the general manly strength, symmetry and bodily beauty of the natives."[60] Later authors idealized the African as an example of physical perfection. Amanda Berry Smith (1837–1915), a traveling evangelist who worked for a number of years in Liberia in the 1880s, was especially entranced by the women. In her *Autobiography,* first published in 1893 and reissued several times within the decade, Smith marveled at everything she saw. Her travels had taken the preacher to many exotic places since 1870, including Italy, India, and Burma. God had been preparing her, however, for her most important work: "He had to send me to India to educate me a little before He could tell me to go to Africa." Although her principal labors kept her in Monrovia, in 1887 she visited Old Calabar, West Africa. There was much to be deplored, she thought, and the natives evinced no "sympathy with Jesus." The women were treated especially badly, she noticed, and the multiple wives of the chiefs and kings could not even leave their compound without permission. But they were beautiful people, and Smith displayed clear admiration in her evocative descriptions. Most of the women had "good features" and were "beautifully formed." Smith, with her plain, old-fashioned garb and commitment to a life of material simplicity, marveled at the rich silks and expensive accessories, especially those of the "head wife" of the king:

> We looked out, and here came through the town all the women, and this same woman, the king's wife, with two escorts on either side, and beautifully dressed; she had a handsome country cloth, with all sorts of colors, like Joseph's coat, wrapped about her; she was bathed and greased; she had rings in her ears, and bracelets on her wrists; her fingers were covered with rings, and rings on her toes and ankles. She looked beautiful! . . . They have some kind of grass they dye black, and it looks very much like hair; and she had on a head dress of this, beautifully curled, and she looked as beautiful as she could be. Then she had a great, big umbrella, red, and blue, and green and yellow striped. Oh, but she was a swell! And they took her through the town; they danced and sang; children, little boys and girls, and women.[61]

Less significant than the details of Smith's report are the associations that she and others made with what they saw. The queen's garments prompted a biblical parallel: they were "like Joseph's coat." To represent this scene to her readers, Smith placed the event within a narrative framework that she—and they—knew well, the story of the coat of many colors that Israel had made for Joseph (Genesis 37:3). That an advocate of holiness Methodism, a tradition typically repelled by ritual activity, attended so closely to the formal observance of the monarch's entrance indicates the intensity of Smith's interest in the spectacle. Several other observers also noticed the "regal" demeanor of natives. When the AME bishop and ardent emigrationist Henry McNeal Turner toured Sierra Leone in 1891, he was taken by the sight of Muslim "priests." Despite his aversion to their religious practices, he found himself won over by their physical bearing, which he likened to that of royalty: "These black Mohammedan priests, learned to kill, walking around here in their robes with so much dignity, majesty and consciousness of their worth, are driving me into respect for them. . . . What fools we are to suppose these Africans are fools!" The lawyer and minister T. McCants Stewart, who had taught briefly at Liberia College a decade earlier, remarked that the women "carry themselves like queens. . . . There she stands; and you involuntarily repeat what the queen of Sheba may have inspired Solomon to say, 'Thou art black and comely.'"[62]

There is a decided sense of awe in many of these accounts. Native Africans elicited a mixture of wonder, dread, and reverence from African Americans, and writers responded with an acuteness of observation that could be startling in its evocative power. Turner described a meeting with a woman known as the "Queen of the Greggree Bush," "with portly limbs, massive head, all bare except a cloth around the waist, hair done up in the most ornamental style, pure silver cuffs, leopard teeth tied and dangling to the elbows, fetish balls fastened to the rear part of the head, beads strung around the body, dressed to death after the fashion of the Gollah tribe." Turner, not one easily silenced, seemed at a loss for words to sum up the effect that the encounter had on him. "The woman looked frightful and pretty too," he concluded.[63]

The link among Africans, ceremony, and royalty broadly conceived had both personal and religious resonances for many African Americans, filling them with a conflicting set of emotions. Memories of ancient African kingdoms had long inspired black leaders, and the ceremonial accoutrements of the Haitian political structure animated intense interest even among those African Americans most committed to the blessings of evangelical piety and representative democracy. The scriptural logic of the Ethiopian prophecy, a passage that many African Americans took as sacred mandate, pointed directly to the prediction that "princes shall come out of Egypt." On a personal level, too, many black leaders in the nineteenth century traced their own family heritage to princes or kings in Africa. Was it such a leap, then, to link the race itself with a form of divine right? Implicitly, and sometimes explicitly, authors made the association clear to their audiences: this is our land. These are our families. Just like our ancestors, and just like our cousins, we are majestic, regal, and dignified.

Lurking as a subtext beneath many of these accounts was a growing debate, fueled by Euro-American historians, ethnologists, and others, about the "natural capacity" of the negro. Scholarly discussion about racial ability had a long and mostly ignoble history, but by the 1890s biologically based theories of race had hardened the terms of the argument. The emerging science of eugenics and the swelling violence toward African Americans in the Southern states cast an ominous shadow over blacks' hopes for eventual equality. Accusations of permanent inferiority were never far from the minds of black leaders, and such indictments shaped the ways missionaries narrated Africa. On board the ship that took him to Africa in 1891, Henry McNeal Turner overheard a conversation among a group of Europeans. "They all decided that Africa was forever doomed," he wrote, "that white men could not well live there and the black man, whether in Africa or elsewhere, was a failure. They could not understand why God should give the negro the richest spot on earth, and that her people should be the poorest specimens of humanity in the world. They reasoned the negro out as fit for nothing but to play, drink whisky and steal from the white race."[64]

Surely much of Turner's championing of Africa's greatness and his recounting of its peoples as the finest in the world was framed as an implicit counter to those shipboard insults. Alfred Ridgel also expressed open rejection of white indictments when he included in his account an extended section on history. "Prejudice and hatred for the negro race have actuated modern historians to use their utmost endeavors to rob the sons of Ham, not only of Africa, but of every other laudable achievement which they have gained," he lamented.[65] As much as African Americans drew on the intensity of a longstanding historical paradigm by affirming the nobility of their own origins, they were also persistently responding to the stated and unstated criticisms of Euro-American racial "science."

Demonstrations of African bodies as dignified and proud stood as a material refutation of these charges, and so it is no wonder that missionary promoters soon began bringing Africans back to the United States. Such display was, to be sure, part of the script of imperial exploration and discovery, beginning with Captain James Cook's delivery of a native Tahitian to the shores of England in the late eighteenth century. The testimony of a converted native had also played a powerful role in fueling the Protestant missionary movement to Hawaii in the early nineteenth century, when Henry Obookiah charmed the citizens of New Haven, Connecticut, with his "simple" Christian piety. But the display of proud *African* bodies, many missionary proponents assumed, incontrovertibly refuted white claims of inferiority. Moreover, it offered African-American audiences both a physical reunion with the past and the promise of a noble future. Time ran in several directions simultaneously when Etna R. Holderness, a Christianized Bassa woman from the interior of Liberia, spoke before the Congress on Africa at Gammon Theological Seminary in 1895. In between speeches by anthropologists, missionaries, philologists, and educators, Holderness told "the story of her past life" and her conversion to Christ. Her testimony presented a tale of progress from heathenism to Christianity, but her physical presence, that of a striking, very dark skinned woman dressed in modest and respectable Western garb, also promised racial reunion and redemption, a metamorphosis into a proud African Christian body—collectively and individually— free of the historical taint of enslavement.[66]

Not all Africans, of course, were like Etna Holderness, who appeared to meld African physical nobility with Christian civility. More often, stories of Africa depicted an untamed wilderness that called for improvement and even rescue. Most missionaries evinced extreme discomfort with the realities of life in Africa and chose, as did white missionaries, to live at both a geographic and a cultural remove from their native charges. Sheppard's arrival at his station in Luebo was typical: to shield him from the intense heat, the newly arrived missionary was rushed from one cool house to another, and he lived and ate with other missionaries rather than with native Africans. Despite his frequent jocularity with locals, Sheppard's narrative often depicts natives as menacing strangers hiding in the jungle or as servants, rendered invisible by status differences. In like manner, C. C. Boone detailed how the missionaries shipped in all of their food to Mpalabala from Montgomery & Ward in Chicago rather than eat indigenous items, and he complained frequently about the troubles that he and his wife had with the servant "boys."[67]

Many missionary narratives contained vivid images of unconverted Africans—without the trappings of Western clothing or even any dress at all. If the appeal of Etna Holderness is understandable because it demonstrated the malleability of the African character and its potential for being civilized, it is perhaps less obvious why African Americans would also produce and consume images of African savagery. Yet black as well as white spectators flocked to speeches, congresses, and meetings wherever Africa was mentioned, including the 1895 address on "Africa and America" advertised in the pages of the AME *Christian Recorder* and given by Dr. Joseph E. Roy, president of the World's Fair Congress on Africa in 1893 and field secretary for the American Missionary Association. "This unique representation of the progressive and educated Negro in America," the paper reported, "as contrasted with the native African in his uncivilized state, has been in great demand ever since it was presented at Chicago."[68]

Even at their most "uncivilized," the display of African bodies had critical psychic import for African Americans. Whereas Holderness demonstrated the power of Christian civilization to transform the individual—and thereby the collective—body, the photographs of warriors and cannibals bespoke a different message, but one no less crucial to the reimagining of African-American communities. *We are their better selves,* these representations seemed to suggest; *we are what they can become.* But even more than simply representing the gulf between African Americans and Africans, Christian and heathen values, or the glories of African ceremonialism, the exhibition of dark-skinned bodies—quite frequently nearly naked figures—communicated about race and sex. Late Victorian America expressed profound disquiet with black sexuality, an anxiety that emerged most malignantly in the racial stereotypes of fiction, cartoons, and other iconography that depicted black men as near-beasts consumed by lustful desires for white women. Black women, in turn, fought consistently against their own typecasting as oversexed and "unladylike."[69] Missionary literature furnished race authors with an opportunity to counter those negative images, to replace them in the popular imagination with new representations.

Even photographs of bare-breasted women and men with waist-strings could be transformed from potentially pornographic material to childlike and unself-conscious purity by being placed in a narrative of unspoiled innocence rather than wanton sexual license—and could thereby serve as an antidote to illustrations of black bodies mauling whites or swinging from trees.[70] Just the fact that African Americans found ways, however minor, to manage representations of African bodies reflected a significant shift of cultural power.

Gender also figured centrally in these narratives, inasmuch as African male bodies symbolized a masculine vigor that black Americans associated with collective racial politics. As in the rhetoric of Haitian emigration, African-American observers linked both masculine and race pride to the establishment of a nation, a physical space that would make manifest collective political power. Liberia had been founded not simply as a refuge for oppressed blacks but as a place for blacks to develop "real manhood in every sense of the word."[71] William Heard's second published volume on Africa made the link between masculine power and nationality even more explicit and countered the unstated assumption that enslavement called into question the potency of a community. He began his history of the founding of Liberia with the enslavement of Israel in Egypt, and continued with the observation that every nation had endured periods of subjection, including the early American settlers, many of whom were indentured servants.[72]

For Stewart and other missionaries, this masculine, racialized nationalism was thoroughly Christian. In his 1886 history of Liberia, Stewart heralded the advent of what he termed the "Christian Negro Nationality" in Africa. Africa had been the protector of Christianity in the ancient world, he asserted, "when Herod threatened to destroy its divine Founder." Now, African-American Christians needed in turn to reach out and help save the continent. Liberia was the natural gateway for such a movement, given its distinguished national history. With a "brave and heroic spirit," the early American settlers of the country had fought against their greatest obstacle, "a trying, a hostile, a deadly climate." He likened the eminence of the first Liberian president to that of both Toussaint L'Ouverture and George Washington. The negro had to redeem Africa himself, Stewart insisted. Whites could help, but they would never be able to "evangelize the Ethiopian" without the guidance of African Americans.[73] Thus Christianity and racial nationalism would work hand-in-hand, driven by the strength of black male leadership.

Other authors expressed concern about the potential for religious conflict between American "redeemers" and African natives. C. C. Boone's and Alexander Camphor's laments, for example, suggest that for them, one of the most salient facts about natives was not racial similarity but religious difference. Kinship or not, these evangels were in the business of saving souls. As Alexander Priestly Camphor put it, "Millions of little lambs . . . are lost in the thickets of heathen Africa, only waiting the tender Shepherd's care."[74] Those working among Americo-Liberians could at least rely on a minimal amount of Christian influence (although some complained about the lack of piety among the settlers), and several rarely ventured beyond the Monrovia city limits. Amanda Berry Smith worked in Liberia for five years before she toured any inland areas. But those like Boone and Sheppard whose work took them into "uncivilized" regions, and others who moved beyond the emigrant settlements, found the differences between Christians and non-Christians to be stark. They shared the widespread American sense that "civility" and Christianity were closely affiliated, and that matters of comportment such as modest dress, physically and emotionally restrained behavior, and the ability to eat at a table with a knife and fork were indications of morality. In a particularly notable and telling intercultural encounter, C. S. Smith visited King Bell of Cameroons Town in the early 1890s, offering as gifts his "Knight Templar accouterments and a banner representing the AME Church and its Sunday School Union." This present communicated clearly the legacy that Smith wished to carry—literally and figuratively—to the motherland.[75]

To attribute missionary responses in any simple way to cultural discomfort and Christian condescension would be to miss the complexity and pathos of their encounters with Africans. Sheppard found in the Kuba kingdom renewed ties with family, and he enthusiastically assumed the role of the reincarnated Kuba monarch. C. C. Boone, although he eschewed indigenous foods, attributed some of the forms of civilization he saw in Congo to ancient African societies rather than to the influence of white culture.[76] Africans and African Americans were kin. The question was, what kind of relationship did they have to one another? And how would they ultimately knit together this family? This tension was one of the great paradoxes that emerged from the African enterprise: black leaders, Christians all, viewed natives simultaneously as long-lost kin and long-lost sheep.

In response, African-American missionaries used narratives to parse the "essence" of African virtue from the chronology of history. One could simultaneously admire African bodies or luxuriant personal adornment and still lament the dark ignorance in which natives were (temporarily) mired. Their descriptions of religious differences displayed the most intricate understandings of this tension. After all, missionaries narrated these accounts to raise money for and awareness of Christianization, so they could not openly admire indigenous practices or Islamic rituals. But in important respects, their narratives changed the significance of religious difference by plotting it temporally in new ways. We might envision this best on a graph, in which time is measured along one axis and distance from the religious ideal of Christianity on another: African customs could be simultaneously admirable (at this particular point) and ignoble (because they were spatially so removed from Christianity). One could both appreciate and lament the state of the natives, and in turn understand that the differences between Africans and African Americans were chronological rather than moral. One people, separated by time and space, had proceeded along two separate spiritual paths. But in the narratives of missionaries they could once again be reunited.

African-American missionaries used this technique in a variety of ways, some more elaborately than others. Two examples illustrate the range of approaches. Alexander Priestly Camphor labored for eleven years as the president of the College of West Africa in Monrovia beginning in the late 1890s. A child of the Deep South in the first years of Emancipation, Camphor was born on a sugar farm in Louisiana and trained at a Freedman's Aid school. From there he went to New Orleans University, and later to graduate work at Gammon Seminary, Columbia University, and Union Theological Seminary in New York. Like many other missionaries, Camphor later reminisced that Africa had entered his heart and imagination at an early age. While studying at New Orleans he helped form a "Friends of Africa" chapter and served as its first president. At Gammon in the mid-1890s, Camphor participated in the height of the African missionary push. Shortly after graduation, he became an educator and missionary for the Methodist Episcopal Church and received an appointment in Monrovia. During and after his African sojourn he spoke frequently to groups in the United States about his experiences in Liberia and eventually published numerous books and essays.[77]

Like Thomas Johnson, Camphor believed that the mission to Africa would recapitulate in religious form the emancipation of African Americans, and that black Christians were under a special obligation to enact this rescue.[78] As part of his training at the missionary-minded Gammon, Camphor excelled in rhetoric that encouraged the American bearers of light to bring the gospel to darkest Africa. The winner of the first prize in the seminary student competition for his hymn of 1894, Camphor elaborated in his composition on the binaries of freedom versus bondage, sight versus blindness, and knowledge versus ignorance:

Africa, 'tis named, that country,
Far away from this bright shore,
Far removed from light and knowledge,
Far remote from Christian lore;
There, for many, many ages,
Ling'ring still in blackest night,
Africa, dark land of hist'ry,
Void of light, is void of light.

How can we remain contented
In illuminated homes,
While our brother gropes in darkness,
And in heathenism roams?
Should not his complete salvation
Be our earnest, prayerful plea,
Till that long-neglected country
Shall be free, yes, wholly free?[79]

After reaching Liberia, Camphor continued to maintain a sharp distinction between the "civilized" African Christians and the "superstitious" Muslims and pagans. His descriptions of local practices evoked a gothic sensibility as he portrayed the "dark and grewsome [sic] recesses" in which "the natives assemble for sacrifice and worship." Camphor's images suggested a people helplessly trapped by their own blindness: "Attracted by the awe which the mountain and huge rocks inspire, and the dark mystery which lurks about the spot, the Gibi people in their deep need for God imagine that they find Him here. In their groping search for some higher power than themselves, they make pilgrimages and offer sacrifices in this mountain, claiming protection and achieving victories over their enemies in war." His florid rhetoric notwithstanding, Camphor clearly wanted to elicit sympathy of a sort—not in the form of identification with the groping, blinded Gibi, but in the guise of compassion on the part of the American rescuer who could save those helpless victims: "Moral and spiritual night rests like a pall upon the people and continent. Rescue must come from without. Africa, in its superstition and degradation, can not save itself. With outstretched hands she pleads for help."[80]

Despite his conviction of spiritual superiority on the temporal plane, Camphor found points of moral connection. Contrary to popular opinion, he noted, Africans shared many laudatory qualities with African Americans, such as familial affection: "The close observer will find that there is a tender relation existing, especially between mother and children. We witnessed scenes that were pathetic and touching when parents had been separated from their children and were united again. Mothers take their children in their arms and lavish upon them the same affection that a civilized mother would." Presumably those domestic traits, so near to the heart of evangelical Protestants, would make for an easy and natural transition to Christianity; Camphor's evocation of familial sentiment urged his readers to see Africans as recognizable relatives rather than as unsaved heathens. Camphor filled his accounts with stories of individuals, tales that illustrated (without moral judgment) the myths, legends, and folklore of African peoples, but that also pointed to parallels with more familiar customs in the past. He asserted, for instance, that the naming practices of African groups were like those of the ancient Hebrews.[81] Camphor suggested that Africans displayed in nascent form the same qualities possessed by their New World cousins. He therein urged emotional and relational linkages, ushering Africans and African Americans into a common moral universe.

From a distinctly different direction, Henry McNeal Turner (1834–1915), a native of Abbeville, South Carolina, and bishop in the AME Church, portrayed Africans as both familiar relatives and exotic strangers. The two men's political positions on race, in some respects, could not have been more different. Unlike Camphor, who worked energetically within the biracial setting of the Methodist Episcopal Church and who rarely raised the matter of race overtly, Turner spent his career as a politician and minister advocating racial equality and protesting the racist conventions of the postbellum South. Whereas Camphor urged Christian missions to Africa, Turner by the 1890s advocated African emigration, which he saw as the only practical solution to a hopelessly oppressive situation in the United States.

Turner had been in the spotlight ever since his involvement in the celebration surrounding the embarkation of the *Azor*, one of the first ships of settlers to sail for Africa after the end of Reconstruction. He delivered a stirring speech to the crowd that inundated the wharf at Charleston, South Carolina, that day in 1878, and his words—sometimes witty, often biting, and always impassioned—had been rousing Southern blacks ever since.[82] In October 1891 he finally had the chance to visit Africa on an extended tour, and during his journey he wrote a series of letters home for public consumption. Turner's observations began on shipboard, where his first encounters challenged the prevalent racist assumptions that Africans (like African Americans) were uneducated and uncultured. He was deeply impressed by the "regular African" from Lagos he met, a young scholar who spoke five languages and read four, including Greek, Latin, and Arabic. But the landing in Sierra Leone disheartened him, as the crew members who rowed out to greet them were naked except for their small waistcloths. "Things look gloomy here," he said to his companion. Turner's emotions continued to seesaw as he encountered evidence both of Christian progress ("men and women rushed upon me and exclaimed, 'Glory to God, Hallelujah!' etc., till I was melted with tears") and of what he took to be heathen degradation.[83]

Turner nonetheless proceeded, in the certainty that Africans were highly teachable, "ready to lay down any habit, custom and sentiment for a better." Despite his professional interests in evangelization and his theoretical commitment to Christianity, Turner could not help being emotionally captivated by the unconverted Africans he met. While he was staying at the home of J. R. Frederick, the presiding AME elder, a local Muslim "bishop," as Turner called him, came by to pay his respects. "He came in splendid robes and looked grandly," he recounted. "He is a man of rare learning and his bear-

ing was kingly. I tried to look big, but felt small, in his presence." These human interactions gradually transformed his opinions of Islam. Turner, like
Amanda Smith, was especially impressed by the Muslims' abstention from
alcohol and regular patterns of prayer and individual reading, practices that
fit well with his own Methodist inclinations. He finally concluded that Islam
served as a precursor to the evangelization of Africa, the "morning-star to
the sun of pure Christianity." The placement of Islam in a larger, racially
specific chronology allowed Turner even to countenance polygamy, at least
in the short run: "Say what you please about the Mohammedans and their
plurality of wives (which of course no Christian can endorse), I verily believe that God is holding these Mohammedans intact, and that they will
serve as the forerunners of evangelical Christianity."[84] Unlike Blyden, Turner
did not advocate a universalist faith as a result of his high opinion of Islam.
He remained convinced that Protestant Christianity would ultimately triumph and bring Africa to its rightful destiny.[85]

The issue of polygamy also prompted another distinction. *Faith* was one
thing. Acceptance—or at least tolerance—of "heathen" religious *practices*
proved a more difficult prospect, if only because many customs did not
originate in the Abrahamic traditions or resemble anything that missionaries, Turner included, could categorize as "religion." Because narrators did
not have any handy system with which to classify "heathen" practices, they
described particular *activities,* such as healing, dancing, and feasting, in
great detail. The terms that they used to characterize indigenous religions or
practitioners frequently came either from anthropological discourses of the
day ("witch doctor," "evil spirits") or directly from the Bible, referring to the
terms employed by the Israelites to describe the worship of other peoples
(those who worship a "wooden or brass god").[86] In either case, missionaries
almost universally condemned indigenous practices.

Turner carefully distinguished between the "visible sciences" practiced by
the "white man" and the "invisible sciences" employed by Africans. Each
community, in its own way, controlled and manipulated those forces with
which it was familiar. And he concluded that one was not necessarily superior to the other: "I believe that the black man is acquainted with secret
agents in the realm of nature that the white man has never dreamed of, and
will offset any telegraph, telephone or phonograph ever invented by white

men." Lest anyone think that he was thereby advocating indigenous religious practices, Turner later elaborated: "the African is not a pagan, but a child of superstition; he worships no wooden or brass god, but believes more strongly in the invisible forces than we do; so it is an easy matter to have him transfer his faith from superstition to Christ Jesus the Lord."[87] Having a basis of belief in some forces already, Turner reasoned, Africans would unproblematically shift their allegiances to Christianity.

As an AME bishop, of course, Turner believed that not all Christianity was alike. With ever an eye toward denominational interests, Turner argued that the AME Church was the best organization for Africa. "There is no church on earth that can grow like ours if we will half work," he reported. "The heathen kings will drive out other denominations, so I am told, and declare our church the church of their kingdoms." He was not alone in mapping ecclesiastical interest onto the continent. Just as denominational infighting had marked the Haitian missionary enterprise, so did Africa present a field fresh for rivalry. Alfred Lee Ridgel, a fellow AME clergyman and the presiding elder of the Liberia Annual Conference in the 1890s, believed that only a black-controlled organization could Christianize Africa, and only a black Methodist church was appropriate, since Africans "like the Methodist fire."[88] Conversely, Alexander Crummell expressed his conviction that the Episcopal Church was by far the most suitable for Africans. In these instances and others, Christian infighting complicated the racial affiliations that so attracted African Americans to missionary work.

For both Turner and Camphor, narrating African religions involved an intricate mapping through time and space. As was true for other African-American writers, their ethnographic observations were informed by a keen historical awareness, understandings of the past and its bearing on the present that shaped what they saw and dictated how they reinterpreted their experiences for domestic audiences. Thus biblical models, ancient African precedents, denominational affiliations, and American national stories all came into play as African Americans worked to understand the call to their homeland. Yet their accounts were also molded by an awareness of diaspora. Their reports sought to explain how American blacks and Africans had been separated and how they eventually could be reunited—spiritually, culturally, and geographically. Missionary encounters with Africans, however, reveal both intimacy and distance, a profoundly ambivalent mix of impressions that had to be narrated into the story of racialized Christian progress. How else could the Israelites live together peaceably in Canaan?

By the first decade of the twentieth century, with Jim Crow at its acme and dozens of blacks being lynched each year, the outlook for African-American collective survival in the United States once again looked bleak. The initial euphoria of Reconstruction had been followed by a steady decline in political fortunes, as blacks systematically were shut out of public life in Southern states. Many fled westward and northward to escape the choking confines of Southern racism and economic hardship. In this atmosphere of dimming hopes at home, the light of Africa shone even brighter for race leaders like Henry McNeal Turner, who, after serving as a Union Army chaplain and helping to found the Republican Party in Georgia, gradually gave up on the United States as a suitable place for African Americans to thrive.

These declining hopes coincided with a broad Christian missionary interest in Africa that had its heyday in the two decades just prior to World War I. For many Protestant evangelicals, Africa stood as one of the chief benchmarks of worldwide Christian progress. For African-American Christians in particular, its significance meshed well with earlier understandings of the African past and future. At the 1895 Congress on Africa, E. W. S. Hammond, editor of the *Southwestern Christian Advocate* (New Orleans), depicted the continent of Africa as the center of world attraction, and his narrative connected its destiny with familiar historical elements. "In Africa we have all the elements out of which to construct such a civilization that will evoke the admiration of the entire civilized world. In ancient history, its place in prophecy, its place in the commercial world, its place in literature and art and science, has already attracted the attention of the great powers of the earth." In a final dramatic flourish, Hammond also reminded his audience of the scriptural importance of Africa, for it was "on this great continent, Israel's matchless leader and lawgiver received that training which made him the most conspicuous character upon the pages of either sacred or profane history."[89]

But Hammond's dramatic focus on past and future eclipsed the primary significance of Africa for contemporary African Americans. Africa was a historical drama, and its narration provided a site for social unity and coherence for a people torn apart both abroad and at home. For if the gap between African Americans and Africans loomed large, the chasm separating African Americans by class, religion, and region remained a considerable obstacle to racial unity. As Alfred Lee Ridgel and others pointed out, American blacks were far from united themselves. "We, as a race, have not as yet learned the importance of *unity* and race love," he wrote in 1898. "I am sure that many who pose as race leaders and wiseacres upon the negro question, have not studied the subject sufficient to arrive at intelligent conclusions." Ridgel believed that establishing a Christian civilization in Africa would both prove the worth of the race to whites and religiously save Africans. But perhaps even more important, the task itself would redeem African Americans:

> To my mind the negro in foreign lands must return home and become renegroized, if you please, before he can fully appreciate himself and his people. For nearly three hundred years the American negro has been away from home; two hundred and forty-seven years of this time he served as a slave, subjected to the most inhuman treatment; whipped, sold, terrorized in numberless ways; in every instance he was reminded of his inferiority, as reckoned from the white man's stand-point. He was taught as a slave that the most commendable thing he could do was to be an honest, obedient negro to the laws of master and mistress; everywhere he turned the white man was lord and ruler; finally, with such strong environments, many of the weaker minds succumbed to the almost inevitable and formed the opinion that *God* created the white man to rule and the negro to serve. Such convictions are dangerous to the race, for when the negro becomes satisfied to occupy a secondary position in the affairs of the world, his aspirations will never rise higher. Under such conditions we would virtually be a slave. Voluntary slavery is far more dangerous and destructive than compulsory slavery. One controls the mind, while the other controls the body.[90]

Ridgel's words reveal the many ways in which he believed that a common racial history, a past that had been stolen from slaves in the New World, would change collective consciousness and unite the race. Not unlike Malcolm X, who a half-century later would call for the expurgation of Euro-American customs, values, and history from African-American life, Ridgel articulated a conviction that communal memories mattered greatly. Much was at stake in Africa, even before Christian expansion could succeed: masculinity, self-respect, and race pride. History had to be rewritten in the minds of African Americans, as well as Christianity etched into the hearts of Africans, before Canaan could be reborn.

5

The Negro Race History

Every man that writes is writing a new Bible, or a new Apocrypha.

THOMAS CARLYLE, *Two Notebooks*

In 1883, in the early years of Jim Crow and scientific racism, the African-American Baptist preacher George Washington Williams published his *History of the Negro Race in America, 1619–1880.* The book, a fundamentally optimistic account of the black presence in the New World, represented an attempt by the well-educated Northern clergyman to balance his commitments to an American evangelical tradition with an awareness of the ongoing oppression of his fellow African Americans. "I commit this work to the public, white and black," he noted in the preface, "to the friends and foes of the Negro in the hope that the obsolete antagonisms which grew out of the relation of master and slave may speedily sink as storms beneath the horizon; and that the day will hasten when there shall be no North, no South, no Black, no White,—but all be American citizens, with equal duties and equal rights." The work revealed much about Williams: his upbringing in antebellum Pennsylvania as the child of an interracial union, his training at Howard University and Newton Theological Seminary, and his work experiences at Baptist churches in New England and Ohio. But most important, it revealed Williams's desire to recast much of the American past. His historical account was, at heart, an attempt to impart moral meaning to the present by reconstructing the historical consciousness of both blacks and whites.[1]

Although African Americans had been writing both personal and communal narratives for many decades before the Civil War, it was not until after Emancipation that the genre of "race history" emerged as an increasingly popular form of black literary expression. Between 1867 and 1920, several dozen writers authored book-length studies of the negro past, present, and future, in an effort, as Edward Johnson put it, to record "the many brave deeds and noble characteristics" of the race. Dozens of articles within the periodical press amplified, drew on, reviewed, and praised the new histories. Writing in the years prior to the professionalization of history as a "scientific" mode of discourse, many early race historians were ordained ministers; some had theological training. All were interested in the possibilities of history, the potential for narrative to shape the future of the free community. As blacks and as Protestants, these writers imbued the past, present, and future of the negro with moral and spiritual significance. Their histories reflected a wide-ranging public discourse among post-Reconstruction black leaders regarding representations of the race that were essential to counter white racial images and to reimagine the African-American community on its own terms.[2] For these narrators, Reconstruction and its aftermath encompassed the reconfiguration of racial, religious, and national stories and, even more fundamentally, the reimagining of time and space.[3]

As Northern missionaries moved into the Southern states in the years following Emancipation, they brought with them an emphasis on education as the key to morality and middle-class respectability. Limited literacy among ex-slaves allowed Protestant clergy and laity systematically to shape their beliefs and ritual lives. As literacy rose in the freed population in the 1880s and 1890s, church-sponsored presses stood ready with journals, newspapers, and books to fill the new demand for printed materials.[4] But the new religious media also provided widespread access to racial representations intended to mold character. J. Max Barber, author of *The Negro of the Earlier World. An Excursion into Ancient Negro History,* commented that "a race without traditions and without a history is most likely to be a race without backbone and without self-respect." Race historians served as self-appointed leaders of the effort to provide a history, and thus a moral identity, for a people often characterized as lacking both. The African-American public, in turn, had access to these depictions of moral identity through the predominantly Northern, urban, and often denominationally based publishing houses that controlled their production.[5]

Historical narratives functioned somewhat differently from Sunday school tracts, exegetical sermons, or other types of written religious discourse. They offered "an overall vision of the historical world," which systematically placed the story of African-American suffering in a reconstructed temporal context and afforded a new collective identity through the act of reading.[6] Race histories created expanded notions of religious and racial communities that had persevered through time. Their dissemination through black denominational presses, and increasingly through Northern white-controlled presses as well, fostered racial and religious commitments to an enlarged African diasporic community.

Equipped with this newly available "technology of power," black Protestant leaders hoped to influence the development of Southern freedmen through conversion of the head and heart.[7] Their various approaches reflected the contentiousness of Protestant roots as well. Race historians may have been similarly motivated by historical circumstances, but their narratives differed greatly in their diagnoses of past ills and their prognoses for future improvement.[8]

One of the most exhaustive and imaginative recastings of sacred history came from the pen of Lorenzo Dow Blackson, a Methodist preacher from Christiana, Delaware. Appearing shortly after the close of the war in 1867, Blackson's *Rise and Progress of the Kingdoms of Light and Darkness; or, The Reign of Kings Alpha and Abadon* combined racial, biblical, national, and ecclesiastical commentary as a way of situating African Americans and steering them toward a brighter future. Blackson's lengthy study has often been categorized as fiction, but it becomes easier to discern the author's intentions when *Rise and Progress* is placed alongside the labors of other African-American race narrators. The work featured many themes integral to collective cultural work—the prominent role of Africa in biblical history and the ancient world; the triumph of Protestantism and African Methodism; a qualified glorification of republican values and the Constitution; the celebration of black manhood; explanations for the enslavement and degradation of Africans from their position of former glory; and a description of the "final battle" that would banish racism and usher in the Kingdom of Light on earth—thus extending the racial narratives of the antebellum period into a new dispensation.

Rise and Progress underscores the autodidacticism of many antebellum blacks. Blackson was born in 1817, the ninth of eleven children—and the second born free—to Thomas and Hanna Blackson. He knew little about his family background, aside from the fact that some of his relatives were "very powerful men physically"; his mother's father was reported to have been an African prince named Palice Abrutas Darram. Lorenzo's own name, an homage to the famous Methodist backwoods revivalist preacher Lorenzo Dow, reflected his parents' intimate connection to the Methodist Church in Delaware, where his father worked as an exhorter, a church leader who could not preach but who read Scripture and spoke about it at prayer meetings. After several years of schooling, Lorenzo, along with two of his brothers, followed his father's footsteps into the Methodist Church. All three became preachers, although Lorenzo ultimately joined the African Union Church, a small black Methodist denomination established in Delaware under the leadership of the Reverend Peter Spencer. Later Blackson moved to Philadelphia and spent the rest of his life there.[9]

Beyond these spare details contained in an introduction, Blackson provided little justification for his comprehensive historical work. "My motives have been to glorify God," he claimed. His use of Matthew 13:34–35 provides an additional hint of an aim: in that passage, Jesus spoke to the multitudes in parables as the fulfillment of Old Testament prophecy (Asaph in Psalm 78:2) that the new Messiah would "utter things which have been kept secret from the foundation of the world." Was Blackson claiming to speak cryptically as Jesus had, revealing ancient sacred secrets? Such a reading makes sense of his convoluted and maddeningly oblique prose style. Reflecting a Methodist commitment to humble speech, Blackson referred to his 1867 work of more than three hundred pages as a "feeble essay," but in its pages he spun an elaborate and often meandering tale of militant and heroic battles against the cosmic forces of evil.

Blackson began with the creation of the world, describing the means by which "a certain King" at the beginning of time created the earth and heavens. Loosely paraphrasing Genesis and reiterating much of the theological commentary of John Milton's *Paradise Lost,* Blackson recounted the creation of men and women and their fall, and the rise of an evil competitor to the King of Light, Satan, or Abadon, a former colleague in Heaven who was cast out of the kingdom and would challenge the king's reign throughout the remainder of the story. Taking a variety of allies, Satan reappeared throughout the ages. Under the guidance of divine inspiration, Blackson predicted a war

between good and evil "which is to determine on which side the final victory will rest forever and ever."[10]

Such was the skeletal outline, marked by a moral contest that served as a
fulcrum for human history. In the course of his tale, however, Blackson
moved quickly through biblical accounts (the flood, the building of the
Tower of Babel), to the rise of the Christian Church, the Reformation, and
into American history. Not surprisingly, given its publication immediately
following the Civil War, the story is saturated with martial and apocalyptic
imagery. God became "King Alpha" or the "King of Light," and the heroes
became the "Soldiers of Light" consisting of various "regiments" that the
king led into battle. Blackson was thorough in his enumeration of church
history: Protestant denominations, including the Quakers, Lutherans, Baptists, Methodists, and Episcopalians ("and many others too tedious to mention"), were rendered as regiments of the Kingdom of Light, commanded by
religious luminaries such as the English Protestant martyrs Hugh Latimer
and Nicholas Ridley, John Foxe, and John Wesley. The work was also explicitly anti-Catholic, portraying the pope and his legions as a false army because of their "cruel torturing of men and its much blood-shed."[11]

Blackson also focused extensively on other cultures and believers of the
world, from Muslims to Hindus to Buddhists. All were portrayed as false armies, serving the King of Darkness by worshipping idols and living in ignorance; their ranks were being thinned systematically by the incursion of
Protestant missionaries into their strongholds. Africa presented a singular
case, however. The author admitted that much of the continent was currently under the control of Abadon. But he also related the story of its origins through the descendants of Ham, Noah's son. The King of Light himself
had recorded in his sacred book that Nimrod, the grandson of Ham, had
been the builder of great cities in the ancient world. This demonstrated,
according to Blackson, that "however far they may at present be behind
civilized and enlightened nations, they were nevertheless, once the first most
powerful and enlightened people on earth." Egypt was particularly ac-
claimed for its culture, attracting men from around the world to its centers
of learning; European civilizations had gained much of their knowledge
through the early teachings of Africans. Moreover, some early inhabitants of
north Africa had been part of the king's regiment, notably Cyprian and
other church fathers: "We merely notice this to show that though they of the

African division have not now the true light of the gospel, yet they were once in it in advance of many others, but by their not walking in the light while they had it, they stumbled and fell into the great darkness and ignorance in which they now are."[12]

At this point the tale zeroes in on racism as a major weapon exploited by Satan. It was Abadon who commanded his armies to steal Africans away from their homeland and transport them into bondage in America. Within the American ranks of the armies of light, held together by the professed principles of life, liberty, and the pursuit of happiness, racism had created disunity: "many of those who should have been the watchmen on the walls, to see the sword coming and warn the people, they miserably and shamefully failed to do so." Blackson did not go so far as to say that white Christians had moved entirely to the dark side, but he detailed explicitly the many institutional effects of their corruption. He described the separation of African Methodists from their white counterparts and argued that the King of Light had himself freed the sons of Africa.[13]

At the same time, Blackson balanced his attack on racism by expressing a thoroughly evangelical focus on personal morality and its perversion through worldliness. As a member of the African Union Church, a relatively small church among the separate black denominations, Blackson used his tale to account for the fact that the AME Church was much larger than his own (although "not so original"). Finally, he worried that the introduction of innovations such as choirs and instrumental music into worship signaled that Methodists were straying from the purity of their Wesleyan roots. Ultimately, it is impossible to distinguish between Blackson's longing for Christian harmony and his call for racial unity. The foundational "secret" he suggests is that the two can never be separated.

Blackson's work anticipated many of the themes that would be recurring features of postbellum race histories, but none more explicitly than the entwining of religious and racial progress. Like Blackson, other narrators, in their attempts to reformulate historical consciousness, had to confront and resolve a number of philosophical problems in the present. One of the most pressing was the perceived political and religious apathy promoted by enslavement. For many decades black Protestants had pondered the religious meaning of African slavery in the providential scheme: why had God allowed African enslavement?[14] Race historians were not satisfied that the results had been salutary or entirely Christian. Further, some argued that it was preferable not to remember at all. Theophilus Gould Steward, AME missionary to the South at the close of the war, observed that slavery divided rather than united African Americans: "slave history is not history; the colored people have made no history which has the least tendency to unite." Committed to the transformative social powers of organized religion, narrators wrestled with the passivity of Southern blacks. Joseph T. Wilson, in his 1882 study *Emancipation: Its Course and Progress from 1481 B.C. to A.D. 1875*, lamented the "absurd extravagancies" of slave worship that still kept blacks in a position of spiritual inferiority. Writers criticized most harshly the continuing tendency of freed men and women to trust the fatalism and superstition of their old religious practices. It was not always healthy, George Washington Williams pointed out, for blacks to rely on a "divine helper" for guidance.[15]

One of the most scathing indictments of black fatalism came from the pen of William Hannibal Thomas. Born in 1843, Thomas was a mixed-blood lawyer with seminary training. While growing up in Pickaway County, Ohio, Thomas witnessed his parents' service as conductors on the Underground Railroad. After a brief preparatory school education, Thomas tried to enlist as a Union Army volunteer in 1860 but was turned away because of his color. Eventually he found his way into the war, fought to the end, and after professional training at a Presbyterian seminary, headed south in 1871 to organize schools for freed blacks. In 1876 he was elected to the legislature of South Carolina. Over the following quarter-century Thomas contributed regularly to the pages of the *Christian Recorder* and *AME Church Review*, combating white racism and encouraging uplift through the channels of the AME Church. By the turn of the century, however, Thomas expressed unmitigated anger toward Southern blacks. In *The American Negro*, a highly contentious work published by Macmillan in 1901, he wrote that "the social side of negro life has been to me an open page of execrable weakness, of unblushing shame, of inconceivable mendacity, of indurated folly and ephemeral contrition." While well aware of the obstacles that had blocked racial progress since the end of Reconstruction, Thomas believed that much of the blame had to be placed at the door of the ex-slaves themselves. He wrote his book, he explained, out of "an intense desire to awaken the negro people out of their sleep of death." "To the negro," he claimed, "religion is a transient impulse, a kind of hypnotic sensation, a thing entirely apart from and outside of ordinary life and duty." It "accentuates individual helplessness and emphasizes dependence on unknown forces by a prominence which it gives through songs, texts, sermons, and prayers to a weird psychic guidance." While it lay within the power of negroes to change their situation, Thomas argued that the best means to do so would be to place blacks once again under "a superior white Christian supervision." Negroes now have the promised land of Liberty spread out before them, Thomas explained, but they do not know how to take it for themselves.[16]

Few writers went so far as Thomas in openly castigating other blacks, but his critique of slave religion was common. Race historians all saw the need for change, although they disagreed about whether slave spirituality needed to be rooted out or could provide a necessary basis for the growth of "true" Christianity. Like many middle-class black religious leaders in the late nineteenth century, race historians had an ambivalent relationship to the black masses for whom they wished to speak. Most were, in fact, relative outsiders to the dilemmas faced by ex-slaves: many had been educated or had lived in the North. Separated from their Northern Protestant colleagues by race, black Protestant leaders were thus distinguishable from Southern blacks along class-based and often regional lines. Ironically, Williams's and Stanford's nicknames as the "Negro Bancroft" and the "Negro Beecher," respectively, while intended as compliments, symbolized their distance from both other blacks and other Protestant divines. Race histories provided African-American leaders with a means of rhetorically uniting the various religious, social, and racial loyalties that constituted their singular stations in life. But in doing so, their narratives often revealed division more than unity, distancing them from the people they sought to improve.

Most race historians, like their missionary counterparts throughout the South, posited an understanding of religious faith that stressed rationality and ethical behavior as the focus of the Christian life. True religion, Thomas asserted, is characterized by "clearness of spiritual perception" and "purity of ideal." The "mass of Negro religionists" do not have this perception of the principles of truth but are instead irrational and worship a God of "personal characteristics and human idiosyncrasies."[17] Other authors agreed with the substance of Thomas's judgment but expressed less vitriol and more optimism about the ability of ex-slaves to rise from the "extreme fanaticism" of slave spirituality to religious rationalism. George Washington Williams, another biracial Civil War veteran who had served Baptist churches in both New England and Cincinnati, saw more to encourage him concerning the growth of Protestant institutions among ex-slaves. Black churches, as he saw it, were "the best proof of the Negro's ability to maintain himself in an advanced state of civilization." The race would progress as blacks learned to do for themselves. As a salient example, Williams pointed to the recent exodus to Kansas: "It was but the natural operation of a divine law that moved whole communities of Negroes to turn their faces toward the setting sun." In other words, the divine will was operating through human agency, and blacks would gradually lift themselves up as they learned to turn their religious piety into social action.[18] In keeping with theistic evolutionary schemes current in white liberal theology, Thomas and other black authors stressed the workings of providence through human processes and "higher laws." They envisioned God as an impersonal force, a natural law removed from the daily cares of the black community.

Race leaders also hoped to shift popular standards of appropriate commemoration through their recasting of history. The early years after Emancipation witnessed a surge of black popular celebrations in Southern towns and cities, as newly freed men and women felt empowered to claim public space for themselves. Many of these were continuations of antebellum festivities that satirized elite black and white efforts to impose order. On holidays a wide assortment of people, in varied styles of dress, would parade in the streets on mules or in wagons, taunting figures of authority in "a vivid burlesque that both mirrored and distorted contemporary power relations in their communities." In counterpoint to these, black elites and Northern missionaries hoped to elevate standards by providing new patterns of ceremony and remembrance.[19]

The very notion of civilized progress assumed in the writing of race histories was indebted both to liberal notions of steady advance and to the development of a documentary record in which previous historical steps could be known and evaluated with precision. In this respect, Protestant authors were thoroughly influenced by the dominant liberal strains of Euro-American philosophy and history; yet even this degree of cultural assimilation was put to the purpose of forming an African-American collective identity, an entity called the "Negro race."[20] Black Protestants could make sense of religious discord and diversity and still maintain the superiority and eventual triumph of their own beliefs, within an organic community; they could write themselves into the same story with the black masses by pointing to historical moments of solidarity within an unfolding, progressive historical drama; and, significantly, they could attempt to exert social and cultural control over less-educated blacks through the rhetorical power of collective self-definition.

Race authors drew on their own biblical and classical traditions to situate Southern blacks in a noble lineage. A number of writers began their works by outlining the glorious and mighty culture of the negro race in Egypt.[21] The Baptist minister L. T. Smith, born in Virginia, employed as a teacher by the Freedmen's Relief Association of Pennsylvania, and later educated at Hampton Institute in the 1870s, advised readers of his 1883 history *A Great Truth in a Nutshell* to "Wake up! Arise from the bed of dead lethargy . . . and, as I shall draw back the curtains of time, look! if you please, twenty-five hundred years back into the grim face of antiquity and see! O! see the elevated and lofty positions of honor, integrity, and so forth, your race once occupied in the scientifical world." Rufus Perry, a Baptist journalist and educator from Smith County, Tennessee, also focused on past nobility, asserting proudly that the early religions of the East, of India, and of the Greco-Roman world all had roots in Egyptian and Ethiopian thought, making the Cushites the foundation of what Perry construed as the ultimate unity of all faiths.[22] African participation in ancient history was a useful counter to the white claim that negroes had always been, and would remain, a degraded race.

The recovery of ancient Egypt signaled more than the placement of African figures in a previously white classical landscape. Perry, Smith, and the Baptist journalist J. Max Barber all argued that Europeans and Americans had actively distorted the past by conspiring to prevent African Americans from recognizing their contributions to it. "We are taught to believe that the history of the race began with slavery," Barber noted. "The white man has tried to rob us of Egypt because Egypt is the mother of modern civilization." Perry asserted that during slavery, "the white man wrote for white men; and now the black man must write for black men." Nonetheless, these authors did not recommend dispensing with the Christian tradition because of its associations with the evils of a Euro-American culture and the subsequent "regression" of Africans to a condition of "barbarism and heathenism." All saw the hand of providence working even in the dimmest light. "God has a purpose in all of this," concluded Barber, "and He will bring it to pass that all men shall have their turn at the wheel." Smith similarly asserted that "its purpose for good is yet veiled from our eager eyes."[23]

As prominent as the culture of ancient Egypt was and in spite of its growing importance as a symbol of cultural nationalism in the pan-African movement, race historians generally used it as a foundation and stepping-stone to link the biblical origins of the Cushites to the Christian era. Most of the survey histories briefly mentioned Africans in the ancient world to establish firmly the monogenetic account of human origins.[24] However, they concentrated on the Euro-American tradition, and particularly on American history. In doing so, race historians did not depict the era of African enslavement, for all its moral complexities, as a period of unmitigated suffering. By restructuring American history through their narratives, Protestant leaders both lauded human heroism and simultaneously rejected the Anglo-Saxon triumphalism of white accounts. One of the most consistent features of these revisions is the simultaneous effort to sacralize the history of slavery and revise sacred history to highlight the current spiritual dilemma of the negro. Put another way, race historians used elements of the Christian paradigm to explain the significance of black Emancipation and to indicate the dawn of a new spiritual era in the late nineteenth century.

Echoing the gospel message, some histories hinged on the acts of Civil War and Emancipation as the harbingers of a worldwide spiritual and social transformation. Several overtly invoked the analogy to Christ's birth. Joseph Wilson, the Virginia-born colonel who expressed anxieties about religious superstitions, realigned sacred history to focus on black activism. His 1882 book *Emancipation* emphasized not merely the specifics of American military engagement but also the sustained war of which the American skirmishes were a part. He centered his tale on the inexorable march of events leading to Emancipation, beginning with the assertion that "no event, save that of the coming—the birth of the Savior—is so rejoiced in as that of the abolition of slavery." Wilson read all of history as an ongoing struggle toward the goal of human freedom: "history proves beyond a doubt that the advancing spirit of freedom has always been met by a relentless war waged by the oppressors of mankind."[25] The climax of history, then, came with the issuing of the Emancipation Proclamation, a document included, along with the Declaration of Independence and the U.S. Constitution, in the appendix to Wilson's book.[26] Peter Thomas Stanford also connected the abolition of slavery to the life of Christ, claiming that the nineteenth century would be viewed by later generations as the most important since the time of Christ "in results of beneficence to human life."[27]

By setting Emancipation as the axis around which the rest of history turned, race historians identified a host of antislavery activists and other friends of the cause of abolition as prophets of the coming new order. American history thus became a sacred drama of black activism. The chronicling of these prophets sometimes differed radically from white accounts of important American heroes, religious or otherwise. The most popular object of affection and reverence for writers was John Brown. Stanford hailed the leader of the Harper's Ferry revolt as a "Puritan hero, Christian philosopher," and "martyr for the slaves." Using an intriguing combination of Protestant and abolitionist titles of honor, Stanford applauded Brown's religious activism: "Baxter and Bunyan were the men with whom he sat and talked, through their books, and the bible was his chief advisor and guide." In George Washington Williams's account, Brown was a martyr who "ranks among the world's greatest heroes": "his ethics and religion were as broad as the universe, and beneficent in their wide ramification."[28]

Nat Turner also occupied a prominent place in many race histories. Edward Johnson's *School History of the Negro Race in America* called him a prophet and mused that "he was, undoubtedly, a wonderful character." Williams was more guarded in his praise, owing, perhaps, to his awareness of white ambivalence toward a rebel slave who had incited the murders of scores of women and children. Nonetheless, he too compared Turner to Moses and John the Baptist: the abolitionist was a remarkable prophet who "preached with great authority" and whose early years were characterized by a steady stream of divinely inspired visions and spiritual growth. Perhaps trying to appeal to whites and blacks alike, Williams carefully avoided the subject of the massacre itself; in addition, he placed both the word "prophet," when referring to Turner, and the word "tragedy," when referring to the slave revolt, in quotation marks, as if to buffer against criticism from either side. But his admiration was unmistakable: he concluded by noting that although no stone marked Turner's grave, his image was "carved on the fleshy tablets of four million hearts."[29]

Despite the generous space accorded to Turner, Brown, the slave rebel Gabriel Prosser, Denmark Vesey, and other heroes of the abolitionist cause, race authors did not simply write a black-centered history of America. Most also accorded space to white harbingers of liberty. In this respect, these histories were not limited to the African-American story in any easily identifiable pattern; narratives were racialized to be sure, but they were also marked by national and religious loyalties. By invoking Euro-American examples, moreover, they implicitly presented even more of a challenge to traditional renderings of American history by relativizing them. The Puritans were praised for being earnest and God-fearing, as opposed to the "idle, dissolute, and mercenary" settlers of Jamestown. Several authors located Emancipation in a long line of religious struggles for independence and freedom, from the Israelites in Egypt, to the French Huguenots, to the Pilgrims. And a number of works stressed the parallels between the American struggle for independence from Britain and the antislavery crusade. Joseph Wilson reasoned that just as whites (with the help of many blacks, he pointed out) had fought for their freedom from an oppressive power, so too had the negro demonstrated his "unquenchable thirst for liberty." Both events, he concluded, confirmed the "religious reverence for man and his natural rights."[30] Race historians claimed selected events in Euro-American history as part of their own sacred heritage but subordinated them to the unfolding drama of race emancipation. Rather than assimilating African Americans into "white" history, these narratives incorporated the tragedies and triumphs of American life into a lengthier account of moral and spiritual struggle. Previous battles, from the Reformation to the American Revolution, served as prophetic preludes to the central drama of the black jubilee.

Peter Thomas Stanford captured well the twists of thought that many contemporary observers have dismissed as simple capitulation to white values. A child of the South, Stanford was born a slave in Hampton, Virginia, lived briefly in a home for black orphans, and was subsequently sent to the family of Perry L. Stanford in Boston. After running away to New York City at age twelve, he was converted to Christianity during a revival conducted by the evangelist Dwight Moody. He received an education thanks to the largesse of Harriet Beecher Stowe, Henry Ward Beecher, and Henry Highland Garnet. From then on, his life reflected both indebtedness to white Protestant support and a commitment to the unity of African Americans. In *The Tragedy of the Negro in America,* Stanford insisted on understanding the history of slavery, the "record of iniquity," not on the temporal plane of human history, but within the realm of "God's record," in which all human history was subordinated to recognition of the clarity of divine justice. This view compelled Stanford to be mindful of "fairness to both black and white"; although he condemned specific social ills such as the convict lease system and the scourge of lynching, he interpreted the evil of slavery as one of many human failings throughout sacred history.[31] Stanford's focus on history as the story of God's dealings with humanity moved his critique away from the mere exercise of judgment over the failings of Euro-Americans. For good or for ill, Stanford's narrative of historical progress represented a distinctive religious outlook.

Although they differed in detail, these stories provided blacks with a new sacred narrative, one that extended beyond the bounds of God's dealings with his people in a land of bondage. To varying degrees, they incorporated some of the more salient features of recent Christian and American history into the account of the African-American journey to freedom. They held up new saints and martyrs, and some even incorporated new documents, such as the Emancipation Proclamation, into the sacred canon. These were histories for a new community, one that had moved beyond the need for supernatural deliverance from the world's woes. Race authors, motivated by their own understandings of the progressive nature of sacred history, stressed the dawning of a distinctive era, one in which blacks would take their rightful places as equals among the races of the world.

Because most writers were so cognizant of the perceived "failings" of Southern blacks, moreover, they did not place full blame for the failures of Reconstruction on the shoulders of white Southerners. Blacks had a future in the South, many of these histories implied, if only they would embrace a new self-definition and a new view of history, one that could accord them the dignity, civility, and religious beliefs that Northern blacks thought they lacked. History, in a real sense, could redeem Southern blacks by remaking their views of the world around them.

Still other authors saw the intrinsic spiritual unity of the African-

American race residing in future events. Calling such prophetic accounts "histories" reflects their grounding in a linear narrative structure that began (implicitly) with biblical precedents. In these stories, African Americans were the chosen people who had always been unified through their accountability to God's will, and who would be united once again in a future moment when called upon to enact the final stages of the providential drama. These authors seemed to agree that the stage was set for action, and that the immutable laws of progress guaranteed the race an important and glorious future.

But as was the case with their Northern, white Protestant counterparts, the Civil War itself raised profound questions for black historians about how God might choose to act in history. As Christians, race authors accepted the biblical prophecy that Christ would return to rule over the earth in a future "golden age" or "millennium." Although the notion of millennialism pervaded both white and black evangelical thought throughout the nineteenth century, the bloody battles of the war itself, so similar to the predicted armed engagement of Armageddon, raised the issue of whether, indeed, the war had set in motion the sacred events prophesied in the Book of Revelation. Is this how the end times would arrive? If so, what role did Christians now play in that story?[32]

The war, therefore, had deep and lasting effects on views of sacred history. As life settled into new routines, blacks and whites alike pondered how to interpret the return to normalcy—and the eruption of new societal fissures. Some foresaw a "postmillennial" future in which the golden age would come about primarily through the efforts of faithful Christians to realize an ideal society here on earth; such believers, in turn, advocated Christian social efforts and often a progressive political agenda as one means to this end. Even if the war had initiated the end times, in this view, human beings still had much work left to do. For other "premillennialists," the war may have foreshadowed the sacred battle to come, but it also reinforced the fact that only God could redeem the world. Christ would return to earth only after a prolonged apocalyptic battle between the powers of good and evil, one fought after the end of human history as they knew it. Christians were relatively powerless to help bring about this foreordained conclusion.

The views of race historians were further complicated by their conviction that Emancipation was assuredly the work of an equitable God overturning past injustices. But if racial issues had initiated Armageddon, of what significance would race be in the future? Most African-American authors interpreted the present and future in ways that mediated—or at least combined—premillennialist and postmillennialist views and reasserted the significance of race. They upheld the tragic vision of a world disabled without the radical intervention of a retributive God, and they also maintained that African Americans, as a community, would play a central role in the steady progress toward the end of time. Yet they parted company over the status of race during the millennium itself. For race authors, the ancient past invariably included a monogenetic account of human development, inasmuch as equality in the present required an affirmation of equality before God in creation.[33] We might assume, then, that these historians would posit an eventual return to a period without racial differentiation, a paradise of human equality. But writers in fact disagreed about the ultimate significance of racial distinctions, especially as race hatred on the part of whites hardened into institutionalized segregation and violence, and they came to hold differing views on whether those differences would continue into the millennium.

J. Max Barber envisioned a dramatic, violent reversal of racial fortunes in the years after Emancipation, predicting a future based on the continuing moral distinctions of race. "The present is the white man's," he conceded, "but the future belongs, not to the degenerating, morally putrid and cruelly avaricious white man, but to the virile, puissant races in whose hearts there is mercy and justice."[34] Arguing a point that may have been implicit in the works of even the more moderate historians, Barber indicated that blacks were the true heirs to the American tradition of freedom and independence; Emancipation had signaled the beginning of a new era, one in which the hierarchy of the races would be reversed. Because of their moral and spiritual superiority forged in a history of oppression, blacks would eventually occupy a correspondingly elevated social position.

The most well known proponent of this latter theme was Theophilus Gould Steward, a journalist, educator, and member of the African Methodist Episcopal Church who had been born in New Jersey in 1843 and served as a missionary during Reconstruction. Steward's 1888 study *The End of the World; or, Clearing the Way for the Fullness of the Gentiles* carried the notion of racial reversal to its eschatological extreme, asserting that the triumph of the negro race was linked directly to the end times of biblical prophecy. Acknowledging that his work would most likely appear "quite novel and in some respects startling" to his audience, Steward associated the present age, the age of the Gentiles, with the rise of Euro-American power, or the Saxon race. Through consistent historical demonstrations of "acquisition and conquest, subjugation or extermination," Saxons had proven that they were the race that the prophet Daniel had foreseen. "The writer feels bound to believe the Saxon race has well-nigh accomplished its mission," Steward asserted. He characterized the Saxon clan as at once energetic and fierce, ingenious and cruel; he described a culture that would destroy itself through its own greed. The "bloody wave will soon have spent its force, and then the end shall come."[35]

While he criticized the hypocritical theology of the white race, Steward also pulled the true mantle of Christianity around himself and other African Americans. The Saxon God was merely a divinity fashioned to serve the whims of a dominant race: "What a very useful God! Oh, that each of the other races had one just as good!" he noted sarcastically. The corruption of Christianity had made it impossible for the majority of the world's peoples to hear the true message of Christ. "The white races of the earth," he wrote, "have modified the Christian idea to an alarming extent by [the] clan principle, so that it has become a white man's religion, and is so recognized by the darker races." This religion would be replaced in the end times, Steward asserted, by the superior moral power of the darker races, those peoples who were not ruled by a devotion to the principle of "clan." Once the darker races were dominant, the church could be purified and liberated entirely from notions of racial difference.[36]

Although Steward's vision sounded like a liberal version of a premillennialist apocalypse, he stressed that this racial transformation could be brought about by Christians and would take place within human history. "We may dismiss from our thoughts alarming ideas of physical catastrophe," he explained. The coming change marked not the end of the world but only the "completion of the current age" through a series of ordinary historical events.[37] Once again using the paradigm of Christian history, Steward, like other race historians, sacralized the social and political advance of the negro by placing it in a religious framework.

Most writers did not match Steward's high-pitched drama, but the theme of ultimate racial triumph recurred in the writings of other prominent religious leaders. James Theodore Holly, the Protestant Episcopal bishop of Haiti, argued in the pages of the *AME Church Review* that racial differences would play a significant role in the final redemption of humanity. Holly took a dispensational approach to sacred history, asserting that just as the descendants of Shem and Japheth had had their turn in history and had fulfilled certain functions along the road to salvation, the "millennial phase" of the sacred drama would feature the descendants of Ham. In the coming dispensation, the servant of all would become the most blessed: "When, therefore, our Savior shall be crowned and seated upon His Throne of Glory, He will doubtless remember in a peculiar manner the race whose son carried His cross for Him, and choose from that race the crowned nobles who shall minister around His person in His Royal Palace."[38] In a striking combination of Christian universalism and racial collectivism, Holly's narrative secured for African Americans a prominent place in the redemption of the world.

Perhaps the most distinctive feature of these race histories is the way they simultaneously called attention to, and then attempted to eradicate, distinctions between Southern and Northern blacks. The two native-born Southerners—L. T. Smith and Peter Thomas Stanford—both came north at early ages for education and training, and they quickly adopted a distinctive Northern black disdain for what they saw as an "inferior" Southern way of life. All race authors emphasized the failings of Southern blacks in the decades after Emancipation, arguing that if only Southerners would accept their own "superior" religious ideas and practices, they too could become civilized members of the newly united country. Yet in remapping history, race authors downplayed and even denied the continuing importance of regional distinctions. In the (Christian) future, they seemed to suggest, the overarching loyalties of race would eradicate any differences between Northern and Southern blacks. Indeed, Barber, Steward, and Holly hardly mentioned geography at all in their discussions of the destiny of the race; presumably, future racial unity would render current regional distinctions pointless.

After the end of Reconstruction the increasing virulence of racism and growing violence toward blacks raised the intellectual stakes for race historians. Although they continued to be concerned about the moral state of Southern blacks, writers were also compelled to respond directly to white attacks on black potential. Increasingly, those attacks came from white professional historians. Between 1834, when the illustrious U.S. historian George Bancroft published his first volume, and the end of the century, Euro-American historical narration had undergone a realignment every bit as momentous as—and deeply indebted to—the transformation of scientific thinking catalyzed by the work of Charles Darwin. By the 1880s academics such as Moses Coit Tyler and J. W. Burgess sought explanations for human behavior and national ascendancy in enduring racial characteristics rather than in the political innovations of Western Europe. Applying comparative philology and evolutionary philosophy to the study of social development, scholars identified certain ideas and features of a given civilization as indicative of cultural "genius." Thus, U.S. historical progress became linked to the singular genius of the Teutonic people and the Anglo-Saxon race as it had been passed along among Aryan peoples from the Greeks to the Romans to Western Europeans. In the eyes of these Anglo-Saxon historians, American civilization was both the heir to those traditions and, as a successor linked through evolutionary progress, their superior.[39]

The racial implications of the new national history were explicit and conclusive. Edward Augustus Freeman, a British historian and proponent of this "universal history," reflected, "My whole line of thought and study leads me to think, more perhaps than most men, of the everlasting ties of blood and speech, and less of the accidental separation wrought by political and geographical causes."[40] During a visit to the United States in the early 1880s, Freeman had witnessed the intractable problem of the negro. As he described it, the race could never become the equal of white people despite legal mandate. "The eternal laws of nature, the eternal distinction of colour, forbid the assimilation of the negro. You may give him the rights of citizenship by law; you cannot make him the real equal, the real fellow, of citizens of European descent."[41] Herbert Baxter Adams would later assert that the origins of democracy were to be found in the forests of Western Europe, not those of Africa; as a result, African-descended peoples would never have the inherited ability to sustain democratic institutions.

Although not all Euro-American historians accepted this emphasis on genealogy as destiny, its proponents were central to the creation of history as a professional discipline and instrumental in the training of graduate students across the nation. Several, such as the Harvard-trained scholar John Fiske, the Columbia political scientist John W. Burgess, and James K. Hosmer, were also active opponents of immigration and ardent imperialists, believing that American institutions and values were dependent on the predominance of certain racial strains. Their commitment to promoting a view of American history based on the kernels of civilization found in Anglo-Saxon and Teutonic societies was linked closely to their desire to rid national leadership, if not the nation itself, of unassimilable others.[42] Late nineteenth-century white commentators, eager to justify the implementation of Jim Crow and armed with theories of social evolution provided by Herbert Spencer, began to question the ability of blacks ever to attain intellectual and moral equality with whites.

Their theories of history provided the ideal fodder for white neglect or outright attacks on black potential. Commemorations and expositions in the late nineteenth century, many of which touted the glories of U.S. nationalism, edited out black experience as not worthy of comment because it did not demonstrate, in the eyes of most whites, the march of civilization. A signal event in this regard was the 1876 celebration of the nation's centennial, at which African-American contributions were almost entirely neglected. One Philadelphia journalist at that event remarked that prejudice and their former condition of enslavement had prevented the participation of blacks, "save that of a menial, the water-drawers and hat-takers, to the assembled races now to be found there." The reception of blacks at the 1893 World's Fair was little better, although both events spurred African-American leaders to highlight racial achievement.[43] A decade later the even more virulently racist attacks of writers such as Thomas Dixon and Charles Carroll, fueled by theories of permanent black inferiority, cemented racist stereotypes in American popular culture.[44]

Negro authors, drawing on a long tradition of narrating the origins of the African race, increasingly confronted white racialized history directly. J. Augustus Cole confessed in 1888 that African-American leaders had been "driven into this species of mania" to research their history by the claims of whites. At the same time, black historians did not reject all the philosophical premises of white authors. They used some of the intellectual tools, especially the emphasis on racial origins as kernels of collective abilities and an organic understanding of social development, to frame their own work.

Black narrators countered Aryan beginnings with their own claims to ancient origins, and a pronounced rhetoric of social progress was ubiquitous in race histories by 1900.[45] But by century's end their accounts also grew more angry and confrontational as authors became increasingly convinced of the conspiracy of whites to denigrate African-American contributions.

At the same time, African-American race narrators hewed ever more closely to what might be termed the antiprogressive biblical accounts of human origins, hitching their own destinies to Christian Scripture. It is easy to see why: as professionalized historians increasingly moved away from scriptural accounts of human origins and sought a more scientific approach based on verifiable data and evolutionary theory, their findings also steered them toward a hierarchy of races that invariably placed "the negro" toward the bottom of the heap. White liberal Protestants, eager to incorporate new intellectual currents in their work, embraced this move away from biblical literalism to an evolutionary and metaphorical view of Scripture. Even worse, challenges to the accuracy of biblical chronology reinvigorated speculation in mainstream Protestant journals about whether the races had emerged independently in separate creations. As Augustus Cole and other blacks saw it, many white writers had become "wilfully [sic] demented, and in the paroxysm attribute [the negro's] origin to the ourang-outang, date his existence from a pre-Adamic age, or teach him that he is a developed chimpanzee."[46] Liberal notions of progress, for many black leaders, looked just like another form of intellectual and cultural segregation that, whether through the assimilation or the eradication of "lesser" races, would justify radical inequalities in American society.

African Americans saw that older ways of reading Scripture were being renounced to justify social inequality, and thus they grew even more insistent on the historical accuracy of the Bible—a source they trusted as the foundation for racial justice. This did not mean that they rejected entirely newer evolutionary and geological theories. But they interpreted them with a suspicion shaped by sensitivity to their contemporary implications. The AME minister Henry McNeal Turner anticipated this intellectual challenge in "The Negro in All Ages," a lecture he delivered in 1873 in Savannah, Georgia. The talk was later published, and on its title page was an explanatory note: "Being an examination into several abominable, anti-scriptural, and pseudo-philosophical theories, designed as a degradation to humanity, by a few malevolent vampires of the age, reviewed and discussed, ethnologically, scientifically and historically." Feeling under siege, Turner insisted that, while the exact age of the Earth is not clarified by the Bible, the record furnished several incontrovertible facts: first, all human beings came from one original source; second, the first human beings were neither "white" nor dark-skinned, as those designations were currently understood, and therefore the curse of Cain could not have referred to the creation of a distinct race; third, the descendants of Ham in Africa, including the Egyptians and the Ethiopians, were among the most distinguished civilizations on earth:

> They instituted the first national police. They formed the priesthood and literati of Egypt and Chaldea. They originated the worship of departed heroes. They were the authors of all that complicated machinery of gods and goddesses, which have been handed down in classic history. For a thousand years they held aloft the blazing torch of science to a darkened world, while philosophy strode, and nations learned the wisdom of temples, the obelisks and pyramids.

Finally, Turner traced the history of the Christian Church in Africa as a mark of superiority: "Africa has given her fathers, her prelates of every grade to the church of God; her bishops rank first in the order of apostolic succession if any such a fact be in history."[47]

This intellectual context helps explain the dozens of articles in black periodicals after 1880 insisting on the origins of blacks through the lineage of Ham. We might well wonder why African-American leaders would continually reiterate Hamitic roots when the biblical account had been used by earlier generations of white commentators to justify African enslavement. The lineage of Ham offered a way to talk about racial distinctiveness without questioning the unitary creation of humanity. It enabled race differences without hierarchy, in other words—or, at least, within a hierarchy ordained by a just God rather than by a racist white society. Benjamin Tucker Tanner, editor of the *AME Church Review,* wrote copiously about Hamitic origins. In 1887 he reviewed Rufus L. Perry's book *The Cushite,* noting enthusiastically that it "brought lustre to the race" by linking Ham to Africa: "Without any blare of trumpets he quietly hands over Europe to the white Japhethite, Asia to the yellow Shemite, and as justly, and as incontrovertibly, Africa—all

Egypt included—to the black Hamite." As Tanner saw it, this ordained division afforded Africans an independent sphere of influence and a civilization that they could properly point to as created by African hands alone: "Three continents: Europe, Asia, Africa; three patriarchs, Shem, Ham and Japheth. Each continent for a patriarch; each patriarch for a continent."[48] Just as Haiti provided an important touchstone as an example of independent black governance, the Hamitic legacy of Africa furnished a cultural referent that refuted white denigrations of black civility and intellect.[49]

In their reading of Scripture, African-American Protestants found common ground with conservative white biblical critics, who were also eager to shore up biblical chronology as established fact. As blacks saw it, conservatives, owing to their devotion to the divine inspiration of scriptural text, also appreciated the contributions of ancient African societies to world history. Religious periodicals such as the *AME Church Review* reprinted articles from orthodox Protestant luminaries such as the Princeton theologian Benjamin B. Warfield. His "Africa and the Beginnings of Christian Latin Literature," which appeared in the *AME Church Review* in 1912, reaffirmed the role of North Africa in the origins of Christian literature, claiming that "it is from African soil, enriched by African intellect, watered by African blood, that the tree of Western Christianity has grown up until it has become a resting place for all the nations of the earth. . . . there is a true sense in which North Africa is the mother of us all."[50] Their commitment to the Bible as God's revelation meant that African-American Protestants never fit neatly into the increasingly contentious divisions between white conservative and liberal biblical interpreters; progressive in some respects but resolute in their commitment to biblical chronology, black narrators steered a course that provided the best arsenal against the barrage of white attacks on their humanity.

African-American race historians parted company with conservatives in other respects as well, especially in the claim—made by numerous black writers in the years before 1920—that Jesus himself may well have been "a negro." Henry McNeal Turner had voiced the possibility in the late nineteenth century that God was black, but interest in the physiognomic characteristics of Jesus also rose as racial theory yoked biology to intellect and morality. In 1913 Arthur Anderson called for racial unity in demanding a separate territory for dark-skinned people. One of his main arguments was that the first human beings, including Abraham, had dark skin; since Christ was descended from the Jewish lineage, Anderson reasoned that Christianity originally was a religion of negro people: "If the Negro can give to the white man a Christ, a God, surely his dark skin should command more respect."[51]

The most extensive exploration of the concept of Jesus as a dark-skinned man came from James Morris Webb. A minister in the Church of God, Webb worked on the margins of black mainstream denominational life but shared many of the same concerns for race pride and rehabilitation. He looked to Frederick Douglass, Booker T. Washington, and Henry McNeal Turner as heroes, and he wrote a defense of the race bolstered by both ancient and modern writers. Advising his readers to keep a Bible at their fingertips as they read, he proclaimed the absolute authority of biblical history and its account of human origins. The black man was the "father of civilization," he asserted, and his proof began with Ham. Webb conceded that Noah, "in a fit of intoxication," did curse Ham's son, Canaan. But he immediately pointed out that the curse never stopped Canaan from producing seven prosperous nations, including the Canaanites, the Phoenicians, and the Sidonians. In turn, Solomon chose a Sidonian, Hiram of Tyre, whom he recognized as a superior human being, to build his temple. Webb asserted that the house of David was filled with negro blood through intermarriages with Egyptians and Ethiopians. Thus, he concluded, Jesus was black: "God honored the black man by allowing some of his Ethiopian blood to flow in the veins of His only Son Jesus Christ, and I unhesitatingly assert that Jesus would in America be classed a Negro."[52]

Webb's invocation of the "black man," while typical of the contemporary convention of using the masculine figure to stand in for the universal, should not pass unnoticed. Another important aspect of many white claims about the racial inferiority of blacks included slanders on their ability to live up to "appropriate" gender ideals. For black males, the accusation that they could never be acceptably "manly" was deeply disquieting. By the late nineteenth century dominant American understandings of dignified manliness, whiteness, Christianity, and Americanness were intricately bound; conversely, black males were frequently stereotyped by whites as oversexualized and no better than beasts on the evolutionary ladder. Race narrators responded to these gendered insults as part and parcel of their claims to be fully human, celebrating the achievements of black manhood at every opportunity. The arguments they put forth were intended to provide inspiring models for lower-class blacks who had not yet—according to many community leaders—shed completely the blinders of their enslavement, a condition that had systematically "unmanned" them. The passivity of the ex-slave had to be countered with a legacy of action, aggression, and discipline. Defining black manhood required a tricky balancing act—presenting the ideal black man as a combination of controlled aggression and morally guided virility.[53]

The role of the soldier fit the part ideally: in these accounts, the black soldier was courageous, patriotic, physically robust, disciplined, and moral. Race narrators had sung the praises of Crispus Attucks and other black war heroes for decades, but the postbellum era witnessed a surge of studies devoted to the model of the black soldier. Joseph T. Wilson, a Civil War veteran himself, published several race histories; his book *The Black Phalanx* (1888) was dedicated entirely to recording the heroic deeds of blacks in uniform, "that all might know the sacrifices they made for the freedoms their descendents were so long denied from enjoying." Emblazoned on the front of the book was an image of the author in his military regalia. His study surveyed African-American service in the Revolutionary War and the War of 1812, but the bulk of the book was devoted to accounts of black heroism in the Civil War. At every possible juncture, Wilson emphasized the patriotism and courage of black soldiers, who were ready to give themselves at a moment's notice for their country. He also argued that service in wartime led to other virtues, such as frugality and discipline, habits that continued to serve blacks as model citizens in the postwar period.[54]

Beyond instilling virtuous practices, military service to the ideals of the United States countered perceived passivity by proving that black men had actively fought their enslavement. Edward Johnson's *School History of the Negro Race* contained a section about black service in wartime, in which he stated that the black revolutionary war soldier "began to loosen the chains of his own bondage" through his actions. George Washington Williams concurred that the negro soldier had "fought his way to undimmed glory." Military service, therefore, came to serve as a way of demonstrating that blacks had indeed helped to free themselves: both Blackson's *Rise and Progress* and Wilson's *Emancipation,* using martial metaphors for the longer war against racism, further implied that all blacks had been continually enlisted in the fight, members of a regiment that engaged in incessant battle throughout human history. Several full-length studies of soldiers appeared in this period, including Edward A. Johnson's *History of Negro Soldiers in the Spanish American War* and George Washington Williams's *History of the Negro Troops in the War of the Rebellion, 1861–1865*.[55] Both these and a host of smaller studies, often chapters within longer group biographical portraits, created an image of the black soldier as a type—and by implication, the most admirable type—of black male.

The spread of interest in race history was facilitated by an explosion of new sources and new audiences. By the 1880s American periodical literature (including dailies as well as journals and tracts) was enmeshed in a "revolution" precipitated by low prices, efficient mass circulation, and advertising revenues that transformed the industry and brought literature to a large-scale reading public for the first time. This was true for both black- and white-sponsored publications, but its coincidence with the conscious attempt among middle-class blacks to forge a race-based African-American community lent added significance to the emergence of black publishing as a major social force. Black writers wrote not simply to express their opinions but to provide a voice for a race that often lacked public and positive modes of expression in postbellum society. Black Protestant denominations played a major role in this revolution. Although a number of church-sponsored papers had appeared in the antebellum period, with the singular exception of the AME *Christian Recorder,* churches did not build enough financial support to sponsor long-running and widely circulated papers until after the war. The *AME Church Review,* established in 1884, proved the most enduring—as well as the most financially solvent—black periodical of the nineteenth century.[56] Several other church-based papers, including the quarterly *AME Church Review* and the *Christian Recorder* (the AME-sponsored weekly), the *Star of Zion* (the AMEZ-sponsored weekly), and later the quarterly *National Baptist Magazine,* boasted both readerships and authors drawn from across (and occasionally beyond) the United States.

Distinctive features of African-American life in this period encouraged a new emphasis on the links between reading and religion. In 1870, census statistics identified nearly 80 percent of the black population in the United States as illiterate; by 1910, that number had dropped to approximately 30 percent. This rapid rise in literacy spawned a tremendously expanded market for literature of all sorts. Black denominations, among the best-funded organizations within African-American communities, were some of the first to take advantage of this new source of income and outreach. By the 1890s, observers noted that reading had become a more common pastime among the black middle classes and had even come to rival oral presentations and sermons for the attention of listeners. Mrs. N. F. Mossell remarked in 1891 that the press was encroaching on the power of the pulpit: "People are coming to prefer to sit by their own cosy firesides and read sermons at their leisure, to traveling in inclement weather to the house of worship." And by 1897, a contributor to the *National Baptist Magazine* placed the press alongside the pulpit as the primary shaping force in society: "I believe the press a divine institution," she noted.[57]

The growth of periodical literature and the development of denominational consciousness among African-American Methodists and Baptists enjoyed a symbiotic relationship that served both economic and evangelistic purposes. Religious publications fostered racial loyalty: the AME Church had long billed itself as the "voice of the race," and the *AME Zion Quarterly* claimed to represent the general interests of "the Afro-American Race in America." The rapid rise of the National Baptist Convention in the 1890s provides a telescopic example of this organizational development. Well into the 1890s, black Baptists (not yet nationally consolidated into a denomination) regularly used white Baptist Sunday school literature; many blacks subscribed to one of several white-sponsored Baptist periodicals of the day. But tensions began to rise as the movement toward race-based denominational consolidation began early that decade. Richard Boyd, a prominent Baptist and entrepreneur who would later establish the National Baptist Publishing Board in Nashville, articulated the joining of religious identity and literary production with his encouragement of the creation of negro Sunday school literature, stamped with "Negro personality, thought, and feeling." Along with a growing number of black Baptists, Boyd believed there could be no separate black Baptist denomination without its own self-produced religious literature. Between 1900 and 1903, less than a decade after the founding of the National Baptist Convention and the Publishing

Board, the denomination claimed to have circulated over thirteen million tracts and booklets. Its periodical, the *National Baptist Magazine,* positioning itself in competition for the reading public with both black Methodist journals and white Baptist publications, claimed to be "devoted to the interests of the Negro Race in general." Even as the young Baptist denomination encouraged the production of "race literature," the impulse toward literary production shaped and even catalyzed religious identification with the Baptist Church. Thus not only did religious literature, particularly the new interest in "race literature," contribute to the growth of the black publishing industry but competition for audiences also served to strengthen denominational consciousness among black Protestants.[58]

Religious leaders encouraged blacks to purchase these materials and advised them how to read for the purposes of racial improvement. By the 1890s "race literature" was advertised and talked about everywhere. All literature was significant as a marker of racial advance, but the promotion of race literature focused intensely on collective history as a means to unite black communities and fight the negative racial images promulgated by whites. Benjamin Tucker Tanner spoke at a banquet in 1883, where, after reiterating the verity of the biblical division of the races and the primacy of Hamitic civilization, he concluded that early African civilizations must have had their own great literature—it just had not been discovered yet. He felt certain that in time scholars would "brush away the clouds" of the last three centuries and reveal the founding documents of the race.[59] The Reverend Edward H. Bryant promoted a more active approach, calling for race leaders to pay writers and found literary clubs: "We need speller, readers, arithmetics, geographies, grammars, histories, philosophies, Greek and Latin courses, for our boys and girls, written by our own race; we need commentaries, theologies, and theological works by our own race; as far as possible we need novels, story books, biographies, poetry, and books of travel for our readers by our own race; we want a literature which deals in the trials, troubles, successes and failures of the Negro in all ages." In 1901 the Baptist minister Harvey Johnson urged readers to take seriously the need for independent literature written by the race. "A race without literature, is a race without standards," he argued. Just as whites had their own writings, blacks needed "a real tangible literature which is in its character at once moral, Christian, racial, denominational and national."[60]

Black writers clearly regarded the production of their own literature as more than just a pleasant pastime or a helpful educational tool. This was about collective self-defense in its most fundamental form. In June 1895 Victoria Earle Matthews, a journalist and organizer who had been born to enslaved parents in Fort Valley, Georgia, in 1861, was invited to give a speech to the First Congress of Colored Women in July of that year. The congress had been called quickly in response to a specific offense: the president of the Missouri Press Association, John W. Jacks, had circulated an open letter criticizing black women, stating that all were immoral "prostitutes, thieves and liars." Matthews agreed to speak, and at the Boston conference she delivered an address entitled "The Value of Race Literature." While her chosen theme might initially have seemed slightly off-topic given the urgency of the occasion, she argued for the absolute necessity of an "original school of race literature, of racial psychology, of potent possibilities, an amalgam needed for this great American race of the future." Anticipating the themes of W. E. B. Du Bois in *The Souls of Black Folk,* Matthews argued that like the genius of negro music, negro race literature would express the very soul and true sentiment of a people. It would raise the standing of blacks in the eyes of the world, refute all that had been written about blacks by others, and expand the capabilities of the community by promoting examples of greatness. Women, she asserted, had an important role to play in this enterprise as writers and producers of children with education and talent who would continue the transmission of these traditions.[61]

Teaching people how to read was as important as encouraging the creation of race literature. Authors moved well beyond the mechanics of spelling and grammar to studies of reasoning, judgment, and interpretation. Orishatukeh Faduma composed a series of articles in the *AME Church Review* in the late 1890s titled "How to Make Reading Profitable." He covered subjects such as "methodical reading," "purposive reading," "select reading," and "critical reading," sprinkling his essays with examples drawn from history and literature. Faduma's lessons, in their inclusions and exclusions, provided a road map of subject matter, from classical authors, to philosophy and history, to newspapers and magazines. The North Carolina Baptist newspaper editor Archibald Johnson, also writing in the *AME Church Review,* advised readers how to study history. Blacks must study the past, he insisted, because "to a people like us just emerging from the most abject sub-

jection, and still substantially a servant class, education is political salvation."
He described how one could distinguish truth from falsehood in history,
and he ended his essay with a brief on important topics from each century
since the creation of the earth.[62]

Periodicals also served the crucial purpose of providing general education—and historical education in particular—in graphic form. The *Indianapolis Freeman,* an independent political journal founded in 1888, was the
first black illustrated newspaper. Its elaborate engravings explained broad
topics such as "The Great Southern Exodus." That 1889 image depicted a
large group of blacks standing in a railroad station, holding bags, bedrolls,
and banjos; in the upper-left corner are insets of whipping, lynching, and
dogs searching, flanked by "The Negro in Kansas" and "In Dixie's Land,"
scenes that evince promises of land, jobs, and happier times. The illustration
accompanied editorial encouragement of black migration out of the Deep
South to Arkansas, Texas, and Kansas. A year later the paper featured an image entitled "Historical data of the Negro since his arrival in this country
in 1620." A series of dates and subjects following the title indicated the art-
ist's understanding of significant milestones: "1620—Leaving Africa. 1700—
Coming to America in large cargoes. 1800—in slavery. 1830—Turner's Insurrection. 1865—Fighting for the flag. 1870—In Congress. 1890—On fame's
great ladder." These dates were then repeated in the image itself over smaller
drawings, like overlapping photos, of each scene. In every case—including
the "1800" setting that showed two slaves working in the fields with a white
overseer in the background and the 1865 battle scene with black soldiers—
the foregrounded actors in the vignette were black. Framing the image was a
tattered and torn piece of paper that read "Historical Events" and "The Record." The vignettes of African-American milestones looked as though they
had been hidden underneath "the record," which had been ripped away to
reveal the true story. This powerful image provided a pointed history lesson and simultaneously critiqued the official white version of events, literally shredding and replacing it with another narrative. In the upper-left
corner a small banner ironically commented, "Note what civilization hath
wrought."[63]

Such illustrations served as a tool for the inculcation of communal history. Equally important were the advertising and canonization of race histories within the pages of magazines. Periodical literature was, of course,

a business, and advertising revenues were crucial to its success. In selling race literature, advertisers promulgated specific versions of what constituted the race and its appropriate reading material. An 1891 edition of the *Indianapolis Freeman* advertised Johnson's *School History of the Negro Race* and announced that it had been adopted as a textbook by Livingstone College, Shaw University, and public schools in Raleigh, North Carolina. "Every member of the race should have a copy," the writer insisted.[64] Such appeals were typical fare. *The Christian Index,* the official publication of the Colored Methodist Episcopal Church, was perennially strapped financially and more dependent on advertising revenues than most papers. Sandwiched among pitches for groceries, pharmacies, and hair straighteners, its book ads— some addressed to general readers, some to ministers, and some to families—insisted that particular sets of books were essential purchases for black Christians. "Important Books that should be in the hands of every minister and in every family," announced one ad in 1888; such calls typically ended with the assertion that "this book should be read by every methodist," or "all of the above books are very useful and should be circulated in the church and school." In advertising race literature and "race authors," periodicals were themselves participating in the normalization of certain types of literature as indispensable purchases for educated blacks. To be a race member, such advertising implied, one had to read race authors.

Lists of books thus became prescriptions for racial advance among the middle class, just as surely as dressing well or speaking correctly signaled the attainment of respectability. This impulse to canonize harks back to the lists of the first black ministers drawn up by Daniel Coker in 1810, or the enumeration of black churches in Philadelphia by William Catto in 1857. It was, on the one hand, a continuation of the impulse to "gather up the fragments, let nothing be lost," to collect the scattered sheep of the African diaspora and bring them into community once more. On the other hand, it also regulated and disciplined literature into specific patterns relevant to race leaders eager to represent themselves and their brethren in particular ways. Overwhelmingly, the books recommended were race histories, Christian histories, and other genres of historical studies.

Such lists of books taught African-American readers what it meant to construct a comprehensive view of the world through canonization and bibliographic incorporation. Many of these books are almost entirely unknown to readers of the twenty-first century. Aside from Frederick Douglass, Edward Blyden, Alexander Crummell, Frances Harper, and a few other names that were rediscovered by scholars in the 1980s, most of these authors have been forgotten by subsequent generations. But in 1900, black narrators were looking back, commemorating and assessing the state of their community. By this time, alongside histories of the ancient past, of African and Haitian lands, and of Christian and American legacies, narrators were building another layer of history by writing their own century of struggle into the story. Group biographies and encyclopedias, emblematic literary productions of the 1890s, recounted traditions that enshrined dozens of late nineteenth-century heroes and heroines, including their contemporaries, alongside earlier figures. The Rev. William J. Simmons's book *Men of Mark* contained brief biographies of figures that included Toussaint L'Ouverture and the Revolutionary War hero Crispus Attucks as well as the music historian James Trotter, the AME bishop Henry McNeal Turner, and James Walker Hood. James Haley's 1895 *Afro-American Cyclopedia* arranged in alphabetical order a sprawling series of entries that included brief histories of black denominations and schools, individual biographies of contemporary leaders, a history of tobacco (accompanied by a New Testament injunction to avoid such impure substances), and discussions of female dentists; within his pages one could find a bricolage of options for African Americans, one that included historical examples from the preceding hundred years. The many genres of communal narration, including ancient history, denominational studies, accounts of Haiti and Africa, and patriotic renderings of black achievement, had been conjoined in group portraits that told the story of a diverse but unified racial community moving forward into the future.[65]

Postbellum race narrators attempted to place their own "maps of the world" at the center of debate over African-American identity and destiny. This was a remarkable and courageous feat in an era in which whites were doing all they could to define the negro as degraded, inferior, and historyless. Despite many disagreements over the specific interpretation of racial history, race historians were more alike than not. Heirs to an ongoing debate in the United States about race, and newly armed with technologies and institutional networks that facilitated the ability to speak on behalf of a community, religious leaders fashioned a novel form of historical narrative aimed at the representation of a renewed African-American collectivity in the years after Emancipation. Much of their art, as they themselves knew, sprang from wishful thinking. Late nineteenth-century blacks were far from united in their views on nationality, race, or religion. Race historians hoped that their accounts would be both self-fulfilling prophecies of racial unity and prophetic indictments of contemporary racial and religious practices. In hindsight, their fragile attempts to unite middle-class evangelical values, progressive views of history, and an appeal to the fundamental verities of scriptural authority, all within a racialized vision of the world, would soon be obsolete. The trope of the "New Negro," increasingly promulgated by African-American intellectuals after the turn of the century, had little use for biblical paradigms or sacred histories. Few narrative accounts published after 1920 carried the same religious and racial valences. The writing of race histories, in general, was turned over to scholars trained in the "science" of historical inquiry.

Yet this genre met the pressing social and cultural needs of newly emancipated blacks who now labored to make sense of the collective ordeal out of which they emerged. Freed men and women, as a result of their relative isolation from the intellectual currents of black cultural production in the North, proved a receptive audience for education about the history and fate of the race as it had been compiled by others. Race history furnished a vigorous response to the growing racism of Euro-Americans by the 1880s and 1890s, a racism institutionalized in Jim Crow laws and conceptualized in U.S. history books—"white" race histories presented as national histories. The negro race history challenged those national narratives by presenting contrasting Christian and patriotic versions of the American past. The genre responded directly to white attacks on collective black efficacy and morality. The advertisement and distribution of negro race histories educated two generations of black readers and canonized a set of interpretive lenses through which the newly unified race, North and South, was forged as a political and theological entity.

6

"The Grand Traditions of Our Race"

I was asked a few years ago by a white friend, "How is it that the men of your race seem to outstrip the women in mental attainment?" "Oh," I said, "so far as it is true, the men, I suppose, from the life they lead, gain more by contact; and so far as it is only apparent, I think the women are more quiet. They don't feel called to mount a barrel and harangue by the hour every time they imagine they have produced an idea."

ANNA JULIA COOPER, *A Voice from the South*

In 1869 Frances Ellen Watkins Harper, one of the most prolific and best known African-American authors of the nineteenth century, published an epic poem entitled *Moses: The Story of the Nile.* Moses had long fascinated the ardent antislavery activist. In 1859 she commented admiringly on his ability to forsake the "glittering splendors" of Pharaoh to suffer with the enslaved. In Harper's hands, Moses's fate unfolds through a series of encounters with women. The poem opens as Moses informs Pharaoh's daughter, the Egyptian princess, that he is leaving the palace to "join / The fortunes of my race." The account then backtracks and rehearses a history of Moses's earlier years, lavishing considerable attention on his Hebrew mother: "From her lips I / Learned the grand tradition of our race . . . / She would lead us through / The distant past: the past, hallowed by deeds / Of holy faith and lofty sacrifice. / How she would tell us of Abraham, / The father of our race, that he dwelt in Ur."[1]

Harper's poem is intriguing in its reduction (or elevation) of one of the most powerful and politically potent biblical stories to a series of domestic encounters with maternal figures. Rather than narrating the story through a progression of Israelite patriarchs, Harper placed a racialized religious history squarely in the hands of women: Moses's mother is acknowledged as the curator of "the grand traditions of our race." While nodding to male religious leaders—the fathers—such as Moses and Abraham, Harper imbued women with the power of narrative, and thus of communal as well as individual agency. Her heroines are figures who "would tell us / Of a promise, / handed down from sire to son, / That God, the God our fathers loved and / worshiped, / Would break our chains, and bring to us a great / Deliverance." Despite the homage paid to men's roles as leaders of the community and conveyors of tradition, it is women who do the work of preserving cultural memory, of handing down "a promise" from mother to child.[2]

In spite of her intimation that women must preserve collective memory, it is doubtful that Harper would have thought of herself as a historian. *Moses* hardly resembled the formal, book-length race histories that African-American men were just beginning to write and publish by the 1870s. And Harper was not one to have made great claims for the importance of her work. Even if she had, it would be difficult to categorize her poem: it is filled with multiple voices, many of them ordinary and hardly the usual agents of heroic tales, and it implies—but never overtly states—an analogy to the contemporary plight of African Americans. Yet it is clear that, like male authors of race histories, the author understood her literary work as an act of service to the race: just as Moses chose to "suffer with the enslaved [rather] than rejoice with the free," Harper declared that the race needed "earnest self sacrificing souls that will stamp themselves not only on the present but on the future."[3] Harper talked *around* history, weaving it in and out of a variety of literary forms.

Harper may have been the most famous African-American female author of her day, but she was not the only one who constructed and interpreted collective pasts, nor was she the only one who did so in indirect or circuitous ways. From Phillis Wheatley's poetry in the 1770s to the plays and pageants of Alice Dunbar-Nelson and Rachel Grimké in the 1920s, black women narrated histories that, like the accounts of their black male counterparts, contained racial, religious, and national themes. But over and above their labors to forge a cultural place for black communities, these women produced knowledge that was shaped decisively by their gender. Organizationally, women's narrative voices emerged in a contested landscape of churches and publishing enterprises, arenas that set particular rules about appropriate sites for, and forms of, female speech. But their distinctive experiences of the past—especially their understandings of community as defined by family, children, domestic life, and other women—allowed black women to push back against both black male authorities and white representations of the race, redefining in the process the terrain of permissible "feminine" speech and writing. In doing so, they began to build a historical tradition of their own, creating representations of a black female community that had been repressed in male-authored accounts.[4]

Just as black men struggled to legitimate their own right to speak and write within a racist culture, so, too, did women bump up against gendered restrictions within their own communities. The "race histories" related by women, while grounded in a commitment to historical narrative as a vehicle of race advancement, also bore the marks of many other kinds of allegiances, including loyalties to other women.

Black women experienced the world differently from men. And those differences—determined by gender conventions of the time and the material distinctions and behaviors that resulted from them—influenced how they perceived community, identity, and memory. Just as African-American men in the early part of the century had taken biblical passages and classical texts and woven them into new and often subversive narratives of a collective past, so, too, did African-American women engage in creative acts of storytelling that challenged older paradigms, and that enfolded women's experiences as a crucial element of the plot. Women's accounts were every bit as diverse as the tales told by men, of course, but their content inevitably was shaped in part by the gender-defined worlds inhabited by nearly all American women of the nineteenth century.

African-American women had long been responsible for the informal transmission of historical knowledge. Numerous accounts of slaves and ex-slaves describe grandmothers, sisters, and mothers who had passed along information about family and community lineage. In his narrative of 1772, one of the earliest penned by an African who had been enslaved, James Albert Ukawsaw Gronniosaw recalled his exchanges with his mother about his own lineage. Similarly, Martin Delany notes that his "Grandma Grace" had vested him with knowledge of his royal African forebears. Delany and Gronniosaw were emblematic of many other enslaved Africans who had come from cultures in which women bore a heavy responsibility for the transmission of vital historical knowledge—especially of lineages—within families and kinship groups.

Arrival in the Americas began to transform black women's roles as transmitters of tradition. The middle passage and its aftermath ushered Africans into a new world—not just physically, but technologically and epistemologically as well. This transition altered the communal status of the historical knowledge for which African women apparently had oversight. Increasing numbers of blacks, aided by Christian conversion and manumission in the Northern states, gained access to a classical Euro-American education and prized the new cultural and political power that it afforded. Despite the nostalgia with which many black men recalled family-centered historical knowledge, they knew that their future lay in the power of print. It provided a new and potent political tool for nascent free black communities, and particularly for black men, to communicate their ideas widely and to associate with broader collectivities. In printed essays and in an increasing number of black-run periodicals published after the 1820s, black men created communal histories of a more abstract sort—premised on national, racial, and political relationships less localized and tactile than the familial knowledge that had preceded them.

Traditional women's knowledge and authority as caretakers for the past, while not disappearing by any means, received less and less visibility and acknowledgment as a shaping cultural force. Framed in terms of individual and collective relationships—mothers, children, families, and the endurance of connections over generations—women's ways of narrating the past were largely excluded from the public discourse found in sermons, newspapers, and other publications. Historical knowledge shifted from a female task to a male prerogative as new forms of technology, first within free black and later within ex-slave communities, heightened the visibility and availability of print-based knowledge.

Any effort to narrate collective history in the new manner required two things: an authoritative knowledge of the past (including information sanctioned by the literate community) and the means publicly to relate an interpretation of that knowledge. As spotty as educational opportunities were for most antebellum free blacks, women's prospects were further constrained by a sharp distinction between the types of education that were considered appropriate for males and females. Few African-American women could anticipate formal education beyond the rudiments of reading and writing. Sunday schools for blacks provided knowledge of the Bible, but beyond that text-based knowledge was uneven, and it is difficult to gauge the extent to which free black women might have had access to other kinds of books.

That said, a few women went far beyond that starting point. Ann Plato, a schoolteacher and member of the Colored Congregational Church of Hartford, Connecticut, published a book of poems and essays in 1841 that demonstrated a working knowledge of many textual sources. Her allusions were not out of keeping with standard Euro-American historical interpretations. In discussing education, she cited Alexander, Aristotle, Milton, Walter Scott, Cicero, Adam Clarke, and Newton. In an essay on character she drew from Christopher Columbus ("He appeared with a steady and cheerful countenance," and he remained resolute even when his companions criticized his quest for a "far distant country"), Demosthenes, Pompey, Benjamin Franklin, Robert Fulton, and Robert Bruce.[5]

Plato's near contemporary in Boston, Maria Stewart, also demonstrated in her speeches that she had explored a remarkable range of texts. We know almost nothing about how she gained her knowledge, but her later speeches and writings reveal a great deal about what she had learned and read. Clearly, her biblical knowledge was vast. In her 1833 "Farewell Address to Her Friends in the City of Boston," she quoted sequentially from Psalms, Matthew, Isaiah, Romans, Luke, Philomen, Ezekiel, Revelation, Judges, Esther, Ephesians, and Proverbs.[6] She also cited or alluded to classical and contemporary authors with admirable facility, making use of the poetry of Thomas Gray, an eighteenth-century English pastoralist, the historical work of the British John Adams, and the hymnody of Isaac Watts.[7]

The foundation for Stewart's historical awareness was thoroughly biblical—in fact, the fiery orator inhabited biblical stories in a way unmatched by any other orator of her day. For Stewart, the Bible was, first and foremost, a template for God's relationship to humanity, and more specifically, to the African race. Like her contemporary and friend David Walker, she lambasted the sins of white Americans and occasionally made use of the analogy of Israel in Egypt, predicting that those whites in the colonization movement, "like Pharoah, king of Egypt . . . would order every male child among us to be drowned." But Stewart favored the prophet Jeremiah and frequently cited

the books of Jeremiah and Lamentations. This predilection led her to corre-
late America with Babylon more often than with Egypt:

> It appears to me that America has become like the great city of Baby-
> lon, for she has boasted in her heart: "I sit a queen, and am no widow,
> and shall see no sorrow!" She is, indeed, a seller of slaves and the souls
> of men; she has made the Africans drunk with the wine of her fornica-
> tion; she has put them completely beneath her feet, and she means to
> keep them there; her right hand supports the reins of government and
> her left hand the wheel of power and she is determined not to let go her
> grasp.

Stewart's framing of the situation went well beyond a condemnation of the
United States. Indeed, the speaker also cautioned against African-American
complacency. Africa had fallen from its glory, she noted continually, and despite the oppression of whites, African Americans had only themselves to
blame.[8]

This final twist of collective recrimination apparently did not endear her
to all listeners. Stewart, on several occasions, mentioned the obstacles she
encountered within the black community of Boston, "those who endeavored
to discourage and hinder me in my Christian progress." Yet her words reflect
a sophisticated and thoroughly consistent rendering of the Babylonian captivity narrative as articulated by the early prophets. Carrying the model of
Israel in Babylon to its logical conclusion, Stewart placed the blame for the
African "exile" squarely at the feet of the sinful new Israel—the African-
American community. Maria fashioned herself as the latter-day Jeremiah,
called to reveal the sins of whites and blacks alike, "however severe they may
appear to be." She excoriated African Americans for their many transgres-
sions and failure to better themselves. Citing Jeremiah and Lamentations,
she interpreted the ill feeling directed toward her, as well as the current state
of "fallen Africa," as the work of those who, like the Israelites in Babylon,
had turned away from God. Like Jeremiah, she prefaced several speeches
with expressions of steely determination to "withstand the fiery darts of the
devil, and the assaults of wicked men." Even her reading of the Ethiopian
prophecy ("Ethiopia shall again stretch forth her hands unto God"), which
infused so much of her thinking, indicated an interpretation framed by her

own prophetic standing: she understood the passage not as a sign that God would once again bless Ethiopia but as a call to Christian reform. Ethiopians would someday (when they demonstrated the right amount of Christian piety) return to God. Although Stewart presumed that the rejection she encountered from other blacks was part and parcel of the prophetic undertaking, and she answered it with militant language, her audiences and readers most likely also rejected the conservatism of the racial politics that flowed from her appropriation of the Babylonian exodus account.[9]

In keeping with the complex messages about racial worth that Stewart's writings reveal, her awareness of the significance of gender was also colored by a deep-seated biblicism. Like many other female historians, she believed that the future of the community resided squarely with black women: "O, ye mothers, what a responsibility rests on you!" During a speech before the newly formed Afric-American Female Intelligence Society, of which she was a member, Stewart reminded her audience of their importance, "for upon your exertions almost entirely depends whether the rising generation shall be any thing more than we have been or not." In this regard, Stewart voiced a predominant ideology of domesticity that isolated the influence of women to the work of the home and the rearing of children. Yet she also used the Bible and other historical texts to argue for the right of women to act publicly and politically. Stewart, moreover, stated quite baldly that she had little respect for the black men of her generation: "It is true, our fathers bled and died in the revolutionary war, and others fought bravely under the command of Jackson, in defence of liberty. But where is the man that has distinguished himself in these modern days by acting wholly in the defence of African rights and liberty?"[10]

Stewart's appropriation of the Babylonian exile was not simply put to the service of racial awareness and uplift. In fact, the opposite may have been true: her Christian convictions and identification with a particular religious history led her to a controversial, judgmental, and probably unpopular understanding of racial character. In living out the story of the Babylonian exile, Israel had debts to pay and sins to account for; ultimately, Babylon and Israel were part of a larger sacred community and were answerable to the same God. Stewart would not sacrifice her religious duty for the sake of racial unity, no matter how much she valued the latter.

Stewart saw herself as a prophet, and her identification with Jeremiah lent spiritual validity to her role as a female speaker. The fullest exposition of Stewart's gendered historical awareness is found in her farewell speech in Boston, delivered before her move to New York. Stewart intended her address to be another Christian call to arms, a jeremiad not unlike those she had delivered previously. But try as she might to make her point, she returned again and again to the subject of her own abilities, accounting for herself with wide-ranging historical argument. In the final section of her speech, Stewart brought out a full biblical and historical arsenal to justify her authority:

> What if I am a woman; is not the God of ancient times the God of these modern days? Did he not raise up Deborah, to be a mother, and a judge in Israel? Did not queen Esther save the lives of the Jews? And Mary Magdalene first declare the resurrection of Christ from the dead? Come, said the woman of Samaria, and see a man that hath told me all things that ever I did, is not this the Christ? St. Paul declared that it was a shame for a woman to speak in public, yet our great High Priest and Advocate did not condemn the woman for a more notorious offence than this; neither will he condemn this worthless worm.

Stewart then considered earlier examples of strong women from the ancient world: "Among the Greeks, women delivered the Oracles; the respect the Romans paid to the Sibyls is well known." Similarly, she noted, early Egyptians, Romans, and even "the most barbarous nations" respected female abilities. In Europe during the medieval and Renaissance periods, she argued, women preached and occupied professional teaching positions; they knew Latin, Hebrew, and Greek; and they functioned as accomplished orators.[11] Beginning from a biblical framework, Stewart rallied an assembly of examples from ancient and early modern periods to create a lineage of capable and strong female precedents.

Although a small number of free Northern black women including Plato and Stewart secured access to a classical education and public modes of expression in the antebellum period, the resources for such efforts were scarce and limited primarily to abolitionist organizations and churches. In this regard, Frances Ellen Watkins Harper was also an entirely unrepresentative antebellum black woman. Harper was born into the black community of Baltimore in 1825. After the death of her mother in Frances's early childhood, the young girl was reared by William and Henrietta Watkins, her aunt and uncle. The family was well connected in black activist circles in the city. William Watkins, a committed AME Church member, antislavery supporter, ardent opponent of African colonization, and preacher, had energetically advocated the Haitian emigration earlier that decade. He contributed articles regularly to the journals edited by his friends and associates, including Benjamin Lundy's *Genius of Universal Emancipation* and later William Lloyd Garrison's Boston-based abolitionist newspaper, *The Liberator*.[12] The family attended Sharp Street Church, a historic black Methodist congregation often called the "Mother Church" of Baltimore Methodism, which stood at the center of abolitionist activism in the 1820s and 1830s. Indicative of its deep commitment to racial causes (as well as to the political diversity of opinions on African emigration within the community), Sharp Street Church had sent a dozen members as emigrants to Liberia in 1825 as part of the African colonization effort. In this setting, Frances became the heir to a distinctive legacy of Christian piety, protest, and racial advocacy, impulses that remained with her throughout her long career.

Harper attained an education more extensive than that of most free blacks and even many white Northerners of the day. The elder Watkins, a shoemaker by trade, had steeped himself in learning acquired from the range of books available, attaining proficiency in Greek, Latin, and medicine. Committed to making such learning accessible to other free blacks, he ran the prestigious William Watkins Academy for Negro Youth, where Frances enrolled at an early age. There she was introduced to an extensive classical curriculum, including biblical studies, history, natural philosophy, Greek, Latin, rhetoric, geography, and mathematics. After she left school in 1839 to work as a domestic and seamstress, Frances procured employment in a family that owned a bookshop. There she extended her education through free access to the family library.[13] In 1850 Harper left to take a position at Union Seminary, a vocational school near Columbus, Ohio, that had been founded by the AME Church in 1844 (and later became part of Wilberforce University). The first female instructor at the school, Harper was hired to teach sewing classes. But her work brought her into contact with an even wider circle of antislavery activists and intellectuals who would later prove instrumental to her career. For Harper, an independent negro academy, a generous employer, a black denominational school, and most important, her relationship to the antislavery movement, provided an educational route to a new world of historical knowledge.

After 1865, many more African Americans living in the Southern states had access to literacy, education, and opportunities for writing and speaking. With freedom came academic prospects, and with schooling came new sources of knowledge. Initially, freed men and women gained education and literacy largely under the auspices of the federal government and church organizations. Sunday schools often operated as the first place where ordinary men and women might acquire basic literacy through exposure to Webster's speller and the Bible. Those who could afford the time attended one of the many new colleges established in the South. But generally, the first schools for women operated under the paternalistic assumption that their primary task was to train African-American women in "True Womanhood," that is, to rear them to be moral exemplars and domestic icons for a rising generation. If women were compelled to work outside the home, they could be trained in one of the few service professions open to blacks in the South. Spelman College, for example, considered to be the preeminent institution for black women, was founded in the 1880s expressly to prepare teachers, nurses, missionaries, and (non-ordained) church workers. Its white female founders did not see the need to offer a classical education, because those intellectual pursuits were deemed luxuries in a situation where pragmatic concerns—with an emphasis on temperance, thrift, and domestic skills—prevailed.[14] However, college and teacher training for African Americans took place primarily in coeducational institutions as early as the 1870s and 1880s. The first state-supported black normal school in the country, founded in Fayetteville, North Carolina, in 1877, enrolled a majority of women in its first class. Many denominational colleges followed suit, and women took courses in classics and theology alongside men. As Anna Julia Cooper, one of the first female students at the coed Saint Augustine's School in Raleigh,

North Carolina, noted, women were accepted in classes, even if they were not encouraged—in part because there were few overt restrictions in place to stop them from enrolling. The lack of precedents for Southern black women's education left room for creative improvisation, and those women plucky enough to take advantage of such opportunities could receive training equal to that of their male colleagues.[15]

A growing emphasis on collective "uplift" encouraged middle-class black women to pursue educational opportunities beyond what was considered appropriately "feminine" in the eyes of white Southerners. African-American middle-class mores dictated that women, like men, pursue learning that would demonstrate their equality with whites of a similar class standing. Female education thus provided one more opportunity to prove the worth of the race as a whole. More often than their white counterparts, middle-class black women had to work outside the home after marriage, and many took advantage of the opportunity to train as teachers. Unlike the dominant images of middle- and upper-class Southern white women as prizing soft-spokenness and looking askance at too much education, black communities often valued academic training in both men and women. Intellectual skills did not appear adversely to affect black women's chances of making a "good marriage"—indeed, evidence suggests the opposite.[16]

Aside from formal schooling, the late nineteenth-century proliferation of black women's organizations—missionary and temperance societies, benevolent affiliates connected to fraternal groups, antilynching groups, and women's clubs—afforded women access to a wider range of political, social, and historical knowledge. If charity and munificence were the stated concerns of many of these associations, self-improvement and collective enjoyment invariably played significant roles as well. Too often, the important personal and social work undertaken at women's gatherings is dismissed as trivial and "just social," but African-American women knew full well the connection between collective support and social change. Public activism necessitated the cultivation of effective speaking, writing, and critical thinking, and women helped one another gain these skills as they delivered papers, discussed topical events, listened to invited speakers, and read books together. In turn, visits to clubs and organizations in other parts of the country facilitated the spread of knowledge to larger communities of women.[17]

In all these educational settings, formal and informal, black women discussed the past and its meanings. Through study of the Bible, theology, history, philosophy, or classical languages in normal schools and seminaries, and through literary and discussion-oriented gatherings in women's organizations, access to historical arguments and examples was widespread. Even women with limited means might attend Sunday school or missionary societies, or hear speakers at local colleges and churches. The collective conviction in all these settings was that history mattered. Women knew that a careful consideration of the past had consequences for all African Americans— and, indeed, for the nation as a whole.

No longer lone pioneers steering a solitary course, African-American women authors increasingly found themselves supported by race-based institutions and organizations that provided a venue for their public aspirations. By the 1880s new doors, quite literally, opened for them: the doors to church organizations, to publishing houses, to clubs and societies, and even to international women's events. Inhabiting new roles as journalists, lecturers, and writers, black women quickly joined the ranks of "scribbling women": between 1890 and 1910 alone, they published more fiction than black men had published in the previous half-century.[18]

Anna Julia Cooper's career was shaped by many of these new postbellum educational realities. Born in 1858 in Raleigh, North Carolina, to an enslaved woman and her white master, Cooper entered the newly established coeducational St. Augustine's College, founded by the Protestant Episcopal Church, at the age of nine. Despite encountering resistance from male students and teachers, Cooper studied Greek and other subjects geared toward males on the ministerial track. Left widowed after a brief marriage to an Episcopal divinity student, Cooper then went north to Oberlin College, where she, along with two other African-American women, completed the four-year "gentleman's course." From there, Cooper embarked on a career as a writer, speaker, and educator, and spent many years as a teacher and educational administrator in Washington, D.C. In 1925 she was awarded a doctorate from the Sorbonne for a dissertation on the history of French attitudes toward slavery during the French Revolution, becoming only the fourth African-American woman to receive a Ph.D.[19]

Cooper is best known for her 1892 publication *A Voice from the South*, in which she ranged widely through politics, education, history, and literature to demonstrate the many obstacles that lay in the path of African-American progress in U.S. society. Gender and race are certainly the predominant themes in her work, but to demonstrate the severity of the current problem Cooper employed stories of the past as well. In her opening piece on the importance of womanhood to the advancement of the race, Cooper used the history of the Christian church, the feudal system, and Arabic civilization as her benchmarks for women's contemporary treatment—all within the first two pages. She then cited Madame de Stael, an eighteenth-century French woman of letters, Thomas Macaulay's *History of England*, Ralph Waldo Emerson, and the Roman historian Tacitus.[20] Cooper's work demonstrates both the general scholarly conventions of essay writing in her day, in which proofs from a wide range of historical periods and literatures (the broader the better) constituted definitive evidence, and also the myriad resources available to a black woman in an era in which females were actively discouraged from entering careers of "pure" scholarship.

But by the 1890s there were many others like her, women intelligent and tenacious enough to take full advantage of the multiple routes to a mastery of classical, biblical, and Euro-American canons. Those African-American women who became journalists, poets, and public speakers represented a small proportion of the nation's black population, to be sure. They were members of an emerging black middle class that sought, through education, comportment, public activism, and the relating of history, to distinguish themselves as leaders of the race. Some, like Cooper and Mary Cook from Kentucky, had been born into slavery.[21] But most were born either in the North or into free black communities in the urban South.[22] As middle-class women dedicated to the "politics of respectability," they used their talents as writers to promote a genteel vision of black community life, and in doing so they strove to control and "correct" the behavior of the working classes in the name of racial and religious unity.[23]

Their vision was also regionally specific. Centered around Eastern cities in New York, Pennsylvania, and Maryland, as well as Washington, D.C., areas that gave birth to the largest concentration of both black publishing ventures and independent black churches, women writers articulated a communal identity at once cosmopolitan and urbane. As such, it was far out of step with the reality of the vast majority of black Protestants who remained in the rural South. In this regard, the first generation of black women authors were "missionaries" to the ex-slaves as much as were male race historians of the day. Many women, however, spoke in historical voices that corresponded more closely with the family and kin-based knowledges of the past.

The differing expectations for women's writing often were apparent from the first sentences of their works. Whereas George Washington Williams dedicated his *History of the Negro Race in America, 1619–1880,* to "the public, white and black," and expressed hope that the book might help bring about racial equality, the schoolteacher Leila Amos Pendleton, writing in 1912, began *A Narrative of the Negro* by describing her work almost hesitantly as "a sort of 'family story' to the colored children of America."[24] Her turn of phrase and the nature of her chosen audience were significant. Pendleton clearly recognized that the invocation of family and children provided her with a distinctive platform from which to communicate. Other women chose another route to public legitimation: they had a man pen a laudatory introduction to their work, an opening that typically vouched for the piety and "femininity" of the author, since presumably she could not do so herself.[25] Women were acutely aware that they were producing histories different from those of male authors, and they frequently hesitated to make substantial claims for the importance of their own work.

Their reticence reflected an awareness that it might be considered unseemly for women to be writing about history at all. As a result, women as a rule utilized different genres for their work. Men wrote Race Histories— narratives with a vast chronological sweep and controlling themes—while women wrote stories, plays, and tales of the race containing suggestive or qualified assertions of their own significance. Indeed, no textbooks nor large tomes written by black women of the day are directly comparable to the race histories of male writers. For black women, the relating of collective history—sometimes evoked only in brief allusions or in the listing of historical names—emerged in a wide array of rhetorical constructions, including biography, social protest, and poetry. This difference reflected not so much a lack of historical knowledge as a consciousness of the gendered nature of the traditional "grand narrative" format. Significantly, their renderings fundamentally challenged the category of "history writing" as a discrete narrative form.[26]

African-American women thereby found ways of writing history without announcing it as such. For example, Pauline Hopkins, an editor of the

Colored American Magazine, rewrote sacred history in her novella *Of One Blood* by referring to a forgotten civilization in Telassar, a city in the ancient Near East; in quoting Milton and the Bible, Hopkins drew these historical references into her fictionalized history of a sacred African-descended people. Her story was not a formal history, but it made use of and revised history to stress the obligation of African Americans to a holy and trans-historical community.[27]

Women's "histories" were also published in places different from the histories written by men. For many decades women were denied or had limited access to the principal professional venues for historical utterance—the ministry and the periodical press. At least, women could not *use* terms like "sermon" or "editorial" to describe their activities; instead, they simply spoke and wrote under other rubrics. Whereas men employed the pulpit and the editorial pages of the black press, women made use of imaginative literature, periodical publishing, women's club gatherings, and children's literature to spread their knowledge. Women's tales of the past did not always look like formal history (which became more prescribed and subject to scholarly conventions by the late nineteenth century), but female authors nonetheless engaged in historical allusion and argument, using knowledge of the past to make claims about contemporary community life.

Yet history-making offered something distinctive to African-American women. Black men had long used interpretation of the past to validate their own claims to citizenship and equal political standing. So, too, women found it an abundant resource for the contestation of female rights and privileges. In turn, the publication of their writings quickly inspired other women to write, multiplying accounts that valorized the deeds of females. Black women in the 1890s did not fail to notice that Phillis Wheatley, Maria Stewart, and Ann Plato were true intellectual pioneers, outpacing even black men. Frances Harper became a revered godmother to many of the women writers of the late nineteenth century, providing inspiration, encouragement, and a dedicated and tangible place in history for black women.

In the postbellum South churches served as the primary location for female activity. As the influence and financial standing of those organizations grew after 1850, women increasingly used religious communities (and their arms of dissemination such as Sunday schools, temperance organizations, colleges, and periodicals) to establish political authority, legitimate intellectual credentials, and pursue public writing and speaking. By the 1890s the development of the black women's club movement, which was in many respects a logical outgrowth of the early female literary societies, further increased opportunities for public utterance. And a series of high-profile gatherings, including the Columbian Exposition and the World's Congress of Representative Women, both in 1893, afforded some black women an international audience for their views on race, history, nation, and gender.

Black churches also provided the most accessible public space for women's narration. Postbellum Protestant churches did their utmost to encourage the growth of literacy and education within Southern black communities. But if the black church was indeed a public sphere in which women could exercise a degree of power—and a voice—not granted them in American society more broadly, it was still a community with rules that governed practice and speech. The ongoing battles over female ordination in both white and black churches throughout the nineteenth century in large measure had revolved around questions of appropriate speech: who was allowed to speak, what they were allowed to say, and to whom they could address their words. The power to tell stories, even within black churches, was meted out by gender.

Black churches, by and large, denied women access to the ritualized presentation of history, a power vested primarily in the minister. As women sought access to the pulpit, which they did increasingly in the late nineteenth century, they were also requesting authority to interpret and expound Scripture, and thus sacred history, before the religious community. All the mainline black denominations denied this form of historical voice for women, battling against the growing number of females who sought official recognition as preachers in the decades after Emancipation. The assertion of AMEZ minister R. D. Davis was typical: he stated that because Jesus did not call women as his apostles, so they should not be allowed to preach in modern times: "All the Hebrew cannons, Greek torpedoes and the 13 inch English guns fired at the ministerial fort will not win a victory for female preachers."[28]

Female church members did not write formal communal history or explicate it within the context of worship, but they were obligated to learn it in order to pass it on. In church communities, their historical voices most often were channeled in ways thought to coincide with their "natural" roles as mothers and teachers of the young. Praised and even valorized as the primary teachers of children, Protestant women were expected to narrate a tradition established by male leaders. Women were presumed to be the messengers but not the authors of history. Male religious leaders voiced assumptions about the circumscription of women's historical voices in easily penetrable code, often couching them in flattery. In 1889 an article appeared in the AME *Christian Recorder* in which the author, I. D. Roes, characterized women as a "gift from heaven" (presumably to men) and rhapsodized: "What is more lovely than a true, good woman, one who has the courage of her convictions and who having plenty to do for herself, can never find time to meddle in others' affairs?" Such affairs included, seemingly, those skills of leadership and interpretation belonging to male authorities.[29]

Hallie Quinn Brown understood well the gendered politics by which women's voices in the religious community were caught up in a web of male leadership. Born in Pittsburgh and reared in the free black community in Chatham, Ontario, Brown graduated from Wilberforce in 1873. She then taught school in the Reconstruction South but was soon tapped as a skilled speaker to travel around soliciting aid for her alma mater. Like several other notable female writers, Brown first gained fame as an outstanding "elocutionist," speaking in front of huge church audiences around the country. But significantly, she was not speaking her own words; she served as a trained spokeswoman for the words of her male superiors. Decades later, she gained fame as an author in her own right, and was most renowned for *Homespun Heroines* (1926), a collective biography of notable African-American women. Nonetheless, when she was heralded in a book-length tribute to African-American women by a black male author, he legitimated her skills through recourse to the opinions of AME church leaders, citing letters of commendation from Daniel Payne and Benjamin Arnett. Brown's talents and her voice, it seemed, were inextricably linked to her position within a male church hierarchy that simultaneously encouraged and restricted her speech.[30]

The opportunities for women to write and publish outside the walls of the church increased dramatically after 1880. Antebellum black writers such as Plato and Stewart were self-published and supported by local printers. But by the late nineteenth century, women writers were everywhere. The tremendous growth of female authorship was simultaneously enabled and constrained by a coincidence of ideological, social, and economic forces, some that pertained to American culture more broadly, and others that were unique to the situation of African Americans in the post-Reconstruction decades. Those forces included the rapid growth of periodical publishing, new marketing dynamics, denominational consolidation, and demographic trends among African Americans that elevated the importance of religious periodicals to collective identity.

Nowhere was this more true than in the growing numbers of black church–sponsored publications that offered women another medium for self-expression, one not governed by the same gendered principles found within the church itself. Within the world of denominational publishing, women circumvented and even subverted the male monopoly on communal history. Couching their historical interpretations in "female" literary genres, and shifting the content of the histories themselves, women's writings implicitly challenged the authorial voices of male clergy as the sole interpreters of collective identity.[31] Increasingly able to draw African-American Protestants into an "imagined community" of believers that extended beyond the walls of a local church, religious publications can be seen as an alternative sacred locale with the potential either to complement or to compete with the beliefs and behavioral norms promoted within the church edifice itself. Their messages could be communicated to a regional or even a national audience.[32] As women increasingly articulated their roles as keepers of tradition and memory in print, they found ways to voice opinions that circumvented churchly dictates about appropriate female speech.

Female representation within the world of print grew enormously in the ensuing decades; women's voices came to play a larger role in the denominational press than they did within the ritual life of the church. Iconographic presentations of this discrepancy between the pulpit and the religious press bear out the growing divide between a male clergy and an increasingly feminized labor force in the religious press. In May 1900 the AMEZ *Star of Zion* presented the public face of the church when it featured on its front page the "Bishops of the African Methodist Episcopal Zion Church," a gallery of portraits of nine male leaders. In the *National Baptist Magazine* of July 1897, conversely, the frontispiece pictured the staff of the publishing house in a parallel style; unlike the representation of the AMEZ Church, however, the National Baptist publishing house featured the three female and two male staff members in its self-presentation, a more gender-balanced image of a religious organization that still did not reflect the many more women writers who contributed to its pages. As male church leaders increasingly reacted to halt the "contagion" of legitimate female authority in church management, the religious press welcomed the poetry, stories, and articles of female church members in ever greater numbers.

Soon other publications began to make greater use of women's literary abilities. With the proliferation of black periodicals in the postwar decades came a concomitant interest in "women's issues" extending beyond the church milieu. Appealing to the sensibilities of women aspiring to middle-class notions of respectability, black magazines and newspapers actively solicited women's contributions and eventually instituted women's departments within their pages. Specialized magazines for women, some of them connected to the emerging women's club movement, grew in number at the same time, and included *Ringwood's Afro-American Journal of Fashion* (established in Cleveland in 1891), *Woman's World* (Fort Worth, 1900), and the *Colored Women's Magazine* (Topeka, 1907). To compete with these publications denominational periodicals, long the province of clergy and predominantly male writing staffs, added women's pages and departments, and sought female contributors for their issues.[33]

High-profile publications, in turn, opened other doors for many women. Economically, writing could supplement a livelihood outside the confines of domestic labor, teaching, and secretarial work. Socially, it brought women to the attention of prominent African-American male leaders, and even precipitated "good" marriages for enterprising women. Professionally, it introduced the work of female writers to other editors, who then vied for their talents. Unlike male contributors to religious periodicals, who tended to be clergy and whose contributions were localized to the pages of specific denominational publications, women writers attained a status at once more prominent and more diffuse. Writers such as Ida B. Wells, Frances Harper, and Gertrude Mossell became national celebrities, correspondents for numerous publications, and authors of their own books; their words thereby carried a potential for influence unmatched by most of their male counterparts. By the 1890s women began to establish clubs that further encouraged education and political literacy.

Female writers participated in the same processes of cultural reconstitution through narration that male writers did; but gender inflected their work in ways that also forged new communal ground. Religious history—biblical, Protestant, and denominational—provided the single richest resource for African-American narratives throughout the century. This seems to have been particularly true for women, perhaps because the Bible was their most readily available resource, or because (as was also the case among white Protestants) African-American Protestant churchgoers were predominantly female and their lives were shaped more fundamentally through a relationship to their churches. In either case, women employed a wide variety of biblical stories as historical examples in their speeches and writings, and they used them to illustrate and emphasize a range of political and social ends. Their works demonstrated confidence that a changed understanding of the past could reorder the present.

Like their male counterparts, African-American women used many stories from the Bible, and especially from the Hebrew Scriptures, to comment on the plight of contemporary African Americans. Priscilla Jane Thompson (1871–1942), an Ohio-born writer of poetry, based her 1897 poem "David and Goliath" on 1 Samuel 17:32. Although published in a volume entitled *Ethiope Lays,* the poem itself does not make explicit any connections between the Israelites and the predicament of African Americans. Thompson simply meditates on the heroism of the young fighter and celebrates his victory over the Philistines. But apparently Thompson saw the analogy as self-evident. In her introduction, she noted that "in this little volume . . . I have endeavored, as nearly as possible to picture the real side of my race bringing in the foreground, their patience, fortitude and forbearance, devoid of that undertone of sarcasm, generally courted."[34] Olivia Bush, a young author from Providence, took a more direct approach in "Creation's Mystery," a poem that appeared in the *National Baptist* that same year. Using the framework of the creation account in Genesis, Bush emphasized that God's original intention for human societies was equality: "From him sprang all the nations great, / Each kindred, tribe and race."[35]

Choice of biblical passages was not simply random. Certain historical moments obviously resonated more significantly than others. The account of the Israelite exile in Babylon, detailed in books of the Hebrew Scriptures such as Ezekiel, Jeremiah, Second Isaiah, and Lamentations, provided comforting precedents for African Americans both before and after Emancipation. In some ways, too, the Babylonian exile (587–539 B.C.E.) presented a more complicated portrait of exile and suffering than did the Egyptian Exodus. After the destruction of Jerusalem, Israel had become a diasporic community, with some members left behind in a weakened kingdom and others taken to Babylon. This striking image—of a unified community lost, its members separated, with some forced into second-class status in a new environment—appealed to African Americans on a variety of levels. It reinforced a collective connection with those "left behind" in Africa, it eulogized the former unity and glory of the homeland, and it offered solace and explanation for current suffering. Mrs. A. A. Bowie at Selma University in Alabama included in her 1897 speech about Baptist unity a reference to Isaiah 55:1, a passage that eloquently invited the Babylonian exiles to partake of God's abundance. God called his people to the Baptist Church today, Bowie noted, just as he had called the oppressed Israelites: "He will conduct you to this fountain of life that you may drink and never thirst."[36]

Denominational loyalties emerged in women's renderings of history. The Reformation loomed large in the recounting of Hardie Martin, speaking at the anniversary of the Columbia Street Church in Montgomery, Alabama, in 1896, where she asserted that the church must help the condition of "the masses," those members of the race who remained illiterate and "morally depraved." Like the apostle Paul, she ventured, the church could bring education to the surrounding culture. Would that the religious community could take a lesson from the lineage of true Christian heroes: "In the days of Polycarp, Roger Williams, Martin Luther, John Knox, and John Wesley no evil that endangered the interests of the masses was winked at." Mary Cook, arguing for the importance of women's work to the race, justified female leadership by quoting Luther, arguing that "the work of a teacher is next to the office of a preacher."[37]

Women participated enthusiastically as the anniversary of the founding of independent black churches approached in the 1890s. Frances Harper, a life-long member of the AME Church and frequent contributor to denominational papers, penned several odes to commemorate the centennial of the church and the fortieth anniversary of Daniel Alexander Payne's bishopric in 1892. Later that decade, Mary Weston Fordham eulogized Payne as a religious hero in *Magnolia Leaves: Poems* (1897), thanking him for service to the race and the denomination. Katherine Tillman authored a similar verse to the AME bishop Benjamin Arnett, and would later expand her literary homage to the church in dramatic form in "The Spirit of Allen: A Pageant of African Methodism" (1922).

Like male race historians, African-American female authors were, on the whole, a patriotic group. Even the antebellum Maria Stewart, despite her comparison of America to Babylon, celebrated the country's potential and identified strongly with some of the main elements of the national narrative. She extolled the Puritans for their ability to flee the religious persecution of Britain and later to defend themselves against political tyranny: "They first made powerful efforts to raise themselves, and then God raised up those illustrious patriots, WASHINGTON and LAFAYETTE, to assist and defend them." Like many other race historians, Stewart presented blacks as the rightful heirs to the republican legacy. "We will tell you that our souls are fired with the same love of liberty and independence with which your souls are fired," she proclaimed in the pages of the *Liberator* in 1831. Despite the sins of whites, Stewart cherished a national legacy that, in her estimation, was founded "upon religion and pure principles." "O, America, America! Thou land of my birth! I love and admire thy virtues as much as I abhor and detest thy vices."[38]

Alice Dunbar-Nelson, a public schoolteacher and journalist based in Washington, D.C., who worked and wrote tirelessly to integrate the achievement of the negro race into the classical education of black youth, penned a series of stories in 1905 entitled "Romances of the Negro in American History." Her accounts used standard (Euro-American–authored) historical texts and foregrounded the participation of African Americans at key moments. In "Estevanico Explores the Southwest," Dunbar-Nelson described

the Spanish expedition of 1527 in which an enslaved Muslim from North
Africa, Estevanico (Esteban, or Steven the Moor, 1500?–1539) was one of
four surviving members to travel from the Gulf Coast to Mexico City. Her
account depicts Estevanico, not Cabeza de Vaca (traditionally the narrative
focus), as the protagonist of the story—plotting escape from Indians and
leading the others with his "wily strategy" and greater physical endurance.
After arriving in Mexico City Cabeza de Vaca exits the scene to return to
Spain, and Estevanico's further adventures as a colonial authority on Indians
elevates him to the status of a famous leader within the community. Even
when he is killed on a subsequent trip north among the Zuni, the gallantry
of the "black Mexican" with "chili lips" continues to be remarked by the natives who attacked him.[39]

Dunbar-Nelson's histories placed African-descended peoples in a New
World picture without fundamentally challenging triumphal narrative traditions. In contrast, other women's stories from the period thoroughly re-
worked the dominant Euro-American understandings of the past. Amelia
Etta Johnson, the wife of a Baptist minister in Baltimore, depicted the history of the race as part of a larger, cyclical human narrative. Explaining at
the outset that her paper was not "a strict chronicle of data, or a systematic
record of happenings," Johnson pointed out that history does repeat itself.
Beginning with the Norman Conquest of 1066, in which a "rude, bluff people" (Saxons) were virtually enslaved, and continuing through the oppression of the Puritans (who then persecuted others in the colonies), Johnson
traced a lineage of subjugation, fermentation, and ultimate release from
bondage culminating in the recent Emancipation of African Americans.
This history, in her estimation, proved both that blacks were part of the nation and that they must oversee their own social progress. "Let us cease trying to prove to the world that we were born into it for the sole purpose of
admiring the white people of the United States, and that this is all we will
ever be fit for," she concluded. "We must fill our place in the world if we are
to furnish our true and complete parallel to its history."[40] From her standpoint at the century's end, American history was less a tale of inevitable
progress than a romantic morality play with tragedy as a necessary and recurring component.

Awareness of Native-American claims on the land had long complicated
the historical consciousness of race writers. Antebellum African-American

writers had previously invoked native perspectives on European conquest to comment upon their own situation. In "Natives of America" (1841) Ann Plato related the story of the near-extinction of Native Americans after the arrival of Columbus. She narrated the poem from the perspective of a Native-American girl whose father speaks to her about the history of their people. Although it is possible that Plato herself had some Native-American blood, her references to a "happy race" that is subsequently brutalized could just as easily stand in for the situation of enslaved Africans: "Oh! silent the horror, and fierce the fight, / When my brothers were shrouded in night." At the close of the poem, all the "fathers" of the race are gone, "we're silent every one," and the girl is left with an instruction from her father to preserve this racial memory:

Now daughter dear I've done,
Seal this upon thy memory; until the morrow's sun
Shall sink, to rise no more;
And if my years should score,
Remember this, though I tell no more.

It is left, then, within the world of this poem, for women to preserve historical memory for future generations in the face of near communal extinction.[41]

Perhaps most intriguing in Plato's work is the glimmer of an American nationalism that is inherently multiracial and fraught with tensions and ambivalences; from her place of relative marginality, Plato narrated national accounts that navigated a space between unity and diversity. Later black women writers pursued similar themes, and interest in American nationalism gained considerable force in their works by the end of the nineteenth century. That interest correlated, not coincidentally, with the widespread popular memorialization of American foundings. Public interest in the European discovery of America became especially frenetic in the 1890s, spurred on by commemorations of the 400th anniversary of Columbus's voyage and the push to establish a national holiday in his honor. Mary Weston Fordham published an ode to commemorate the Chicago Columbian Exposition in 1893; her work demonstrated a much more enthusiastic and less tragic view of Native Americans than that expressed by Ann Plato decades earlier. In keeping with standard depictions of American Indians as a noble but vanishing race, she rendered natives as innocents whose cultural extinction inevitably would make way for the rise of more advanced civilizations. The body of the poem consists of a description of the native-European encounter from the perspective of the Indians, a narrative choice that complicates the celebratory mood. The native chieftain watches the approach of the "Pale Face crew" with trepidation and worry. But his concern turns to amazement and awe at the sight of the men—a superior race, presumably—on their knees, praying to God "that His blessings e'er / Might this fair land endow." Olivia Ward Bush-Banks, in telling the tale of the Long Island Indian in 1914, articulated an American national pride that was blameless in the face of impersonal natural laws: "How relentless, how impartial, / Is the fleeting hand of time, / By its stroke, great empires vanish / Nations fall in swift decline." One could, according to these historians, admire the "fierce" and "proud" Indians but still celebrate America's evident progress.[42]

Like male race authors, women celebrated the bravery of black soldiers in American wars. Their inclusion was not limited to memorials for the American Revolution (although Crispus Attucks received attention) or the Civil War; in the 1890s, an era of American high imperialism, African-American writers also praised participation in the Spanish American War as a symbol of racialized patriotic manhood. Among homages to Abraham Lincoln, Frederick Douglass, and Wendell Phillips, the poet Olivia Bush included verse addressed to "A Hero of San Juan Hill," a black soldier who "fought for Cuban liberty":

> March on dark sons of Afric's race,
> Naught can be gained by standing still,
> Retreat not, quit yourselves like men,
> And like these heroes, climb the hill.
> Till pride and prejudic shall cease,
> Till racial barriers are unknown,
> Attain the heights, and thou shalt find,
> Equality upon the Throne.

Bush conjoined racial, national, masculine, and Christian progress in her image of the black soldier, who fought not simply for recognition as a black man but for the "crown" of American victory and even religious redemption. Soldiers' inclusion in this volume of poems juxtaposed them with other heroes of the race, placing their efforts in a longer legacy of struggles—and implicitly, into a progressive narrative that would lead them to an ultimate glory.[43]

Black participation in a war in the Caribbean had additional national and racial significance because of the proximity of Cuba to Haiti, another island with a large African-descended population. It would have been difficult for a black writer or reader not to have associated those black soldiers fighting in the Caribbean with blacks who had taken part in the slave revolt nearly a century earlier—as well as with those who had fought for U.S. freedom. Leila Pendleton dealt extensively with the participation of African Americans in American conflicts from the Revolution to the Spanish American War in her *Narrative of the Negro* (1912). She depicted black soldiers as heroically fighting for the freedom of Cubans: "For a hundred years Cuba had been restless under the heavy yoke of Spain and the people had many times arisen in revolt. During the revolution which broke out in 1895, the sympathy of the civilized world was with the Cubans, and when the United States battleship Maine was destroyed in the harbor of Havana in 1898, war was declared with Spain." Making the racial connection explicit, Pendleton noted that "among the Cuban soldiers also, were many intrepid fighters of African descent; Gen. Quentin Bandera, the famous black Chieftain, was noted for his fearlessness and bravery." "So again, you see," Pendleton concluded, "American Negroes proved themselves, as one writer has said of the native Africans, to be the greatest natural warriors of the earth."[44] The story of the war provided a means of demonstrating simultaneously the inherent patriotism, manliness, and racial loyalty of black soldiers.

Like Frederick Douglass and other male narrators, female writers noted the ironic existence of slavery in a "free" American nation. Frances Harper's poetry toyed suggestively with communal terms such as "our native land" and "our country" to accentuate both the achievements and the moral failings of the nation. In "An Appeal to my Country Women" (1894) she brought together Christian ideals, female sympathy, and racial oppression in a powerful historical evocation. Criticizing white American women who would lament the plight of the "sad-eyed Armenian" or the Russian exile while ignoring the "murmurs of pain" emanating from blacks in their own southland, Harper implored them to spare some sympathy for "mothers who dwell 'neath the shadows / Of agony, hatred and fear." Ultimately, in her estimation, the history of the nation would be subsumed within a sacred accounting. Significantly, perhaps, Harper was one of the few race historians to view American imperialism during the Spanish American War from the perspective of Christian pacifism. "Do not cheer, for men are dying," she began her ode to the tragedy of human bloodshed. "Do not cheer until each nation / Sheathes the sword and blunts the spear, / And we sing aloud for gladness; / Lo, the reign of Christ is here."[45]

Women's accounts were distinguished not just by their subject matter but also by their characters and settings. In particular, women's exploration of domestic life as a primary mover of history shaped the content and intellectual concerns expressed in their race histories. Their stories, populated by mothers, children, old men and women, the poor, and everyday heroes, challenged not just white versions of history but the narrative styles employed by black men as well.

The rendering of slavery presents a striking example. The central dilemma for any patriotic African-American historian by the late nineteenth century was slavery, a rupture that challenged nationalist narratives. Slavery as a usable past presented more of a burden than an opportunity for male authors. Black men tended to link the era of African enslavement conceptually to religious degeneracy and male powerlessness, abstracting slavery as a concept from the particulars of slavery as lived experience. Black women, conversely, narrated enslavement as a lived—and living—reality, and took great pains to render the contours of everyday life under the lash in great detail. As Gertrude Mossell argued (several years before W. E. B. Du Bois published his similarly romantic view of Southern slave religion), slavery was an era of heroism, and it ought to be included in historical accounts: "Let us see to it that we despise nothing—the croonings of our aged nurses, the weird monotone of the slave song, the folk-lore. These are our authors' first editions, the source of what will some day become the mighty rivers of our race literature. Let us not undervalue their worth, but gather and string them like pearls of great price upon the chain of memory."[46] Slavery represented a period of intense spiritual trial—and thus of triumph. This victory was both powerfully personal, because individuals had strengthened their faith in the furnace of suffering, and collective, reflecting the mettle of the race as a whole. As a characteristic of many societies throughout history, slavery was a great leveler, according to Mossell. In a tragic way it demonstrated the unity of Africans with all humanity.

Slavery represented an era in which domestic and relational ties were important factors in the building of community. Katherine Davis Tillman's 1901 play "Heirs of Slavery, A Little Drama of Today," created on the pageant model that was becoming ever more popular at the opening of the twentieth century, tells the story of a "negro youth" worn out by the oppression and barriers to equal treatment that he has encountered. As he questions his own desire for achievement in the face of such obstacles, he is visited in a dream by a series of characters who seek to boost his morale: Father Time, History, Poesy, Art, and a handful of historical figures. The most provocative element of Tillman's narrative is her claim, like that of Mossell, that the legacy of slavery is a crucial aspect of racial history. But Tillman goes beyond the straightforward assertion that African Americans have a distinctive history; she also affirms that their history of enslavement is an integral part of world history, an inheritance of suffering that unites blacks across time and space with other communities. Blacks, she asserts, are not the only heirs to this inheritance. As attested by Moses's mother, Miriam; a Greek gladiator; a Roman slave; and an Anglo-Saxon, many nations have been "conquered in the heated fray." At the close of his dream, the young protagonist arises, renewed with optimism, and vows both to defend the honor of his race and to recognize his connections with all humanity: "Allen and Douglass shame my sorry plight / Toussaint and Dumas star my gloomy night. . . . I'll do my best, proving where'er I can / Despite his skin, a man is but a man!"[47]

In her collection of poems *Ethiope Lays*, Priscilla Jane Thompson of Rossmoyne, Ohio, also balanced the particular experience of African Americans with universalism, but her portrait of slavery is more intimate, domestic, and evangelical in tone than Tillman's. In "The Old Saint's Prayer" the intense piety of an elderly woman helps her endure "Satan's host" during her years of enslavement ("Full sixty years she'd faced the brunt, / And still she was not tired"). In "My Father's Story" the father of the narrator relates an "ancient" tale about the horrible fate of a cruel, rich slave owner. Significantly, the telling of the story of slavery itself—a scene of young children with parents sitting around a fire during a cold winter night—instills a feeling of comfort and unity. The "cruel, foul, perverseness" of the slave owner is juxtaposed with the peaceful domestic scene within the home. The father is not exactly nostalgic for the past as he shares horrifying stories with his family, but he finds meaning in imparting the morality tale of the fate of a sinful man.[48] Christian faith was strengthened by endurance in the face of suffering, to be sure; but in Thompson's work the suffering was tactile, measured not in universal laws but in worn hands and warm hearts.

These memories of slavery were not simply markers of the power of racial endurance. They also signaled a worry that others, both black and white, would avoid or forget enslavement. While black men wrote of slavery as divine mandate or lapsed into silence about it, some women turned directly to the pain of familial suffering and collective endurance. Theirs were inspirational stories with layers of community—racial, familial, generational, evangelical, and human—woven in intricate patterns. Slavery, a history that dramatically set off African Americans from all other American groups, was used to explore a range of loyalties and histories—and relating the past around a domestic fireside became in itself a reinforcement of a racial and religious legacy. Thompson's final poem in the volume, "Address to Ethiopia," might seem to be her most racially specific. She begins by identifying herself with "ill-starred Ethiopia," "My weak and trampled race!" Her poem promises to trace the path of this community through time. Calling on her fellow blacks to rise up "and form a nation of thine own," the author seeks racial union. Yet throughout the poem, in an insistent undertone, Thompson alludes to another identity based on a shared faith and a common circumstance apart from the condition of enslavement: "The same God hath created thee, / That did thy fairer brother; / Thinkst thou, that in His justice, great, / He'd prize one 'bove the other?"[49] Race pride, for Thompson, was couched within the broader context of a common Christian community.

Slavery was an important component of collective memory inasmuch as it had threatened to break generational connections that made community recollection possible. Women understood this more viscerally—or at least they conveyed it with more immediacy—than did men, in part because generational continuity among enslaved peoples was dependent on the maternal line in a singular way. The legal status of black children had been defined principally by their relationship to their mother; if she was a slave, they also would be enslaved. Further, because enslaved black women were unable to regulate or protect their own sexual behavior in an economy dominated by the authority of white men, lineage necessarily had to be marked by maternal descent. These political and sexual realities found voice in the views of history articulated by African-American female writers well into the twentieth century; narrators pressed the practical mechanics of the connection between history and procreation vividly and insistently.

Mothers commonly figured in historical vignettes as critical shapers of culture. Frances Harper was the master of this sort of history, as she demonstrated so clearly in her placement of Moses in a domestic world, surrounded by family and other community members. His decision to leave his home has momentous consequences (as one familiar with the biblical story would have known), but Harper portrays it as a decision made within specific human relationships, through dialogue with a mother. While the patriarchs and the central male characters remain in prominent places in the account, the driving subtext of the story is a relational connection nurtured, often invisibly, by mothers and sisters. Many of Harper's other poems reveal how great evils and triumphs play out within particular communities. Slavery is rendered as the tragedy of the wife left behind while her husband flees, or the violence of a child separated from his mother. Harper's narration of the past often traces absence or longing, rather than action or power.

Black women narrators were making fundamental assertions that moved history from the battlefield and halls of government to the parlor, kitchen, and slave quarters. Many were quite straightforward about their intentions: Virginia Broughton noted in her 1894 address that maternal influence was crucial to moral development: "The mother transmits her virtues or her vices to her children; in fact, she reproduces herself in her children." But unlike her male counterparts, who asserted that women should serve as the "elocutionists" of history scripted by male authorities, Broughton elevated the role of women within the story itself. She wedded maternal guidance to God's plan in the unfolding of Israelite—and by extension African-American—history, which occurred primarily as a result of female influence. Echoing Harper's *Moses,* she declared that "in the deliverance of Israel from Egyptian bondage, it was the love and wisdom of woman that preserved, nourished, and trained the man child that God called to be the leader, judge and priest for his people." A year later, Mrs. C. H. Baxter summed up this commonly held view even more succinctly, when she noted that "the influence of woman more or less affects for good or evil, the entire destinies of man."[50]

This ideology of female cultural influence through the invocation of sentiment reflected pervasive American assumptions in the Victorian era about women's roles as nurturers, teachers, and moral paragons. But for black women, the interrelations of cultural inheritance, communal identity, and maternal influence assumed a distinctive and highly charged meaning. Slavery had acted as a potential rupture in the very fabric of collective history, one summed up in a poem published in the *Star of Zion* in May 1886. Written in commemoration of the birthday of the author's mother, it described the collective history of slavery, Civil War, and Emancipation that only a mother could relate to her children: "You have seen poor Afric's children, / Struggling, groaning neath their load, / You have seen those children flee to / Where the North Star points the road."[51] The "you" referred to is the author's mother; standing in here for all black mothers, she is not the only witness to these events, but she is the most reliable vehicle of collective history in a period when families were torn apart and paternity was a precarious bearer of identity.[52] Fanny Jackson-Coppin opened her *Reminiscences of School Life, and Hints on Teaching* with a memory of her grandmother: "Mammy used to make a long prayer every night before going to bed; but not one word of all she said do I remember except the one word 'offspring.' She would ask God to bless her off spring."[53] Without a history of slavery, this passage embodies only the domestic piety of middle-class Victorian America; but seen in light of enslavement, it takes on new meaning as a symbol of collective endurance and transmission refracted through the lens of motherhood.

Not all black women's narratives, however, employed sentimental or evangelical strategies, particularly as the optimism of Reconstruction sank into the despair of early twentieth-century Jim Crow laws and lynchings. The themes of miscegenation, rape, and race suicide, tracing as they did a historical legacy of sexuality and violence, posed more subversive lessons. Frances Harper's only full-length novel, *Iola Leroy* (1893), features a heroine who has grown up as a proslavery Southern belle, only to discover years later that her mother was a slave owned by her father.[54] The theme of miscegenation reflected a sense of the precariousness of individual identity and highlighted the pervasiveness and hypocrisy of white fears of racial impurity. It was used to protest the systematic sexual violence perpetrated against black women that endured as an unfading legacy of enslavement. The mulatto character marked—and physically embodied—the inheritance of the slaveholding past. Since maternal status determined one's history (white or black), miscegenation represented a potential break with community; like Iola Leroy, one could discover, suddenly and without expectation, that one's history was in fact not really one's own. Upon learning her true paternity, Iola Leroy is confronted not only with a dilemma of her own standing in the present but with a problem of her relationship to the past.[55]

Pauline Hopkins's serialized novel *Of One Blood: Or, the Hidden Self* (1902–1903) is a provocative exploration of time, memory, and the connections between family lineage and racial history. Hopkins (1859–1930), a performer, playwright, orator, novelist, journalist, and biographer, was fascinated by history. She believed that biography was the best kind of history, and as the editor of the Boston-based *Colored American Magazine* (1900–1904), she wrote a character study for each issue. Two of these studies, "Famous Men of the Negro Race" and "Famous Women of the Negro Race," read as narrative histories of the race, and they demonstrate her interest in using history as a tool for racial uplift. Hopkins's work presents a familiar example of the interweaving of race with other events in world history: her section on black female educators, for example, rehearses the transmission of civilization from Ethiopia to Egypt, and then on to Greece and Rome, before discussing illustrious figures in the present.[56]

Of One Blood tells the story of Reuel Briggs, a light-skinned young medical student at Harvard who is passing as white. In a fantastic turn of events, Reuel, who has renounced his African lineage, finds himself awakening from a four-day sleep in the Great Pyramid in Telassar, a city containing the modern descendants of Meroe (ancient Ethiopia). Here he discovers his connection to Africa, "the enchanted ground." Moreover, the citizens of the city are awaiting the arrival of the king, "who shall restore to the Ethiopian race its ancient glory," and Reuel has arrived at a propitious moment to help the community fulfill its destiny. They immediately name him as the heir to their legacy.

The novel can be analyzed in any number of ways—for its use of utopian and science fiction themes, and for its exploration of new psychological theories of the unconscious, among others—but its investigation of the link between past and present and its intertwining of personal, familial, and communal identities are particularly significant. Reuel is a mulatto, and his insistent denial of his racial identity is both a concrete disavowal of his family, an act that cuts him off from others, and a failure to recognize his inheritance as a regal redeemer of a hidden civilization. Telassar itself represents a place at once ancient and contemporary; it is both a city hidden from the eyes of outsiders and the purveyor of occluded wisdom. Reuel awakens there to a new identity, to a newly recovered knowledge, and to a destiny that he will fulfill. Hopkins plays with the notion of time, with the conjunction of past and present embodied in a racial community of memory. On the sphinx in Telassar (which, notably, predates the Egyptian sphinx) is inscribed a phrase taken from the Old Testament book of Ecclesiastes: "That which hath been, is now; and that which is to be, hath already been; and God requireth that which is past."[57]

Much of Hopkins's story echoes themes found in earlier race narratives: the tales of secret communal wisdom of black Masonic lore; the notion that civilization began in an Edenic Ethiopia with Hamitic peoples; the use of biblical and classical literature from Herodotus, Milton, and the Euro-American luminaries Cotton Mather and Ralph Waldo Emerson; and even a suggestion that an African-American time-traveling missionary (who needs some educating himself) will reappear in Africa to save the race.[58] Hopkins adds to this the more recent events of enslavement and sexual brutality at the hands of whites that continues well beyond Emancipation (both implied in Reuel's light skin and realized in the rape of another character in the story). Her fictionalized account allows her to represent the intellectual and spiritual emancipation of African Americans through the emblematic awakening of one man. Reuel's "passing," his renunciation of family and community, reflects the broader historical plight of African Americans, who, as later black intellectuals and activists would repeat more directly, have forsaken their collective future through a denial of the past.

As racism became increasingly virulent in the early twentieth century, some female narrators took even more radical steps in their work, calling into question the future of the race on account of its past and present sufferings. Anticipating themes probed in the work of Harlem Renaissance writers such as Nella Larsen and Georgia Douglas Johnson, the playwright Angelina Weld Grimké's work *Rachel: A Play in Three Acts,* first performed in 1916, explored the issue of racial history through the trope of childbearing, and offered the possibility of a fundamental negation of the historical process itself. The play opens with a scene swathed in idealized domesticity, in a "scrupulously neat and clean" if plain living room. Grimké's stage direction furnishes the space in painstaking detail, highlighting the fireplace, the piano with Raphael's *Madonna* perched above it, and the "open, threaded sewing machine," at which an African-American mother, Mrs. Loving, sits surrounded by yards of white fabric. She is immediately joined by her daughter, Rachel, and the two engage in an extended conversation about children and the sacredness of motherhood. "Ma dear," the daughter gushes, "if I believed that I should grow up and not be a mother, I'd pray to die now." For Rachel, childbearing is not simply a hope but a God-ordained blessing to protect children of color. "Ever since I have known how Mary felt at the Annunciation *(almost in a whisper)* God spoke to me. . . . I love the little black and brown babies best of all. . . . More than the other babies, I feel that I must protect them."[59]

On one level, the story can be read as an unsubtle and sentimentalized critique of lynching and an indictment of white Southern communities that allow the abuse of children through systematic violence. Rachel and her brother soon discover that their father and half-brother had been lynched ten years earlier by a white mob, a revelation of the past related through her mother's voice. This unfolding of history transforms Rachel completely, until she becomes embittered and cynical regarding the inevitability of entrenched racism: "The blight—sooner or later—strikes all," she concludes. Finally, on the edge of insanity, "as though her soul had been mortally wounded," as her mother describes it, Rachel rejects the offer of marriage by her longtime suitor and announces her intention never to have children. "I am afraid—to go—to sleep, for every time I do—my children come—and beg me, weeping—not to—bring them here—to suffer. . . . I have promised them again, now. . . . I have damned—my soul to all eternity—if I do."[60]

Rachel's climactic "anti-annunciation" is paired with her earlier reverence for Mary, a gesture that links the experience of racial violence in both past and present to childbearing and to the unfolding of sacred history itself. Rachel's refusal to have children thus becomes a way to stop history entirely, to refuse to play out the divinely ordained role of mother for a God that she has come to see as irredeemably cruel. This antihistoricism reminds us that the premise of history itself depends on generational succession and the cultivation of offspring who will move forward because they are confident about the past and the present. Whereas male race historians focused principally on the notion of lineal succession in institutional terms, that is, through the mechanisms of churches, schools, and public offices, Grimké offers a radical reinterpretation of historical progression, locating it within the personalized and familial reception and transmission of values, sentiments, and hope.[61]

Most African-American female historians were not as pessimistic as Grimké in their predictions. Instead, they sought not just to critique the present but to change it by shifting the historical focus. Blurring the lines between homes and institutions, women narrators ushered a community of black women onto the historical stage. They presented the legacy of black women as an explicit challenge to the male monopoly on racial history, and they also criticized the failure of African-American men to include women in their narratives. The exclusion of women not only reflected an egregious blindness to the historical record, in the opinion of some, but also affected the future of the race as a whole. It was, in short, a moral problem. In 1888 Catherine Casey contributed an article to the *AME Recorder* emphasizing the importance of race histories as a means of instilling pride in children, but she questioned the limitation of "race literature" to that written by black men. She described witnessing a sermon given by Levi Coppin (then an AME elder) in which he held up five books for presentation to a local church library, "calling them his 'black boys.'" "While Elder Coppin was rejoicing over his 'black boys' I was wondering where the 'black girls' were. Why are not Mrs. Harper's poems bound in blue and gold and lying upon our library shelves?"[62]

Throughout black periodical literature beginning in the 1880s, women called attention to the activities of prominent female historical figures. Like Maria Stewart before them, they cited a litany of female leaders such as Joan of Arc, Sojourner Truth, Frances Willard, Harriet Beecher Stowe, and Florence Nightingale to demonstrate the prominence of women in the historical record. Mrs. M. E. Steward, a Kentucky Baptist, opened her article on "Woman in the Church" by noting women's agency since the establishment of Christianity: "through all stages of its history, in prosperity and in adversity, woman has been prominent as a worker." She noted that women had been "last at the cross" and "first at the tomb" and had also served as a "special messenger of the Lord" to carry news of the Resurrection to the disciples.[63]

Others exploited the genre of writing known as prosopography, or group biography. In 1894 Gertrude Mossell published a book-length study of black women that most closely approximated the male-dominated genre of the "race history." Like many of her contemporaries, Mossell was steeped in the overlapping worlds of both the black church and race-based journalism. According to Ida B. Wells, a prominent journalist and activist in her own right, Mossell had "done more varied newspaper work than any other woman of her race in the country." Born into a Quaker family in Philadelphia, Mossell later joined the Presbyterian Church. But she was encouraged by AME editor Benjamin Tucker Tanner to contribute to the pages of the *Christian Recorder,* and thereafter she began writing for the *AME Church Review,* the *Indianapolis Freeman, Our Women and Children,* and many other black periodicals.[64]

In *The Work of the Afro-American Woman* Mossell lauded the accomplishments of women in business, art, law, medicine, journalism, and religion. She covered the historical progress of black women up to the present, and included women within traditional accounts of racial advancement. Many of the women mentioned, including Elizabeth Steward, Mrs. Benjamin T. Tanner, and Grace Douglass, were best known as wives of notable black male leaders and were close friends of Mossell's; but she also lauded the female evangelist Amanda Smith and the club activist Fannie Barrier Williams. Mossell separated the history of the race into three epochs. By "race," she clearly meant African American (she excluded Africans), and despite her faith in the strength of individuals, the history she narrated was not sunny. Part I consisted of enslavement, the departure from Africa, and arrival in the New World; Part II encompassed 250 years of slavery; and Part III comprised the era of freedom, in which the race held "in name citizenship, but [was] defrauded of its substance by every means that human ingenuity could devise."[65]

Mossell's work was perhaps the best known and most widely circulated race history of its day. Its success was attributable in part to Mossell's connections within multiple race-based organizations, including churches, periodicals, and women's groups. But her work and its reception also illustrate the complex layering of communication and authorization through which a narrative became part of collective memory. In placing many of her contemporaries squarely within a longstanding racial lineage, Mossell transformed both past and present. The preeminence of women of the past, a story too little told, lent added importance to the achievements of contemporary women. F. E. W. Harper's novel *Iola Leroy,* Cooper's *A Voice from the South,* and Victoria Earle Matthews's *Aunt Lindy,* by being named as pieces of a common history, changed the larger racial narrative and declared those works to be representative of something beyond themselves. Mossell devoted an entire chapter to a description of important race literature, in which she listed over seventy "race books," declaring that "he who would know the Afro-American of this present day must read the books written by this people to know what message they bear to the race and to the nation."[66]

The genre of group biography created black female communities in print. It also allowed some writers to move away from the "great figures" approach to history to focus more on the common folk. This choice underscored the historical significance of traditional women's work. Mrs. Sarah J. Dorset championed a view of history in which the lowly, the quiet, and the obscure became the primary agents of moral and racial progress. "In the family she quietly labors for the children," Dorset explained. "The outside world knows and thinks little of her trials and perplexities; but patiently and trusting in her God, she quietly discharges her daily routine of work." The first "woman's column" published in the *Star of Zion* in the 1890s, written by Mrs. Pettey (the wife of an AMEZ bishop), consistently touted the virtues of local churches and unseen workers, those "less noted but hard-working self-sacrificing Christian soldiers," as the backbone of the denomination. "The large churches stand as shining lights and towering sentinels to let Christianity and the world know that Zion is alive," she wrote in 1899. "But it is to a certain extent the small churches and the country work producing the motive power propelling our great ship of Church."[67] In her hands, the "church" became a united community of humble servants and workers—primarily female—extending beyond the bounds of worship and ritual life.

To call women's race narratives "revolutionary" stretches the term. For the most part, African-American female authors did not employ a style that counseled protest or social disturbance, even of traditional gender roles. Most spoke in low voices and delivered mild rebukes. Given the multiple obligations of educated women to race, to churches, to middle-class respectability, and to other women, it would be surprising to see anything less complex and multivocal. Virginia Broughton's address on "Woman's Work," delivered to the National Baptist Educational and Foreign Mission Convention in 1893, expressed a representative concern for balance. Beginning her presentation with the creation account in Genesis, Broughton noted that woman "has figured conspicuously" throughout history. Female influence served as a "desirable help to man" rather than as an overpowering force. "In the deliverance of Israel from Egyptian bondage," Broughton asserted, "it was the love and wisdom of woman that preserved, nourished and trained the man child that God called to be the leader, judge and priest for his people." Broughton repeated the words "help" and "help-meet" throughout her address, as if defending preemptively against the charge that she was claiming too much for women's authority. Shifting to the present, she argued that because the biblical record clearly indicated God's desire for gender balance in human societies, women should be included more extensively in the intellectual work of both church and government.[68]

For many middle-class African-American women, history was primarily a tale of relationships among people—mothers and children, husbands and wives, friends and neighbors, and church members. And because they had been designated as the primary caretakers of human relations, the plot was driven principally by women. This was, indeed, a revolutionary claim, one that, if made too loudly, might well endanger other kinds of connections within African-American communities. If we juxtapose these works with those of race histories by black men, we begin to see another kind of reasoning that gauged the morality of history in slightly different, perhaps more local and concrete, terms.

If few women were willing to tout their own innovations, it is also the case that their intellectual efforts were effectively marginalized—not just by whites who ignored or mocked the notion of black historical production but by black men as well. Male commentators consistently attempted to mute the radical implications of women's intellectual work by dismissing it as cloyingly sentimental or containing it within the generic constraints of fiction or children's literature. Benjamin Brawley, for example, a black poet and historian in his own right, deemed Harper's poetry "lacking in technique." "Mrs. Harper was best when most simple," he noted at the First Biennial Conference of the Association for the Study of Negro Life and History in 1917.[69] Whereas black male uses of sentiment could be construed as intellectually daring, women's work was more likely to be dismissed. Du Bois's well-received historical work *The Souls of Black Folk* is extremely romantic, and its most moving passages—"Of the Sorrow Songs," for instance—play on many of the same psychic chords sounded by Harper. Not insignificantly, Du Bois appealed overtly to romanticism: he began his chapters in *Souls* with epigraphs taken from some of the great romantic poets, including Byron, Schiller, and Elizabeth Barrett Browning.

The silencing of a female historical voice demonstrated the increasing organizational exclusion of women in an era of historical professionalization. As black men worked to define an objective and scholarly science of history, and to lay claim to a racial legacy that countered the rise of white-dominated historical societies, they drew ranks around their own visions of what constituted historical data and interpretation in part by defining women out of the arena entirely. The founding of the Bethel Literary and Historical Association (1881), the American Negro Historical Society (1897), the American Negro Academy (1897), and the Negro Society for Historical Research (1911) marked a new turn toward the professionalization of communal history, offering unique opportunities for African-American men to write and promote race-based scholarship. But most of these groups closed their membership entirely to women, and only a few accepted the occasional female speaker, such as Anna Julia Cooper. The American Negro Academy, founded by Alexander Crummell in 1897 to promote collegiality among black scholars and poets, initially limited its membership to men.[70] At the first biennial meeting of the Association for the Study of Negro Life and History in 1917, the only woman present was one of the several visiting white dignitaries, and only a handful of articles by women (including Alice Dunbar-Nelson, Leila Amos Pendleton, and Mary Church Terrell) appeared in the *Journal of Negro History* during its first five years of publication.[71]

Black women writers were better represented in periodical publishing, but that venue was still embedded within a larger nexus of publishing regulated by men. The editors of religious publications invariably were male; men decided what constituted "suitable" work; they even controlled what ended up on the "woman's page" of the paper. Only a few intrepid women, including Pauline Hopkins and Frances Harper, ever held the reins of their own literary destinies for any length of time. As Gertrude Mossell commented in the 1890s, despite all the strides made by women writers, they still played supporting roles: "They are admitted to the press association and are in sympathy with the male editors; but few have become independent workers in this noble field of effort, being yet satellites, revolving round the sun of masculine journalism." Increasingly after 1900, black periodicals targeted the growing audience of African-American women by creating women's departments and columns. While the creation of a special section of a publication geared toward women certainly reflected an attempt to attract a larger female readership, it did not necessarily amplify women's voices within the periodicals. Indeed, once women's "concerns" were relegated to a separate section, their voices were less audible elsewhere.[72]

At the same time, women discovered a new and burgeoning venue for their work: historical textbooks for African-American children. New schools in the Jim Crow South required books that would train young people in the history excluded from most white-authored texts. In 1920 Leslie Pinckney Hill, the first president of the Cheyney School for Teachers in Pennsylvania, noted the important links among history, family, and the future of the race that were becoming standard views among African-American educators: "What the children read the fathers will believe. What the fathers believe will constitute the ideals of the race." Both Alice Dunbar-Nelson and Leila Pendleton wrote historical works that were intended to teach youths to read and write. Dunbar-Nelson dedicated her 1920 *Dunbar Speaker and Entertainer,* a work that also schooled children in appropriate speech and comportment, to "the children of the race which is herein celebrated . . . that they may read and learn about their own people."[73]

Leila Pendleton's *Narrative of the Negro* furnished one of the most comprehensive historical accounts of the race written by a woman, and it bore the marks of (by-now) canonized names and places. Like many of the male-authored race histories, Pendleton's work traced "Negro" lineage to Meroe (Ethiopia) and Egypt. She then discussed the growth of the Christian Church in Africa, beginning in Abyssinia and Carthage, and continuing to the nineteenth-century missionary movement of the European explorers Mungo Park and David Livingstone, Paul Cuffe, Edward Blyden, and William Sheppard. Pendleton highlighted native conversions to the faith by

King Mtesa of Uganda and others, and she predicted that pure-blood Africans would eventually produce a "new form" of Christianity for the race. She then took her readers on a lengthy tour of Haiti, where "Negro slaves struck their first blow for freedom." She linked black activism there to negro slave revolts in Brazil, Jamaica, Bermuda, and other New World locales, commenting approvingly on the current participation of blacks in government in the West Indies.[74]

Pendleton did not flinch from a discussion of the history of slavery. Hers was a tale of both black and white subservience and activism. Beginning with ancient slavery, she commented that "members of every great European race" had been enslaved at one time or another. Likewise, Europeans and Euro-Americans had also fought for abolition; she held up the Quakers, William Lloyd Garrison, and Benjamin Lundy for particular endorsement. Her lists of commendable African Americans were lengthy and detailed: Phillis Wheatley, Prince Hall, Benjamin Banneker, Lemuel Haynes, Absalom Jones, and James Varick all spoke out against slavery; Denmark Vesey and Nat Turner (whom Pendleton compared to Joan of Arc) acted against the slave system; and countless others built churches, schools, colleges, fraternal orders, and periodicals. She discussed the politics of Frederick Douglass, Booker T. Washington, and W. E. B. Du Bois, ministers of every denomination, and the many "race women" who had contributed in recent years to the advance of the negro race. Fittingly, in a final chapter entitled "The Light Diffused," Pendleton's recitation of history became a litany of names, one after another, page after page, as if to demonstrate by sheer accumulation how the race itself was progressing into the future. She closed with a prayer, an homage to the God who had directed this sacred account: "May He, who holds Creation in the hollow of His hand, and yet marks the sparrow's fall, behold, and see the Negro, though persecuted and afflicted, though cast down and almost destroyed, still clinging to the Faith once delivered to the saints, still looking up, even though through blood and tears, to the ETERNAL GOD."[75]

By the 1910s the writings of black women, while more prominent in some respects and increasing in number, had been effectively channeled into what were considered female spheres of influence. In children's literature, in

Sunday school pageants, and in women's columns and magazines, African-American women continued to produce race narratives that drew on the patriotic and religious themes of previous generations of black writers. Well into the 1920s and 1930s, the historical work of Drusilla Dunjee Houston's *Wonderful Ethiopians of the Ancient Cushite Empire* (1930), the staged production "Heavenbound" (1931) by Nellie Davis, and the biblically inspired musicals of Eva Jessye such as "The Chronicle of Job" (1934) and "Paradise Lost and Regained" (1936?) transmitted popular historical knowledge to generations of African-American schoolchildren and churchgoers. Mainline black churches increasingly relegated women to the pews and the Sunday schools as male clergy carved out a space for themselves in Protestant pulpits. Occasionally women's stories broke through to the broader American public consciousness, but for the most part they remained sequestered within black communities, where they did not threaten to upset white American and religious self-understandings, the calling of the minister, or the halls of professionalized African-American history.

Conclusion

Out of necessity, the black church had to minister to the whole person. Out of necessity, the black church rarely had the luxury of separating individual salvation from collective salvation. It had to serve as the center of the community's political, economic, and social as well as spiritual life; it understood in an intimate way the biblical call to feed the hungry and clothe the naked and challenge powers and principalities. I was able to see faith as more than just a comfort to the weary; rather, it was an active, palpable agent in the world.

BARACK OBAMA, *The Audacity of Hope: Thoughts on Reclaiming the American Dream* (2006)

Two souls? All thinking people have more than two souls.

WILSON MOSES, "Ambivalent Maybe" (2003)

In October 1913 the 12th Regiment Armory in New York City hosted a new historical pageant, "The Star of Ethiopia," written and produced by the great race leader and scholar W. E. B. Du Bois. Believing that such a production could both demonstrate African-American contributions to history and facilitate the creation of a cultural consciousness, Du Bois provided a visual and aural representation of African-American origins and destiny. Through dance, music, and a historical reenactment in which hundreds participated, he hoped for nothing less than the regeneration of the race. Du Bois was a public relations genius: he stirred up popular interest by discussing the pageant in editorials and essays in the pages of the magazine he edited, *The Crisis*. Opening on the fiftieth anniversary of the Emancipation Proclamation, the play attracted audiences estimated at 30,000 in its New York run alone. It later toured nationally.[1]

Du Bois's historical vision was ambitious. The production featured a prologue and five scenes in thirteen episodes that traced major historical eras: The Gift of Iron, The Dream of Egypt, The Glory of Ethiopia, The Valley of

Humiliation, The Vision Everlasting. The story opened in ancient Ethiopia and Egypt and surveyed early African contributions to art, commerce, and technology. At the end of scene three Africans were enslaved by Europeans. Scene four did not linger on the experience of slavery itself, however; instead, it followed the heroic figures of John Brown, Toussaint L'Ouverture, and Nat Turner as they fought for freedom. The final scene depicted a unified and prosperous future for Ethiopia.[2]

Much of this story is familiar by now. But perhaps the most puzzling element of Du Bois's play is what was omitted. Protestant Christianity—as a set of institutions, as a resource for knowledge of the past, and as a guide to the future—was curiously absent. Never a churchgoing man himself, Du Bois nonetheless understood the power of narrative enacted through ritual. He stated that his goal in producing "Star of Ethiopia" was instrumental, "to teach on the one hand the colored people themselves the meaning of their history and their rich, emotional life through a new theatre, and on the other to reveal the Negro to the white world as a human, feeling thing."[3] Believing, perhaps, that the stage could replace the church as a venue for moral uplift, Du Bois depicted a race history freed from the burdens of Christian discipline and fellowship but still bonded by its African lineage.

This is not to suggest that Du Bois ignored religion, either in this play or elsewhere. His 1915 study *The Negro* presented in textual form a history of the race from Africa to the present. There he wrote at length about the religious life of African peoples, defending them from the charge that their practices of polytheism and animism were mere "senseless degradation." In *The Souls of Black Folk*, published in 1903, he wrote movingly of Southern folk religion, giving life and humanity to the "sorrow songs" and the "frenzy." His sociological study *The Negro Church*, also appearing in 1903, presented a sweeping institutional survey of churches in black communities. Personally, Du Bois was deeply interested in religious faith and wrote constantly about its power and presence in African diasporic life.[4]

But reading his work as well as the numerous African-American historical narratives by scholars that appeared after 1900, one cannot avoid the feeling that something fundamental had shifted. In the studies of Benjamin Griffith Brawley, Kelly Miller, and even Carter Woodson, three more black academics who came to prominence after 1900, the place and role of Protestant churches, as well as the Afro-Christian consciousness that they had fostered, were downplayed if not silenced entirely. The trend toward representation that introduced the trope of the New Negro to black and white audiences after 1900—a trope featured in the work of Du Bois, Woodson, Alain Locke, and the writers and artists of the Harlem Renaissance who explored myriad facets of black cultural expression—was decidedly silent about the Protestant faith.[5] In part this growing absence reflected the professionalization of the disciplines and the rise of the first generation of African-American professors within universities. Held to different standards of what constituted evidence and historical analysis, scholars like Du Bois increasingly marginalized religious experience and assertions of divine causality as vestigial, if romantic, remnants of the negro past. They still studied churches, of course, but they depicted them as either artifacts of a fading past (the rural and "folk" churches) or, as in the case of the growing number of large urban congregations, progressive organizational vehicles for voluntarism, uplift, and philanthropy.[6]

Another notable feature of the literature of the New Negro was its promotion of itself as entirely new, a claim that has followed the work of Du Bois and his compatriots ever since. One recent scholar refers to "Star of Ethiopia" as "the first mass assembly of black people for the purpose of self-determination and cultural pride." Robert Gregg, in his commentary in a recent edition of *The Negro*, asserts that the volume was "the first overall examination of the history of African and African-derived people," and he notes that it "lifted a veil from African history" and successfully refuted European and American claims of negro inferiority. The Du Bois biographer David Levering Lewis claims that *The Negro* is a "pioneering synthesis of the latest scholarship brilliantly beamed through a revisionist lens."[7]

No doubt, Du Bois was able to synthesize and articulate information in compelling ways, and his range of knowledge was vast. But his work also built on a tradition of dozens of African-American intellectuals before him and mined a legacy that was enabled primarily by Protestant institutions and the consciousness that they had fostered. "The Star of Ethiopia" had its roots in black church commemorations such as Allen's Day, Children's Day, Katherine Tillman's play "The Heirs of Slavery," and the parades and celebrations of the Prince Hall Masons. The references to ancient civilizations had been filtered through biblical and Christian lenses. To be sure, Du Bois also anchored his work in contemporary sociology and European and

istian worldview in which race was one among a number of social allies and loyalties.

he negro race history as it would have been known a half-century earlier
not disappeared. If anything, it continued to flourish in the hands of
men and church leaders who persisted in asserting the themes of ancient
can origins, Protestant piety, rich and regal ceremonialism, and Ameri-
patriotism. They worked in relative obscurity, at least to the veiled
lds inhabited by white Americans. Drusilla Dunjee Houston is a case in
it. Born in Winchester, Virginia, in 1876, Houston was the daughter of a
tist fundraiser for the American Baptist Home Mission Society. After
ing as a young bride to Oklahoma, Houston worked as an educator and
nalist, helping to publicize white atrocities perpetrated against blacks.
also became interested in African history and began to research what
proposed would be a three-volume work on ancient Africa and its peo-
When her first volume, *Wonderful Ethiopians of the Ancient Cushite Em-
Book I: Nations of the Cushite Empire. Marvelous Facts From Authentic
rds* appeared in 1926, it was met with critical acclaim in black commu-
s and was favorably reviewed in the *Amsterdam News,* the *Pittsburgh
rier,* and A. Philip Randolph's *Messenger.* The book was a fascinating
hesis of anthropological data, literature, and historical studies, and she
erstood it as a bold strike against white and black elite historians who
sed to tell the true story of the African past. "Out of anthropology, eth-
gy, geology, paleontology, archaeology, as well as history," she explained,
ive dug up an irrefutable arsenal of facts that Harvard or Yale or cow-
scholarship in our race dare not refute. How can a leadership point the
ard way that is utterly ignorant of the past?" Almost unknown today by
ut a few scholars of African-American history and literature, Houston
inued to work through the 1930s as a syndicated columnist for the As-
ited Negro Press, although she never published the other two volumes
r monumental work.[9]

so lost in the desire to celebrate political and instrumental achieve-
ts was the emphasis on kingship and ceremony, seen in Prince Hall
nic ritual and the monarchical musings of Prince Saunders and Baron
istey; lauded by Martin Delany; picked up in the admiration of African
doms and royal bodies; and threaded through pageants and fiction in
arly twentieth century. This predilection has always existed alongside

American literary trends; but even as he marked the (
lem" of the twentieth century, he looked back to the
solve the problem with many of the same narrative to
nities had relied on previously.

The books representing the "New Negro" were visible
a way that the older tradition was not. Making any v
cans noticeable in the mainstream was difficult, a re
astonishing fact that the only article published by a
1895 and 1980 in the premier historical journal of
Historical Review, was a 1910 article by Du Bois (
Bois, Woodson, Brawley, Miller, Locke, and other wi
naissance, mostly males trained in predominantly w
ferociously for racial equality and presented the re
race to most of white America. In their work, religio
a sociological and documentary exercise, and the
for the political contributions it made to black socia
nities, with their disciplines and odd practices, were
and even remembered fondly, but they were not live
way that Benjamin Tucker Tanner or Frances Har
roles within churches.

African-American leaders had been reconstru
worlds for many decades before the arrival of the
single novel act of reconstruction, a single "New
steady waves of constitution and reconstitution, be
narratives composed by Prince Hall Masons and b
bellum North, moving through literature on Haiti a
missionary organizations, and cresting in the att
reach out to freed men and women after Emancip
novel, in retrospect, is that when the advocates (
their claims in the 1910s and 1920s, they did so by
the Christian piety of their forebears. The New Ne
as an adamant repudiation of the "Old Darky" of t
reotypical negro, but it was also a rejection of a b
ment, common in the South by 1900, that was s

American literary trends; but even as he marked the color line as the "problem" of the twentieth century, he looked back to the nineteenth century to solve the problem with many of the same narrative tools that black communities had relied on previously.

The books representing the "New Negro" were visible to white Americans in a way that the older tradition was not. Making any work by African Americans noticeable in the mainstream was difficult, a reality exemplified by the astonishing fact that the only article published by a black scholar between 1895 and 1980 in the premier historical journal of the day, the *American Historical Review,* was a 1910 article by Du Bois on Reconstruction.[8] Du Bois, Woodson, Brawley, Miller, Locke, and other writers of the Harlem Renaissance, mostly males trained in predominantly white institutions, argued ferociously for racial equality and presented the representative face of the race to most of white America. In their work, religious experience figured as a sociological and documentary exercise, and the church became relevant for the political contributions it made to black social life. Religious communities, with their disciplines and odd practices, were observed, romanticized, and even remembered fondly, but they were not lived in—at least not in the way that Benjamin Tucker Tanner or Frances Harper had inhabited their roles within churches.

African-American leaders had been reconstructing their intellectual worlds for many decades before the arrival of the New Negro. Instead of a single novel act of reconstruction, a single "New Negro," history reveals steady waves of constitution and reconstitution, beginning with the earliest narratives composed by Prince Hall Masons and black pastors in the antebellum North, moving through literature on Haiti and Africa encouraged by missionary organizations, and cresting in the attempts by Northerners to reach out to freed men and women after Emancipation. What seems most novel, in retrospect, is that when the advocates of the New Negro staked their claims in the 1910s and 1920s, they did so by self-consciously rejecting the Christian piety of their forebears. The New Negro may have been forged as an adamant repudiation of the "Old Darky" of the South, the passive, stereotypical negro, but it was also a rejection of a black Protestant establishment, common in the South by 1900, that was steeped in a patriotic and

Christian worldview in which race was one among a number of social alliances and loyalties.

The negro race history as it would have been known a half-century earlier had not disappeared. If anything, it continued to flourish in the hands of women and church leaders who persisted in asserting the themes of ancient African origins, Protestant piety, rich and regal ceremonialism, and American patriotism. They worked in relative obscurity, at least to the veiled worlds inhabited by white Americans. Drusilla Dunjee Houston is a case in point. Born in Winchester, Virginia, in 1876, Houston was the daughter of a Baptist fundraiser for the American Baptist Home Mission Society. After moving as a young bride to Oklahoma, Houston worked as an educator and journalist, helping to publicize white atrocities perpetrated against blacks. She also became interested in African history and began to research what she proposed would be a three-volume work on ancient Africa and its people. When her first volume, *Wonderful Ethiopians of the Ancient Cushite Empire, Book I: Nations of the Cushite Empire. Marvelous Facts From Authentic Records* appeared in 1926, it was met with critical acclaim in black communities and was favorably reviewed in the *Amsterdam News,* the *Pittsburgh Courier,* and A. Philip Randolph's *Messenger.* The book was a fascinating synthesis of anthropological data, literature, and historical studies, and she understood it as a bold strike against white and black elite historians who refused to tell the true story of the African past. "Out of anthropology, ethnology, geology, paleontology, archaeology, as well as history," she explained, "I have dug up an irrefutable arsenal of facts that Harvard or Yale or cowardly scholarship in our race dare not refute. How can a leadership point the forward way that is utterly ignorant of the past?" Almost unknown today by all but a few scholars of African-American history and literature, Houston continued to work through the 1930s as a syndicated columnist for the Associated Negro Press, although she never published the other two volumes of her monumental work.[9]

Also lost in the desire to celebrate political and instrumental achievements was the emphasis on kingship and ceremony, seen in Prince Hall Masonic ritual and the monarchical musings of Prince Saunders and Baron de Vastey; lauded by Martin Delany; picked up in the admiration of African kingdoms and royal bodies; and threaded through pageants and fiction in the early twentieth century. This predilection has always existed alongside the black Protestant commitment to thrift and aesthetic wariness. Seeing it as a persistent motif helps to explain the astounding popularity of Marcus Garvey among African-Americans in the 1920s. His emphasis on black self-help and pan-African community was crucial to his success. But the fact that he dressed in military regalia, accompanied his processions with bands, and injected a ceremonialism into the proceedings of his organization, the Universal Negro Improvement Association, captured perfectly the tenor of a community for whom those images resonated with a well-developed history. Many whites laughed at what they saw as a clownish donning of meaningless costume, and black intellectuals like Du Bois ridiculed the "new comic opera" of Garvey's presentation. But Garvey knew better than they the power of a narrative that linked African Americans to a ceremonial lineage.[10]

Afro-Christian intellectual culture in the nineteenth century shared the enduring political dilemma of how to respond to white racism. It also forged creative understandings of the specific events that characterized this time period, including abolition, institution-building, Emancipation, Reconstruction, and Jim Crow. African Americans responded in different ways to these calls, providing divergent answers to pressing questions. But they were conversation partners, arguing their cases from the same epistemological premises: the Bible is a trustworthy authority; ancient history provides a lineage that will move a community into the future; Protestant denominations are family units that knit Christians together in common purpose; and diasporic Africans are connected in fundamental ways to one another. Most important, they believed, history is critically important not simply because it helps us to shape our future, but because it demonstrates how a transcendent God, one who stands outside of the vicissitudes of this world, wants us to act. The point of history is to rise above ourselves and this world to an unmoving vantage point.

All the tools used by African-American narrators were designed to liberate them from the present time and place by connecting them with the past and future and with sites outside their own imperfect society. Ancient history, including biblical stories and church history, furnished a long view of world order, providing insights that facilitated the move forward. In their telling, American history freed them from the falsehoods of white narration but provided an inspiring view of what political equality might really mean and why it was worth defending. Narratives of Haitian and African societies unchained them from the constraints of their American situation, allowing them to imagine both a wider community of which they were a part and a people who provided inspiration about their own courage, nobility, and place in the world.

Yet the paradox of these narratives of liberation is that they were all, simultaneously, narratives of obligation, stories that compelled action and discipline for specific purposes. Ancient Egypt and Ethiopia were legacies to aspire to; God called his people through biblical accounts to live up to their promises; American values had to be defended and preserved; Haitians and Africans needed to be rescued from their own sins, a salvation that only African Americans were able to offer. Ultimately, this call to arms motivated cultural consensus, such as it was—not just the recognition of liberation from white intellectual constraints. Freedom alone would not liberate a community, because it would not define and compel common purpose. That is why churches, missions, tithing, adherence to familial and gender roles, and discipline were critically important. If many of these narratives now seem quaint or overly rigid in their inscribing of social duties and divisions, it was because race narrators saw such discipline as the only way to progress; liberation without marching orders would lead only to anarchy.

For better or for worse, the heralds of the "New Negro" had different understandings of how to motivate action, and they worked with different intellectual assumptions about human agency and progress. Their story is left in other hands. Meanwhile, Afro-Christian intellectual culture is still alive and well. While most often invisible outside of black communities, expressed in Sunday school pageants and sermons, it erupts into white public consciousness in surprising ways: an "angry" black preacher gets national airtime for his critique of traditional American patriotism; a black church brings ancient Egyptian symbols or rituals into its liturgy; or a dark-skinned Jesus finds its way to the wall of a church building. Outsiders are shocked because they see these incidents as anomalous and revolutionary affronts to "real" American Christianity, rather than as the counternarratives that have thrived among African Americans for nearly as long as they have been in this country.

If white Christians are surprised by these "disruptions" of their own stories, so, too, are academics. In the rush toward objectivity and scientific racialism, twentieth-century historians largely have forgotten the worldview that motivated early race authors. Indeed, their self-understanding has long eluded description by even the most careful historians. Wilson Moses, in discussing the views of racial destiny espoused by the black Episcopalian Alexander Crummell, quite candidly concluded, "I can think of no simple explanation for Crummell's optimistic view of history, his reliance on Providence, his belief in progress."[11] The key to Crummell's mystery, as well as to the puzzle provided by a generation of race historians in the four decades preceding World War I, is grounded in a historical consciousness that was at once thoroughly Protestant and thoroughly African American. Synthesized in a new way by a new generation of middle-class black Christians, this consciousness took into account a temporal sweep measured in centuries rather than in decades, evaluated by providential rather than by human means. This sweep frequently allowed for the acknowledgment both of universal human strengths, weaknesses, and ultimate forgiveness and for an unyielding commitment to a historically specific collective destiny embodied in the suffering and future triumphs of the negro race. Neither assimilationist nor separatist, but inspired by Euro-American philosophy and African-American cultural unity, this worldview was articulated in the only form that could fully represent its dependence on a linear and progressive notion of time: chronological narrative. The difficulty that some contemporary observers have in identifying the moving force behind these self-understandings is perhaps attributable to the polarized racial lenses through which the dominant American culture views these histories, as well as to the failings of a discourse about race that conceives of choices, both metaphorically and literally, as being either "black" or "white."[12]

NOTES

ACKNOWLEDGMENTS

INDEX

Notes

Introduction

1. Dennis Saleebey, *Human Behavior and Social Environments: A Biopsychosocial Approach* (New York, 2001), 46.

2. Lorenzo Dow Blackson, *The Rise and Progress of the Kingdoms of Light and Darkness. Or, the Reign of Kings Alpha and Abadon* (Philadelphia, 1867), 209, 211.

3. Vernon Loggins, *The Negro Author: His Development in America* (New York, 1931), 305–306; Blyden Jackson, *A History of Afro-American Literature,* vol. 1, *The Long Beginning, 1746–1895* (Baton Rouge, 1989), 383–388.

4. B. Clark, *The Past, Present, and Future in Prose and Poetry* (Toronto, 1867).

5. See Arnold Rampersand, "W. E. B. Du Bois as a Man of Literature," *American Literature* 51, no. 1 (March 1979): 50–68.

6. Kōnstantinos Dēmaras, *A History of Modern Greek Literature,* trans. Mary P. Gianos (Albany, N.Y., 1972), 42–44.

7. Hans W. Frei, *The Eclipse of Biblical Narrative: A Study in Eighteenth and Nineteenth Century Hermeneutics* (New Haven, 1974), 2.

8. On community formation, see Joanna Brooks, *American Lazarus: Religion and the Rise of African American and Native American Literatures* (New York, 2003); Dickson D. Bruce, *The Origins of African American Literature (1680–1865)* (Charlottesville, 2001); and John Ernest, *Liberation Historiography: African American Writers and the Challenge of History, 1794–1861* (Chapel Hill, N.C., 2003). On the disciplining of historical voices, see Stephan Palmié, *Wizards and Scientists: Explorations in Afro-Cuban Modernity and Tradition* (Durham, N.C., 2002), ch. 1.

9. On other African-American textual traditions, see Henry Louis Gates, Jr., *The Signifying Monkey: A Theory of African American Literary Criticism* (New York, 1988). On African American autobiography, see William L. Andrews, *To Tell a Free Story: The First Century of Afro-American Autobiography, 1760–1865* (Urbana, Ill., 1986); on religious narratives, see Andrews, *Sisters of the Spirit: Three Black Women's Autobiographies of the Nineteenth Century* (Bloomington, Ind., 1986).

10. On modern notions of race, see Steven Jay Gould, *The Mismeasure of Man* (New York, 1996); and George W. Stocking, *Victorian Anthropology* (New York, 1987).

11. Pierre Hadot, *Philosophy as a Way of Life: Spiritual Exercises from Socrates to Foucault* (Oxford, 1995); see also the introduction to Laurie F. Maffly-Kipp, Leigh Eric Schmidt, and Mark R. Valeri, eds., *Practicing Protestants: Histories of Christian Life in America, 1630–1965* (Baltimore, 2006).

12. On the Exodus theme, see Eddie S. Glaude, Jr., *Exodus: Religion, Race, and Nation in Early Nineteenth-Century Black America* (Chicago, 2000); Albert J. Raboteau, "African Americans, Exodus, and the American Israel," in *A Fire in the Bones: Reflections on African-American Religious History* (Boston, 1995), 17–36; and David W. Wills, "Exodus Piety: African American Religion in an Age of Immigration," in Jonathan D. Sarna, ed., *Minority Faiths and the American Protestant Mainstream* (Urbana, Ill., 1998).

13. On racial theories, see George M. Fredrickson, *The Black Image in the White Mind: The Debate on Afro-American Character and Destiny, 1817–1914* (New York, 1971); Gould, *Mismeasure;* and Mia Bay, *The White Image in the Black Mind: African American Ideas about White People, 1830–1925* (New York, 2000). On the origins of nationalism see Benedict Anderson, *Imagined Communities: Reflections on the Origin and Spread of Nationalism* (London, 1983); Anthony W. Marx, *Faith in Nation: The Exclusionary Origins of Nationalism* (New York, 2003); and Anthony D. Smith, *Nationalism and Modernism: A Critical Survey of Recent Theories of Nations and Nationalism* (New York, 1998).

14. On history and collective memory see Paul Connerton, *How Societies Remember* (Cambridge, 1989); Eric Hobsbawm and Terence Ranger, eds., *The Invention of Tradition* (Cambridge, 1983); and Bernard Lewis, *History: Remembered, Recovered, Invented* (Princeton, 1975).

15. On black nationalism, see St. Clair Drake, *The Redemption of Africa and Black Religion* (Chicago, 1970); Wilson Jeremiah Moses, *The Golden Age of Black Nationalism, 1850–1925* (New York, 1978); and Sterling Stuckey, *Slave Culture: Nationalist Theory and the Foundations of Black America* (New York, 1987). Wilson Moses and St. Clair Drake have done the most to emphasize the significance of Anglo-Christianity to the development of black nationalist ideology. Yet Moses dismisses the Christian beliefs of Edward Blyden and Alexander Crummell as "mystical, pseudo-Christian racial rhetoric" (*Golden Age,* 90). Sterling Stuckey, in *Slave Culture,* sees Christianity as another form of dissemblance in the face of white oppression.

16. Laurie F. Maffly-Kipp, "Denominationalism and the Black Church," in Robert Bruce Mullin and Russell E. Richey, eds., *Reimagining Denominationalism: Interpretive Essays* (New York, 1994). On race as a metalanguage, see Evelyn Brooks Higginbotham, "African American Women's History and the Metalanguage of Race," *Signs* 17, no. 2 (Winter 1992): 251–274.

17. Charles Taylor, *Multiculturalism: Examining the Politics of Recognition*, ed. Amy Gutmann (Princeton, 1994), 32, 33. On the history of selfhood, see Charles Taylor, *Sources of the Self: The Making of the Modern Identity* (Cambridge, Mass., 1989).

18. Ira Berlin, *Many Thousands Gone: The First Two Centuries of Slavery in North America* (Cambridge, Mass., 1998).

1. Wonders of the Ancient Past

1. Jacob Oson, *A Search for Truth; Or, An Inquiry for the Origin of the African Nation: An Address, Delivered at New-Haven in March, and at New York in April, 1817* (New York, 1817).

2. Erasmus Darwin, *Zoomania, or, The Laws of Organic Life* (London, 1794–1796).

3. Founded in 1809 by John Murray, the *Quarterly Journal* was notable for its conservative politics and promotion of romantic literature. Vastey's piece appeared in vol. 21, no. 42 (April 1819).

4. Vernon Loggins, *The Negro Author: His Development in America* (New York, 1931), 55; Bruce Dain, *A Hideous Monster of the Mind: American Race Theory in the Early Republic* (Cambridge, Mass., 2002), 112–113; and Joanne Pope Melish, *Disowning Slavery: Gradual Emancipation and "Race" in New England, 1780–1860* (Ithaca, N.Y., 1998), 252; Albert J. Raboteau, *A Fire in the Bones: Reflections on African-American Religious History* (Boston, 1996); Eddie S. Glaude, Jr., *Exodus! Religion, Race, and Nation in Early Nineteenth-Century Black America* (Chicago, 2000); and John Ernest, *Liberation Historiography: African American Writers and the Challenge of History, 1794–1861* (Chapel Hill, N.C., 2003).

5. See Alon Confino, "Collective Memory and Cultural History: Problems of Method," *American Historical Review* 102, no. 5 (December 1997): 1386–1403. Patrick Rael points out that discussion of a common Africanness is removed from the lived experience of social difference (class, gender, religious, etc.). His discussion of William Hamilton's 1815 celebration presents his rhetoric as a "discursive process" of creating a fictive family; he concludes that "such a nation existed primarily as a rhetorical gesture" separated from black folk culture or lived experience. See Rael, *Black Identity and Black Protest in the Antebellum North* (Chapel Hill, N.C., 2002), 46. This is both true and not true: yes, the rhetoric quite self-consciously obscured social differences; but by contrast, it also created commonality in its performance of unity. The term "African American" is, of course, the contemporary fruit of the sort of cultural work performed by Hamilton, Oson, and others; as such, it testifies to the significance of these early efforts at imagining a collective black identity grounded in the narrative of a shared African past.

6. On the concept of "narrative acts" see Nina Baym, *American Women Writers and the Work of History, 1790–1860* (New Brunswick, N.J., 1995).

7. On Hall's life in Nova Scotia, see Joanna Brooks, "John Marrant's Journal: Providence and Prophesy in the Eighteenth-Century Black Atlantic," *The North Star* 3 (1999), http://northstar.vassar.edu/volume3/brooks.html; Cedrick May, "John Marrant and the Narrative Construction of an Early Black Methodist Evangelical," *African American Review* 38 (Winter 2004): 553–570.

8. On theology during the Civil War, see Harry S. Stout, *Upon the Altar of the Nation: A Moral History of the Civil War* (New York, 2007).

9. Most often cited on this point is Friedrich Hegel (1770–1831), who in his *Philosophy of History* declared that Africa "is no historical part of the world; it has no movement or development to exhibit" (J. Sibree, trans., 1899; reprint ed., New York, 1956), 99. See also John Willinsky, *Learning to Divide the World: Education at Empire's End* (Minneapolis, 1998), 116–121; and B. Jewsiewicki and V. Y. Mudimbe, "Africans' Memories and Contemporary History of Africa," *History and Theory* 32, no. 4, Beiheft 32: History Making in Africa (December 1993): 1–11.

10. Lawrence Levine, *Black Culture and Black Consciousness: Afro-American Folk Thought from Slavery to Freedom* (1977; Thirtieth Anniversary Edition, New York, 2007). See also Michael A. Gomez, *Exchanging Our Country Marks: The Transformation of African Identities in the Colonial and Antebellum South* (Chapel Hill, N.C., 1998), esp. 280–281; and Sterling Stuckey, *Going Through the Storm: The Influence of African American Art in History* (New York, 1994), 15.

11. David P. Henige, *The Chronology of Oral Tradition: Quest for a Chimera* (Oxford, 1974), 7, 14–15; and Gomez, *Exchanging*. On Roman Catholicism see Thornton, "The Development of an African Catholic Church in the Kingdom of Kongo, 1483–1750," *Journal of African History* 25 (1984): 147–167.

12. Sandra Gustafson, *Eloquence Is Power: Oratory and Performance in Early America* (Chapel Hill, N.C., 2000); and David Waldstreicher, *In the Midst of Perpetual Fetes: The Making of American Nationalism, 1776–1820* (Omohundro Institute of Early American History and Culture, Williamsburg, Virginia, 1997).

13. Hallie Quinn Brown, *Homespun Heroines and Other Women of Distinction* (Xenia, Ohio, 1926), 6; Frank A. Rollin, *Life and Public Services of Martin R. Delany* (Boston, 1883), 16; Dorothy Sterling, *The Making of an Afro-American: Martin Robison Delany, 1812–1885* (Garden City, N.Y., 1971), 2.

14. On free black communities see Leon Litwack, *North of Slavery: The Negro in the Free States* (Chicago, 1965); Patrick Rael, *Black Identity*, ch. 1; Shane White, *Stories of Freedom in Black New York* (Cambridge, Mass., 2002); Julie Winch, *Philadelphia's Black Elite: Activism, Accommodation, and the Struggle for Autonomy, 1787–1848* (Philadelphia, 1988).

15. Ira Berlin, "Time, Space, and the Evolution of Afro-American Society on British Mainland North America," *American Historical Review* 85, no. 1 (February 1980); John Thornton, *Africa and Africans in the Making of the Atlantic World, 1400–1800*, 2nd ed. (Cambridge, 1998); and Gomez, *Exchanging*.

16. Berlin, "The Revolution in Black Life," in Alfred F. Young, ed., *The American Revolution* (DeKalb, Ill., 1976), 362, 376; and Berlin, "Time, Space," 51–54; Rael, *Black Identity*, ch. 3, esp. 84–91.

17. According to James Fentress and Chris Wickham, textualized knowledge evolves in predictable ways that differ greatly from oral forms. See James Fentress and Chris Wickham, *Social Memory* (Oxford, 1992), 10.

18. The vast majority of books available to American Christians were what would now be termed religious works (if such a distinction had existed then): Sermons, tracts, histories, and elegies. The majority of motifs were drawn from the Bible or from a traditional set of cosmic frameworks, most of which described the journey of the individual through this life as a chronological narrative. See David D. Hall, *Cultures of Print: Essays in the History of the Book* (Amherst, Mass., 1996), 163. On the ritual of memorialization as a Christian practice, see Jacques Le Goff, *History and Memory*, trans. Steven Randall and Elizabeth Claman (New York, 1996), 68; and Frances A. Yates, *The Art of Memory* (Chicago, 1984), 83–84.

19. Henry Louis Gates, Jr., begins his analysis of African-American literature with the 1770 publication of Gronniosaw's narrative. See *The Signifying Monkey: A Theory of African-American Literary Criticism* (New York, 1989), 132.

20. *A Narrative of the Most Remarkable Particulars in the Life of James Albert Ukawsaw Gronniosaw, an African Prince, as Related by Himself*, ed. James Albert Ukawsaw Gronniosaw and Walter Shirley (Bath, England, 1770), 4.

21. This psychic distancing process has also been characteristic of Christian conversion in many other settings, in which new believers have been called upon to forsake parents, friends, and past lives to "put on Christ." See, for example, Christine Heyrman, *Southern Cross: The Beginnings of the Bible Belt* (Chapel Hill, N.C., 1997), 3; Michele Renee Salzman, *The Making of a Christian Aristocracy: Social and Religious Change in the Western Roman Empire* (Cambridge, Mass., 2002), 2.

22. For another perspective on this account, see Adam Potkay, "Olaudah Equiano and the Art of Spiritual Autobiography," *Eighteenth-Century Studies* 27, no. 4, African-American Culture in the Eighteenth Century (Summer 1994): 677–692.

23. Phillip Richards, "The 'Joseph Story' as Slave Narrative: On Genesis and Exodus as Prototypes for Early Black Anglophone Writing," in Vincent L. Wimbush, ed., *African Americans and the Bible: Sacred Texts and Social Structures* (New York, 2001), 221–235; and John Saillant, "Origins of African American Biblical Hermeneutics in Eighteenth-Century Black Opposition to the Slave Trade and Slavery," in Wimbush, *African Americans*, 236–250. See also Allen Dwight Callahan, *The Talking Book: African Americans and the Bible* (New Haven, 2006); and Theophus H. Smith, *Conjuring Culture: Biblical Formations of Black America* (New York, 1994).

24. Frank Lambert, "'I Saw the Book Talk': Slave Readings of the First Great Awakening," *Journal of African American History* 87, The Past before Us (Winter 2002), 12–25.

25. "A Narrative of the Lord's Wonderful Dealings with John Marrant, a Black" (London, 1802), in Dorothy Porter, ed., *Early Negro Writing, 1760–1837* (Boston, 1971), 433, 438; Hall, *Cultures,* 31.

26. Leonard P. Curry, *The Free Black in Urban America, 1800–1850* (Chicago, 1981), 210.

27. On the history of black Freemasonry, see Harry Davis, *A History of Freemasonry among Negroes in America* (New York, 1946); Lorenzo Greene, "Prince Hall: Massachusetts Leader in Crisis," *Freedomways* 1, no. 3 (1961): 238–258; William Grimshaw, *Official History of Freemasonry among the Colored People in North America* (New York, 1903); William A. Muraskin, *Middle-Class Blacks in a White Society* (Berkeley, 1975); Edward N. Palmer, "Negro Secret Societies," *Social Forces* 23 (December 1944): 207–212; Harold Van Buren Voorhis, *Negro Masonry in the United States* (New York, 1949); and Loretta J. Williams, *Black Freemasonry and Middle-Class Realities* (Columbia, Mo., 1980).

28. Maurice Wallace, "Are We Men? Prince Hall, Martin Delany, and the Masculine Ideal in Black Freemasonry, 1775–1865," *American Literary History* 9, no. 3 (1997): 404. On the blending of New Divinity theology and black Freemasonry see Peter P. Hinks, "John Marrant and the Meaning of Early Black Freemasonry," *William and Mary Quarterly* 64, no. 1 (January 2007) at <http://www.history cooperative.org/journals/wm/64.1/hinks.html> (accessed Feb. 15, 2008).

29. "Masonry," *Massachusetts Sentinel,* May 5, 1787, cited in Adam Potkay and Sandra Burr, eds., *Black Atlantic Writers of the Eighteenth Century* (New York, 1995), 16.

30. On the Masonic use of lineage and Marrant's sermon, see Hinks, "John Marrant."

31. For further analysis of Marrant's speech and Hall's Masonic speeches, see Joanna Brooks, "Prince Hall, Freemasonry, and Genealogy," *African American Review* 34, no. 2 (Summer 2000): 197–216.

32. Stephen J. Harris, *Race and Ethnicity in Anglo-Saxon Literature* (New York, 2003), 65–66.

33. Joanna Brooks argues that Prince Hall wrote a significant portion of John Marrant's earlier speech, a fact that may explain the close convergence of historical narratives. See Brooks, "Prince Hall," 214n10.

34. Prince Hall, "A Charge Delivered to the Brethren of the African Lodge. On the 25th of June, 1792" (Boston, 1792).

35. Prince Hall, "A Charge Delivered to the Brethren of the African Lodge on the 24th of June, 1797" (Boston, 1797), in Porter, *Early Negro Writing,* 71, 72, 74, 77.

36. Martin Bernal, *Black Athena: The Afroasiatic Roots of Classical Civilization,* vol. 1 (London, 1987), 182, 245; and E. S. Shaffer, *'Kubla Khan' and the Fall of Jerusalem: The Mythological School in Biblical Criticism and Secular Literature, 1770–1880* (Cambridge, 1975), 118.

37. William Hutchinson, *The Spirit of Masonry* (1775; reprint ed., New York, 1982), 47–49, 50, 53–55.

38. Bernal, *Black Athena,* 245.

39. "The African Lodge, An Oration delivered before the Grand Master, Wardens, and Brethren of the most Ancient and venerable Lodge of African Masons," *Columbian Magazine* 2, no. 8 (August 1788): 467–469.

40. On antiblack political cartoons and broadsides see Barbara E. Lacey, "Visual Images of Blacks in Early American Imprints," *William and Mary Quarterly,* 3rd ser., 53, no. 1 (January 1996): 137–180; and Shane White, "'It Was a Proud Day': African Americans, Festivals, and Parades in the North, 1741–1834," *Journal of American History* 81, no. 1 (June 1994): 35–37.

41. On Delany's early life see Victor Ullman, *Martin R. Delany: The Beginnings of Black Nationalism* (Boston, 1971).

42. Martin Delany, *The Origin and Objects of Ancient Freemasonry; Its Introduction into the United States and Legitimacy Among Colored Men* (Pittsburgh, 1853), 10, 13, 28.

43. The New York procession of 1809 is described in Joseph Sidney, "An Oration, Commemorative of the Abolition of the Slave Trade in the United States; delivered before the Wilberforce Philanthropic Association, in the City of New York, on the second of January, 1809," in Porter, *Early Negro Writing,* 363. See also Mitchell Alan Kachun, *Festivals of Freedom: Memory and Meaning in African American Emancipation Celebrations, 1808–1915* (Amherst, Mass., 2003), 26, 28.

44. Kachun, *Festivals,* 17–18; White, "'It Was a Proud Day,'" 13–50.

45. Leonard I. Sweet, "The Fourth of July and Black Americans in the Nineteenth Century: Northern Leadership Opinion within the Context of the Black Experience," *Journal of Negro History* 61, no. 3 (July 1976): 260; Frederick Douglass, "The Meaning of July Fourth for the Negro," at http://www.pbs.org/wgbh/aia/part4/4h2927t.html (accessed February 20, 2008); Dickson D. Bruce, Jr., *The Origins of African American Literature, 1680–1865* (Charlottesville, 2001), 106; and Kachun, *Festivals,* 39.

46. William Hamilton, "An Oration, on the Abolition of the Slave Trade, delivered in the Episcopal Asbury African Church, in Elizabeth-St., New York, January 2, 1815," in Porter, *Early Negro Writing,* 391, 392–393.

47. Hamilton, "Oration," 394, 395, 396.

48. Adam Carman, "An Oration delivered at the Fourth anniversary of the Abolition of the Slave Trade, in the Methodist Episcopal Church, in Second-street, New-York, January 1, 1811" (New York, 1811), 10, 14. On Carman's speech see

Manisha Sinha, "To 'cast just obliquy' on Oppressors: Black Radicalism in the Age of Revolution," *William and Mary Quarterly* (January 2007) <http://www.history cooperative.org/journals/wm/64.1/sinha.html> (accessed February 20, 2008).

49. Absalom Jones, "A Thanksgiving Sermon, preached January 1, 1808, in St. Thomas's, or the African Episcopal Church, Philadelphia; on account of the abolition of the African slave trade, on that day, by the Congress of the United States," in Porter, *Early Negro Writing*, 337.

50. Peter Williams, "An Oration on the Abolition of the Slave Trade, delivered in the African Church in the city of New York, January 1, 1808" (New York, 1808), in Porter, *Early Negro Writing*, 350–351; Hamilton, "Oration," 398.

51. This is a paraphrase of Isaiah 20:5, "And they shall be afraid and ashamed of Ethiopia their expectation, and of Egypt their glory."

52. Isaiah 19:2: "And I will set the Egyptians against the Egyptians: and they shall fight every one against his brother, and every one against his neighbour; city against city, and kingdom against kingdom."

53. Miller, *A Sermon*, 8. The reference comes from Jeremiah 5:6: "Therefore a lion from the forest will attack them, / a wolf from the desert will ravage them, / a leopard will lie in wait near their towns / to tear to pieces any who venture out, / for their rebellion is great / and their backslidings many."

54. Miller, *Sermon*, 12. The quotation is from Isaiah 35:1.

55. On Puritan rhetoric in early African-American sermons, see John Saillant, "Lemuel Haynes and the Revolutionary Origins of Black Theology, 1776–1801," *Religion and American Culture* 2, no. 1 (Winter 1992): 79–102; and "Slavery and Divine Providence in New England Calvinism: The New Divinity and a Black Protest, 1775–1805," *New England Quarterly* 68, no. 4 (December 1995): 584–608.

56. Miller, *Sermon*, 14.

57. Hall, *Cultures*, 42, 46; Richard S. Newman, "'We Participate in Common': Richard Allen's Eulogy of Washington and the Challenge of Interracial Appeals," *William and Mary Quarterly* 64, no. 1 (2007): 26 pars. <http://www.historycoop erative.org /journals/wm/64.1/newman1.html> (accessed August 13, 2008).

58. Carl F. Kaestle, *Pillars of the Republic: Common Schools and American Society, 1780–1860* (New York, 1983), 31, 32, 38, 172.

59. Ruth Miller Elson, *Guardians of Tradition: American Schoolbooks of the Nineteenth Century* (Lincoln, Neb., 1964), 5.

60. E. Jennifer Monaghan, *A Common Heritage: Noah Webster's Blue-Black Speller* (Hamden, Conn., 1983), 11, 31, 95–96; Noah Webster, *The American spelling book: containing the rudiments of the English language; for the use of schools in the United States* (Philadelphia, 1809), 118; John Alfred Nietz, *Old textbooks: spelling, grammar, reading, arithmetic, geography, American history, civil government, physiology, penmanship, art, music, as taught in the common schools from colonial days to 1900* (Pittsburgh, 1961), 65–66, 264.

61. Elson, *Guardians*, 4.

62. Delany was likely referring here to the *New York Primer, or Second Book* (New York, 1811). The reference to Ossian suggests a fascinating set of parallels. In the 1760s the Scottish poet James Macpherson published a volume of poetry that he claimed he had translated from ancient Scots Gaelic sources. The edition achieved international success and was heralded as the Celtic equivalent of classical writers such as Herodotus or Homer. Throughout the early nineteenth century a furor raged over the true origins of the poems: some thought they came from Irish writers, and others thought that Macpherson himself had creatively appropriated work from a variety of ethnic sources. Despite the unresolved disputes, the work inspired a generation of romantic authors including Walter Scott and Goethe. See Dafydd Moore, "Ossian," *The Literary Encyclopedia,* http://www.litencyc.com/php/stopics.php?rec=true&UID=1287 (accessed June 15, 2007); Dorothy Sterling, *The Making of an Afro-American: Martin Robison Delany, 1812–1885* (Garden City, N.Y., 1971), 18, 30, 45.

63. Mia Bay, *The White Image in the Black Mind: African-American Ideas about White People, 1830–1925* (New York, 2000), 15–22.

64. On the life of Jacob Oson, see Randall K. Burkett, "The Reverend Harry Croswell and Black Episcopalians in New Haven, 1820–1860," in *North Star* 7, no. 1 (Fall 2003) <http://northstar.vassar.edu/volume7/burkett.html> (accessed January 18, 2007); and Stephen G. Hall, "A Search for Truth: Jacob Oson and the Beginnings of African American Historiography," *William and Mary Quarterly* 65, no. 1 (January 2007): 139–148. See also E. F. Hening, *History of the African Mission of the Protestant Episcopal Church in the United States* (New York, 1853), 17–18; and "The late Rev. Jacob Oson," *African Repository* 4 (November 1828): 283–284.

65. Randall K. Burkett, "The Reverend Harry Croswell and Black Episcopalians in New Haven, 1820–1860" (unpublished manuscript in author's possession), 5–7. On race relations in New Haven in this period, see Robert Austin Warner, *New Haven Negroes: A Social History* (New York, 1969). Paul Cuffe referred to Oson as the "President of the Union Society and A M New Haven" in a comment made in 1814; I have been unable to learn anything else about this society. Cuffe later addressed a letter to a "Jacob Jon" dealing with educational matters; in all likelihood this is a mistranscribed reference to Oson: Rosalind Cobb Wiggins, *Captain Paul Cuffe's Logs and Letters, 1808–1817* (Washington, D.C., 1996), 271, 320; Edward D. Smith, *Climbing Jacob's Ladder: The Rise of Black Churches in Eastern American Cities, 1740–1877* (Washington, D.C., 1988), 67.

66. French theorists, influenced by the radical Enlightenment, were among the earliest and most avid proponents of polygenesis. As early as 1684, the *Journal des Savants* argued that blacks were not part of the same species as whites. Many scientists, it should also be noted, despite their embrace of new systems of classification, refuted this assertion. See David Brion Davis, *The Problem of Slavery in Western Culture* (New York, 1966), 446–482; Samuel Stanhope Smith, *An Essay on the*

Causes of the Variety of Complexion and Figure in the Human Species, ed. Winthrop D. Jordan (Cambridge, Mass., 1965), xv.

67. Smith, *Essay,* xxi. Oson mistakenly cites the excerpt from Acts as having come from ch. 24, but he quotes 17:26.

68. On the curse of Ham argument, see David Goldenberg, *The Curse of Ham: Race and Slavery in Early Judaism, Christianity, and Islam* (Princeton, N.J., 2003); and Colin Kidd, *The Forging of Races: Race and Scripture in the Protestant Atlantic World, 1600–2000* (Cambridge, 2006). On American iterations, see Stephen R. Haynes, *Noah's Curse: The Biblical Justifications of American Slavery* (New York, 2002); and Sylvester A. Johnson, *The Myth of Ham in Nineteenth-Century American Christianity: Race, Heathens, and the People of God* (New York, 2004).

69. Dwight's epic, according to critics, was as boring as it was ambitious. Even Dwight's friends, such as John Trumbull (1750–1831), remained unenthusiastic. Trumbull quipped that so much thunder and lightning raged in the melodramatic battle scenes that the epic ought to be provided with lightning rods.

70. Harry Croswell, *Diary,* 1:199 (January 16, 1823), cited in Burkett, "The Reverend Harry Croswell," 4. Croswell's diaries are located in the Manuscripts and Archives Division, Sterling Memorial Library, Yale University.

71. Lloyd S. Kramer, "Historical Narratives and the Meaning of Nationalism," *Journal of the History of Ideas* 58, no. 3 (July 1997): 525–545; Le Goff, *History and Memory,* 87–88; and Elson, *Guardians,* 2.

72. David Nicholls, *From Dessalines to Duvalier: Race, Colour and National Independence in Haiti* (1979; rev. ed., New Brunswick, N.J., 1996), 43; Nicholls, "Pompée Valentin Vastey: Royalist and Revolutionary," in *Jahrbuch für Geschichte von Staat, Wirtschaft und Gesellschaft Lateinamerikas* (Cologne, 1991), 109.

73. William Woodis Harvey asserted that Vastey "was said to have been educated at Paris about the time of the French Revolution." Because he was born in 1781, and joined L'Ouverture's cause in Saint Domingue at the age of fifteen, it is unclear exactly when and in what manner he was educated. However, he was clearly a well-read individual. See Harvey, *Sketches of Hayti: From the Expulsion of the French to the Death of Christophe* (1827; rep. ed., London, 1971), 221, 222.

74. Nicholls, "Pompée," 110–111; Harvey, *Sketches,* 147. The anonymous translator of the text termed Vastey "as distinguished for the urbanity and polish of his manners, as for the extent of his understanding and the brilliancy of his wit" (W.H.M.T., "Translator's Preface," *Remarks upon a Letter,* 11). Yet Harvey witnessed another side of Vastey's character. He admired Vastey's accomplishments, but recalled that "had the character of de Vastey been as consistent, as his abilities were respectable, he would have deserved our admiration; but this unhappily was not the case. His fierceness, his duplicity, and his meanness, rendered him at once despicable and odious." Harvey, *Sketches,* 223.

75. Nicholls, *Dessalines to Duvalier,* 43; Harvey, *Sketches,* 223.

76. Nicholls, "Pompée," 108, 112, 113.

77. See Sismondi's *De l'intérêt de la France à l'égard de la traite des Nègres* and *Nouvelles réflexions sur la traite des Nègres,* both in *Recueil de diverses pièces et des discussions qui eurent lieu aux Cortès générales et extraordinaires d'Espagne, en l'année 1811* (Paris, 1814). F. Mazères, *Lettre à J.-C.-L. Simonde de Sismondi sur les nègres, la civilization de l'Afrique* (Paris, 1815). It should be noted, however, that Mazères was only the latest in a line of French colonial (and ex-colonial) officials to argue that blacks were by nature incapable of freedom. In 1775, Pierre Victor Malouet, formerly a high official in Guiana and Saint Domingue, made a similar argument. See Davis, *Slavery,* 460.

78. On anthropological theory during this period, see George W. Stocking, Jr., *Victorian Anthropology* (New York, 1987).

79. Buffon (1707–1788) published his *Histoire Naturelle,* a thirty-six-volume production, between 1749 and 1789; in it he gave the first naturalistic account of the history of the Earth. *Etudes de la Nature,* first published in 1784 by Saint Pierre (1737–1814), took a more pious tack, vindicating the work of divine providence but placing it within a naturalized framework.

80. David Brion Davis suggests that eighteenth-century French theorists (notably Voltaire) were particularly enamored with polygenetic theories, because they could be used as a powerful weapon against revealed religion. This may explain Vastey's need to counter polygenesis at a time when it was falling out of favor in British and American intellectual circles. See Davis, *Slavery,* 454; and Edward D. Seeber, *Anti-Slavery Opinion in France During the Second Half of the Eighteenth Century* (Baltimore, 1937).

81. See Park, *Travels in the Interior Districts of Africa: performed under the direction and patronage of the African Association, in the years 1795, 1796, and 1797,* 2nd ed. (London, 1799); and James Bruce, *Travels to Discover the Source of the Nile,* 5 vols. (Edinburgh, 1790).

82. Herodotus was a fifth-century B.C.E. Greek historian whose work, *The Histories,* provided the first extended ethnography of North African peoples. Hanno, a fifth-century B.C.E. Carthaginian, was said to have been the first sailor to circumnavigate Africa; his account of the west coast of that continent remained the standard guide for seafarers until Portuguese explorations of the fifteenth century. Porphyry (234–305 C.E.), a Neo-Platonist and follower of Plotinus, wrote many philosophical works as well as critical attacks on Christianity. Lucan (39–65 C.E.) was a Roman poet whose major work, the epic *Pharsalia,* described the Roman Civil War. Lantantius, a fourth-century C.E. Christian apologist, is best known for *The Divine Institutions.* Tacitus (c. 55–117 C.E.) wrote the most detailed early description of the German peoples at the end of the first century C.E. in *Germania.* Baron de Montesquieu (1689–1755) was a social theorist who ruminated broadly on commerce, slavery, and politics; Vastey drew extensively on Montesquieu's knowledge of classic works in *The Spirit of Laws* (1758). Alain René Le Sage (1668–1747), a novelist, composed a picaresque novel titled *Gils Blas* that served as

a model for later British picaresques. Ambroise Marie François Joseph Palisot de Beauvois (1752–1820) was a botanist and explorer who visited both Africa and North America; he drew pictures of flora and fauna unknown to Europeans at the time, and speculated about the native inhabitants of both continents (comparing, as Vastey points out, African peoples to orangutans). Constantin-François Chasseboeuf comte de Volney (1757–1820), whose most famous work was *The Ruins* (1791), championed the notion that the ancient Ethiopians were the founders of the first human civilization; later white and black abolitionists drew extensively on his ethnographic research and historical hypotheses. René de Chateaubriand (1768–1848) was a romantic writer whose *Genius of Christianity* (1802) gained enormous popularity in France and influenced later European and American romantics.

83. On British theories of the diffusion of culture, see Philip D. Curtin, *The Image of Africa: British Ideas and Actions, 1780–1850,* vol. 1 (Madison, Wis., 1964), 253.

84. See Stocking, *Victorian Anthropology,* 17.

85. Volney theorized that the "Negro" features resulted from the mixing of African blood with that of Romans and Greeks. See St. Clair Drake, *Black Folk Here and There: An Essay in History and Anthropology,* vol. 1 (Los Angeles, 1987), 133.

86. Robert D. Richardson, Jr., Introduction to *A New Translation of Volney's Ruins,* 2 vols. (New York, 1979), 1:30–35, 66, 78–79, 88.

87. Vastey had no trouble finding classical sources to bolster his argument about the incivilities of ancient Gaul and Germany. Lucan, Caesar, and other Roman historians of the campaigns against Gaul gave him plenty of ammunition to demonstrate their lack of morality and strange customs. Similarly, Tacitus provided a detailed description of the Germans, including their practice of human sacrifice (a practice that many Europeans took to be a signal feature of African "barbarism"): "Mercury is the deity whom they chiefly worship, and on certain days they deem it right to sacrifice to him even with human victims. Hercules and Mars they appease with more lawful offerings. Some of the Suevi also sacrifice to Isis. Of the occasion and origin of this foreign rite I have discovered nothing but that the image, which is fashioned like a light galley, indicates an imported worship. The Germans, however, do not consider it consistent with the grandeur of celestial beings to confine the gods within walls, or to liken them to the form of any human countenance. They consecrate woods and groves, and they apply the names of deities to the abstraction which they see only in spiritual worship." Alfred John Church and William Jackson Brodribb, trans., *The Agricola and Germany of Tacitus, and the Dialogue on Oratory,* rev. ed. (London, 1877), 93.

88. Comte de Limonade to Grégoire, June 10, 1814, Letter in Bibliothèque de l'Arsenal, MS 6339, in Thomas Cassirer and Jean-François Brière, trans., *On the Cultural Achievements of Negroes* (Amherst, Mass., 1996), xliii.

89. Richard H. Brodhead, *Cultures of Letters: Scenes of Reading and Writing in Nineteenth-Century America* (Chicago, 1993), 193.

90. The governors of North Carolina and Virginia both sent special messages to their legislatures about the *Appeal,* and the governor of Georgia even wrote to the mayor of Boston requesting its suppression (Loggins, *Negro Author,* 87). For more on the Appeal see Peter P. Hinks, *To Awaken My Afflicted Brethren: David Walker and the Problem of Antebellum Slave Resistance* (University Park, Penn., 1997).

91. *Liberator,* January 29, 1831, cited in Loggins, *Negro Author,* 87.

92. Curry, *Free Black in Urban America,* 204, 207.

93. For more on the broader ramifications of early African-American print culture, see Frances Smith Foster, "A Narrative of the Interesting Origins and (Somewhat) Surprising Developments of African-American Print Culture," *American Literary History* 17, no. 4 (Winter 2005): 714–740.

2. The Children of Gilead

1. William Catto, *A Semi-Centenary Discourse, delivered in the First African Presbyterian Church, Philadelphia, with a short history of the church from its first organization* (Philadelphia, 1857), 15, 17. The pastor was quoting John 6:12, a passage in which Jesus has distributed the loaves and the fishes to the five thousand and is cautioning his disciples to collect all the fragments that are left behind. As a story of a meal served during Passover, this chapter is commonly interpreted as a foreshadowing of the Last Supper.

2. Catto, *Semi-Centenary Discourse,* 77.

3. Richard Allen and Jacob Tapsico, *The Doctrines and Discipline of the African Methodist Episcopal Church,* 1st ed. (Philadelphia, 1817), 3.

4. Of the many excellent studies of antebellum life among free urban blacks, see especially Leslie M. Harris, *In the Shadow of Slavery: African Americans in New York City, 1626–1863* (Chicago, 2003); Gary B. Nash, *Forging Freedom: The Formation of Philadelphia's Black Community, 1720–1840* (Cambridge, Mass., 1988); Patrick Rael, *Black Identity and Black Protest in the Antebellum North* (Chapel Hill, N.C., 2002); Shane White, *Somewhat More Independent: The End of Slavery in New York City, 1770–1810* (Athens, Ga., 1991); Julie Winch, *Philadelphia's Black Elite: Activism, Accommodation, and the Struggle for Autonomy, 1787–1848* (Philadelphia, 1988).

5. "The African Methodist Episcopal Church," *Independent* 43 (March 5, 1891), 11.

6. See Caroline Walker Bynum, *Holy Feast and Holy Fast: The Religious Significance of Food to Medieval Women* (Berkeley, 1987); *Fragmentation and Redemption: Essays on Gender and the Human Body in Medieval Religion* (New York, 1991); and R. Marie Griffith, *God's Daughters: Evangelical Women and the Power of Submission* (Berkeley, 1997).

7. Jonathan Z. Smith identifies within the formation of a canon and its interpretation the "basic cultural process of limitation and of overcoming that limitation through ingenuity," a "sacred persistence" that functions as a form of cultural

capital. In all religious systems, Smith argues, human beings work to surrender their freedom through the creation of a canon and simultaneously rediscover freedom through the exercise of reinterpretation "within their self-imposed limits." See Jonathan Z. Smith, "Sacred Persistence: Toward a Redescription of Canon," in *Imagining Religion: From Babylon to Jonestown* (Chicago, 1982), 52.

8. Will B. Gravely, "The Rise of African Churches in America (1786–1822): Re-examining the Contexts," *Journal of Religious Thought* 41 (1984), 68; and Nathan O. Hatch, *The Democratization of American Christianity* (New Haven, Conn., 1989).

9. My interest lies not so much in the kinds of factual evidence provided in a denominational account as in the worldview or "metanarrative" described therein. See Russell E. Richey, "Institutional Forms of Religion," in Charles H. Lippy and Peter W. Williams, eds., *Encyclopedia of the American Religious Experience: Studies of Traditions and Movements,* vol. 1 (New York, 1988), 33.

10. Albert J. Raboteau, *A Fire in the Bones: Reflections on African-American Religious History* (Boston, 1995), 25–26.

11. Those lists were later noted by Daniel Alexander Payne in a biography of Coker from the *Repository of Religion and Literature* (July 1861), cited in James A. Handy, *Scraps of African Methodist Episcopal History* (Philadelphia, 1902), 37.

12. Catto, *Semi-Centenary Discourse,* 12.

13. Daniel Coker, "Sermon Delivered Extempore in the African Bethel Church in the City of Baltimore, on the 21st of January 1816," in Herbert Aptheker, ed., *A Documentary History of the Negro People in the United States,* 1st ed. (New York, 1951), 68.

14. Catto, *Semi-Centenary Discourse,* 56.

15. John W. Prout, *An Oration, on the Establishment of the African Methodist Episcopal Church, in the United States of America. Delivered on the Third Anniversary Day, in the African Bethel Church, in the City of Baltimore, before the Members of the Annual Conference, on the Seventeenth of April, 1818* (Baltimore, Md., 1818), 9–22.

16. Christopher Rush, *A Short Account of the Rise and Progress of the African M.E. Church in America, Written by Christopher Rush, Superintendant of the Connexion, with the Aid of George Collins. Also, a Concise View of Church Order or Government, from Scripture, and from Some of the Best Authors on the Subject of Church Government, Relative to Episcopacy* (1843; reprint ed., New York, 1866), 6.

17. Cannon, *A History of the African Methodist Episcopal Church, the Only One in the United States of America, Styled Bethel Church* (Rochester, 1842), 3, 8.

18. Cannon, *History,* 14.

19. Cannon concluded his history by returning explicitly to the apostolic image of the "little ship Bethel" that had been launched onto the sea: "A victory so brilliant, so unexpectedly achieved by our Rev. father, R. A. and his little crew, a brave patriot of Christ—the Lord will protect all such. Jam. i. 25." See Cannon, *History,* 44.

20. Richard Allen, *The Life, Experience, and Gospel Labours of the Rt. Rev. Richard Allen. To Which is Annexed the Rise and Progress of the African Methodist Episcopal Church in the United States of America. Containing a Narrative of the Yellow Fever in the Year of Our Lord 1793: With an Address to the People of Colour in the United States* (Philadelphia, 1833), 9, 14.

21. Rush, *Short Account,* 13, 26, 57; Gravely, "Rise of African Churches," 65–66.

22. Benjamin Tucker Tanner, *An Outline of Our History and Government for African Methodist Churchmen, Ministerial and Lay, in Catechetical Form* (Philadelphia, 1884), 21. Joanna Brooks, *American Lazarus: Religion and the Rise of Native American and African American Literatures* (New York, 2003), ch. 2; on American hymnody, see Stephen A. Marini, *Sacred Song in America: Religion, Music, and Public Culture* (Urbana, Ill., 2003); and Edith L. Blumhofer and Mark A. Noll, eds., *Singing the Lord's Song in a Strange Land: Hymnody in the History of North American Protestantism* (Tuscaloosa, Ala., 2004).

23. Richard Allen, *A Collection of Spiritual Songs and Hymns Selected from Various Authors by Richard Allen, African Minister* (Philadelphia, 1801), 53, 38. The first printing of the hymnbook contained fifty-four hymns; the second, published later the same year, contained sixty-four. See David Nicholls, ed., *The Cambridge History of American Music* (Cambridge, 1999), 127.

24. Richard Allen, *The Life Experience and Gospel Labors of the Right Reverend Richard Allen,* with an introduction by George A. Singleton (Nashville, Tenn., 1960), 29–30.

25. George A. Levesque, "Inherent Reformers-Inherited Orthodoxy: Black Baptists in Boston, 1800–1873," *Journal of Negro History* 60, no. 4 (October 1975): 491–525. On Wesley Church, see Richard S. Newman, *Freedom's Prophet: Bishop Richard Allen, the AME Church, and the Black Founding Fathers* (New York, 2008), 210–213.

26. Rush, *Short Account,* 28, 32, 42, 62.

27. Tanner's introduction to Alexander Walker Wayman, *My Recollections of African M.E. Ministers, or Forty Years' Experience in the African Methodist Episcopal Church* (Philadelphia, 1881), vi–vii.

28. William E. Montgomery, *Under Their Own Vine and Fig Tree: The African-American Church in the South, 1865–1900* (Baton Rouge, 1993), 117–118, 342–343.

29. Montgomery, *Under Their Own Vine,* 343; Paul Harvey, *Redeeming the South: Religious Cultures and Racial Identities among Southern Baptists, 1865–1925* (Chapel Hill, N.C., 1997), ch. 2.

30. Benjamin Lee, introduction to Tanner, *Outline,* 9.

31. Benjamin Tucker Tanner, *An Apology for African Methodism* (Baltimore, 1867), 18; Benjamin W. Arnett, *Proceedings of the Semi-Centenary Celebration of the African Methodist Episcopal Church of Cincinnati* (Cincinnati, 1874), 16; Richard R. Wright, *Centennial Encyclopaedia of the African Methodist Episcopal Church. Containing Principally the Biographies of the Men and Women, both Ministers and Laymen, Whose Labors During a Hundred Years, Helped Make the A. M. E. Church*

What It Is; Also Short Historical Sketches of Annual Conferences, Educational Insti-
tutions, General Departments, Missionary Societies of the A. M. E. Church, and Gen-
eral Information about African Methodism and the Christian Church in General; Be-
ing a Literary Contribution to the Celebration of the One Hundredth Anniversary of
the Formation of the African Methodist Episcopal Church Denomination by Richard
Allen and others, at Philadelphia, Penna., in 1816 (Philadelphia, 1916), 5.

32. Alfred Lee Ridgel, *Africa and African Methodism* (Atlanta, 1896), 27.

33. H. T. Kealing, the editor of the *AME Church Review,* gushed that the campaign to commemorate Mother Bethel as the "abbey of African Methodism" was
fulfilled. Now, as he described it, "every loyal son of that church may see and touch
the relics that connect the present with the motives of its foundation." See *AME*
Church Review 17, no. 4 (1900), 393–394, 392. On the growth of Allen's Day, see
Mitch Kachun, *Festivals of Freedom: Memory and Meaning in African American*
Emancipation Celebrations, 1808–1915 (Amherst, Mass., 2003), 161–165.

34. Josephine Heard, *Morning Glories* (Philadelphia, 1890), ii, 92.

35. Horace Talbert, *The Sons of Allen: Together with a Sketch of the Rise and*
Progress of Wilberforce University, Wilberforce, Ohio (Xenia, Ohio, 1906), 22, 26, 25.

36. Talbert, *The Sons of Allen,* viii; J. T. Jenifer, "What has African Methodism to
say for itself?" in Wright, *Centennial Encyclopedia,* 9; Gail Bederman, *Manliness*
and Civilization: A Cultural History of Race and Gender in the United States, 1880–
1917 (Chicago, 1995); Clark, *Defining Moments,* ch. 3.

37. Katherine Davis Tillman, "The Spirit of Allen: A Pageant of African Methodism," in Claudia Tate, ed., *The Works of Katherine Davis Chapman Tillman* (New
York, 1991), 398, 401, 412.

38. Daniel Alexander Payne, *History of the African Methodist Episcopal Church*
(Nashville, Tenn., 1891), ix. On Payne's views about the mission of the AME
Church in the context of the universal Christian church, see David W. Wills, "As-
pects of Social Thought in the African Methodist Episcopal Church, 1884–1910"
(Ph.D. diss., Harvard University, 1975), 34–38.

39. *The Semi-Centenary and the Retrospection of the African Methodist Episcopal*
Church (1866; reprint ed., Freeport, N.Y., 1972), 22.

40. Payne, *History of the AME,* 2–7.

41. Payne, *Semi-Centenary and the Retrospection,* 33; *History of the AME,* 12;
Payne, "Thoughts About the Past, the Present and the Future of the African M.E.
Church," *AME Church Review* 1 (July 1884), 3, quoted in Wills, "Aspects of Social
Thought," 35.

42. "The African Methodist Episcopal Church," *Independent* 43 (March 5,
1891), 11; *An Outline of Our History and Government for African Methodist*
Churchmen, Ministerial and Lay, in Catechetical Form (Philadelphia, 1884), 10, 13–
14. Interestingly, in his extensive catechism Tanner required the catechumen to say
not that the AME Church was the *best* church but instead that it was "better for
me" than other denominations (Baptist, Presbyterian, Episcopal, Catholic). Tanner

pointed out that the church contained Euro-American members, "to say nothing of the host who by reason of mixture cannot be so written."

43. Wills, "Aspects of Social Thought," 35.

44. Tanner, "African Methodist Episcopal Church," 10–11.

45. John Jamison Moore, *History of the A. M. E. Zion Church in America. Founded in 1796, in the City of New York* (York, Penn., 1884), 5, 11, 382.

46. James Walker Hood, *One Hundred Years of the African Methodist Episcopal Zion Church; or, The Centennial of African Methodism* (New York, 1895), 1–2, 6–7, 14, 22, 23.

47. Hood, *One Hundred Years,* 133.

48. James Walker Hood, *Sketch of the Early History of the African Methodist Episcopal Zion Church with Jubilee Souvenir and Appendix* (Charlotte, N.C., 1914), 62. According to the AMEZ Historical Catechism of 1922, new members were instructed that they had left the John Street (white) Church in 1797 "with the consent and good will" of that group. In contrast, their histories noted, AME members had departed in anger and without appropriate sanction. See Cicero Richardson Harris, *Historical Catechism of the A. M. E. Zion Church. For Use in Families and Sunday Schools* (Charlotte, N.C., 1922), 13.

49. Hood, *One Hundred Years,* 12; Benjamin Franklin Wheeler, *The Varick Family* (Mobile, Ala., 1906), 6; Harris, *Historical Catechism,* 11.

50. Fayette Montgomery Hamilton, *A Plain Account of the Colored Methodist Episcopal Church in America. Being an Outline of Her History and Polity; Also, Her Prospective Work* (Nashville, Tenn., 1887), 10.

51. Charles H. Phillips, *The History of the Colored Methodist Episcopal Church in America: Comprising Its Organization, Subsequent Development and Present Status* (Jackson, Tenn., 1925), 35.

52. Hamilton, *Plain Account,* 45.

53. Hamilton, *Plain Account,* 83–84.

54. Phillips, *History,* 76.

55. Emanuel King Love, *History of the First African Baptist Church, from its Organization, January 20th, 1788, to July 1st, 1888. Including the Centennial Celebration, Addresses, Sermons, etc.* (Savannah, Ga., 1888), 202; Charles Octavius Boothe, *The Cyclopedia of the Colored Baptists of Alabama: Their Leaders and Their Work* (Birmingham, Ala., 1895); E. C. Morris, *Sermons, Addresses and Reminiscences and Important Correspondence, With a Picture Gallery of Eminent Ministers and Scholars* (Nashville, Tenn., 1901); Eugene Carter, *Once a Methodist; Now a Baptist. Why?* (Nashville, Tenn., 1905).

56. Love, *History,* page D.

57. Love, *History,* iii.

58. James Meriles Simms, *The First Colored Baptist Church in North America. Constituted at Savannah, Georgia, January 20, A.D. 1788. With Biographical Sketches of the Pastors* (Philadelphia, 1888), 21.

59. Simms, *The First Colored Baptist Church,* 21; Love, *History,* 233.

60. Love, *History,* 3; on the ideological functions of early Christian martyrologies, see Elizabeth A. Castelli, *Martyrdom and Memory: Early Christian Culture Making* (New York, 2004), ch. 2.

61. E. C. Morris, *Sermons, Addresses and Reminiscences and Important Correspondence, With a Picture Gallery of Eminent Ministers and Scholars* (Nashville, Tenn., 1901), 27.

62. C. T. Walker, "The Introductory Sermon," in Love, *History,* 216.

63. Lawrence N. Jones provides an important reminder in his assertion that "there is no 'black church' in the conventional understanding of that term. There are denominations, composed of congregations of black persons and under their control, and there are countless free-standing congregations, but there is no one entity that can be called the black church." See "The Black Churches: A New Agenda," in Milton C. Sernett, ed., *Afro-American Religious History: A Documentary Witness* (Durham, N.C., 1985), 491. See also Curtis Evans, *The Problem of Black Religion* (New York, 2008).

64. W. E. Burghardt Du Bois, *The Souls of Black Folk* (1903; reprint ed., New York, 1969), 213–215, 225; Sernett, *Documentary Witness,* 309.

65. *The Story of the Negro* (New York, 1909), I: 278, quoted in Sernett, *Documentary Witness,* 3–4.

66. Carter G. Woodson, *The History of the Negro Church,* 2nd ed. (Washington, D.C., 1945) esp. chs. 12–15; W. E. B. Du Bois, *The Rural Negro* (Washington, D.C., 1930), quoted in Sernett, *Documentary Witness,* 331.

67. Du Bois characterized the AME as the "greatest Negro organization in the world" (*Souls,* 217).

68. Mays and Nicholson, *The Negro's Church* (New York, 1933), 292, cited in Sernett, *Documentary Witness,* 348; Drake and Cayton, *Black Metropolis: A Study of Negro Life in a Northern City* (New York, 1945).

69. E. Franklin Frazier, *The Negro Church in America* (New York, 1964).

3. The Serpentine Trail

1. Mary Hassal, *Secret History, or, The Horrors of St. Domingo, in a Series of Letters Written by a Lady at Cape Francois, to Colonel Burr, Late Vice-President of the United States, Principally during the Command of General Rochambeau* (Philadelphia, 1808), 100.

2. On the dramatic effects of the Haitian Revolution on Americans, see Elizabeth Rauh Bethel, "Images of Hayti: The Construction of an Afro-American Lieu De Mémoire," *Callaloo* 15, no. 3, *Haitian Literature and Culture,* Part 2 (Summer 1992): 827–841; David Brion Davis, *Revolutions: Reflections on American Equality and Foreign Liberations* (Cambridge, Mass., 1990), 49–54; Chris Dixon, *African Americans and Haiti: Emigration and Black Nationalism in the Nineteenth Century*

(Westport, Conn., 2000); and Alfred N. Hunt, *Haiti's Influence on Antebellum America: Slumbering Volcano in the Caribbean* (Baton Rouge, 1988), 2. The best overview of the history of the revolution itself is Laurent Dubois, *Avengers of the New World: The Story of the Haitian Revolution* (Cambridge, Mass., 2004).

3. Hunt, *Haiti's Influence,* 3. See also Bruce Dain, "Haiti and Egypt in Early Black Racial Discourse in the United States," *Slavery and Abolition* 14, no. 3 (December 1993): 139–161.

4. The best treatment of David Walker is Peter P. Hinks, *To Awaken My Afflicted Brethren: David Walker and the Problem of Antebellum Slave Resistance* (University Park, Penn., 1997).

5. David Walker, *Walker's Appeal in Four Articles* (2nd ed., 1830; reprint ed., New York, 1969), 31.

6. Walker, *Appeal,* 47, 69, 70, 81, 88.

7. As Joan Dayan has expressed it, "Haiti forced imagination high and low: expression moved uneasily between the extremes of idealization and debasement." See Joan Dayan, *Haiti, History, and the Gods* (Berkeley, 1998), 5.

8. Ruth Miller Elson, *Guardians of Tradition: American Schoolbooks of the Nineteenth Century* (Lincoln, Neb., 1964), 95; James Franklin, *The Present State of Hayti (Saint Domingo), with remarks on its agriculture, commerce, laws, religion, finances, and population, etc. etc.* (1828; reprint ed., Westport, Conn., 1970), 9, 395. Franklin, a British merchant, wanted to warn other merchants about the perils of investment in Haiti; his arguments also related to debates in England over the abolition of slavery in the British Empire, an event that presumably would have detrimentally affected his own business.

Médéric-Louis-Élie Moreau de Saint-Méry, *A Civilization that Perished: The Last Years of White Colonial Rule in Haiti,* trans., abridged, and ed. Ivor D. Spencer (1797–1798, 2 vols.; reprint ed., Lanham, Md., 1985), ix, 1, 6.

9. Anonymous, *North American Review* (1821), 113, 118, 120, 131.

10. Benjamin Seebohm, ed., *Memoirs of the Life and Gospel Labors of Stephen Grellet,* vol. 1 (Philadelphia, 1860[?]), 336, 338–339, 343.

11. Arthur O. White, "Prince Saunders: An Instance of Social Mobility among Antebellum New England Blacks," *Journal of Negro History* 60, no. 4 (Oct. 1975), 526–528; and Julie Winch, *A Gentleman of Color: The Life of James Forten* (New York, 2002), 211. Henri Christophe controlled the northern part of Haiti from 1807 to 1820, while President Alexandre Pétion ruled the south until his death in 1818; American emigrants considered both locations for settlement.

12. *Haytian Papers: A Collection of the very interesting proclamations, and other official documents; together with some accounts of the rise, progress, and present state of the kingdom of Hayti* (London, 1816), 184, 219–220. The authorship of much of the *Papers* is unclear: Saunders did not distinguish between his own writings and excerpts he collected elsewhere. For this reason, the last piece is especially problematic because its rhetorical style is not the same as that of other pieces authored

by Saunders. I have been especially careful to note him as the compiler rather than as the author of this document.

13. Saunders, *Haytian Papers*, 148.

14. White, "Prince Saunders," 529–532.

15. James G. Leyburn, *The Haitian People* (1941; reprint ed., New Haven, 1966), 33–34, 119–120.

16. On Haitian narrations of its postrevolutionary history, see Dayan, *Haiti, History and the Gods;* and Michel-Rolph Trouillot, *Silencing the Past: Power and the Production of History* (Boston, 1995). See also Prince Saunders's translation of the *Manifesto* of King Henry (1814) in *Haytian Papers*, 154–191.

17. Floyd J. Miller, *The Search for a Black Nationality: Black Emigration and Colonization, 1787–1863* (Urbana, Ill., 1975), viii.

18. Julie Winch, "American Free Blacks and Emigration to Haiti, 1804–26," Working Paper no. 33, *Centro de Investigaciones Del Caribe y América Latina* (Puerto Rico, 1988), 12.

19. Winch, "Free Blacks," 1, 8, 12–15, 17, 21. The Society of Friends was particularly active in encouraging manumission and supporting the transportation abroad of newly freed slaves.

20. Haiti shifted from the most productive island in the Caribbean in the 1790s to one of the poorest nations in the world in a span of some thirty years. It is little wonder that the president looked to its wealthy neighbor to the north, the United States, for economic rehabilitation. On the Haitian economy, see Leyburn, *The Haitian People.*

21. Miller, *Search*, 77–78; Boyer to Dewey, April 30, 1824, in *Correspondence Relative to the Emigration to Haiti of the Free People of Colour in the United States, together with Instructions to the Agent Sent by President Boyer*, comp. Loring Dewey (New York, 1824), 6; Winch, *Gentleman*, 215.

22. *Genius of Universal Emancipation*, 3:4 (June 1824). See also the letter of Haitian visitor John G. Alexandre, *U.S. Gazette*, December 28, 1824; reprint from the *National Journal* in the *U.S. Gazette*, April 19, 1825.

23. Dewey to Boyer, March 4, 1824, 4; Boyer to Dewey, April 30, 1824, 10, both in Dewey, *Correspondence.*

24. Excerpt from the *National Gazette*, July 21, 1824, cited in Jonathas Henri Théodore Granville, *Biographie de Jonathas Granville, par son fils* (Paris, 1873), 154.

25. Cited in *U.S. Gazette*, December 24, 1824, and in *Genius*, June 1825; from the *National Gazette*, cited in Granville, *Biographie*, 128.

26. "Haiti," *American Baptist Magazine, and Missionary Intelligencer* n.s., 4 (July 1823): 133–136; "Mission to Haiti," *The Latter Day Luminary* 5 (April 1824): 110–111; on Paul, see Russell L. Adams, *Great Negroes Past and Present* (Chicago, 1969), 98.

27. In an account from the *National Gazette*, this phrase is attributed to Bryan Edwards. However, it recurs throughout the promotional literature in the 1820s.

National Gazette, June 21, 1824, cited in Granville *Biographie,* 124; Boston *Sentinel,* July 1, 1824, cited in Granville, *Biographie,* 142.

28. Kenrick's poem was originally published in the *Boston Sentinel* and reprinted in the *Genius of Universal Emancipation,* February 11, 1826.

29. *Genius of Universal Emancipation,* March 1825 and June 3, 1826.

30. Eddie Glaude, *Exodus! Religion, Race, and Nation in Early Nineteenth-Century Black America* (Chicago, 2000), part 1.

31. *Genius of Universal Emancipation,* February 11, 1826.

32. Black use of this image provides an intriguing counterpoint to Thomas Paine's more famous poem, "Liberty Tree" (1775), the last lines of which contain the following:

> But hear, O ye swains, 'tis a tale most profane,
> How all the tyrannical powers,
> Kings, Commons, and Lords, are uniting amain
> To cut down this guardian of ours;
> From the east to the west blow the trumpet to arms
> Through the land let the sound of it flee,
> Let the far and the near, all unite with a cheer,
> In defence of our Liberty Tree.

33. *Genius of Universal Emancipation,* August 1825.

34. Thomas Jefferson to William Stevens Smith, November 13, 1787, in *The Yale Book of Quotations,* Fred R. Shapiro, ed. (New Haven, Conn., 2006), 393; Will B. Gravely, "The Dialectic of Double Consciousness in Black American Freedom Celebrations, 1808–1863," *Journal of Negro History* 67 (Winter 1982): 302–317; and Gregg D. Kimball, "African, American, and Virginian: The Shaping of Black Memory in Antebellum Virginia, 1790–1860," in W. Fitzhugh Brundage, ed., *Where These Memories Grow: History, Memory, and Southern Identity* (Chapel Hill, N.C., 2000), 57–77.

Celebrations connected to Haiti that did take place in the United States were more often linked to the achievement of foreign *recognition* of Haitian independence than to the initial feat of black liberation. In August 1825, the "colored people of Baltimore" met to celebrate the French acknowledgment of Haiti as a sovereign nation, and the custom later spread to other Southern cities. See Christopher Phillips, *Freedom's Port: The African American Community of Baltimore, 1790–1860* (Urbana, Ill., 1997), 174.

35. B. Inginac to John Kenrick, January 20, 1824, and free black man to "his friend in New York City," November 5, 1823, both in *Genius of Universal Emancipation,* June 1824, 3:14.

36. *Genius of Universal Emancipation,* August 12, 1826.

37. Leslie G. Desmangles, *Faces of the Gods: Vodou and Roman Catholicism in Haiti* (Chapel Hill, N.C., 1992), 4–5.

38. Leyburn, *The Haitian People,* 137–140.

39. Leyburn, *The Haitian People,* 120–122.

40. *U.S. Gazette,* April 5, 1825.

41. *Colored American,* August 5, 1837. See also Letter from the Reverend A. A. Phelps, *National Era* 1, no. 1 (January 7, 1847), 3; and Solomon P. Hood, "The A.M.E. Church in the West Indies," AME *Christian Recorder* 28, no. 48 (November 20, 1890), 1.

42. Munroe to Dr. Bolles, June 1835, William Munroe papers, Virginia Baptist Historical Society, Richmond, VA; Rev. S. W. Hanna, *Notes of a Visit to Some Parts of Haiti, Jan., Feb., 1835* (London, 1836), 150.

43. *Minutes of the Virginia Branch of the American Colonization Society,* January 17, 1825, Virginia Historical Society. The ACS argument asserted that African Americans would find themselves *more* at home in Africa, where the immigrant would encounter "a people speaking the same language, professing the same religion, and governed by laws dictated by themselves." In this case, it was the ACS that was eager to overlook cultural and political differences to make its point.

44. *National Gazette,* September 15, 1824, cited in Granville, *Biographie,* 172.

45. *Genius of Universal Emancipation,* December 1824 and November 1824.

46. *Genius of Universal Emancipation,* July 1825; February 1825; April 1825; December 1824; and Granville, *Biographie,* 208.

47. *Genius of Universal Emancipation,* June 24, 1826; Cromwell to Allen, January 14, 1825, in *U.S. Gazette,* April 5, 1825; *Genius of Universal Emancipation,* July 1825.

48. Alexander W. Wayman, *My Recollections of African M.E. Ministers, or Forty Years' Experience in the African Methodist Episcopal Church* (Philadelphia, 1881), 3–4.

49. Granville letter of March 24, 1825, in *U.S. Gazette,* April 19, 1825.

50. *Genius of Universal Emancipation,* July 8, 1826.

51. Beaubrun Ardouin, *Période Haïtienne, quatrième époque, livre quatrième,* vol. 9 of *Etudes sur l'histoire d'Haïti suivies de la vie du general J.-M. Borgella,* annotated by François Dalencour (1860; reprint ed., Port-au-Prince, Haiti, 1958), 68, trans. Patricia Holland. Ardouin was also a close associate—and longtime defender—of President Boyer.

52. *U.S. Gazette,* June 14, 1825. African Americans would almost certainly have been considered mulattoes by natives.

53. Effie Lee Newsome, "Early Figures in Haitian Methodism," *Phylon* 5 (1944), 51.

54. *U.S. Gazette,* April 19, 1825.

55. Lundy, *Genius of Universal Emancipation,* April 1825.

56. "A Letter from Santo Domingo, January 1, 1830," in *Christian Recorder* 15, no. 59 (February 22, 1877); the brief career of William C. Munroe in Haiti is an interesting case in point. Appointed by the Baptist General Convention, Munroe sailed for Haiti in 1835 and established a small church in Port-au-Prince. Meeting

in Munroe's home, the church grew to approximately twenty people. Munroe held three services on the Sabbath, established a Sunday school, and held a weekly lecture and prayer meeting. His efforts were limited, however, because he could only preach in English; his communicants most likely were immigrants themselves. He was also hampered by his inability to find a public meeting space. In 1837, after the death of his wife, Munroe quit the mission station and the Baptists decided to suspend it entirely because of lack of funds. See Joseph Tracy, Solomon Peck, Enoch Mudge, William Cutter, Enoch Mack (Joseph Tracy, compiler), *History of American Missions to the Heathen, from Their Commencement to the Present Time* (Worcester, Mass., 1840), 557.

57. Russworm, "The Condition and Prospects of Haiti," in Philip S. Foner, ed., *The Voice of Black America: Major Speeches by Negroes in the United States, 1797–1971* (New York, 1972), 36–37. Russworm likely was making reference to Isaiah 23:8, "Who hath taken this counsel against Tyre, the crowning city, whose merchants are princes, whose traffickers are the honourable of the earth?"

58. On Haiti's political history in this period, see Leyburn, *The Haitian People,* ch. 4.

59. Redpath published the work of John Relly Beard, *Toussaint L'Ouverture: A Biography and Autobiography* (Boston, 1863); Wendell Phillips, "Toussaint L'Ouverture" (1861), in Louis Filler, ed., *Wendell Phillips on Civil Rights and Freedom,* 2nd ed. (Washington, D.C., 1982); James McCune Smith, "A Lecture on the Haytien Revolution; with a Sketch of the Character of Toussaint L'Ouverture" (New York, 1841); Lydia Maria Child, *The Freedmen's Book* (Boston, 1865); C. W. Mossell, *Toussaint L'Ouverture, The Hero of Saint Domingo, Soldier, Statesman, Martyr; or Hayti's Struggle, Triumph, Independence, and Achievements* (Lockport, N.Y., 1896).

60. Brown, "St. Domingo: Its Revolutions and Its Patriots, delivered before the Metropolitan Athenaeum, London, and St. Thomas's Church, Philadelphia, 1854" (Boston, 1855), 12, 22. Brown drew from John R. Beard, *The Life of Toussaint L'Ouverture, the Negro Patriot of Hayti: Comprising an Account of the Struggle for Liberty in the Island, and a Sketch of Its History to the Present Period* (London, 1853).

61. Brown, "St. Domingo," 13, 37.

62. On romantic racialism, see George M. Fredrickson, *The Black Image in the White Mind: The Debate on Afro-American Character and Destiny, 1817–1914* (New York, 1971), ch. 4. As Fredrickson notes, Euro-American historians such as Francis Parkman and William H. Prescott also made use of these ideas, although typically they used them comparatively to celebrate the superiority of Anglo-Saxon "racial character."

63. David M. Dean, *Defender of the Race: James Theodore Holly, Black Nationalist and Bishop* (Boston, Mass., 1979), 2–22; Howard B. Bell, introduction to Holly's *Vindication of the Capacity of the Negro for Self-Government and Civilized Progress*

(1857), in Bell, ed., *Black Separatism and the Caribbean, 1860* (Ann Arbor, Mich., 1970), 9.

64. Dean, *Defender of the Race,* 23–29.

65. James Theodore Holly, "The Church at Hayti," *Churchman* 25, no. 36 (November 1, 1855), 288.

66. Holly, *Vindication,* in Bell, *Black Separatism,* 60.

67. Holly, "Thoughts on Hayti," *Anglo-African Magazine* 1, no. 6 (June 1859), 185–186; and Holly, *Vindication,* 25.

68. This theme was echoed later by the Rev. John W. Lewis, an emigrant in Holly's party. He even suggested that Haitians were, at their best, what might be termed "crypto-Protestant"—tolerant, individualistic, divinely inspired Bible readers—called by the true God despite the outward formalism of their religious beliefs: "Although theirs was, and mine is, a country full of ceremonies, they need no Te Deum chanted for the repose of their souls, nor a virgin saint to commend them to God or good angels. As master-spirits of their age, they were moved by an inward holy inspiration, which made their deeds heroic." *Pine and the Palm* 1, no. 4 (June 8, 1861).

69. Holly, "The Church at Hayti," 288.

70. Holly, *Vindication,* 65; "Thoughts," 187.

71. Holly, "Thoughts," 328, 364.

72. Holly, "Appeal for a farewell benefit for the Haytian Emigrants from New Haven," *Weekly Anglo-African* (April 27, 1861); Lewis, letter of April 6, 1861, *Pine and the Palm* 1, no. 4 (June 8, 1861); Miller, *Search,* 242.

73. J. Dennis Harris, *A Summer on the Borders of the Caribbean Sea* (1860), in Bell, *Black Separatism,* 167.

74. Miller, *Search,* 80–86, 248; Solomon P. Hood, "The AME Church in the West Indies," AME *Christian Recorder* 28, no. 48 (November 20, 1890), 2. Samuel E. Cornish, later the editor of the first black newspaper, *Freedom's Journal,* initially had supported the Haitian emigration movement. By the late 1820s his paper ran an active anti-emigration campaign. For criticism of the second migration, see especially the scathing letters written by Mary Shadd Cary to the *Weekly Anglo-African* in the fall of 1861.

75. On Steward's experiences in Haiti, see Albert G. Miller, *Elevating the Race: Theophilus G. Steward, Black Theology, and the Making of an African American Civil Society (1865–1924)* (Knoxville, Tenn., 2003); and William Seraille, *Voice of Dissent: Theophilus Gould Steward (1843–1924) and Black America* (Brooklyn, N.Y., 1991).

76. In C. W. Mossell, *Toussaint L'Ouverture: The Hero of Saint Domingo* (Lockport, N.Y., 1896), 406. For Steward's study of the Haitian Revolution, see *The Haitian Revolution, 1791 to 1804: Or, Side Lights on the French Revolution* (New York, 1914).

77. Bethel, "Images of Hayti"; Winch, "Free Blacks," 16; Dain, "Haiti," 142; Chris

Dixon, "An Ambivalent Black Nationalism: Haiti, Africa, and Antebellum African-American Emigrationism," *Australasian Journal of American Studies* 10 (1991), 22, n. 11.

4. Exodus and Ethiopia

1. Daniel H. Peterson, *The Looking-Glass: being a true report and narrative of the life, travels and labors of the Rev. Daniel H. Peterson, a colored clergyman; embracing a period of time from the year 1812 to 1854, and including his visit to western Africa* (New York, 1854), 72.

2. Peterson, *Looking-Glass*, 61–62, 63.

3. On African-American interchange with Africa, see Kwame Anthony Appiah, *In My Father's House: Africa in the Philosophy of Culture* (New York, 1992); James Campbell, *Middle Passages: African American Journeys to Africa, 1787–2005* (New York, 2006); Paul Gilroy, *The Black Atlantic: Modernity and Double Consciousness* (Cambridge, Mass., 1993).

4. Peterson, *Looking-Glass*, 118.

5. Anna Johnston, *Missionary Writing and Empire, 1800–1860* (Cambridge, 2003), 32.

6. Johnston, *Missionary Writing and Empire*, 28. Johnston, citing Catherine Hall's work, *Civilising Subjects: Metropole and Colony in the English Imagination, 1830–1867* (Chicago, 2002), makes the important point that for British readers of missionary literature, the "identity of colonizer is a constitutive part of Englishness." So, too, with African Americans. The complex layering of American and racial national allegiances should not obscure the struggles for control that raged between native Liberians and Americo-Liberians throughout this period.

7. Floyd J. Miller, *The Search for a Black Nationality: Black Emigration and Colonization, 1787–1863* (Urbana, Ill., 1975), 3; on oral accounts of Africa and their transmission among slaves see Lawrence W. Levine, *Black Culture and Black Consciousness* (New York, 1977). James A. McMillin demonstrates that the slave trade continued well into the nineteenth century, shifting into the lower South ports of Savannah, Charleston, and New Orleans. *The Final Victims: Foreign Slave Trade to North America, 1783–1810* (Columbia, S.C., 2004).

8. Philip D. Curtin, *The Image of Africa: British Ideas and Actions, 1780–1850*, vol. 1 (Madison, Wis., 1964), 34.

9. For white views on colonization as a positive goal see P. J. Staudenraus, *The African Colonization Movement, 1816–1865* (New York, 1961). Jefferson and many other white political leaders at the turn of century supported the idea. In all these efforts (including British settlement of Sierra Leone), we see a fine distinction between, on the one hand, colonizing and repaying blacks by sending them "home," and, on the other, penalizing them for their color (e.g., in Sierra Leone blacks were considered wards of the state). New Jersey–born Robert Finley, a Presbyterian

minister, launched the idea for a colonization society, and it was supported by many notable political figures, including Thomas Jefferson and Andrew Jackson.

10. Miller, *Search*, 4, 15; Chris Dixon, "An Ambivalent Black Nationalism: Haiti, Africa, and Antebellum African-American Emigrationism," *Australasian Journal of American Studies* 10 (1991), 10, 11.

11. Paul Cuffe, *A Brief Account of the Settlement and Present Situation of the Colony of Sierra Leone in Africa* (New York, 1812), 7.

12. Staudenraus, *African Colonization*, 100.

13. Robert Millar, *The History of the Propagation of Christianity and Overthrow of Paganism wherein the Christian religion is confirmed, the rise and progress of heathenish idolatry is considered, the overthrow of paganism and the spreading of Christianity in the several ages of the New Testament Church are explained, the present state of heathens is enquired into and methods for their conversion offered*, 2 vols. (Edinburgh, 1723). Millar (1672–1752), the minister of Paisley Abbey, published two subsequent editions of his highly successful work.

14. Daniel Coker, *Journal of Daniel Coker, A Descendent of Africa* (1820; reprint ed., New York, 1970), 13, 21.

15. Coker, *Journal*, 43–44, cited in Josephus R. Coan, "Daniel Coker: Nineteenth-Century Black Church Organizer, Educator and Missionary," *Journal of the Interdenominational Theological Center* 3 (Fall 1975), 28.

16. Anonymous, "African Belief," *African Repository and Colonial Journal* 20, no. 12 (December 1844), 380.

17. Sandy Dwayne Martin, *Black Baptists and African Missions: The Origins of a Movement, 1880–1915* (Macon, Ga., 1989), 21.

18. Patrick Brantlinger, "Victorians and Africans: The Genealogy of the Myth of the Dark Continent," *Critical Inquiry* 12 (Autumn 1985), 175–176.

19. Martin R. Delany, *Official Report of the Niger Valley Exploring Party*, in Howard Bell, ed., *Search for a Place: Black Separatism and the Caribbean, 1860* (Ann Arbor, Mich., 1970), 57, 74–75, 84.

20. Delany, *Official Report*, 104, 108, 77, 106. Christianity, of course, meant Protestantism: Delany also attributed the continuance of the slave trade to Islam and Roman Catholicism; slavery was, he reported, the "legitimate successor of Roman Catholicism" (103).

21. Delany, *Official Report*, 41.

22. David Wills, Eddie Glaude, and others have argued for the centrality of "Exodus piety" among nineteenth-century African Americans. See David W. Wills, "Exodus Piety: African American Religion in an Age of Immigration," in *Minority Faiths and the American Protestant Mainstream*, ed. by Jonathan D. Sarna (Urbana, Ill., 1998), 136–190; on the theme of Israel in Canaan, see Regina M. Schwartz, *The Curse of Cain: The Violent Legacy of Monotheism* (Chicago, 1997), introduction.

23. Hollis Lynch, *Selected Letters of Edward Wilmot Blyden* (Millwood, N.Y., 1978), 10, 30; letter to Gladstone, April 20, 1860, in Lynch, *Letters,* 30.

24. Blyden, *Christianity, Islam, and the Negro Race* (1887; reprint ed., Edinburgh, 1967), 278.

25. Edward Wilmot Blyden, *African Life and Customs* (London, 1908), 12.

26. Blyden, *Christianity, Islam,* v; Lynch, *Letters,* 98, 125, 136.

27. Blyden, *Christianity, Islam,* 24, 31–32. Blyden asserted that "the Mohammedan Negro is a much better Mohammedan than the Christian Negro is a Christian, because the Muslim Negro, as a learner, is a disciple, not an imitator" (*Christianity, Islam,* 37); Blyden, "'The Problems before Liberia,' a lecture delivered in the Senate Chamber at Monrovia, Jan. 18, 1909" (London, 1909), 19.

28. Blyden, *African Life and Customs,* 61, 62, 69.

29. Blyden, *African Life and Customs,* 10.

30. This was true of many black leaders at the end of the nineteenth century. See Wilson Moses, *The Golden Age of Black Nationalism, 1850–1925* (Hamden, Conn., 1978), esp. ch. 1.

31. Blyden, "'Problems before Liberia,'" 11–12, 15, 19, 22.

32. Alexander Crummell, "Africa and Her People," in *Destiny and Race: Selected Writings, 1840–1898* (Amherst, Mass., 1992), 61.

33. Wilson Jeremiah Moses, introduction, Crummell, *Destiny and Race,* 3–4; Sylvia M. Jacobs, *The African Nexus: Black American Perspectives on the European Partitioning of Africa, 1880–1920* (Westwood, Conn., 1981), 22–23.

34. "Our National Mistakes and the Remedy for Them," in Alexander Crummell, *Africa and America: Addresses and Discourses* (Springfield, Mass., 1891), 196–197; Crummell, "The Race-Problem in America," in John R. Oldfield, ed., *Civilization and Black Progress: Selected Writings of Alexander Crummell on the South* (Charlottesville, Va., 1996), 167.

35. "Destined Superiority," in *Civilization and Black Progress,* 50, 52; "Report from Caldwell," *Spirit of Missions* 36 (1871), 485–489, cited in Crummell, *Destiny and Race,* 79; Oldfield, Introduction to *Civilization and Black Progress,* 9.

36. "Emigration, an Aid," in Crummell, *Africa and America,* 411; *Christian Recorder* 5, no. 38 (September 23, 1865), 151.

37. "'The Need of New Ideas and New Aims for a New Era,' An Address to the Graduating Class at Storer College, Harper's Ferry, West Virginia, May 30, 1885," Crummell, *Africa and America,* 17. For more on Crummell's thoughts about historical memory, see David W. Blight, *Race and Reunion: The Civil War in American Memory* (Cambridge, Mass., 2001), 315–319.

38. Crummell, "'The Duty of a Rising Christian State to Contribute to the World's Well-Being and Civilization and the Means by Which It May Perform the Same,' Delivered before Common Council and the Citizens of Monrovia, July 26, 1855" (1856; reprint ed., Boston, Mass., 1857), 7, 8, 9.

39. Crummell, "The Greatness of Christ," *Destiny and Race*, 133. Crummell also included Greece and Rome in his list of debased cultures; as we have seen, in other speeches he included the Greeks and Romans as part of the Western political and cultural tradition that should be embraced.

40. Crummell, "The Duty," 30. He reminded his audience that "we speak the language / Shakespeare spake; the faith and morals hold / Which Milton held!"

41. In 1812 he had indentured himself to purchase his own mother's freedom. He blamed slavery on Great Britain rather than on the United States: "Dear brethren, I want you to consider at this time, that this nation was not the cause of our forefathers being plunged into bondage. It was the British nation, who, in an age of darkness, made slaves of the colored people." Peterson, *Looking-Glass*, 62.

42. Peterson, *Looking-Glass*, 52–53.

43. Peterson, *Looking-Glass*, 102, 50, 62.

44. James T. Campbell, *Songs of Zion: The African Methodist Episcopal Church in the United States and South Africa* (New York, 1995), 79.

45. Walter Williams, *Black Americans and the Evangelization of Africa, 1877–1900* (Madison, Wis., 1982), 85, 87, 6–8; Campbell, *Songs of Zion*, 92; Henry McNeal Turner, *African Letters* (Nashville, Tenn., 1893), 30.

46. On black women and missionary work see Sylvia M. Jacobs, "Their 'Special Mission': Afro-American Women as Missionaries to the Congo, 1894–1937," in Jacobs, *Black Americans and the Missionary Movement in Africa* (Westport, Conn., 1982), 155–176; Williams, *Black Americans;* and Campbell, *Songs of Zion*, 93.

47. Annual Minutes, Consolidated American Baptist Convention, 1877, 31; cited in Martin, *Black Baptists*, 18.

48. Letter of May 7, 1873, addressed "To the Members of the Colored Baptist Churches and Associations in the United States of America," *African Repository* 49, no. 8 (August 1873), 252.

49. Williams, *Black Americans*, 7.

50. Thomas L. Johnson, *Africa for Christ. Twenty-Eight Years a Slave* (London, 1892), 14.

51. Johnson, *Africa for Christ*, 77, 78, 80, 86; Johnson, *Twenty-Eight Years a Slave, or the Story of My Life in Three Continents* (Bournemouth, U.K., 1909), 196. See also the reference from the *Pittsburgh Courier*, January 21, 1887, in *Twenty-Eight Years*, 188.

52. Walter L. Williams, "William Henry Sheppard, Afro-American Missionary in the Congo, 1890–1910," in Jacobs, *Black Americans*, 144; Maggie Pogue Johnson, an African-American poet from Virginia, heralded Sheppard in a 1910 poem in a way that expressed the admiration of many Southern blacks. Her final stanza concluded with a reverential "All Hail to thee, oh Sheppard, / Who carried them the light." Maggie Pogue Johnson, "Dedicated to Dr. W. H. Sheppard," in *Virginia Dreams: Lyrics for the Idyl Hour, Tales of the Time told in Rhyme* (n.p., 1910), 39.

53. Donald F. Roth, "The 'Black Man's Burden': The Racial Background of Afro-American Missionaries and Africa," in Jacobs, *Black Americans,* 37.

54. Pagan Kennedy, *Black Livingstone: A True Tale of Adventure in the Nineteenth-Century Congo* (New York, 2002), 82–111; William E. Phipps, *William Sheppard: Congo's African American Livingstone* (Louisville, Ky., 2002); and Williams, *Black Americans,* 94.

55. Despite his display of simple piety, Thomas Johnson was well versed in African-American historical literature; in his text he relies on the work of at least two contemporary authors: Edward Johnson, *School History of the Negro Race in American from 1619–1890* (Raleigh, N.C., 1890); and Joseph Thomas Wilson, *The Black Phalanx: A History of the Negro Soldiers of the United States in the Wars of 1775–1812, 1861–'65* (Hartford, Conn., 1890).

56. Williams, *Black Americans,* 94; William Henry Sheppard, *Presbyterian Pioneers in Congo* (Richmond, Va., 1917), 108, 101; Kennedy, *Black Livingstone,* 92. Sheppard's narrative of this encounter is strikingly reminiscent of the plot of Pauline Hopkins's novel *Of One Blood,* in which an African-American man is transported to a hidden and ancient African city that declares him to be its long-lost ruler.

57. C. C. Boone, *Congo as I Saw It* (New York, 1927), v, 24, 8–9.

58. Boone, *Congo as I Saw It,* 28, 66–67; Peterson, *Looking-Glass,* 120–121.

59. Sheppard, *Presbyterian Pioneers,* 137, 143.

60. Crummell, "'Africa and Her People': Lecture Notes," in *Destiny and Race,* 64.

61. Smith, *An Autobiography: The Story of the Lord's Dealings with Mrs. Amanda Smith the Colored Evangelist* (1893; reprint ed., New York, 1988), 285, 379–380, 388–389.

62. Turner, *African Letters,* 41; T. McCants Stewart, *Liberia: The Americo-African Republic* (New York, 1886), 60, 61.

63. Turner, *African Letters,* 59–60.

64. Turner, *African Letters,* 18.

65. Alfred Lee Ridgel, *Africa and African Methodism* (Atlanta, Ga., 1896), 42.

66. J. W. E. Bowen, *Africa and the American Negro: Addresses and Proceedings of the Congress on Africa: Held under the Auspices of the Stewart Missionary Foundation for Africa of Gammon Theological Seminary in Connection with the Cotton States and International Exposition December 13–15, 1895* (Atlanta, Ga., 1896), 113–115.

67. Sheppard, *Presbyterian Pioneers,* 30, 47; Boone, *Congo as I Saw It,* 26, 58.

68. *Christian Recorder,* December 12, 1895, 6.

69. On the valence of the term "lady" for African-American women in this period, see Evelyn Brooks Higginbotham, "African-American Women's History and the Metalanguage of Race," *Signs* 17, no. 2 (Winter 1992): 255–274.

70. See, for example, Bishop Levi J. Coppin, *Observation of Persons and Things in South Africa, 1900–1904* (Philadelphia, 1904), 75.

71. William H. Heard, *The Bright Side of African Life* (1901; reprint ed., New York, 1969), 8. When T. McCants Stewart assumed a teaching position at Liberia College in 1883, he explained his decision as part of a communal destiny: "That the Negro must develop a Nationality, a civilization somewhere, before he will be able to stand erect among the races and nations of the earth, becomes clearer and clearer to us as we travel and observe, and read and reflect. We feel that our brethren have a great work in America, but ours is to where Ethiopia shall soon stretch forth her hand unto God." *New York Globe,* August 4, 1883; cited in Albert S. Broussard, *African-American Odyssey: The Stewarts, 1853–1963* (Lawrence, Kan., 1998), 39. See also Michelle Mitchell, *Righteous Propagation: African Americans and the Politics of Racial Destiny after Reconstruction* (Chapel Hill, N.C., 2004), ch. 1.

72. Although Heard clearly understood nation-building as a demonstration of masculinity, he lauded the exploits of Matilda Newport, the early Americo-Liberian whom he nominated the "Joan of Arc" of Liberia (Heard, *Bright Side,* 20). Liberians celebrate December 1 in honor of this "Sainted Mother" of the national cause. The Matilda Newport story forcefully represents the triumph of Americo-Liberians over attacks by indigenous Africans; the national rights of ex-slave migrants were thereby pitted against the "uncivilized" tribes. Matilda Newport is still a subject of considerable tension, representing as she does the divide between Americo-Liberian nationalist sentiments and natives; as stated in a speech by Liberian activist Togba-Nah Tipoteh in 1977: "End the Matilda Newport thing now. . . . To honor Matilda Newport in any way whatsoever is to push the Liberian people backwards," in H. Boima Fahnbulleh, ed., *Voices of Protest: Liberia on the Edge, 1974–1980* (Boca Raton, Fla., 2004), 85.

73. Stewart, *Liberia,* 92, 98.

74. Alexander Priestley Camphor, *Missionary Story-Sketches: Folk-Lore from Africa* (Cincinnati, 1909), 156.

75. C. S. Smith, *Glimpses of Africa, West and Southwest Coast* (Nashville, Tenn., 1895), 174. Along with an explanation of the Knights Templar regalia, Smith also tried to convince the king—with little apparent success—that alcohol was an evil substance.

76. Boone, *Congo as I Saw It,* 26, 44.

77. Camphor, *Missionary Story-Sketches,* 8.

78. Camphor, "Our Work in Liberia, West Africa: Its Need for Help," (n.p., 1901), 7.

79. Bowen, *Africa and the American Negro,* 236.

80. Camphor, *Missionary Story-Sketches,* 48, 50, 77.

81. Camphor, *Missionary Story-Sketches,* 114, 288.

82. On the Azor incident see Campbell, *Songs of Zion,* 80; and Wills, "Exodus Piety," 6. For biographical information on Turner, see Steven Ward Angell, *Bishop Henry McNeal Turner and African-American Religion in the South* (Knox-

ville, Tenn., 1992); and Edwin S. Redkey, *Black Exodus: Black Nationalist and Back-to-Africa Movements, 1890–1910* (New Haven, Conn., 1969).

83. Turner, *African Letters,* 15, 32, 34.

84. Turner, *African Letters,* 56, 44, 72. The issue of African-American reactions to African polygamy is a fascinating subject for further research. Perhaps the most intriguing and sustained examination of the issue by a Christian missionary was undertaken by Levi Coppin, the first resident bishop of South Africa in the AME Church. Coppin wrote at length about the positive virtues he saw in polygamy: its systematic quality, care for widows, and so on, although ultimately he denounced the practice. See Campbell, *Songs of Zion,* 228–229.

85. The debate over the status of Islam continued (and continues) within African-American communities. At the 1912 conference at Tuskegee at least one participant suggested that Islam was better adapted to African life than was Christianity (echoing Blyden), while others argued that Islam needed to be eradicated; "The Negro in Conference at Tuskegee Institute," *African Times and Orient Review* (July 1912), 11.

86. The Book of Daniel 5:4 refers specifically to the practices of Belshazzar, the son of Nebuchadnezzar: "They drank wine, and praised the gods of gold, and of silver, of brass, of iron, of wood, and of stone." The significance of this invocation of the Babylonian Exile is an interesting topic for further investigation, especially given the predilection of African-American Protestants to cite the exilic experience as a collective touchstone.

87. Turner, *African Letters,* 53, 55.

88. Turner, *African Letters,* 35; Ridgel, *Africa and African Methodism,* 58, 61.

89. Hammond, "Africa in Its Relation to Christian Civilization," in Bowen, *Africa and the American Negro,* 207.

90. Ridgel, *Africa and African Methodism,* 45–46.

5. The Negro Race History

1. George Washington Williams, *History of the Negro Race in America, 1619–1880: Negroes as Slaves, As Soldiers, and As Citizens* (1883; reprint ed., New York, 1968), x. On Williams's life, see John Hope Franklin, *George Washington Williams: A Biography* (Chicago, 1985). Williams fit precisely Friedrich Nietzsche's characterization of "historical men," those who "believe that ever more light is shed on the meaning of existence in the course of its *process,* and they look back to consider that process only to understand the present better and learn to desire the future more vehemently." Nietzsche, *On the Advantage and Disadvantage of History for Life,* trans. Peter Preuss (Indianapolis, 1980), 13.

2. Edward A. Johnson, *A School History of the Negro Race in America from 1619 to 1890* (New York, 1911); Benjamin Quarles, "Black History's Antebellum Origins," *Proceedings of the American Antiquarian Society* 88, no. 1 (April 1979): 89–

122; J. Max Barber, *The Negro of the Earlier World. An Excursion into Ancient Negro History* (Philadelphia, n.d.), 5. On the use of black history as a counter to the late nineteenth-century proslavery argument, see John David Smith, "A Different View of Slavery: Black Historians Attack the Proslavery Argument, 1890–1920," *Journal of Negro History* 65, no. 4 (Fall 1980): 298–311. On representation as racial construction, see Henry Louis Gates, Jr., "The Trope of a New Negro and the Reconstruction of the Image of the Black," *Representations* 24 (Fall 1988): 129–155.

3. Jonathan Z. Smith helpfully suggests that when we study religion, we are examining "one mode of constructing worlds of meaning, worlds within which men find themselves and in which they choose to dwell," as well as "the variety of attempts to map, construct and inhabit . . . positions of power through the use of myths, rituals and experiences of transformation." *Map Is Not Territory: Studies in the History of Religions* (Leiden, 1978), 290–291.

4. From just 5 percent of the black adult population in 1860, black literacy rose dramatically to 70 percent by 1910. See Evelyn Brooks Higginbotham, *Righteous Discontent: The Women's Movement in the Black Baptist Church, 1880–1920* (Cambridge, Mass., 1993), 11, 44. See also Eric Foner, *Reconstruction: America's Unfinished Revolution, 1863–1877* (New York, 1988), 88–102; Leon Litwack, "The Gospel and the Primer," in *Been in the Storm So Long: The Aftermath of Slavery* (New York, 1979); and William E. Montgomery, *Under Their Own Vine and Fig Tree: The African-American Church in the South, 1865–1900* (Baton Rouge, La., 1993).

5. Barber, *Negro of the Earlier World*, 5. Richard Brodhead, *Cultures of Letters: Scenes of Reading and Writing in Nineteenth-Century America* (Chicago, 1993), 193.

6. Paul Ricoeur, *Time and Narrative,* trans. Kathleen McLaughlin and David Pellauer, vol. 1 (Chicago, 1984), 162. Ricoeur provides a helpful definition of narrative as a semantic innovation created through employment of a plot, through which "goals, causes, and chances are brought together within the temporal unity of a whole and complete action" (ix).

7. Through use of the phrase "technology of power," I distinguish between the possession of historical consciousness, which antebellum African Americans surely had in the form of oral traditions and limited access to education, and the possession of a mobile and complex "representational technology" that later enabled the large-scale dissemination of ideas. See Stephen Greenblatt, *Marvelous Possessions: The Wonder of the New World* (Chicago, 1991), 9–12. Lawrence Levine makes a case for the strength of oral narrative traditions in the antebellum era in *Black Culture, Black Consciousness: Afro-American Folk Thought from Slavery to Freedom* (New York, 1977).

8. Some accounts, such as Benjamin Tucker Tanner's *Negro's Origin* (1869), Rufus L. Perry's *Cushite or the Descendants of Ham* (1893), Barber's *Negro of the Earlier World* (n.d.), and Augustus T. Bell's *Woolly Hair Man of the Ancient South* (n.d.), concentrated on the ancient and scriptural origins of the Negro race. Oth-

ers focused on the roles played by blacks in American history, as in Williams, *History of the Negro Race in America* (1883); William T. Alexander, *History of the Colored Race in America* (1887); Joseph T. Wilson, *The Black Phalanx* (1888); Peter Thomas Stanford, *The Tragedy of the Negro in America* (1898); H. M. Tarver, *The Negro in the History of the United States* (1905); and Edward A. Johnson, *A School History of the Negro Race in America* (1911). Still other authors, including William Wells Brown, *The Rising Son: Or, The Antecedents and Advancement of the Colored Race* (1874); Joseph T. Wilson, *Emancipation, Its Course and Progress from 1481 B.C. to A.D. 1875* (1882); L. T. Smith, *A Great Truth in a Nutshell* (1883); and William Hannibal Thomas, *The American Negro* (1901), attempted topical overviews of racial history. Several more works, including James T. Holly's "Divine Plan of Human Redemption in its Ethnological Development" (1884); and Theophilus Gould Steward's *End of the World; or, Clearing the Way for the Fullness of the Gentiles* (1888), forecast future events within a broad scriptural narrative framework. Evidence internal to both Barber's and Bell's histories leads me to date them both to the first decade of the twentieth century, probably between 1904 and 1910.

9. Lorenzo Dow Blackson, *The Rise and Progress of the Kingdoms of Light and Darkness; or, The Reign of Kings Alpha and Abadon* (1867; reprint ed., Upper Saddle River, N.J., 1968), 3–18.

10. Blackson, *Rise and Progress,* 209, 211.

11. Blackson, *Rise and Progress,* 116, 118. Latimer and Ridley were burned at the stake side-by-side in Oxford, England, in 1655 during the reign of the Catholic queen Mary I. John Foxe was the famous martyrologist and author of *Foxe's Book of Martyrs* (1563). On John Wesley, the founder of Methodism, see ch. 2.

12. Blackson, *Rise and Progress,* 123, 128.

13. Blackson, *Rise and Progress,* 155.

14. Albert J. Raboteau discusses the larger context for some of these theological concerns in "'Ethiopia Shall Soon Stretch Forth Her Hands': Black Destiny in Nineteenth-Century America," in *A Fire in the Bones: Reflections on African-American Religious History* (Boston, 1995), 37–56.

15. *Christian Recorder,* December 14, 1876, cited in Kathleen Ann Clark, *Defining Moments: African American Commemoration and Political Culture in the South, 1863–1913* (Chapel Hill, N.C., 2005), 180; Wilson, *Emancipation: Its Course and Progress from 1481 B.C. to A.D. 1875* (Hampton, Va., 1882), 150; Williams, *History of the Negro Race,* vol. 2, 547. Williams also criticized Harriet Beecher Stowe's antislavery novel *Uncle Tom's Cabin* for the "terrible fatality" of its leading black characters.

16. Thomas, *The American Negro: What He Was, What He Is, and What He May Become* (New York, 1901), xii–xvii, xxi, xxiv, 165, 145, 44. On Thomas's life see John David Smith, *Black Judas: William Hannibal Thomas and the American Negro* (Athens, Ga., 2000).

17. Thomas, *The American Negro,* 146–148.

18. Williams, *History of the Negro Race,* vol. 2, 464, 534.

19. Clark, *Defining Moments,* 40.

20. Elizabeth J. Eisenstein, "Some Conjectures about the Impact of Printing on Western Society and Thought," *Journal of Modern History* 40 (1968), 25. On the connections between collective identity and the rise of print-capitalism, see Benedict Anderson, *Imagined Communities: Reflections on the Origin and Spread of Nationalism* (London, 1983), 44. On Anglocentric understandings of identity, see Wilson Moses, *The Golden Age of Black Nationalism, 1850–1925* (New York, 1978).

21. Contemporary debates over "Afrocentricity," which are often reliant on black precedents in ancient Egypt, have been surprisingly neglectful of the history of those representations. Ironically, much of the nineteenth-century impetus for the study of African antiquity came from black Protestants, whose reliance on Christian tradition was subsequently rejected by Afrocentrists. See John H. Bracey, Jr., and August Meier, "Black Ideologies, Black Utopias: Afrocentricity in Historical Perspective," *Contributions in Black Studies* 12 (1994): 111–116.

22. Smith, *A Great Truth in a Nutshell. A Few Ancient and Modern Facts of the Colored People, by One of their Number* (n.p., 1883), i–ii, 9; Perry, *The Cushite, or the Descendants of Ham* (Springfield, Mass., 1893), 97–98.

23. Barber, *Negro of the Earlier World,* 6, 16, 24; Perry, *Cushite,* ix–x, v; Smith, *A Great Truth,* 9.

24. All of the race histories written by African Americans that I have consulted adhere to a monogenetic biblical interpretation. See George Fredrickson, *The Black Image in the White Mind: The Debate on Afro-American Character and Destiny, 1817–1914* (New York, 1971); Steven Jay Gould, *The Mismeasure of Man* (New York, 1981); and H. Shelton Smith, *In His Image, But . . . Racism in Southern Religion, 1780–1910* (Durham, N.C., 1972).

25. Wilson, *Emancipation,* 9, 99. For biographical information on Wilson, see James T. Haley, comp., *Afro-American Encyclopaedia; or, the Thoughts, Doings, and Sayings of the Race* (Nashville, Tenn., 1895), 228.

26. Wilson also raised an interesting question that he never answered: if the Emancipation Proclamation was the acme of modern history, was Abraham Lincoln an instrument of the divine will (72)? If so, what does this reveal about white agency in the abolitionist struggle? It is intriguing, in any event, that John Brown is seen as a martyr for the slaves, but Lincoln's role is somewhat more ambiguous.

27. Stanford, *The Tragedy of the Negro in America* (Boston, 1898), 43.

28. Stanford, *Tragedy,* 62, 66; Williams, *History of the Negro Race,* vol. 2, 214, 223.

29. Johnson, *School History,* 92; Williams, *History of the Negro Race,* vol. 2, 86, 90, 91.

30. Thomas, *American Negro,* 2–3, 12; Williams, *History of the Negro Race,* vol. 2, 534–535; Wilson, *Emancipation,* 100–101, 121.

31. "The outrages of to-day are merely repetitions of previous outrages, the

bad, poisonous fruit of seed sown in the distant and near past." Stanford, *Tragedy*, iii, 9.

32. James Moorhead, *American Apocalypse: Yankee Protestants and the Civil War, 1860–1869* (New Haven, 1978), 81.

33. Timothy E. Fulop, "'The Future Golden Day of the Race': Millennialism and Black Americans in the Nadir, 1877–1901," *Harvard Theological Review* 84, no. 1 (1991), 85; Ernest Lee Tuveson, *Redeemer Nation: The Idea of America's Millennial Role* (Chicago, 1968), 78.

34. Barber, *Negro of the Earlier World*, 28.

35. Steward, *End of the World* (Philadelphia, 1888), 68–69, 7, 71. For more on Steward's views of African-American destiny, see Fulop, "'The Future Golden Day of the Race'"; Raboteau, "'Ethiopia shall soon stretch forth her hands'"; and David W. Wills, "Aspects of Social Thought in the African Methodist Episcopal Church, 1884–1910" (Ph.D. diss., Harvard University, 1975). On Steward's career, see William Seraile, *Voice of Dissent: Theophilus Gould Steward (1843–1924) and Black America* (Brooklyn, N.Y., 1991).

36. Steward, *End of the World*, 76, 3–4.

37. Steward, *End of the World*, 14, 16–17.

38. James Theodore Holly, "The Divine Plan of Human Redemption, in Its Ethnological Development," *AME Church Review* 1 (October 1884), 83. Holly asserted that Shem's heirs had their dominance during the "Hebrew dispensation," before the destruction of the temple, and Japheth's during the "Gospel phase," or Christian dispensation.

39. Edward Norman Saveth, "Race and Nationalism in American Historiography: The Late Nineteenth Century," *Political Science Quarterly* 54, no. 3 (September 1939), 421–423.

40. Freeman, *Some Impressions of the United States* (London, 1883), 15–16, cited in Saveth, "Race and Nationalism," 427.

41. Freeman, *Some Impressions* (New York, 1883), 143–144.

42. See Adams, "The Germanic Origin of New England Towns, Read before the Harvard Historical Society, May 9, 1881," *Johns Hopkins University Studies in Historical and Political Science,* 1st ser., 2, Local Institutions, no. 2; Saveth, "Race and Nationalism," 434–438. On the professionalization of history see Peter Novick, *That Noble Dream: The "Objectivity Question" and the American Historical Profession* (Cambridge, 1988).

43. Quotation by Colonel Forney in Philip S. Foner, "Black Participation in the Centennial of 1876," *Phylon* 39, no. 4 (4th quarter, 1978), 295. See also Clark, *Defining Moments*, 120–124.

44. Thomas Dixon, *The Leopard's Spots: A Romance of the White Man's Burden, 1865–1900* (New York, 1902), and *The Clansman: An Historical Romance of the Ku Klux Klan* (New York, 1905); Charles Carroll, "*The Negro Is a Beast*," or, "*In the Image of God*"; *The Reasoner of the Age, the Revelation of the Century! The Bible as it*

is! The Negro and His Relationship to the Human Family . . . The Negro is Not the Son of Ham (St. Louis, Mo., 1900).

45. J. Augustus Cole, "The Negro at Home and Abroad: Their Origin, Progress and Destiny," *AME Church Review* 4 (April 1888), 394; Clark, *Defining Moments,* 164.

46. See, for example, Benjamin Tucker Tanner's refutation of an article in the Methodist *Sunday School Journal for Teachers and Young People,* in which the author had questioned whether "the negro race are descended from Ham." See "The Hamitic Origin of the Negro," *AME Church Review* 4 (July 1887), 550; Cole, "The Negro at Home and Abroad," 394.

47. Henry McNeal Turner, "The Negro in All Ages: A Lecture delivered in the Second Baptist Church of Savannah, GA" (Savannah, Ga., 1873), 23, 24; Mia Bay, *The White Image in the Black Mind: African-American Ideas about White People, 1830–1925* (New York, 2000), 81–82. Kathleen Ann Clark notes that AME missionary to Africa William Heard witnessed Turner giving this speech in 1876 while Heard was a teenager. Years later, in his autobiography, Heard noted that "I was so impressed with the pictures and historic facts he presented of the Race in past ages, and of the men of the present, that my life is largely what it is because of the impressions made at this meeting" (cited in Clark, *Defining Moments,* 75–76).

48. Benjamin Tucker Tanner, Review of *The Cushite; Or, the Children of Ham, AME Church Review* 3 (April 1887), 437; Benjamin Tucker Tanner, "The Hamitic Origin of the Negro," *AME Church Review* 4 (July 1887), 555.

49. The Baptist Harvey Johnson, author of several works on ethnology beginning in the 1890s, also reinforced the biblical division of races while insisting on unitary creation, a pairing that allowed for both equality and difference; Harvey Johnson, *The Nations from a New Point of View* (Nashville, Tenn., 1903); Bay, *The White Image,* 105–106.

50. *AME Church Review* 29, no. 2 (October 1912), 99.

51. Arthur A. Anderson, *Prophetic Liberator of the Coloured Race of the United States of America: Command to His People* (1913), reprinted in John H. Bracey, Jr., August Meier, and Elliott Rudwick, eds., *Black Nationalism in America* (New York, 1970), 178.

52. James Morris Webb, *The Black Man, the Father of Civilization, Proven by Biblical History* (n.p., 1914), 11.

53. Gail Bederman, *Manliness and Civilization: A Cultural History of Gender and Race in the United States, 1880–1917* (Chicago, 1995). See Clark, *Defining Moments,* 57, on the centrality of manliness to constructions of black male identity after Emancipation. She observes that black males avoided the problem of referring to slavery as a male problem by talking instead about the sexual exploitation of black women; in this way they also avoided the potential implication that black men had been passive (76–77).

54. Joseph Thomas Wilson, *The Black Phalanx: A History of the Negro Soldiers of*

the United States in the Wars of 1775–1812, 1861–'65 (Hartford, Conn., 1888), n.p., 504.

55. Johnson, *School History*, 27; Williams, *History*, 369; Edward A. Johnson, *History of Negro Soldiers in the Spanish American War and other items of Interest* (Raleigh, N.C., 1899); George Washington Williams, *A history of the Negro troops in the War of the Rebellion, 1861–1865: preceded by a review of the military services of Negroes in ancient and modern times* (New York, 1888).

56. In Penelope Bullock's study of the black periodical press (in which she excluded daily newspapers), she counted ninety-seven titles that appeared between 1838 and 1909. Of those, eleven appeared before or during the Civil War, and eighty-five in the three decades following the war, with the largest number appearing in the decade 1900–1909: *Afro-American Periodical Press, 1838–1909* (Baton Rouge, 1981), 2, 3, 71–72, 92.

57. *Afro-American Periodical Press*, 9; I. Garland Penn, *The Afro-American Press and its Editors* (1891; reprint ed., New York, 1969), 487; Hardie Martin, "How the Church Can Best Help the Masses," *National Baptist Magazine* 4–5 (October 1896–January 1897), 281.

58. James D. Tyms, *The Rise of Religious Education among Negro Baptists* (New York, 1965), 153, 169; Higginbotham, *Righteous Discontent*, 12.

59. Tanner, "The Races: Their Literature," *Christian Recorder* 21, no. 11 (March 15, 1883), 2.

60. Rev. Edward H. Bryant, "Our Duties, Responsibilities: Negro Literature," *AME Church Review* 1, no. 3 (January 1885), 261; Harvey Johnson, "The Need of a Distinct Race and Denominational Literature," *National Baptist* 8, no. 4 (August 1901), 327, 329.

61. Victoria Earle Matthews, "The Value of Race Literature: An Address Delivered at the First Congress of Colored Women of the United States" (1895), in Shirley Wilson Logan, ed., *With Pen and Voice: A Critical Anthology of Nineteenth-Century African-American Women* (Carbondale, Ill., 1995), 120, 128, 129.

62. Orishatukeh Faduma, "How to Make Reading Profitable," *AME Church Review* 13, no. 4 (April 1897); Archibald Johnson, "The Study of Universal History in Liberal Education," *AME Church Review* (January 1896), 371.

63. *Indianapolis Freeman*, April 13, 1889; January 18, 1890.

64. *Indianapolis Freeman*, April 1891.

65. William J. Simmons, *Men of Mark: Eminent, Progressive and Rising* (Cleveland, Ohio, 1887).

6. "The Grand Traditions of Our Race"

1. Harper, "Our Greatest Want," *Anglo-African Magazine* 1 (May 1859), 160; *Moses: The Story of the Nile*, in Harper, *Idylls of the Bible* (1901; reprint ed., New York, 1975), 3, 9–10.

2. Harper, *Moses,* 10.

3. Harper, "Our Greatest Want," 160.

4. On gender as a form of knowledge that is both articulated and constructed by language, see Joan Wallach Scott, "Some More Reflections on Gender and Politics," in *Gender and the Politics of History,* rev. ed. (New York, 1999), esp. 200–201; Judith Butler, *Bodies That Matter: On the Discursive Limits of "Sex"* (New York, 1993); and Donna J. Haraway, "'Gender' for a Marxist Dictionary: The Sexual Politics of a Word," in *Simians, Cyborgs, and Women: The Reinvention of Nature* (New York, 1991), 127–148.

5. Ann Plato, *Essays; Including Biographies and Miscellaneous Pieces, in Prose and Poetry* (1841; reprint ed., New York, 1988).

6. Maria Stewart, "Mrs. Stewart's Farewell Address to Her Friends in the City of Boston" (Boston, 1833).

7. In her 1832 "Lecture delivered at The Franklin Hall," Stewart quoted several lines from Thomas Gray, "Elegy Written in a Country Churchyard" (1751); in her "Farewell Address" she mentioned her indebtedness to "Sketches of the Fair Sex," a reference to John Adams, *Woman, Sketches of the History, Genius, Disposition, Accomplishments, Employments, Customs and Importance of the Fair Sex in all Parts of the World Interspersed with Many Singular and Entertaining Anecdotes By a Friend of the Sex* (London, 1790); and she cited four different Isaac Watts hymns in her speeches.

8. "An Address Delivered at the African Masonic Hall," in Marilyn Richardson, ed., *Maria W. Stewart, America's First Black Woman Political Writer* (Bloomington, Ind., 1987), 61, 63, 58.

9. "An Address Delivered Before the Afric-American Female Intelligence Society of America," in Richardson, *Maria W. Stewart,* 50, 52, 53.

10. "Religion and the Pure Principles," in Richardson, *Maria W. Stewart,* 35; "Address Before the Afric-American," in Richardson, *Maria W. Stewart,* 55. This female black literary society met regularly and had an elaborate structure. Its founding suggests that middle-class black women were very interested in intellectual pursuits. The group collected 25 cents at the first of the year, then 12.5 cents per month thereafter to buy books, hire a room, and pay for other incidentals, and they heard from a wide variety of speakers. Stewart seemed at her most defensive in front of this gathering, but one might speculate that the ability of the group to entertain dissenting opinions demonstrated its strength. And it is almost certain that Stewart made use of its growing book collection for her own research: Elizabeth McHenry, *Forgotten Readers: Recovering the Lost History of African American Literary Societies* (Durham, N.C., 2002), 69; "An Address Delivered at the African Masonic Hall," in Richardson, *Maria W. Stewart,* 57.

11. "Farewell Address," Richardson, *Maria W. Stewart,* 69–70.

12. Dickson D. Bruce, Jr., *The Origins of African American Literature (1680–1865)* (Charlottesville, Va., 2001), 153, 186; Melba Joyce Boyd, *Discarded Legacy:*

Politics and Poetics in the Life of Frances E. W. Harper, 1825–1911 (Detroit, 1994), 37.

13. Boyd, *Discarded Legacy,* 36; Maryemma Graham, ed., *The Complete Poems of Frances E. W. Harper* (New York, 1988), xxxiv.

14. Sally G. McMillen, *To Raise Up the South: Sunday Schools in Black and White Churches, 1865–1915* (Baton Rouge, 2001), 21. On attitudes toward the education of African-American women, see Beverly Lynn Guy-Sheftall, *Daughters of Sorrow: Attitudes towards Black Women, 1880–1920* (Brooklyn, N.Y., 1990). See also W. H. Harthorn and George W. Penniman, *An Era of Progress and Promise* (Boston, 1910), 116.

15. Glenda Elizabeth Gilmore, *Gender and Jim Crow: Women and the Politics of White Supremacy in North Carolina, 1896–1920* (Chapel Hill, N.C., 1996), 37–39.

16. Gilmore, *Gender and Jim Crow,* 43.

17. McHenry, *Forgotten Readers,* 202–210.

18. Henry Louis Gates, Jr., introduction to Schomburg Library of Nineteenth Century Black Women Writers (New York, 1988), xvi.

19. Her husband was George A. C. Cooper, a Greek instructor at St. Augustine's. He died in 1879, just a few months after becoming the second African-American ordained clergyman in the church. Elizabeth Alexander, "'We Must Be about Our Father's Business': Anna Julia Cooper and the In-Corporation of the Nineteenth-Century African American Woman Intellectual," *Signs* 20, no. 2 (Winter 1995), 338–339.

20. Cooper, *A Voice from the South* (Xenia, Ohio, 1892), 9–10. Thomas Babington Macaulay's book *The History of England from the Accession of James the Second* was published serially in the United States between 1849 and 1861; excerpts from this and other writings also appeared in popular periodicals such as the *North American Review,* the *Atlantic Monthly,* and *Putnam's Monthly.*

21. Cook was born in Kentucky in 1862. Her education was later financed by Northern whites. Evelyn Brooks Higginbotham, *Righteous Discontent: The Women's Movement in the Black Baptist Church, 1880–1920* (Cambridge, Mass., 125).

22. Hallie Quinn Brown, for example, was born in Pittsburgh but grew up in the black community centered around Chatham in Canada; Pauline Hopkins came of age in the middle-class black society of Boston. Mary Church Terrell and Frances Harper, conversely, were products of the urban South who came north for education reasons: Terrell grew up in Memphis and later graduated from Oberlin College in 1884. Harper, born in 1825 in Baltimore to free black parents, eventually moved to Ohio, and later to Pennsylvania to teach, lecture, and write. L. A. Scruggs, *Women of Distinction: Remarkable in Works and Invincible in Character* (Raleigh, N.C., 1893), 17, 227; Hazel V. Carby, *Reconstructing Womanhood: The Emergence of the Afro-American Woman Novelist* (New York, 1987), 65.

23. Hazel V. Carby, "Policing the Black Woman's Body in an Urban Context,"

Identities, ed. Anthony Appiah and Henry Louis Gates, Jr. (Chicago, 1995), 124. The useful term "politics of respectability" is defined by Evelyn Brooks Higginbotham in *Righteous Discontent,* ch. 7.

24. George Washington Williams, *History of the Negro Race in America, 1619–1880: Negroes as Slaves, As Soldiers, and As Citizens* (1883; reprint ed., New York, 1968), x; Pendleton, *A Narrative of the Negro* (Washington, D.C., 1912), 3.

25. William Still, for example, wrote an introduction to *Iola Leroy,* by Frances Ellen Watkins Harper (1892), in which he praised her efforts and used her own prolific writing history and political activism to demonstrate her fitness for the cause. Maria W. Stewart, who published a new, enlarged edition of her *Meditations* in 1879, included not one but five separate letters of commendation: from Amos Hunt (a notary public in Washington, D.C.), William Lloyd Garrison (the noted white abolitionist), Louise C. Hatton (an acquaintance), Alexander Crummell (a black writer and African colonizationist), and William B. Jefferson (the pastor of the Third Baptist Church of Washington, D.C.). This particular form of literary legitimation had long been practiced by black male authors: many slave narratives opened with the testimony of a white male who could "vouch" for the authenticity and integrity of the author. In like manner, black (and white) men here authorized the work of black women.

26. McHenry, *Forgotten Readers,* 74. History writing eventually became a professional category as well, a fact that had important consequences for both black men and black women.

27. *Of One Blood: Or, the Hidden Self,* was first excerpted in the *Colored American Magazine* (1902–1903) and was reprinted in *The Magazine Novels of Pauline Hopkins* (New York, 1988).

28. "A Female Ministry," *Star of Zion* 23 (January 26, 1899).

29. "Woman," AME *Christian Recorder* (March 1889).

30. L. A. Scruggs, *Women of Distinction: Remarkable in Works and Invincible in Character* (Raleigh, N.C., 1893), 17–22.

31. This production of texts was not simply a reflection of women's activities in other spheres of life but also, in and of itself, a conscious attempt to shape and define what it meant to be an African-American church member. What Hazel Carby notes with respect to women's novels also pertains to the sphere of religious publishing; she astutely observes that early black women's novels are not simply "socially determined by the conditions within which they were created"; they are "also cultural artifacts which shape the social conditions they enter." So, too, the writings of women in religious periodicals continuously created and replicated notions of black Protestant life. See Carby, *Reconstructing Womanhood,* 95.

32. Many of these periodicals were read by people who were not members of the church, or who belonged to other churches. The AME *Christian Recorder* was among the most widely circulated black periodicals in the South in the 1880s, and its pages contained letters and articles by members and non-members alike. Simi-

larly, the *AME Church Review* and the *National Baptist Magazine* both featured pieces by unaffiliated African-American readers.

33. Bullock, *Afro-American Periodicals,* 167. According to Bullock, the AME Church even authorized publication of a "Ladies' Magazine" at the 1880 General Conference, but there is no evidence that the journal was ever published (166).

34. Priscilla Jane Thompson, *Ethiope Lays* (Rossmoyne, Ohio, 1900), n.p.

35. *National Baptist* 5, no. 2 (April 1897), 354.

36. Bowie continued, "Every one that thirsteth, come ye to the waters, and he that hath no money; come ye, buy, and eat; yea, come, buy wine and milk without money and without price." "The Call of God to the Church," in *National Baptist* 5, no. 2 (April 1897), 360. See also Mary Fordham, "By the Rivers of Babylon," in *Magnolia Leaves: Poems* (Charleston, S.C., 1897).

37. "Our Women," *National Baptist* 2, no. 3 (July 1895), 138.

38. "Lecture Delivered at the Franklin Hall," in Richardson, *Maria W. Stewart,* 49; "Religion and the Pure Principles of Morality," in Richardson, *Maria W. Stewart,* 40; "Cause for Encouragement, Composed Upon Hearing the Editor's Account of the Late Convention in Philadelphia," from the *Liberator,* July 14, 1832, in Richardson, *Maria W. Stewart,* 43.

39. "Romances of the Negro in History," manuscript in Alice Dunbar-Nelson Papers, University of Delaware, Box 21, F. 405.

40. "Some Parallels of History," *Baptist Magazine* 7, no. 1 (July 1899), 5.

41. Plato, "Natives of America," *Essays,* in Joan R. Sherman, *African-American Poetry of the Nineteenth Century* (Urbana, Ill., 1992), 53.

42. Fordham, "Chicago Exposition Ode," in *Magnolia Leaves,* 30–32; Olivia Ward Bush-Banks, "On the Long Island Indian," in *Driftwood* (Providence, R.I., 1914), 86.

43. Olivia Ward Bush-Banks, "A Hero of San Juan Hill," *Driftwood,* 39.

44. Pendleton, *Narrative of the Negro,* 183, 184–185.

45. Harper, "An Appeal to My Country Women," Graham, ed., *Complete Poems,* 194, 197.

46. "Life and Literature," *AME Church Review* (January 1898), 325.

47. Tillman, "Heirs of Slavery, A Little Drama of Today," *AME Church Review* (January 1901), 201, 203.

48. Thompson, *Ethiope Lays,* 3, 45.

49. Thompson, *Ethiope Lays,* 94, 95.

50. "Woman's Work," *National Baptist Magazine* (January 1894), 31. Broughton did not mention Harper's *Moses,* but it is possible that she was alluding to it here; C. H. Baxter, "Woman's Sphere in Society," *National Baptist Magazine* (January 1895), 26.

51. Mrs. H. Brown, "To Mother," *Star of Zion* 10 (May 7, 1886).

52. Emblematic was a passage included in Thomas Johnson's *Twenty-Eight Years a Slave* in which he recalls the role his mother played in communicating informa-

tion about religion, race, and family history. He recounted that his mother taught him the little she knew about Africa and about heaven, where "God would think as much of the black people as he did of the white." "I cannot forget her tears as she looked upon me with a mother's love, more than sixty years ago, and told me what little she knew. To her, as to thousands of poor slaves, the Bible was almost a sealed book." *Twenty-Eight Years a Slave, or The Story of My Life on Three Continents,* 7th ed. (Bournemouth, U.K., 1909), 4.

53. Fanny Jackson-Coppin, *Reminiscences of School Life, and Hints on Teaching* (1913; reprint ed., New York, 1987), 9.

54. Scholars have noted that miscegenation and the dilemma of the biracial heroine or hero figure prominently in African-American novels written before World War I, but they have interpreted the prevalence of this theme principally as a response to white fears about racial mixing. See J. Lee Greene, *Blacks in Eden: The African American Novel's First Century* (Charlottesville, Va., 1996).

55. Carby, *Reconstructing Womanhood,* 90. See also Barbara Christian, *Black Feminist Criticism: Perspectives on Black Women Writers* (New York, 1985), 167.

56. Carby suggests that Hopkins got this from Herodotus (156), but it seems clear that there is a much more recent lineage within African-American historical accounts.

57. Hopkins, *Of One Blood,* 552.

58. Reuel quotes Milton as he begins to recover his lost memory of this hidden world:

> Eden stretched her lines
> From Auran eastward to the royal tow'rs
> Of great Seleucia, built by Grecian kings,
> Or where the sons of Eden long before
> Dwelt in Telassar. (547)

59. Angelina Weld Grimké, *Rachel: A Play in Three Acts,* in Kathy A. Perkins and Judith L. Stephens, eds., *Strange Fruit: Plays on Lynching by American Women* (Bloomington, Ind., 1998), 33, 34.

60. Grimké, *Rachel,* 60, 67, 77.

61. Peter Brown suggests that celibacy presented the same challenges to early Christian communities: it called into question the very basis of society and its reproduction. See Peter Brown, *The Body and Society: Men, Women, and Sexual Renunciation in Early Christianity* (New York, 1988). See also the analysis of the work of Grimké and Georgia Douglas Johnson in Katharine Capshaw Smith, *Children's Literature of the Harlem Renaissance* (Bloomington, Ind., 2004), 20–21.

62. "Our Woman's Column," AME *Christian Recorder* (February 9, 1888). Casey did not confront Coppin about his books within the church itself, but she did feel free to do so within the medium of the *Christian Recorder.* Noting the genius of Harper's poem about Moses, Casey continued with a more general com-

plaint: "Why is it always necessary when we want to quote a poetess to go all the way back to Phillis Wheatley, when we have such poems as those of Mrs. Harper's shining in our faces from the newspapers and the magazines of the present day?"

63. See, for example, Mattie Roberts, "The Power and Influence of Woman," AME *Christian Recorder* (January 1886); Mrs. M. E. Steward, *National Baptist* 6, nos. 4–5 (August–October 1898), 147.

64. Scruggs, *Women of Distinction,* 24.

65. Mossell, *Work,* 49.

66. Mossell, *Work,* 60, 64–67.

67. "Woman's Relation to the World," *Star of Zion* 10 (January 1886); Mrs. Pettey, "Woman's Column," *Star of Zion* 23 (June 1899).

68. Broughton, "Woman's Work," *National Baptist* 1, no. 1 (January 1894), 31, 34. The U.S. president, Broughton related, employs both a cabinet and an errand boy. "Now," she modestly asserted, "we would like to whisper to man that he needs woman's help more in his cabinet than as an errand girl."

69. "Three Negro Poets: Horton, Mrs. Harper, and Whitman," *Journal of Negro History* 2, no. 4 (1917), 386.

70. Mary Helen Washington, ed., *Invented Lives: Narratives of Black Women, 1860–1960* (Garden City, N.Y., 1987), xviii.

71. *Journal of Negro History* 2, no. 4 (October 1917), 442–448.

72. I. Garland Penn, *The Afro-American Press and Its Editors* (Springfield, Mass., 1891), 490; "Woman's Department," *AME Church Review* (January 1901). In 1901, for example, the *AME Church Review* established a "woman's department." But the pieces that ran there, edifying numbers such as "why women nag," were not on the whole written *by* women; they included snippets from other journals and short articles selected or written by the male editor intended for the *improvement* of women. One might fruitfully compare this phenomenon to women's magazines, and now women's television stations, which invariably make decisions about what constitute "women's concerns," thus prescribing appropriate female roles.

73. Alice Dunbar-Nelson, *The Dunbar Speaker and Entertainer* (Naperville, Ill., 1920), 9, 3.

74. Pendleton, *Narrative,* 37, 54.

75. Pendleton, *Narrative,* 78, 217.

Conclusion

1. Anne Elizabeth Carroll, *Word, Image, and the New Negro: Representation and Identity in the Harlem Renaissance* (Bloomington, Ind., 2005), 91.

2. David Krasner, *A Beautiful Pageant: African American Theatre, Drama, and Performance in the Harlem Renaissance, 1910–1927* (New York, 2002), ch. 4; David W. Blight, *Race and Reunion: The Civil War in American Memory* (Cambridge, Mass., 2001); Wilson J. Moses, "The Poetics of Ethiopianism: W. E. B. Du Bois and

Literary Black Nationalism," *American Literature* 47, no. 3 (November 1975): 411–426.

3. Katharine Capshaw Smith, *Children's Literature of the Harlem Renaissance* (Bloomington, Ind., 2004), 56.

4. W. E. B. Du Bois, *The Negro* (New York, 1915), 74; *The Souls of Black Folk* (Chicago, 1903); Du Bois, ed., *The Negro Church. Report of a Social Study Made under the Direction of Atlanta University; Together with the Proceedings of the Eighth Conference for the Study of the Negro Problems, held at Atlanta University, May 26th, 1903* (Atlanta, 1903). For a recent study of Du Bois's religious thought, see Edward J. Blum, *W. E. B. Du Bois: American Prophet* (University Park, Penn., 2007).

5. One of the latest anthologies about the trope of the New Negro contains well over one hundred representative texts and is divided into thirteen sections, but the church is decidedly absent from the list. See Henry Louis Gates, Jr., and Gene Andrew Jarrett, *The New Negro: Readings on Race, Representation, and African American Culture, 1892–1938* (Princeton, N.J., 2007).

6. As Hayden White explains, "The politicalization of historical thinking was a virtual precondition of its own professionalization, the basis of its promotion to the status of a discipline worthy of being taught in the universities, and a prerequisite of whatever 'constructive' social function historical knowledge was thought to serve." White, "The Politics of Historical Interpretation: Discipline and De-Sublimation," *Critical Inquiry* 9, no. 1 (September 1982), 118.

7. Krasner, *Beautiful Pageant*, 2, cited in Smith, *Children's Literature*, 61; Robert Gregg, Afterword to W. E. B. Du Bois, *The Negro* (University Park, Penn., 2001), 245; David Levering Lewis, *W. E. B. Du Bois—Biography of a Race, 1868–1919* (New York, 1993), 461.

8. Jacqueline Goggin, "Countering White Racist Scholarship: Carter G. Woodson and the *Journal of Negro History*," *Journal of Negro History* 68, no. 4 (Autumn 1983), 358.

9. Drusilla Dunjee Houston, *Wonderful Ethiopians of the Ancient Cushite Empire, Book I: Nations of the Cushite Empire. Marvelous Facts From Authentic Records* (1926; reprint ed., Baltimore, Md., 1985). See especially the introduction by William Paul Coates. The manuscript of the second volume of Houston's trilogy was discovered within the last few years and published by Peggy Brooks-Bertram, *Origin of Civilization from the Cushites* (Buffalo, N.Y., 2007).

10. For Du Bois's statement about Garvey, see his article in *Century Magazine* 105 (February 1923), 539–548.

11. Wilson J. Moses, *Golden Age of Black Nationalism, 1850–1925* (New York, 1978), 78. Moses, like many other observers of nineteenth-century black nationalism, is well aware of the religious character of virtually all its manifestations. He asserts that "in the nineteenth century, black nationalism was almost inseparable from religion. . . . Rather than thinking of religious black nationalism as one of the varieties of black nationalism, one might almost say that black nationalism is a va-

riety of religion." *The Wings of Ethiopia: Studies in African-American Life and Letters* (Ames, Iowa, 1990), 35, 113. St. Clair Drake makes similar arguments in *The Redemption of Africa and Black Religion* (Chicago, 1970). Yet neither Moses nor Drake traces the institutional means, especially the black churches, through which black nationalist ideologies were disseminated.

12. Sandra Lipsitz Bem analyzes the various cultural "lenses" that govern our perceptions and articulations of gender difference in the United States. They can usefully be applied to race. See Bem, *The Lenses of Gender: Transforming the Debate on Sexual Equality* (New Haven, 1993).

Acknowledgments

Like all communal histories, this one features many friends, generous gestures of support, and fortuitous encounters along the way. The journey has been long enough that I will undoubtedly forget to acknowledge someone. I can only hope that that person knows what their help has meant even if my own historical accounting falls short.

To Cornel West, David Wills, and David Brion Davis, who long ago made me curious about the treasures that I had in front of me.

To many wonderful research assistants who have labored to find materials for me, including Michele Easter, Julius Bailey, David Weaver-Zercher, Alan Love, Quincy Newell, Katie Lofton, and Mary Ellen O'Donnell. Whenever I run across their handwriting in my notes it makes me smile.

To good listeners and readers, including my Young Scholars in American Religion cohort, the History of the Book seminar at Harvard, the American Studies seminar at the University of Western Ontario, the Yale Seminar in American Religion, and the History of Christian Practice Project, especially Bill Hutchison, David Hall, Margaret Kellow, Harry Stout, Jon Butler, Leigh Schmidt, and Mark Valeri. I am also grateful to the seminars Reimagining Denominationalism, Women and Twentieth-Century Protestantism, and the seminar on missions convened by Grant Wacker, for terrific advice.

To my graduate students at the University of North Carolina and Duke who read my drafts and helped me think more clearly.

To colleagues here and there who read and commented on drafts, including Jason Bivins, Fitz Brundage, Lisa Lindsay, and Don Mathews.

To practical support from many sources: the National Humanities Center, the National Endowment for the Humanities, the Mellon Foundation, the Louisville Institute, and the Lilly Foundation, Inc. The University of North

Carolina at Chapel Hill, my academic home, has provided very generous help, especially the Institute for the Arts and Humanities, the McLester Fund in the Department of Religious Studies, the University Research Council, the College of Arts and Sciences, and the Provost's office. Thanks to Hope Toscher, Myra Quick, and Cathy Ashworth, my departmental ballasts.

To staff and colleagues at the African American Religion Documentary History Project at Amherst College, my home away from home on many occasions. Special thanks to Sue Peabody, Scott Sessions, Albert Raboteau, Randall Burkett, Patricia Holland, Judith Weisenfeld, and David Wills, friend and general editor.

To the unfailingly supportive members of my writing groups over the years: Margaret Wiener, Sarah Shields, Sylvia Hoffert, Tim Marr, Jane Thrailkill, Barbara Ambros, Lauren Leve, and Randall Styers.

To Joyce Seltzer, a remarkable editor whom I found just in time to save me from excess verbiage; to Christine Thorsteinsson for copyediting; to Jane Merryman for thorough indexing; and to the sharp-eyed anonymous reviewers who corrected my course.

To my best readers and listeners, Katie Lofton and Grant Wacker, for just about everything that has made this a better book, including many cups of coffee.

To Peter, Wesley, Joseph, and David, for keeping it all real.

You are all my community of memory, and I am grateful for your nudging, correcting, and boosting along the way.

Index